Intellectual Capital as a Precursor to Sustainable Corporate Social Responsibility

Bartolomé Marco-Lajara
University of Alicante, Spain

Patrocinio Zaragoza-Sáez
University of Alicante, Spain

Javier Martínez-Falcó
University of Alicante, Spain

A volume in the Advances in Business Strategy
and Competitive Advantage (ABSCA) Book Series

Published in the United States of America by
    IGI Global
    Business Science Reference (an imprint of IGI Global)
    701 E. Chocolate Avenue
    Hershey PA, USA 17033
    Tel: 717-533-8845
    Fax: 717-533-8661
    E-mail: cust@igi-global.com
    Web site: http://www.igi-global.com

Library of Congress Cataloging-in-Publication Data

Names: Marco Lajara, Bartolomé, editor. | Zaragoza-Sáez, Patrocinio, 1974- editor. | Martinez Falcó, Javier, 1997- editor.
Title: Intellectual capital as a precursor to sustainable corporate social responsibility / edited by Bartolomé Marco-Lajara, Patrocinio Zaragoza-Sáez, Javier Martínez Falcó.
Description: Hershey, PA : Business Science Reference, [2023] | Includes bibliographical references and index. | Summary: "The book is intended to serve as a study guide, reflection and critique to understand the role of intellectual capital in achieving a sustainable approach by the organization. The book sheds light on the new trends and challenges around intellectual capital management and sustainable practices, making it a must-read for academics and managers who want to deepen their understanding of the link between organizations' intangible assets and their sustainable management. The book could therefore become a thought-provoking work in the field of intellectual capital and sustainability, as it addresses its renewal and future directions"-- Provided by publisher.
Identifiers: LCCN 2022045617 (print) | LCCN 2022045618 (ebook) | ISBN 9781668468159 (hardcover) | ISBN 9781668468166 (paperback) | ISBN 9781668468173 (ebook)
Subjects: LCSH: Social responsibility of business. | Management--Social aspects.
Classification: LCC HD60 .I537 2023 (print) | LCC HD60 (ebook) | DDC 658.4/08--dc23/eng/20220927
LC record available at https://lccn.loc.gov/2022045617
LC ebook record available at https://lccn.loc.gov/2022045618

This book is published in the IGI Global book series Advances in Business Strategy and Competitive Advantage (ABSCA) (ISSN: 2327-3429; eISSN: 2327-3437)

British Cataloguing in Publication Data
A Cataloguing in Publication record for this book is available from the British Library.

All work contributed to this book is new, previously-unpublished material. The views expressed in this book are those of the authors, but not necessarily of the publisher.

For electronic access to this publication, please contact: eresources@igi-global.com.

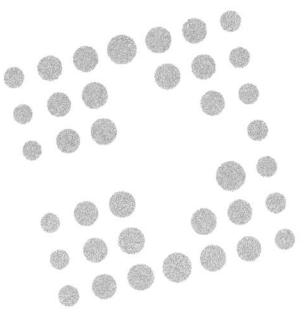

Advances in Business Strategy and Competitive Advantage (ABSCA) Book Series

Patricia Ordóñez de Pablos
Universidad de Oviedo, Spain

ISSN:2327-3429
EISSN:2327-3437

MISSION

Business entities are constantly seeking new ways through which to gain advantage over their competitors and strengthen their position within the business environment. With competition at an all-time high due to technological advancements allowing for competition on a global scale, firms continue to seek new ways through which to improve and strengthen their business processes, procedures, and profitability.

The **Advances in Business Strategy and Competitive Advantage (ABSCA) Book Series** is a timely series responding to the high demand for state-of-the-art research on how business strategies are created, implemented and re-designed to meet the demands of globalized competitive markets. With a focus on local and global challenges, business opportunities and the needs of society, the **ABSCA** encourages scientific discourse on doing business and managing information technologies for the creation of sustainable competitive advantage.

COVERAGE

- Business Models
- Differentiation Strategy
- Value Chain
- Competitive Strategy
- Strategic Alliances
- Entrepreneurship & Innovation
- Co-operative Strategies
- Customer-Orientation Strategy
- Ethics and Business Strategy
- Adaptive Enterprise

IGI Global is currently accepting manuscripts for publication within this series. To submit a proposal for a volume in this series, please contact our Acquisition Editors at Acquisitions@igi-global.com or visit: http://www.igi-global.com/publish/.

Titles in this Series

For a list of additional titles in this series, please visit: www.igi-global.com/book-series

The Transformation of Global Trade in a New World
Bartolomé Marco-Lajara (University of Alicante, Spain) Ahu Coşkun Özer (Marmara University, Turkey) and Javier Martínez Falcó (University of Alicante, pain)
Business Science Reference ● © 2023 ● 308pp ● H/C (ISBN: 9781668459508) ● US $250.00

Exploring the Economic Opportunities and Impacts of Migrant Entrepreneurship Success Stories and Case Studies
Meena Chavan (Macquarie University, Australia) and Sheba Nandkeolyar (Multiconnexions, Austalia)
Business Science Reference ● © 2022 ● 231pp ● H/C (ISBN: 9781668449868) ● US $215.00

Analyzing the Relationship Between Corporate Governance, CSR, and Sustainability
Ayberk Soyer (Istanbul Technical University, Turkey) and Umut Asan (Istanbul Technical University, Turkey)
Business Science Reference ● © 2022 ● 315pp ● H/C (ISBN: 9781799842347) ● US $215.00

Handbook of Research on Digital Innovation and Networking in Post-COVID-19 Organizations
Ana Pego (Nova University of Lisbon, Portugal)
Business Science Reference ● © 2022 ● 539pp ● H/C (ISBN: 9781668467626) ● US $315.00

Antecedents and Outcomes of Employee-Based Brand Equity
Muhammad Waseem Bari (Government College University, Faisalabad, Pakistan) Muhammad Abrar (Government College University, Faisalabad, Pakistan) and Emilia Alaverdov (Tbilisi State University, Georgia)
Business Science Reference ● © 2022 ● 297pp ● H/C (ISBN: 9781668436219) ● US $250.00

Cases on Emerging Market Responses to the COVID-19 Pandemic
Raj K. Kovid (Sharda University, India) and Vikas Kumar (Central University of Haryana, India)
Business Science Reference ● © 2022 ● 332pp ● H/C (ISBN: 9781668435045) ● US $240.00

Impact of Digital Transformation on the Development of New Business Models and Consumer Experience
Maria Antónia Rodrigues (Polytechnic of Porto, Portugal & CEOS.PP, Portugal & SIIS Porto, Portugal) and João F. Proença (Faculty of Economics, University of Porto, Portugal & Advance/CSG, University of Lisbon, Portugal & ISEG, University of Lisbon, Portugal)
Business Science Reference ● © 2022 ● 347pp ● H/C (ISBN: 9781799891796) ● US $240.00

701 East Chocolate Avenue, Hershey, PA 17033, USA
Tel: 717-533-8845 x100 ● Fax: 717-533-8661
E-Mail: cust@igi-global.com ● www.igi-global.com

Table of Contents

Detailed Table of Contents

  Gazala Yasmin Ashraf, Amity University, Raipur, India
  Disha Sharma, Amity University, Raipur, India
  Reshma Shrivastava, Amity University, Raipur, India

Corporate social responsibility can be a narrative in many different ways, from one's personal and social intentions to coming together to forge toward the collective goals of empowerment. Corporate social responsibility is already on its way to replace human social responsibility. The study involves the study of the standing on CSR activity and its relationship between CSR spending and value creation. This article, however, argues that much of the past literature reviewed the complex process of interaction and negotiation evolving between businesses and consumers. This study is focusing on reflecting a clearer picture of brand interaction, challenges, and exchanges within the disclosure and consumer perception of CSR. Then, the chapter will identify the relationship between CSR and value creation. In this chapter, the authors are going to discuss the practical and theoretical implications, as well as give suggestions for future research.

  Jonai Wabwire, Kisii University, Kenya

This chapter reviews literature on the role of social capital and intellectual capital in the economy, and their contribution to corporate social responsibility with a particular emphasis on their importance for corporations. The chapter relates social capital and intellectual capital to concepts such as trust and corporate culture; and discusses and proposes various metrics that capture them at the firm level, including firms' corporate social responsibility (CSR) efforts. A summary of the existing research on the relation between social capital, intellectual capital, and firm value and stock market performance has been done. Finally, an analysis of whether firms are investing enough in intellectual capital and social capital in its corporate social responsibilities has been done.

Chapter 3

The purpose of this book chapter is to assess information governance in South African organizations. The book chapter assess corporate governance, data privacy, legislation, information security, big data, access, and training. The success of corporate governance is dependent on executive management buy in, the alignment of organisational strategy with mission, and the vision of the organisation. Organisations are to implement systematic disposal of records, effective retention of records, and quality assurance should be proven.

Chapter 4

Government agencies are important due to their contributions to the growth of economy and the benefits they bring to the society. However, there is an increasing need for these agencies to be ethical, especially in the 21st century, an era full of competitors, and also characterized by an increasingly globalized business world and a cascade of corporate corruption and fraud in both developed and developing countries. Government agencies thus require the enforcement of business ethics for long-term business success and sustainability. Although the main objective of business is to earn the money and profit, government agencies should take initiative for the welfare of the society and perform their activities within the framework of environmental norms and social responsibility. These agencies should provide goods and services legally, and profitably to the society and operate responsibly to address social and environmental issues. The study utilised literature review to critically analyse business ethics and social responsibility practices in government agencies in South Africa.

Chapter 5

Knowledge plays a fundamental role in the achievement of business success. This has led to the intensification of the study of the set of intangible assets of the organization called intellectual capital (IC) as well as its impact on the achievement of sustainable competitive advantages over time. Moreover, IC that incorporates sustainable aspects (i.e., green intellectual capital [GIC]) was only recently introduced in the academic literature and has since become an emerging field of study. The lack of consistency in the terminologies used has made it difficult to establish clear measurements of intangibles, especially of the dimensions of IC, which have posed an additional difficulty in advancing this area of knowledge. To overcome this research problem, the authors analyze the origins and conceptualization of IC and GIC, trying to shed light on the field of study by answering the following questions: (1) What are the origins of IC? (2) How is IC defined? (3) What are the origins of GIC? (4) How is GIC defined?

Chapter 6

José G. Vargas-Hernández, Posgraduate and Research Department, Tecnológico Mario Molina Unidad Zapopan, Mexico
Omar C. Vargas-González, Tecnológico Nacional de México, Ciudad Guzmán, Mexico

This study aims to analyze the conceptual and theoretical approaches to ecology of organizations from the assumption that the unit of analysis of the ecology of organizations can be described, analyzed, and explained from different frameworks of reference. The method employed is the analytically referential and reflective of the main characteristics of the different perspectives already systematized in the theoretical and empirical research literature. It is concluded that the unit of analysis of the ecology of organizations in both the internal and external environments can be approached to be systematized from the perspectives of the open systems, the evolutionary theory, institutional and functionalist, and structural and community theories.

Chapter 7

José G. Vargas-Hernandez, Posgraduate and Research Department, Tecnológico Mario Molina Unidad Zapopan, Mexico
Omar C. Vargas-González, Tecnológico Nacional de México, Ciudad Guzmán, Mexico

This study aims to analyze the implications of green knowledge and technology in organizational green innovation, urban green innovation, and green roofs. The analysis is supported by the assumption that green sharing knowledge and technology is basic to organizational green innovation and urban green innovation areas practices, operations, and activities. The methods employed are based on the analytical-reflective and descriptive supported with the review of theoretical and empirical literature. The analysis concludes that green knowledge sharing is relevant to create and develop the green technology with positive implications for organizational green innovation, urban green innovation areas, and green roofs.

Chapter 8

Hettiwattage Harshani Dedunu, Rajarata University, Sri Lanka
Darshana Sedara, Southern Cross University, Australia

The purpose of the study is to find out how consumer purchasing decisions affect environmental, social, and governance practices. Consumers with recent bachelor's degrees were given the questionnaire. Through smart pls, the survey questions were tested. The findings imply that consumers prioritize two factors, the environment and social. It was verified that the personal concerns regarding the recycling process, resource consumption, and environmentally friendly business practices. Further, customers' health and safety, organizations' healthy and good working environment, human right concentration have shown reasonable importance. However, governance factors consideration is very low in the customer decision-making process due to a low level of awareness about governing practices especially political involvement and fraud and corruption. Thus, the empirical findings of the study serve as a springboard for further investigation in this field and offer marketers and sellers of ESG practices strategic implications.

    Deepak Kumar Nama, Devi Ahilya Vishwavidyalaya, India
    Ranjana Kanungo, Sica College, India

Many businesses select business sustainability to satisfy the needs of the environment, society, and economy in order to be optimal in the long run. To do this, businesses must fully and efficiently utilize their resources. Intellectual capital, which increases market value and establishes long-lasting competitive advantages, is one of their most precious resources. This research advances the growth of two distinct but related fields of study: sustainability and intellectual capital. Purpose of the study is to comprehend the notion in its whole and how each component of intellectual capital contributes to a company's sustainable growth. The realization in an organization occurs at every level of management, whether on the basis of interactions with people, human resources, or effective life cycle processes or structures, as we have seen in all prior researches. A crucial or significant part of intellectual capital is played in the long-term sustainability of corporations. Intellectual capital boosts market value and solidifies long-lasting competitive advantages.

    Osman Arslan, Maritime Faculty, Kocaeli University, Turkey

The concept of "green port" reflects ecological practices aimed at protecting the environment during port activities. Green port practices are a long-term strategic approach in terms of ensuring the environmental sustainability of a port. The study focuses on the environmental dimension of sustainability, which is a popular concept today. By conducting a literature search on the green port strategy, important indicators were determined, and it was aimed to analyze these indicators. As a result of the study, important indicators such as air quality, climate change energy efficiency, noise pollution, relations with the local community, water quality and ship waste, dredging operations and port development, and garbage/port wastes have been reached.

    José G. Vargas-Hernández, Posgraduate and Research Department, Tecnológico Mario
       Molina Unidad Zapopan, Mexico
    Omar C. Vargas-González, Tecnológico Nacional de México, Ciudad Guzmán, Mexico

This study aims to analyze the implications of organizational innovation to green technological innovation departing from the assumption that organizational innovation and technological innovation are the dimensions that lead to the creation and development of green technological innovation capacities that have the potential to alleviate and ease the ecological and environmental crises. The method used is the analytical reflective based on the theoretical and empirical literature. It is concluded that the development of green technological innovation organizations tends to develop the competence to innovate and survive for a longer period in their domains.

Reshma Shrivastava, Amity University, Raipur, India
Imran Nadeem Siddiqui, Amity University, Raipur, India
Suresh Kumar Pattanayak, Amity University, Raipur, India

The majority of businesses have adopted human resource strategies that promote environmental sustainability while taking into account minimizing environmental damage and contamination. The chapter investigates how business organizations can create a sustainable environment with reference to selected companies in India. The senior management of an organization is therefore also responsible for making sure that the staff is encouraged to pursue the social, ecological, and financial benefits of living in a greener environment. The chapter highlights the value of a green environment as well as the initiatives taken by various businesses to preserve a sustainable environment. Evaluation of the green human resource management (GHRM) predicted results and anticipated challenges while attempting to create a greener environment. The chapter focuses on the corporate social responsibility effort of selected companies and how much they are spending in CSR initiatives toward a green environment.

Javier Martínez Falcó, University of Alicante, Spain
Bartolomé Marco Lajara, University of Alicante, Spain
Patrocinio Zaragoza-Sáez, University of Alicante, Spain

In recent years, interest in intangible assets has grown, and their identification, measurement, and management has become a topical issue. It is considered important to the recognized value of these invisible assets, called intellectual capital (IC), because they add information to traditional financial indicators that are used both to improve decision making and to demonstrate their potential to potential external users. In this context, IC that incorporates environmental and sustainable aspects (i.e., green intellectual capital [GIC] and sustainable intellectual capital [SIC]) were recently introduced in the academic literature to emphasize the importance of sustainable performance. In order to contribute new knowledge to the subject under study, the research aims to answer the following six research questions through a literature review: (1) What are the origins of IC? (2) How is IC defined? (3) What are the origins of GIC? (4) How is GIC defined? (5) What are the origins of SIC? (6) How is SIC defined?

Preface

In an increasingly changing and complex environment, sustainable development, corporate social responsibility, effective knowledge management and intellectual assets represent the basis of today's innovations and therefore the new ways for organizations to compete in the marketplace. In this regard, organizations need to incorporate a sustainable approach to their operations because: (1) there is a growing awareness of environmental issues among customers, (2) they are faced with increasingly stringent environmental regulations, and (3) the development of sustainable practices can lead to sustainable competitive advantages over time.

This book provides a body of research that aims to explore the theoretical and practical aspects of linking corporate profitability, intangible assets, corporate social responsibility and sustainability with respect to business management practices. Covering a wide range of topics, this book is ideally designed for business practitioners, small business owners, entrepreneurs, academics, researchers and business students who wish to delve into the study of the intangible assets of organizations and sustainable business practices.

The book is structured in 13 book chapters. Chapter 1 reflects on how corporate social responsibility can be conceived as a narrative in many different ways, from personal and social intentions coming together to forge a part towards collective empowerment goals. Corporate social responsibility is already in the process of being replaced by people's social responsibility. The status of CSR activity and its relationship to CSR spending and value creation is also studied. However, the authors argue that much of the previous literature reviewed the complex process of interaction and negotiation that takes place between companies and consumers. In this book chapter, the authors focus on reflecting a clearer picture of the interaction, challenges and brand exchange within consumer disclosure and perception of CSR.

Chapter 2 reviews the literature on the role of social capital and intellectual capital in the economy and their contribution to corporate social responsibility, with particular emphasis on their importance for companies. The chapter relates social capital and intellectual capital to concepts such as trust and corporate culture, and discusses and proposes several metrics that capture them at the firm level, including CSR efforts by firms. The author summarizes existing research on the relationship between social capital, intellectual capital, and firm value and stock market performance. In addition, he analyzes whether companies are investing enough in intellectual capital and social capital in their corporate social responsibilities.

Chapter 3 assesses information governance in South African organizations. The authors discuss corporate governance, data privacy, legislation, information security, big data, access, and training. The chapter findings reveal that successful corporate governance depends on executive management buy-in, alignment of organizational strategy with the organization's mission and vision. In addition, organizations must implement systematic disposal of records, effective retention of records, quality assurance must be tested.

Chapter 4 highlights the role of government agencies for their contribution to the growth of the economy and the benefits they bring to society. However, there is an increasing need for these agencies to be ethical, especially in the 21st century, an era filled with competitors and also characterized by an increasingly globalized business world and a cascade of corruption and corporate fraud in both developed and developing countries. As a result, government agencies require the application of business ethics for the long-term success and sustainability of companies. Although the main objective of business is to make money and profit, government agencies must take the lead for the welfare of society and conduct their activities within the framework of environmental standards and social responsibility. These agencies must provide goods and services legally and profitably to society and act responsibly to address social and environmental problems. The author conducts a literature review to critically analyze business ethics and social responsibility practices in South African government agencies.

Chapter 5 argues that knowledge plays a fundamental role in achieving business success. This has led to the intensification of the study of the set of intangible assets of the organization, called Intellectual Capital (IC), as well as its impact on the achievement of sustainable competitive advantages over time. Moreover, IC that incorporates sustainable aspects, i.e., Green Intellectual Capital (GIC), was recently introduced into the academic literature and has since become an emerging field of study. The lack of consistency in the terminologies used has made it difficult to establish clear measurements of intangibles, especially the dimensions of IC, which has posed an additional difficulty for the advancement of this area of knowledge. To overcome this research problem, the authors analyze the origins and conceptualization of IC and GIC, attempting to shed light on the field of study by answering the following questions: (1) What are the origins of IC? (2) How is IC defined? (3) What are the origins of GIC? (4) How is GIC defined?

Chapter 6 aims to analyze the conceptual and theoretical approaches to organizational ecology based on the assumption that the unit of analysis of organizational ecology can be described, analyzed and explained from different frames of reference. The method employed is the analytical and reflexive referential of the main characteristics of the different perspectives already systematized in the theoretical and empirical research literature studying the ecology of organizations. The authors conclude that the unit of analysis of the ecology of organizations, both internally and externally, can be approached to be systematized from the perspectives of open systems, evolutionary theory, institutional and functionalist, structural and community theories.

Chapter 7 aims to analyze the implications of green knowledge and technology in organizational green innovation, urban green innovation and green roofs. The analysis assumes that green knowledge and technology are basic to the practices, operations and activities in the areas of organizational green innovation and urban green innovation. The methods employed by the authors are based on the analytical-reflective and descriptive methods supported with theoretical and empirical literature review. The authors conclude that green knowledge sharing is relevant to create and develop green technology with positive implications for organizational green innovation, urban green innovation areas and green roofs.

Chapter 8 aims to find out how consumers' purchasing decisions affect environmental, social and governance practices. The questionnaire was given to newly graduated consumers. Through smart pls, the author checked the survey questions. The results imply that consumers prioritize two factors, environmental and social. The chapter shows that personal concerns relate to the recycling process, resource consumption and environmentally friendly business practices. In addition, customer health and safety, good working environment and focus on human rights have shown reasonable importance. However, the consideration of governance factors is very low in the decision-making process of customers due to the low level of knowledge about governance practices, especially political participation and fraud and corruption. Thus, the author's empirical findings serve as a springboard for further research in this area and offer marketers and sellers of ESG practices strategic implications.

Chapter 9 emphasizes that many companies opt for corporate sustainability to meet the needs of the environment, society and the economy in order to be optimal in the long term. To do so, companies must use their resources fully and efficiently. Intellectual capital, which increases market value and establishes lasting competitive advantages, is one of their most precious resources. This research advances the growth of two distinct but related fields of study: sustainability and intellectual capital. The authors' purpose is to understand the notion as a whole and how each component of intellectual capital contributes to the sustainable growth of a company. Realization in an organization occurs at all levels of management, whether it is based on interactions with people, human resources or effective life-cycle processes or structures. Intellectual capital, according to the authors, plays a crucial or significant role in the long-term sustainability of companies.

Chapter 10 focuses on the "green port" concept, which reflects environmentally friendly practices aimed at protecting the environment during port activities. Green port practices constitute a long-term strategic approach to ensure the environmental sustainability of a port. The book chapter focuses on the environmental dimension of sustainability, which is a very popular concept today. Through a literature search on green port strategy, the author tries to identify important indicators and then analyzes them. The author identifies important indicators such as air quality, climate change energy efficiency, noise pollution, local community relations, water quality and ship waste, dredging operations and port development, and garbage/port waste.

Chapter 11 analyzes the implications of organizational innovation for green technological innovation based on the assumption that organizational innovation and technological innovation are the dimensions that lead to the creation and development of green technological innovation capabilities that have the potential to alleviate and facilitate ecological and environmental crises. The method used is the reflective analytical method based on theoretical and empirical literature. The authors conclude that the development of green technological innovation organizations tends to develop the competence to innovate and survive longer in their domains.

Chapter 12 highlights that most companies have adopted human resource strategies that promote environmental sustainability with consideration of minimizing environmental damage and pollution. The authors investigate how business organizations can create a sustainable environment with reference to selected companies in India. Therefore, the top management of an organization is also responsible for ensuring that staff are encouraged to seek the social, ecological and financial benefits of living in a greener environment. The book chapter advocates the value of a green environment as well as the initiatives taken by various companies to preserve a sustainable environment, focusing mainly on the corporate social responsibility effort of the selected companies and the amount they spend on CSR initiatives towards a green environment.

Chapter 13 highlights the fact that in recent years interest in intangible assets has grown and their identification, measurement and management has become a topical issue. It is considered important to recognize the value of these invisible assets, called Intellectual Capital (IC), because they add information to traditional financial indicators that are used both to improve decision-making and to demonstrate their potential to potential external users. In this context, IC that incorporates environmental and sustainable aspects, i.e. Green Intellectual Capital (GIC) and Sustainable Intellectual Capital (SIC), have recently been introduced in the academic literature to highlight the importance of sustainable performance. In order to bring new knowledge to the topic under study, the researchers answer the following six research questions through a literature review: (1) What are the origins of IC? (2) How is IC defined? (3) What are the origins of GIC? (4) How is GIC defined? (5) What are the origins of SIC? (6) How is SIC defined?

The book thus serves as a study guide, reflection and critique to understand the role of intellectual capital in achieving a sustainable approach by the organization. The book sheds light on new trends and challenges around intellectual capital management and sustainable practices, making it a must-read for academics and managers who want to deepen their understanding of the link between organizations' intangible assets and their sustainable management.

Bartolomé Marco-Lajara
University of Alicante, Spain

Patrocinio Zaragoza-Sáez
University of Alicante, Spain

Javier Martínez-Falcó
University of Alicante, Spain

Acknowledgment

The editors would like to point out on this festive occasion the fact that this scientific book entitled Intellectual Capital as a Precursor to Sustainable Corporate Social Responsibility, published by IGI Global, is the result of the vigorous work and the sedulousness that characterized the activity and the actions belonging to the authors, to the members of the Editorial Advisory Board (EAB), and to the members of the Editorial Review Board (ERB).

Furthermore, the editors would like to express the deepest and the profoundest appreciation to the IGI Global team members, who were on top of the situation at every level and who turned this constructive collaboration into a wonderful scientific project that came to life in order to support hard work, creativity, dedication, knowledge, and education, in times in which the ability of organizations to promote sustainable development and foster environmental protection is a key feature for the survival and health of our Planet.

Editorial Advisory Board

Luis A. Millán-Tudela, *University of Alicante, Spain*
Vicente Sabater-Sempere, *University of Alicante, Spain*
Jorge Valdes Conca, *University of Alicante, Spain*

Chapter 1
A Review of Corporate Social Responsibility in Shaping the Brand Value in Context to the Spending on Rural Urban Development

Gazala Yasmin Ashraf

Amity University, Raipur, India

Disha Sharma

https://orcid.org/0000-0003-2124-0970

Amity University, Raipur, India

Reshma Shrivastava

Amity University, Raipur, India

ABSTRACT

Corporate social responsibility can be a narrative in many different ways, from one's personal and social intentions to coming together to forge toward the collective goals of empowerment. Corporate social responsibility is already on its way to replace human social responsibility. The study involves the study of the standing on CSR activity and its relationship between CSR spending and value creation. This article, however, argues that much of the past literature reviewed the complex process of interaction and negotiation evolving between businesses and consumers. This study is focusing on reflecting a clearer picture of brand interaction, challenges, and exchanges within the disclosure and consumer perception of CSR. Then, the chapter will identify the relationship between CSR and value creation. In this chapter, the authors are going to discuss the practical and theoretical implications, as well as give suggestions for future research.

DOI: 10.4018/978-1-6684-6815-9.ch001

INTRODUCTION

Corporate social responsibility can be a narrative in many different ways, from one's personal and social intentions to coming together to forge toward the collective goals of empowerment. Corporate social responsibility is already on way to replace human social responsibility. To scale corporate social responsibility, there could be several parameters. Lately, there has been an increased focus on the branding of corporate and establishing an identity as a potential source for building the image of the brand. There is a phenomenon called 'the second wave of corporate branding' which shifted the core focus from the brand and products to the company. This perspective focuses more on the fundamentals of uplifting the locus of differentiation and corporate advantages. The development of CSR strategies has been particularly pressing for brand-based and multi-national companies such as Nike etc. The inclination of public interest recently has highlighted the importance of protecting the brand image and demonstrating the brand image with a view of a corporate socially responsible attitude in order to maintain social capital with customers and suppliers.

The relationship between corporate governance and corporate performance is mostly measured using variables of the corporate governance mechanism. Thus, recent literature on CSR strategy and corporate branding quotes numerous reasons why a company can benefit by acting in more socially responsible and environmentally aware ways. Through this phenomenon, the company can achieve a competitive advantage, build a strong corporate image and end up winning the war for talent. However, there are multiple parameters that define the values and justification for corporate social responsibility that has a direct relationship between the motive and the act of the company and an indirect relationship with the vision of the company. Nevertheless, the practice of CSR is Subject to major criticism and full of trial and error, seems like CSR is no more like window-dressing. Though past researchers have commented on the significance of CSR over many external factors and internal factors implemented in building the brand image and framing business strategy. By strengthening the company's CSR structure, a company can contribute to developing a positive, strong corporate brand image.

The purpose of this study is to develop new knowledge on corporate branding from a CSR perspective. The study involves the study of the standing on CSR activity and its relationship between CSR spending and brand value. This article, however, argues that much of the past literature reviewed the complex process of interaction and negotiation evolving between businesses and consumers. This study is focusing on reflecting a clearer picture of brand interaction, challenges, and exchange within the disclosure and consumer perception of CSR. In the flow of this chapter, the article will first identify the factors that have a direct involving corporate social responsibility impact on building the brand image through secondary literature review. Secondly, the chapter will identify the relation between CSR and value creation. In this chapter, we are also going to discuss through bibliometric analysis the scenario and will give suggestions for future research.

Literature Review

According to Carroll (1979) Corporate Social Responsibility came into prominence after 1950s. He holds the view that social responsibility of business includes varied expectations from the society. According to Clarkson (1995) proposes in his study that the primary stakeholder group as "one without whose continuing participation the corporation cannot survive as a going concern." With the primary group including shareholders and investors, employees, customers and suppliers, together with what is defined as the public stakeholder group; the governments and communities that provide.

According to Webb and Mohr (2006) says that CSR helps in building corporate reputation. It is found that consumers take CSR activities positively. Crouch (2006) observes that companies practicing CSR will be able to anticipate change and disturbances.

According to Chatterji (2011) writes that Government is very well aware that CSR plays a very significant role for developing the socio-economic development. The government also understands that CSR helps in managing costs and benefits of business for both internal as well as external stakeholder. In her book she writes that the government of India conducted some review and gave conclusion that there are some aspects that have to be followed by Indian Companies like CSR policy, planning for CSR activities, fixing targets for CSR activities, budget allocation for CSR activities and monitoring mechanism for CSR activities.

World Business Council for Sustainable Development holds the view that "Corporate Social Responsibility is the continuing commitment by business to behave ethically and contribute to economic development while improving the quality of life of the workforce and their families as well as of the local community and society large". So we see that the CSR concept is largely focusing on the stakeholder concept. Doing business ethically is the bottom line of the CSR concept today. As Kotler and Lee 2005 hold the view that CSR has become an important issue today and stakeholders are very enthusiastic about it which has made CSR popular among marketing professionals it has become a corporate identity and consumers' purchase intentions are dependent on it. According to (Malik 2015) CSR plays a significant role in enhancing firm value by promoting employee productivity, ensuring better operating performance and helping in building a relationship with society and other stakeholders. CSR has an impact on brand and it creates brand value it has been found that it creates financial impact too. (Pope 2021).

CSR also has a potential contribution to brand value and it can be maximized by market-based performance by the organizations. (Melo et al 2011). It also determines the most important investment point and it promotes sustainable development. (Qi et al 2021). As stated by (Fatma & Khan 2019) there stands indirect relationships between CSR and brand loyalty with the mediation effect of brand experience and brand trust, CSR does not influence brand loyalty directly, it is required to provide a better brand experience to enhance trust and that ultimately create brand loyal customers. The managers of the region should line up their efforts toward CSR activities directed at improving corporate social performance for the overall betterment of the organization as well as society. (Mahmood & Bashir 2020). The concept of corporate social responsibility (CSR), which links societal ideals and company objectives, is well-known in management disciplines. CSR is used as a strategic approach that gives competitive differentiation through the coagulation of both business and overarching societal goals. Companies think that the goodwill generated by CSR initiatives contributes to sustainable development and strategic competitive advantage. (Rahman et al. 2019,) According to polls of businesses, one of their corporate social responsibility's primary goals is branding (CSR). With advantageous data from Brand Finance, it addresses there are many factors responsible for the relationship between CSR and brand value. CSR has a positive impact on brand value regardless of industry and it has a strong impact on stakeholder (Chiang, H.-T. and Lin, Y.-C. and Chen, W.-W.,2022), CSR initiatives not only have a positive impact on brand value but it also impacts the firm competitive advantage and helps firm to sustain in the competitive market. (Qi, Chai, & Jiang, 2021).There is relationships among perceived corporate social responsibility (CSR), perceived team CSR, social identities, and corporate brand equity. Corporate brand equity is directly benefited by CSR. Corporate brand equity has been positively impacted by CSR actions (Ma & Kaplanidou, K 2021).

Corporate social responsibility (CSR) actions both directly and indirectly (through brand value dimensions) have an impact on consumers' willingness to pay a premium price (WTPP) for luxury brand products. A long-term orientation (LTO) may also moderate these links (Dahmane at al., 2021).

In order to provide expected value for the business and society, corporate social responsibility is emerging as a major trend in business operations that links sustainable development with fundamental values. Corporate social responsibility (CSR) helps a company's reputation, brand value, and quality. CSR can dramatically improve brand value and importance for businesses. (Tam, P.T.2021). Corporate investments in social responsibility initiatives have a positive indirect impact on the company's financial performance, including return on assets and market capitalization. This is because a high level of corporate social responsibility and ethical behavior has a stronger impact on brand value (Melikova & Yu, 2021).

Corporate social responsibility (CSR) is a crucial tactical instrument for boosting a company's legitimacy and competitive advantage. This study applies stakeholder theory to examine how different CSR actions may relate to global brand value in different ways. It also examines the potential effects of firm size on these relationships. (Kim & Wang, 2021). In a developing, Islamic nation, CSR actions for financial services brands are perceived. Results indicate that the attribute of CSR, the amount of CSR, and attitude toward CSR are the three main areas of focus for CSR activities. According to the findings, there are two primary reasons to participate in CSR activities: practical and moral considerations. (Roy et al., 2020). While enterprises without international participation make up only 40% of the total, nearly 86% of food companies with foreign presence engage in CSR initiatives. The biggest discrepancies in how people view the value of CSR initiatives can be seen in foundations and charitable endeavors, as well as in sponsorship and donations; however, these differences are less obvious in regards to ecology, corporate transparency, and collaboration with non-profit organizations. CSR initiatives are promoted and employed in the environmental protection sector to increase brand value. (Kádeková et al., 2020).

It was evident that the company should focus more on CSR activities to persuade its customer-based brand equity since 70% of respondents can distinguish the "Activia" brand among other rival companies. (Pashkina, Fernandes, & Vasiukov, 2019). Through mediating effects of improved brand image and brand loyalty, CSR actions have a favourable effect on brand value. According to the findings, managers should be aware that CSR presents a chance to improve organizational value and should be implemented at all operational levels. (Verma & Singh, 2018). We contend that CSR initiatives in businesses with strong investor interest and visibility are swiftly taken note of. Given that CSR initiatives could be thought of as a mean to enhance value.

The Research Objective

The study's primary goal is to analyze various topics related to CSR practices and its relationship with Brand value and CSR Spending (Rural-Urban spending), which has become one of the most popular research topics in the last ten years due to significant changes in government policies as well as societal perception and organizational attitude.

1. To study the trend and growth of "Brand Value" in association with "CSR" practices.
2. To study about various authors, affiliations, disciplines and countries working on the concept of "CSR activities" and its relationship with "Brand value" and CSR spending (Rural-Urban spending).

Research Methodology and Analysis

Data for the current study were gathered from the "Scopus" database. 102 papers were assessed using TITLE-ABS-KEY (impact AND of AND csr AND on AND brand-value/or AND rural-urban/ OR spending) in the choices "Impact of CSR", "Brand value", "rural-urban spending". Statistical and network analyses were carried out in the current bibliometric analysis, and statistical analysis was done with data collected from the Scopus database by analyzing the results. The results and findings of 102 papers that were chosen for the study were discussed. The documents have been organized by year, source, author, affiliation, type, and subject area, and a descriptive analysis has been done. To ascertain the fields, nations, and authors' contributions to the field in terms of conducting research and its influence on other works, published research from 2010 to 2022 was examined using the bibliometric analysis approach. The categories, key research areas, cross-subject connections, and collaborations for the 102 documents under review are all made available to the public. A systematic map that will be created for Impact of CSR on Brand value and Rural-urban spending will show the progression of graphically represented published papers, pinpoint the sectors of the market that are now of interest, and eventually guide anticipated future research. By analyzing/reviewing the years that a particular research topic was most popular in terms of nations, most widely read journals, and contributing authors, this research methodology made it feasible to swiftly discover trends in the study subject.

Figure 1. Documents Published by Year

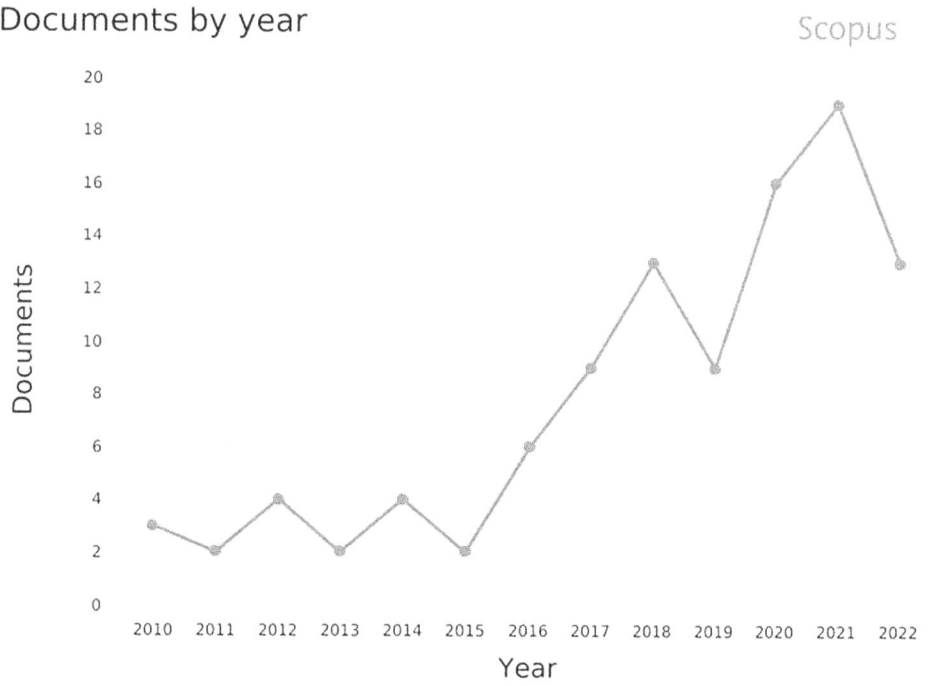

Table 1. Documents Published in Year (Number of results: 102)

Year	Count
2022	13
2021	19
2020	16
2019	9
2018	13
2017	9
2016	6
2015	2
2014	4
2013	2
2012	4
2011	2
2010	3

From the above-mentioned table 1, based on the data supplied on a year-by-year basis, 102 research articles were published between 2010 and 2022. There were less than 5 publications each in the field up till 2015 after the first paper in the area appeared in 2010. When we compare the number of publications by year, we can see that there were less publications up until 2016 (6 papers published), but following that year, there was a comparable rise in research relating to "Impact of CSR", "Brand management" and "Rural- Urban spending". The biggest developments were around 2021, when the companies changed the CSR spending after unforeseen "Covid-19" pandemic hit the world.

From the above-mentioned Table 2, the source states that there were (7) documents in Sustainability Switzerland and (3 each) in Global Business Review, Meditari Accountancy Research and Corporate Social Responsibility and Environment Management. There are 2 contributions in 8 journals and rest are distributed 1 each in other journals.

From the above-mentioned Table 3, The most popular authors in this field are Bhattacharyya A., Jadiyappa N., Aguenaou S., Amor M.A., Bansal M., Bhaduri S.N., Farooq O., Iyer S.R., Rahman M.L., Selarka E. who have contributed there research in area of "Impact of CSR", "Brand management" and "Rural- Urban spending" and rest published (1) document each.

From the above-mentioned Table 4, the most prominent documents by affiliation are BITS Pilani, Universiti Utara Malaysia, National Taiwan University, Prince of Songkla University, Rijks Universite Groningen, The University of Newcastle, Australia, IIT Bombay, Institute of Chartered Financial Analysts of India, American University in Cairo, Al Akhawayn University, Copenhagen Business School, CQ University Australia, The University of New Mexico, Madras School of Economics, Asia University, Taylor's University Malaysia, O.P. Jindal Global University, IIM Ranchi, IIM Raipur, Newcastle Business School, AUC School of Business.

Figure 2. Documents per year by Source

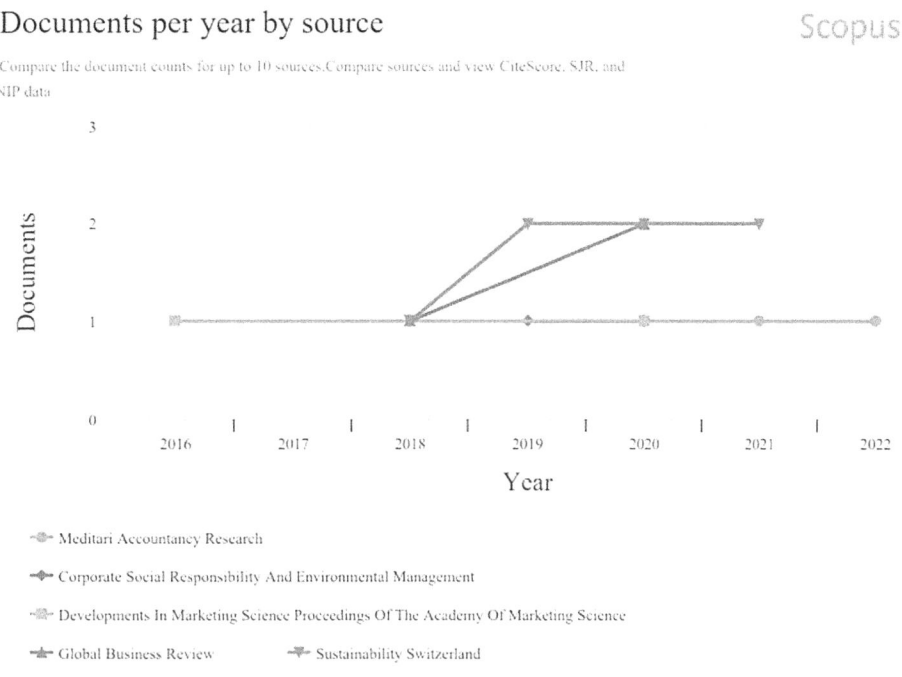

Table 2. Documents Per Year by source

Source Title	Count
Sustainability Switzerland	7
Global Business Review	3
Meditari Accountancy Research	3
Corporate Social Responsibility And Environmental Management	2
Developments In Marketing Science Proceedings Of The Academy Of Marketing Science	2
Emerging Markets Review	2
European Journal Of Marketing	2
Journal Of Applied Business Research	2
Journal Of Cleaner Production	2
Journal Of Contemporary Accounting And Economics	2
Journal Of Product And Brand Management	2
ACM International Conference Proceeding Series	1
ACM Transactions On Internet Technology	1
Accounting Finance Sustainability Governance And Fraud	1

Source Title	Count
Asia Pacific Financial Markets	1
Asia Pacific Journal Of Accounting And Economics	1
Asia Pacific Journal Of Business Administration	1
Benchmarking	1
Business History	1
Business Strategy And Development	1
Canadian Journal Of Economics	1
China Finance Review International	1
Corporate Governance An International Review	1
Economic And Political Weekly	1
Economic Research Ekonomska Istrazivanja	1
Ecs Transactions	1
Energy Policy	1
Engineer	1
Espacios	1
European Journal Of Political Economy	1
Food Science And Technology London	1

continues on following page

Table 2. Continued

Source Title	Count
Gender Technology And Development	1
Global Business And Organizational Excellence	1
Indian Journal Of Corporate Governance	1
Information Switzerland	1
Innovative Marketing	1
International Journal Of Business Excellence	1
International Journal Of Business Governance And Ethics	1
International Journal Of Management And Sustainability	1
International Journal Of Management Practice	1
International Journal Of Market Research	1
International Journal Of Mechanical Engineering And Technology	1
International Journal Of Organizational Analysis	1
International Journal Of Public Sector Performance Management	1
International Journal Of Research In Marketing	1
International Review Of Finance	1
International Review Of Law And Economics	1
Jordan Journal Of Business Administration	1
Journal Of Air Transport Management	1
Journal Of Banking And Finance	1

Source Title	Count
Journal Of Brand Management	1
Journal Of Corporate Finance	1
Journal Of Marketing Theory And Practice	1
Journal Of Services Marketing	1
Journal Of Small Business And Entrepreneurship	1
Journal Of Travel And Tourism Marketing	1
Management International Review	1
Management Science	1
Managerial And Decision Economics	1
Nankai Business Review International	1
Oeconomia Copernicana	1
Prisma Social	1
Procedia Computer Science	1
Research In Developmental Disabilities	1
Research In International Business And Finance	1
Review Of Accounting And Finance	1
Review Of International Business And Strategy	1
Social Responsibility Journal	1
Society And Business Review	1
Sustainability Accounting Management And Policy Journal	1
Sustainable Business	1

From the above-mentioned Table 5, the countries in the world, which has led to an increase in research effort connected to "Impact of CSR" and "Brand Value" and "Rural-Urban spending" are India (32), United States (20) and Australia (10) produced over half of all global papers, indicating that these three countries are critical to the CSR impact on Brand value and spending. In research, United Kingdom has emerged as fourth with contributing (7) whereas Taiwan contributed (6) and Canada (Rest have less than 5 contributions.

From the above-mentioned Table 6, 84 articles, 11 book chapters, 6 conference papers,2 Conference Reviews and 1 Review were the key components of the study that was gathered from the Scopus database.

From the above-mentioned Table 7, following searches in the Scopus database related to Impact of CSR; Brand Value and Spending – most of the publications were from Business, Management and Accounting Discipline (70), Social Sciences being second with count (32) followed by Economics, Econometrics and Finance in third place with (26) publications. Environmental science has (22) publications whereas Energy (12) followed by Computer Science and Engineering with (6) each. Rest comprise of less than (5) papers.

Figure 3. Documents by Author

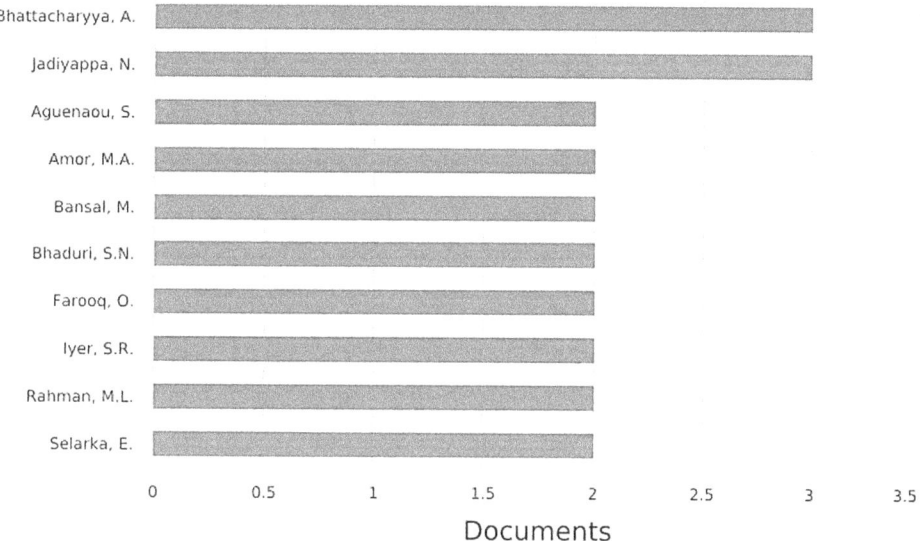

Table 3. Documents by Author

Author Name	Count	Author Name	Count	Author Name	Count
Bhattacharyya, A.	3	David, B.A.	1	Josiassen, A.	1
Jadiyappa, N.	3	Davis, D.	1	Jothi Francina, V.	1
Aguenaou, S.	2	De La Poza Plaza, E.	1	Joy, F.	1
Amor, M.A.	2	Devji, S.	1	Justman, M.	1
Bansal, M.	2	Dharmapala, D.	1	Jyothi, P.	1
Bhaduri, S.N.	2	Dipa Kalyani Sujata, P.	1	Jyrämä, A.	1
Farooq, O.	2	Diplaris, S.	1	Kajalo, S.	1
Iyer, S.R.	2	Dube, L.	1	Karim, S.	1
Rahman, M.L.	2	Dungtripop, W.	1	Khan, M.	1
Selarka, E.	2	Duppati, G.	1	Khan, Q.R.	1
Agus Harjoto, M.	1	Ebrahimpour, M.	1	Khanna, V.	1
Ahmed, I.	1	Ehsan, S.	1	Khusainova, R.	1
Ahn, J.S.	1	Ehsanullah, S.	1	Kim, H.G.	1
Akbar, M.	1	Erfgen, C.	1	Kim, T.	1
Al Mamun, M.	1	Ertugrul, M.	1	Kim, Y.	1
Al Nashef, M.I.	1	Fatemi, H.	1	Kompatsiaris, I.	1
Al-Wugayan, A.A.A.	1	Francken, N.	1	Kotek, K.	1

continues on following page

Table 3. Continued

Author Name	Count	Author Name	Count	Author Name	Count
Alcaide González, M.Á.	1	Fu, Y.	1	Košičiarová, I.	1
Ali, I.	1	Galan, J.I.	1	Kraus, A.	1
Ambilikumar, V.	1	Gambhir, V.K.	1	Kremer, G.E.O.	1
Amin, A.	1	Ganesan, D.	1	Krishnan, G.V.	1
Assaf, A.G.	1	Ganushchak-Efimenko, L.	1	Kumar, N.	1
Aswani, J.	1	Gao, L.S.	1	Kumar, S.	1
Ayuba, I.A.	1	Garito, M.	1	Kumar, S.	1
Babu, A.	1	Garrett, R.D.	1	Kumar, V.	1
Bain, S.	1	Giacomin, V.	1	Kuo, T.C.	1
Bandyopadhyay, P.	1	Gkatziaki, V.	1	Kádeková, Z.	1
Banerjee, G.	1	Glauner, W.	1	Lakkanawanit, P.	1
Bardos, K.S.	1	Good, V.	1	Lambin, E.F.	1
Barnea, A.	1	Goss, A.	1	Le, A.P.	1
Beloskar, V.D.	1	Goswami, S.	1	Lim, W.M.	1
Bhattacharya, A.	1	Gow, J.	1	Lin, H.C.	1
Bhattacharyya, S.S.	1	Guadalajara Olmeda, N.	1	Lin, J.	1
Bianca Sardjono, S.	1	Gupta, N.	1	Lin, S.Y.	1
Bijmolt, T.H.A.	1	Guzmán, F.	1	Lin, W.L.	1
Bird, R.	1	Hall, S.	1	Liu, C.	1
Boots, A.	1	Harms, R.	1	Liu, C.K.	1
Butcher, K.	1	Hasan, I.	1	Liu, C.Y.	1
Cabral, C.	1	Heinkel, R.	1	Long, C.	1
Chacón Cantos, J.	1	Hernàndez, J.A.A.I.	1	Majmudar, N.	1
Chan, E.	1	Hickman, L.E.	1	Malik, M.	1
Chang, Y.	1	Ho, J.A.	1	Manab, N.A.	1
Chastagner, K.	1	Hofmann, J.	1	Manning, L.	1
Chatterjee, B.	1	Hsu, C.W.	1	Manswell, M.N.	1
Chee Keong, O.	1	Ilon, L.	1	Marchoo, W.	1
Chen, C.C.	1	Iqbal, N.	1	Maresova, P.	1
Chen, S.L.	1	Ishola, A.K.	1	Mattila, A.S.	1
Cheng, C.H.	1	Ismail, R.B.	1	Melo, T.	1
Chidambaran, N.K.	1	Iyanar, Y.	1	Merhabi, M.A.	1
Chun, W.	1	Jangili, R.	1	Miguel, A.	1
Cockx, L.	1	Johnen, M.	1	Mills, R.	1
Cordeiro, J.J.	1	Jones, G.	1	Miranda, S.	1
Dahiya, R.	1	Joo, J.	1	Mishra, S.	1

Figure 4. Documents by Affiliation

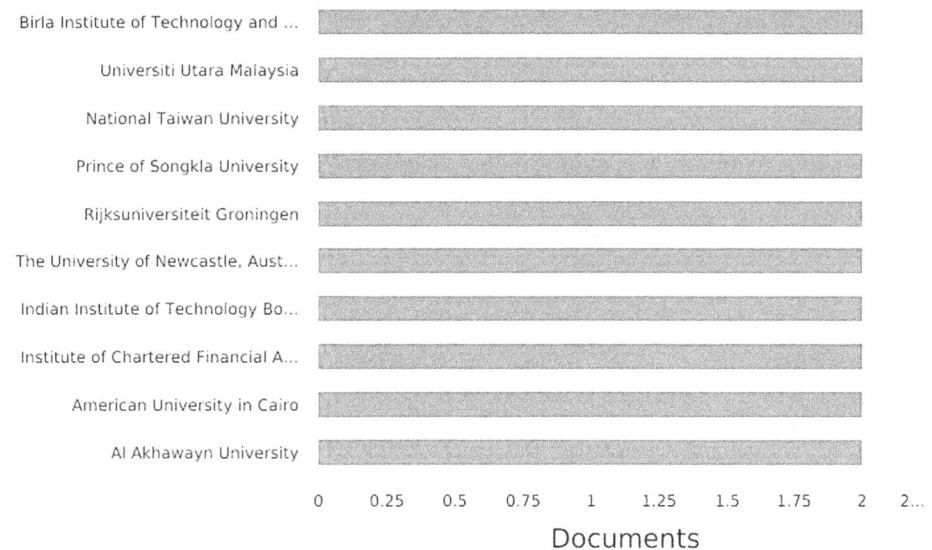

Figure 5. Documents by Country / Territory.

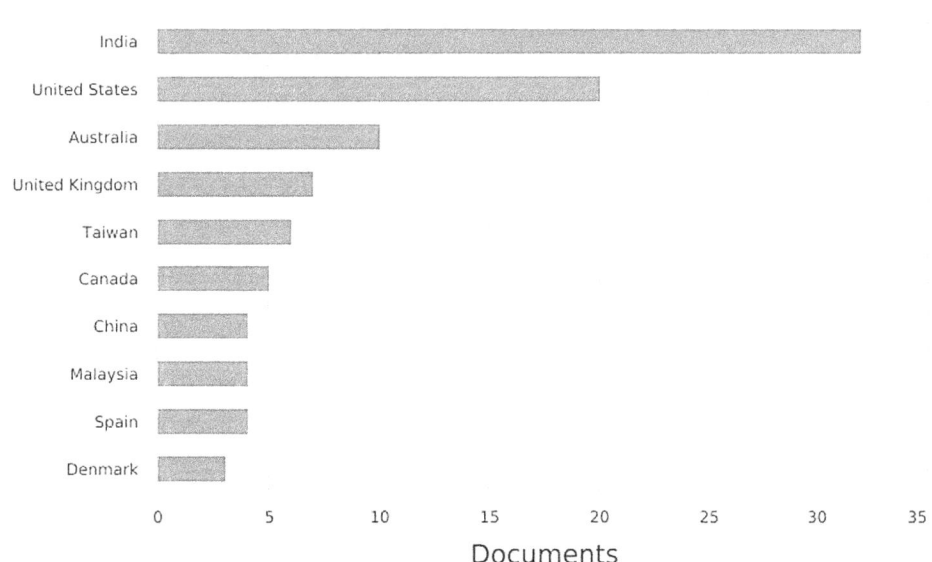

Table 4. Documents by Affiliation

Affiliation	Count	Affiliation	Count
Birla Institute of Technology and Science, Pilani	2	National Yunlin University of Science and Technology	1
Universiti Utara Malaysia	2	B.S.Abdur Rahman University	1
National Taiwan University	2	University of Massachusetts Amherst	1
Prince of Songkla University	2	Hong Kong Baptist University	1
Rijksuniversiteit Groningen	2	Slovak University of Agriculture in Nitra	1
The University of Newcastle, Australia	2	Aston University	1
Indian Institute of Technology Bombay	2	National Cheng Kung University	1
Institute of Chartered Financial Analysts of India	2	Fordham University	1
American University in Cairo	2	Universidad Torcuato Di Tella	1
Al Akhawayn University	2	Florida International University	1
Copenhagen Business School	2	University of Pittsburgh	1
CQUniversity Australia	2	Prince Sultan University	1
The University of New Mexico	2	Manipal Academy of Higher Education	1
Madras School of Economics	2	St. Cloud State University	1
Asia University	2	Khon Kaen University	1
Taylor's University Malaysia	2	University of Sussex	1
O.P. Jindal Global University	2	Coventry University	1
Indian Institute of Management Ranchi	2	Malaviya National Institute of Technology Jaipur	1
Indian Institute of Management Raipur	2	Southwestern University of Finance and Economics	1
Newcastle Business School	2	UBC Sauder School of Business	1
AUC School of Business	2	Indiana University of Pennsylvania	1
Kano State Polytechnic	1	Alpen-Adria-Universität Klagenfurt	1
Estonian Academy of Music and Theatre	1	Harvard Business School	1
University of Southern	1	Boston University	1
Kerala University of Fisheries and Ocean Sciences	1	University of Birmingham	1
Guangzhou City University of Technology	1	University of Southern Queensland	1
Kenson School of Production Technology	1	Universiteit Twente	1
Information Technologies Institute I.T.I.	1	Maulana Azad National Institute of Technology	1
Justice KS Hegde Institute of Management	1	Hope College	1
Kantar Public	1	Madurai Kamaraj University	1
Diploma Superior en Pedagogía Universitaria. Asesoría académica	1	National Institute of Industrial Engineering	1
FECO ENETECH Co., Ltd.	1	Sacred Heart University Fairfield	1
R.M.D. Degree College	1	University of Macau	1
Sustainable Advancements OPC Private Limited	1	National Chi Nan University	1
Jordan Int. Insurance Company	1	Rutgers University–Camden	1
Ministry of Corporate Affairs	1	Aalto University School of Business	1

continues on following page

Table 4. Continued

Affiliation	Count	Affiliation	Count
Centre for Research and Studies in Sociology CIES-ISCTE	1	University of Technology Sydney	1
University of North Florida	1	University of Massachusetts Boston	1
Univerzita Hradec Králové	1	University of North Texas	1
Université Catholique de Louvain	1	Royal Agricultural University	1
Pennsylvania State University	1	Bundelkhand University	1
Universidad Carlos III de Madrid	1	National Central University	1
Kyung Hee University	1	Universidad de Salamanca	1
Bank of Finland	1	KU Leuven	1
University of San Diego	1	Universiti Putra Malaysia	1
Université McGill	1	The University of Sydney	1
Universitat de València	1	Pepperdine University	1
HEC Montréal	1	Walailak University	1
Indian Institute of Forest Management	1	University of Oxford	1
Iowa State University	1	Ben-Gurion University of the Negev	1
Cranfield University	1	St Antony's College University of Oxford	1
The University of Waikato	1	University of Seoul	1
East West University	1	Universität Hamburg	1
Ecole Hôtelière de Lausanne	1	Iscte – Instituto Universitário de Lisboa	1
University of Žilina	1	Yaşar Universitesi	1
James Madison University	1	University of Southern California	1
Kookmin University	1	Chung Yuan Christian University	1
Universidad del Desarrollo	1	Swinburne University of Technology	1
National Changhua University of Education	1	Toronto Metropolitan University	1
La Trobe University	1	University of Cambridge	1
Sungkyunkwan University	1	Swinburne University of Technology Sarawak Campus	1
The College at Brockport, State University of New York	1	Michigan State University	1
University of South Florida, Tampa	1	St. Francis Xavier University	1
Dongguk University, Seoul	1	EM Normandie	1
Central Michigan University	1	Universitat Pompeu Fabra Barcelona	1
The University of British Columbia	1	Griffith University	1
University of KwaZulu-Natal	1	York University	1
Fairfield University	1	Kuwait University	1
Ahmadu Bello University	1	Universidad de Los Andes, Colombia	1
California Polytechnic State University, San Luis Obispo	1	University of the Punjab	1
Guangdong University of Foreign Studies	1	The University of Jordan	1

continues on following page

Table 4. Continued

Affiliation	Count	Affiliation	Count
RMIT University	1	Air University Islamabad	1
Universitat Politècnica de València	1	The University of the West Indies, St. Augustine Campus	1
University of Northern British Columbia	1	University of Mauritius	1
IMC Fachhochschule Krems GmbH	1	Tungnan University	1
University of Windsor	1	Bank of India	1
Julius-Maximilians-Universität Würzburg	1	Amrita Vishwa Vidyapeetham	1
Stanford University	1	Amrita School of Business	1
Yuan Ze University	1	Sona College of Technology	1
University of Florida	1	Thiagarajar School of Management	1

Table 5. Documents by Country / Territory

Country/Territory	Count	Country/Territory	Count
India	32	Colombia	1
United States	20	Czech Republic	1
Australia	10	Ecuador	1
United Kingdom	7	Estonia	1
Taiwan	6	France	1
Canada	5	Greece	1
China	4	Hong Kong	1
Malaysia	4	Indonesia	1
Spain	4	Israel	1
Denmark	3	Italy	1
Netherlands	3	Jordan	1
Pakistan	3	Kuwait	1
Thailand	3	Macao	1
Austria	2	Mauritius	1
Belgium	2	New Zealand	1
Egypt	2	Nigeria	1
Finland	2	Portugal	1
Germany	2	Slovakia	1
Morocco	2	South Africa	1
Saudi Arabia	2	Switzerland	1
South Korea	2	Trinidad and Tobago	1
Argentina	1	Turkey	1
Bangladesh	1	Ukraine	1
Chile	1	Viet Nam	1

Figure 6. Documents by Type

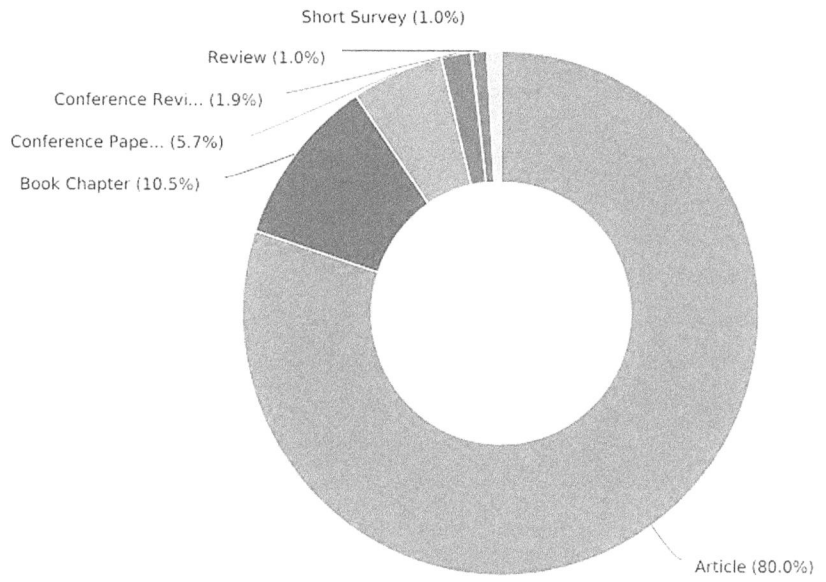

Documents by type

Scopus

Short Survey (1.0%)

Review (1.0%)

Conference Revi... (1.9%)

Conference Pape... (5.7%)

Book Chapter (10.5%)

Article (80.0%)

Table 6. Documents by Type

Document Type	Count
Article	84
Book Chapter	11
Conference Paper	6
Conference Review	2
Review	1
Short Survey	1

CONCLUSION

The paper has tried to justify the intentions, patterns, practices, and results of the acts that have presently become practice and are called as corporate social responsibility. The parameters considered in the present study have explained the overall inclination of CSR towards rural and urban development. The recent practices applied in CSR practices have enabled the company to satisfy the varied expectations of the customers. Theories also suggested that the inclusion of CSR practices has helped in building the brand reputation and socio-economic dimensions. This study also holds the significance of the adoption of CSR help to promote employees' productivity, ensure better performance, and build healthy relationships amongst the stakeholders. The better practices of sustainable development have directly proportional to stakeholders' practices. More than 60% of CSR spending has been dedicated to rural development.

Figure 7. Documents by Subject Areas

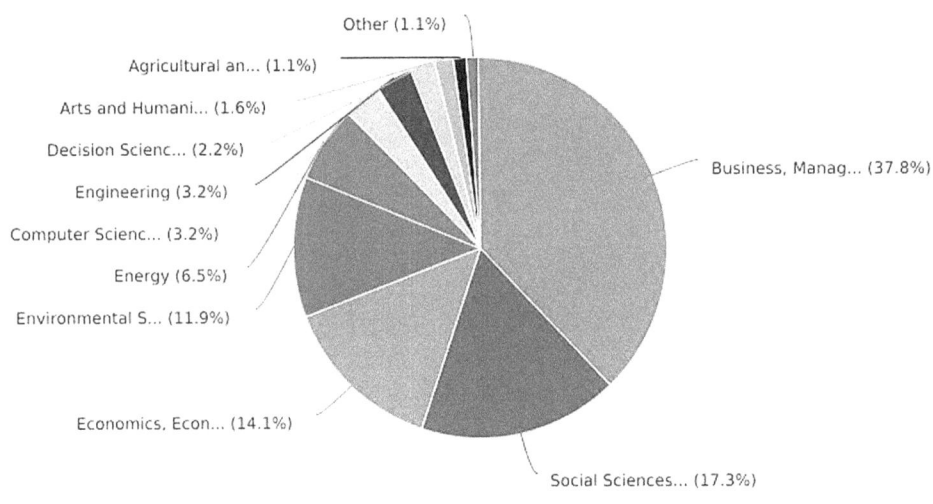

Documents by subject area   Scopus

Table 7. Documents by Subject Areas

Subject Area	Count
Business, Management and Accounting	70
Social Sciences	32
Economics, Econometrics and Finance	26
Environmental Science	22
Energy	12
Computer Science	6
Engineering	6
Decision Sciences	4
Arts and Humanities	3
Agricultural and Biological Sciences	2
Earth and Planetary Sciences	1
Psychology	1

Managerial Implications

An increase in rural spending has a positive impact not only on the development of a rural community but has enhanced the brand value of the business. CSR can be imperative for companies to enhance their brand value. Brand Value creation is focused more on rural and urban spending. It has been observed that more than 80% of the study has been found in the area of business, management, accounting, social sciences, economics, and environmental science. Very few studies have been found in the area of psychology, arts, humanities, and agriculture, hence this gives a future scope to the researcher to explore more in these areas. The study is primarily done in India, US, Australia, and UK very few are found in Taiwan Canada, China, Malaysia, Spain, Denmark, Netherlands Pakistan and Thailand hardly one or two studies have been done in other countries.

REFERENCES

Ajina, A. S., Roy, S., Nguyen, B., Japutra, A., & Al-Hajla, A. H. (2020). Enhancing brand value using corporate social responsibility initiatives: Evidence from financial services brands in saudi arabia. *Qualitative Market Research*, *23*(4), 575–602. doi:10.1108/QMR-11-2017-0145

Carroll (1979). A three Dimensional Conceptual Model Of Corporate Performance. *Academy of Management Review, 4*(4), 497-505.

Chatterji, M. (2011). *Corporate Social Responsibility* (1st ed.). Oxford University Press.

Chiang, H., Lin, Y.-C., & Chen, W.-W. (2022). Does family business affect the relationship between corporate social responsibility and brand value? A study in different industry taiwan. *Asia Pacific Management Review*, *27*(1), 28–39. doi:10.1016/j.apmrv.2021.04.002

Clarkson, M. B. E. (1995). A Stakeholder Framework for Analyzing and Evaluating Corporate Social Performance. *Academy of Management Review*, *20*(1), 92–117. doi:10.2307/258888

Crouch. (2006). Modelling the Firm in its Market and Organisational Environmennt: Methodologies For studying CSR. *Organisation Studies, 27*(10), 1533-1551.

Diallo, M. F., Ben Dahmane Mouelhi, N., Gadekar, M., & Schill, M. (2021). CSR actions, brand value, and willingness to pay a premium price for luxury brands: Does long-term orientation matter? *Journal of Business Ethics, 169*(2), 241–260. doi:10.100710551-020-04486-5

Ellen, S. P., Webb, J. D., & Mohr, A. (2006). Building Corporate Associations:Consumer Attributions for CSR Programs.*Journal of the Academy of Marketing Science,34*,147–157.doi:10.1177/0092070305284976

Farooq, O., Aguenaou, S., & Amor, M. A. (2015). Corporate social responsibility policy and brand value. *Journal of Applied Business Research*, *31*(6), 2013–2024. doi:10.19030/jabr.v31i6.9463

Farooq, O., Aguenaou, S., & Amor, M. A. (2015). Corporate social responsibility policy and brand value. *Journal of Applied Business Research*, *31*(6), 2013–2024. doi:10.19030/jabr.v31i6.9463

Filz, J., Blomme, R. J., & Van Rheede, A. (2016). The marketing value of CSR initiatives and potential brand equity, taste perception, and emotional value. *Advances in Hospitality and Leisure.* doi:10.1108/S1745-354220160000012006

Guzmán, F., & Davis, D. (2017). The impact of corporate social responsibility on brand equity: Consumer responses to two types of fit. *Journal of Product and Brand Management, 26*(5), 435–446. doi:10.1108/JPBM-06-2015-0917

Kádeková, Z., Savov, R., Košičiarová, I., & Valaskova, K. (2020). CSR activities and their impact on brand value in food enterprises in slovakia based on foreign participation. *Sustainability (Switzerland), 12*(12). doi:10.3390/SU12124856

Kádeková, Z., Savov, R., Košičiarová, I., & Valaskova, K. (2020). CSR activities and their impact on brand value in food enterprises in slovakia based on foreign participation. *Sustainability (Switzerland), 12*(12). doi:10.3390/SU12124856

Khan, I., & Fatma, M. (2019). Connecting the dots between CSR and brand loyalty: The mediating role of brand experience and brand trust. *International Journal of Business Excellence, 17*(4), 439–455. doi:10.1504/IJBEX.2019.099123

Kim, H. G., Chun, W., & Wang, Z. (2021). Multiple-dimensions of corporate social responsibility and global brand value: A stakeholder theory perspective. *Journal of Marketing Theory and Practice, 29*(4), 409–422. doi:10.1080/10696679.2020.1865109

Kotler, P., & Lee, N. (2005). *Corporate Social Responsibility.* Wiley.

Ma, S., & Kaplanidou, K. (2021). How corporate social responsibility and social identities lead to corporate brand equity: An evaluation in the context of sport teams as brand extensions. *Sport Marketing Quarterly, 30*(1), 16–29. doi:10.32731/SMQ.301.032021.02

Mahmood, A., & Bashir, J. (2020). How does corporate social responsibility transform brand reputation into brand equity? Economic and noneconomic perspectives of CSR. *International Journal of Engineering Business Management, 12*, 1847979020927547. doi:10.1177/1847979020927547

Malik, M. (2015). Value-enhancing capabilities of CSR: A brief review of contemporary literature. Journal of usiness. *Ethics, 127*(2), 419–438.

Melo, T., & Galan, J. I. (2011). Effects of corporate social responsibility on brand value. *Journal of Brand Management, 18*(6), 423–437. doi:10.1057/bm.2010.54

Pope, S., & Kim, J. (2021). Where, When, and Who: Corporate Social Responsibility and Brand Value—A Global Panel Study. *Business & Society.* doi:10.1177/00076503211019315

Qi, Y., Chai, Y., & Jiang, Y. (2021). Threshold effect of government subsidy, corporate social responsibility and brand value using the data of China's top 500 most valuable brands. *PLoS One, 16*(5), e0251927. doi:10.1371/journal.pone.0251927 PMID:34032810

Rahman, M., Rodríguez-Serrano, M., & Lambkin, M. (2019). Brand equity and firm performance: The complementary role of corporate social responsibility. *Journal of Brand Management, 26*(6), 691–704. doi:10.105741262-019-00155-9

Singh, A., & Verma, P. (2018). Driving brand value through CSR initiatives: An empirical study in indian perspective. *Global Business Review*, *19*(1), 85–98. doi:10.1177/0972150917713270

Tam, P. T. (2021). Impacting corporate social responsibility on brand value: A case study of commercial banks in ho chi minh city. *Academy of Strategic Management Journal, 20*(2), 1-12.

Vasiukov, D., Fernandes, P. O., & Pashkina, O. (2019). Corporate social responsibility and customer-based brand equity. Paper presented at the Proceedings of the 33rd International Business Information Management Association Conference, IBIMA 2019: Education Excellence and Innovation Management through. *Vision (Basel)*, *2020*, 4594–4604. www.scopus.com

Zhukova, N. Y., & Melikova, A. E. (2021). Corporate social responsibility: Strengthening brand value and affecting company's financial performance. Finance. *Theory into Practice*, *25*(1), 84–102. doi:10.26794/2587-5671-2021-25-1-84-102

Chapter 2
A Review of Social and Intellectual Capital From the Lens of Corporate Social Responsibility

Jonai Wabwire
Kisii University, Kenya

ABSTRACT

This chapter reviews literature on the role of social capital and intellectual capital in the economy, and their contribution to corporate social responsibility with a particular emphasis on their importance for corporations. The chapter relates social capital and intellectual capital to concepts such as trust and corporate culture; and discusses and proposes various metrics that capture them at the firm level, including firms' corporate social responsibility (CSR) efforts. A summary of the existing research on the relation between social capital, intellectual capital, and firm value and stock market performance has been done. Finally, an analysis of whether firms are investing enough in intellectual capital and social capital in its corporate social responsibilities has been done.

INTRODUCTION

In contemporary corporate management, managers combine capital and labor in the production process to maximize profits. Companies continue investing until the return on the marginal dollar of investment is equal to the cost of capital. A huge literature has studied the various frictions that prevent firms from investing optimally, either because financing frictions prevent them from exhausting their investment opportunities (Stulz, 1990), or because inefficiencies in the contracting process between the firm and its executives lead firms to over invest. Likewise, there is a large literature on the importance of human capital in the production process and the role of compensation, particularly at the CEO level, in affecting investment and firm performance (Edmans & Gabaix, 2016). The same applies to intellectual capital

DOI: 10.4018/978-1-6684-6815-9.ch002

demands in various firms. It is in this light that this chapter attempts to analyze the relationship that exits between the various capitals (intellectual and social capitals) and corporate social responsibility.

More recently, a literature has also emerged studying a firm's intellectual capital—investments in Research and Development (R&D) (Brown, Fazzari, & Petersen, 2009) and associated patents and patent citations (Trajtenberg, 1990; Hall 2005). Such intangible investments are an obvious necessity to safeguard the future livelihood of the firm, and, in fact, many industries spend more on R&D than on physical capital. Broadly speaking though, investments in both physical and intellectual capital would be considered capital investments. There is another type of capital, however, that has received much less attention in the literature, but may be as important as the other sources of capital. In fact, without it, the return on investments in other capital may well be substantially diminished. This type of capital is called social capital; it consists broadly of the quality of the relationships that the firm has built with a variety of stakeholders. Firms with greater social capital provoke a level of trust and cooperation from stakeholders that can ultimately enhance profitability and firm valuation.

On the other hand, there is intellectual capital. In 1969, Calbraith, an American economist, first put forward the term "intellectual capital". He pointed out that intellectual capital is a dynamic capital, a dynamic process of knowledge generation, and a way to achieve goals (Xu, 2014). However, Calbraith's definition and study of this concept only stay here, without further elaboration. At present, the connotation of intellectual capital lacks a unified standard. Scholars mainly define intellectual capital from three perspectives: intangible assets, knowledge and ability, and enterprise value (Andriessen, 2001). In my opinion, intellectual capital can be defined as the total of knowledge assets that a company owns or controls, which can bring competitive advantages to an organization and create high value. This concept points out that creating high value differentiates intellectual capital from general intangible assets, and emphasizes that intellectual capital is not a single asset. It can play an economic role and is more suitable for the study of the relationship between intellectual capital and enterprise performance in the lenses of corporate social responsibility.

In this chapter, the importance of social capital, intellectual capital and corporate social responsibility for corporations and their relationships to trust building and the notion of corporate culture has been discussed. The chapter starts by discussing the antecedents of the notion of social and intellectual capitals which were originally defined at the level of the society at large and applied to each individual member of that society. Much of the current research on social and intellectual capitals continues to rely on this notion. However, the chapter argues that both, social capital and intellectual capital; can also be defined at the firm level. Investments in social capital can help build trust between the firm and its stakeholders or publics and, thereby, can improve the performance of the firm.

SOCIAL CAPITAL

As a new concept for corporate management, social capital has attracted so much attention that it has become routinized in everyday conversation and policy discourse (Wool-Cock 2010). As a field of research, social capital theory has already been argued to have reached maturity (Kwon & Adler, 2014) because its basic thesis (i.e., the beneficial impact of social capital on information, influence, control, power, and solidarity) has been widely accepted across disciplines. Social capital can be simply said as the resource embedded in the social relationship and can be explored and used for some specific goals, however, since social capital is mainly intangible, there is still no uniform understanding, neither precise definition (Nahapiet et al., 1998), for instance, Burt defined social capital as the structure of relationship networks and information available to an individual (Burt, 1992), while Coleman even simply defined social capital as a type of capital, and can be developed when the relationship between individuals is utilized to facilitate their actions (Coleman, 1998). However, despite the diverse definitions, it is not difficult to find that social capital can be used as an instrument for some specific purpose; undoubtedly, this will influence the individual and organizational performance.

Social capital has been wildly discussed from 1980s, however, there is still no precise and completely accepted definition, for example, Bourdieu defined social capital as the aggregation of actual and potential resources within a specific network, where the network is composed of relationships that involve mutual acquaintance and mutual recognition (Bourdieu, 1980), while Adler and Kwon defined it as the network of relationships which adds value to the network actors by accessing to the resources embedded in the network (Adler et al., 2002). Comparing different definitions about social capital, this chapter attributes them into three broad perspectives, the static perspective and the dynamic perspective, and the mixed perspective.

The former one focus on the static attributes of network, such as the network structure, including density, centrality, triangle relationship, the first and second structural holes, considering the ties, links, relationships within and between networks as the source of social capital, connections and ties mean the chances to access to resources and opportunities, generally speaking, the more ties and connections, the more social capital, one typical example is Burt's structural holes theory, which focus on the advantage of being broker connecting people who are not themselves connected to each other (Burt, 2005); On the contrary, the dynamic perspective focus on the interactions between network actors, compared with the static perspective, it is relative intangible, including norms, trust, values, beliefs, emotional affiliation and so on, in this way, social capital can only be embedded in the social network, unlike the static perspective, social capital cannot be owned by individual actor, and non-existing beyond the network, for example, the trust within a certain group, social value and so on (Roel et al., 2010). The third one is the mixed perspective, mixing the static and dynamic perspective, both considering the network structure and interactions between actors, for instance, Field, (2003) considered social capital as a complex account of people's relationship and their value, as well as the way social ties can be activated to produce particular type of benefits. It seems that the third perspective should be the best one, however, it may be difficult to mix tangible and intangible attributes in one research; Besides, since people are social beings, even networks have the same structure, the social capital may be different significantly, even in the same network, the social capital of actors may still have significant difference, as a result, the dynamic perspective may provide better explanation, however, it still cannot.

Dimensions of Social Capital

The diverse and inconsistent definitions about social capital result in various understanding about its dimensions, different levels, different forms, even different characteristics can divide social capital into different dimensions. From the different levels perspective, social capital can be divided into individual level, including benefits or potential benefits that accrue to an actor as a result of social network, and communal level, including civic spirit, community trust, adherence to beneficial norms (Kilduff et al, 2010); From the forms perspective, the dimensions of social capital can be divided into three forms, including trustworthiness, information flow capacity and norms accompanied by sanctions (Wu, 2008; Coleman, 1988); From the characteristics perspective, it can be divided as structural dimension, relational dimension, and resource dimension (Castro et al, 2013). Moreover, there are still some other opinions about the dimensions of social capital, such as bridging social capital and bonding social capital (Molina-Morales, 2010), instrumental ties and expressive ties (Ibarra & Andrews, 1993), cognitive dimension, relational dimension and structural dimension (Wu, 2008; Nahapiet & Ghoshal, 1998).

Since the mixture of tangible and intangible nature of social capital, it is almost impossible to give precise and clear definition about the dimensions, however, it is still possible to identify some general dimensions from the nature of social capital, including tangible dimension and intangible dimension (in this chapter, it is called interactional dimension), and the chapter only focus on the individual personal network, the actors are only individuals, not including organizations or groups. The tangible dimension mainly including the network structure and resources owned by individual actors, the network structure represents the components and structure of the network, mainly including the network density, size, individual direct and indirect ties, the individual position (for example, brokers or isolate points), the reciprocity, multiplexity (Kilduff et al, 2010), the centrality, the closeness and so on, the structural dimension gives a general graph about the personal network. The resource owned by individual can be simply understood as the quality of the social network, and is the main source of social capital. However, it is not difficult to understand that the resources will affect the network structure significantly, for example, resources owned by people in the same cluster are more similar than others in the other cluster, and this will increase the average path length in social network (Uzzi et al, 2007), in turn, the network structure can also influence the resources individuals owned or accessed, especially the hierarchic connection, such as the external bridging (Magni et al., 2012).

The intangible dimension mainly refers to the things critical to the network, but cannot be easily observed or measured exactly, and usually represented during the interactional process, as a result, it can be called as the interactional dimension, including trust, norms, social value, shared vision, obligation, recognition, social participation and so on. Usually, the intangible dimension can provide great benefits for the actors, for instance, trust can help star employees to prevent information overload (James, et al., 2012), in addition, the network structure can also influence the intangible dimension, for instance, the closure level can influence the diffusion of responsibility (Massimo, et al., 2012); however, unlike the resources and assets owned by individuals, the intangible dimensions can be viewed as the assets and resources that can only be embedded in the network, and cannot be owned by the individuals. Compared with the tangible dimension, the intangible dimension is usually related to the perception, even the same sub-dimension can be perceived different significant.

Effects of Social Capital on the Organizational Performance

Social capital can be viewed from different perspectives, this chapter has only focused on the personal network, and the actors focused are only individuals, however, the tangible and interactional dimensions can influence the organizational performance at different levels; individual level, network level, and organizational level. As such, the direct effects of both tangible and interactional dimensions of social capital are at the individual level. Structural social capital has important influence at the individual level. For instance, people located centrally within network are less likely to be depressed than those on the periphery (Rosenquist et al., 2011), however, the centrality may also cause some negative effects, take the star employee (those employees who have always exceeded the expectations of their managers) as an example, since the high performance and high visibility, star employees are usually located centrally within the network, despite the more information received and sent, they may also experience information overload (James et al., 2012).

Another important sections are about the bonding and bridging, especially the bridging ties connect diverse social groups, while bonding ties only connect actors in the same group (Putnam, 2000), according to the bridging and bonding theory, people in the same group may own similar resources, if connection with the other groups, people can access to different resources, thus can benefit the individuals, many researches have shown that bridging can positively affect individual-level outcomes, including job-seeking prospects (Granovetter, 1985), career success (Podolny et al., 1997). Compared with bridging, bonding is often related to the strong ties and trust, as a result, bonding ties and bridging ties are considered complementary instead of totally contrary, strong ties is the base of trust, and can promote exchanges of high-quality information as well as tacit knowledge (Molina-Morales et al., 2010); however, there are also disadvantages of the strong ties, for example, strong ties may not be benefits for acquiring different information or resources (Burt, 1992): Another important structural social capital is the type of connection ties, in general, expressive ties are positively related to performance at the individual level, even some researches show that the relationship is not significant, however, most researches have showed the positive relationship, for instance, expressive ties in the self-managing team is positive related to procedural justice climate (Quinetta et al., 2012): As for the advice or instrumental ties, it can help to promote the transmission of information (Adler and Kwon, 2002), knowledge sharing, although there are some researches that shows no significant relationship (Bassett etal., 2013), there is rare evidences that show the negative relationship between connection ties and performance, the main reasons may be that most analysis are from the egocentric perspective, rarely from the other alters perspective, such as the actors giving advices, or the data collection, analysis methods are not so precise, perhaps in the future, there will be some improvements. Despite the network structure, the resources owned by the actors also have significant influence at individual level, there is no doubt that the main advantage provided by the social network is the access to different actors, in other words, the access to different resources owned by the actors, especially the brokers and actors with high degree, take the information as a key resource (Bin Zhu etal., 2010), the more quality owned by the actors in the network, the more value actors can get from the social ties

INTELLECTUAL CAPITAL

Continuous innovation has become a key requirement for organizational viability in the present environment characterized by fierce competition and increasing globalization (Chen et al., 2010; Kianto, 2011). As Sáenz and Aramburu (2011) point out, innovation "is a matter of survival in a free market economy" and therefore, the creation of something new (i.e. innovation) is no longer an optional choice but a necessity facing all organizations alike (p. 87). Accordingly, finding ways to maintain the requisite level of renewal and developing capabilities for being more creative and innovative have become imperatives for firms. Intellectual capital (IC), the set of intangible assets that the firm owns or has access to (Edvinsson and Malone, 1997) has been at the forefront of a wide range of studies in the management field. Entrenched within the resource-based view of the firm (Wernerfelt, 1984; Barney, 1991), building strong intangibles provides companies with opportunities for improving business performance (Mention & Bontis, 2013), gaining competitive advantage (Chahal & Bakshi, 2015) and innovating (Wu et al., 2007; Leitner, 2011). Traditionally, IC has been split into three components: human capital (HC) or employees' knowledge, skills and experience (Schultz, 1961;Subramaniam and Youndt, 2005); structural capital (SC) or firms' codified knowledge, databases and culture (Bontis, 1996; Menor et al., 2007); and relational capital (RC) or the knowledge embodied in the networks of internal and external relationships the company manages (Nahapiet & Ghoshal, 1998; Hsu & Fang, 2009) (Bontis, 1998; Subramaniam & Youndt, 2005).

The existing literature has repeatedly demonstrated the connection between IC and innovation (Subramaniam & Youndt, 2005; Wu et al., 2007; Hsu & Fang, 2009; Leitner, 2011). However, the sheer amount of the existing studies as well as the varying methodological choices and approaches taken by different authors to both IC and innovation, beg the question of where the IC-innovation research field currently stands as a whole. As innovation is essential for company survival, gaining a deep and holistic understanding of how this field of research has evolved so far and where it should go from here is of utmost importance. Comprehending what is known about the IC–innovation relationship is significant for both academics, aiming to grasp potential research opportunities, and managers, looking for insights into how to reinforce innovation in their organizations

Dimensions of Intellectual Capital

The concept of intellectual capital is introduced as a relatively new perspective that is an integration of resource oriented and knowledge-oriented perspective (Stam & Andriessen, 2009). In the resource-oriented view, there is no clear distinction between varieties of organizational resources. On the other hand, in the knowledge-based view (knowledge management), all attention is focused on organizational knowledge and its explicit and hidden forms. But in terms of intellectual capital, emphasis is placed on the identification and management of all intangible resources and capital of the organization. In this view, knowledge and other intangible assets as valuable resources along with the resources of work, land, and capital (previously considered in the economy) are presented as assets that, unlike previous sources, their value is increased as they are being used (Afrazeh, 2005). With the advent of the information technology revolution, the information and networking society, and the rapid growth and development of superior technology, the pattern of global economic growth has changed. As a result, knowledge has become the most important alternative to financial and physical capital in today's global economy. In a knowledge-based organization, traditional accounting methods, based on tangible assets of the organization, are inadequate to value intellectual capital, the largest and most valuable intangible assets of organizations.

Studies have shown that, contrary to the decline in the returns of traditional resources such as money, land, machinery, etc., knowledge is really a source of business performance improvement. For example, accountants are interested in measuring it in balance sheets, information technology experts are trying to codify it in information systems, sociologists tend to balance power using it, psychologists tend to develop minds, human resource managers tend to calculate the return on investment through it, and education and development staff are keen to be sure they can put it into human resource development programs. With regard to the elements that comprise intellectual capital and its components, many comments and models have been presented by scientists. It seems that when looking at the literature of intellectual capital research, most intellectual capital models have tried to consider three components of human capital, structural capital, and relational capital for intellectual capital (Bontis, 2003).

In the framework of the dynamic characteristic of current markets, intellectual capital is shown as a set of assets of intangible nature that derive from the knowledge inside the organizations. For this reason, López et al. (2005) claim that, through strategies related to the planning, organization, direction, and control of organizational learning, business capabilities can be developed to generate competitive advantages. For its part, Bradley (1997) considers that the intellectual capital refers to those assets of intangible nature arising from the knowledge generated by the capabilities and mental models of the human resource. From this class of resources, the strategies used by the high management allow to efficiently manage the productive factors of immaterial nature. In summary, the various theoretical references have identified the intellectual capital as an integration of intangible assets that support the generation of competitive advantages, from the development of strategies aimed at the economic use of the knowledge derived from the processes, human resources, and relations with the external sector.

THE IMPACT OF SOCIAL AND INTELLECTUAL CAPITALS ON CORPORATE SOCIAL RESPONSIBILITY

Corporate social responsibility (CSR) is the concept which has gained prominence in business reporting. Every corporation has the policy concerning CSR, which reports, annually, details of its activities. Every corporation could recognize the corporate activity, that is socially responsible and the activities, which are not socially responsible. There are two interesting points regarding CSR. Firstly, there is no consensus about the definition of social responsibility. The comprehensive definition of social responsibility is concerned with what is or should be the relationship between global corporations, governments of countries and individual citizens. More locally, the definition is concerned with the relationship between the corporation and the local society in which it resides or operates. Another definition is concerned with the relationship between a corporation and its stakeholders (Crowther, & Aras, 2008). CSR is the allusion of firm behavior and one of the major issues in the business environment. It deals with a firm's relationship toward stakeholders and the increasingly recognized moral implications in investments (Cheung et.al, 2010). Industrialization on around of the world lead to important social responsibilities which impacted on the financial and non-financial on business.

Firms in developing countries tend to move and engage on global markets because of globalization. Hence, firms to be able to participate and compete in global markets should participate in social responsibilities and disclose them. Altogether, the firms should know that different groups of the society demand different social responsibilities information, because, such information play important role in their decision-makings (Cho, 2007). In other hand, many believe that intellectual assets such as intellectual capital obtain place beyond of material and physical place which could relate to firm's social responsibility. Because disclosure of firm's social responsibilities explains the relationship between individuals among organizations with external users, no doubt that if the firms could enhance intellectual assets such as intellectual capital in addition to their physical assets, they will provide necessary backgrounds to improve disclosure level of social responsibilities. The reason is that literature suggest that the added-value which the firms obtain through intellectual assets is more than physical assets.

In addition to, trade units attempt to improve their performance which high disclosure of social responsibility is one of the factors which is used to measure trade unit performance which it can be realized through investment on intellectual assets. In other words, intellectual capital and disclosure of social responsibility have common goals including attempt to survive in competitiveness environment (Musibah et.al, 2013). In this regard, Yancheshmeh and Hemati (2018) studied the impact of voluntary disclosure of different dimensions of intellectual capital on disclosure level of social responsibility and found that disclosure of different dimensions of intellectual capital positively impacted on the disclosure level of social responsibility. Noryaman (2015) considered the impact of intellectual capital on financial performance and resulted that financial performance significantly is influenced by intellectual capital. Theoretically and experimentally, literature suggested that intellectual assets have so significant added value. Therefore, we could consider the necessity to take attention to such capitals and related factors more and more overtime (Musibah et al., 2013). Moreover, financial performance and its evaluation is one of the subjects in management accounting that has been considered through agency theory. Different stakeholders in particular, shareholders attempt to invest on firms with suitable performance (Olugu & Kuan, 2012).

According to some recent literature of management accounting (Mishra et.al, 2011; Avishek and David, 2017), firms must seek to engage on social responsibility activities to be able to realize stable competitiveness advantage, increased firm value and suitable financial performance. Literature take attention to relationship between social responsibility and financial performance. For example, Navarro et al., (2016) found that firms use economic and social achievements to obtain higher financial performance. Ramanathan et al, (2017) consider the relationship between financial performance considering environmental regulations and found that financial performance positively related to environmental activities. Nekhili et al., (2017) studied the mediating role of family firms on the relationship between social responsibility and firm value and found that market-based performance which is measured by Tubins' Q negatively related to non-family firms CSR disclosure and positively related to family firms CSR disclosure. Yinyoung et al., (2018) suggested that CSR act as competitiveness advantage for all businesses and shareholders with CSR knowledge in restaurant industry could mediate the relationship between social and financial performance which lead to increased financial profit of the firms. Therefore, we could consider some related questions: whether social responsibility could improve financial performance of the firms. If the intellectual capital could improve social responsibility and if the financial performance of firms could mediate the relationship between social responsibility and intellectual capital?

FUTURE RESEARCH DIMENSIONS

Although this chapter has provide important contributions at the theoretical level, literature review reveal some limitations. First, by referring to a holistic perspective, we adopt a synthetic measure of Intellectual Capital efficiency and its contribution to financial performance of organizations. Second, while we separate the intellectual and social capitals pillars from CSR, we keep together the pillars of environmental responsibility and relationships with society. Third, the CSR depends on the willingness of of the board of directors to spend stakeholders money. Therefore, in light of the aforementioned limitations, a new research agenda could expand the current literature review in several ways such as by adopting alternative measures of Intellectual and Social Capitals efficiency, exploring additional Intellectual capital characteristics, and disentangling the other pillars of CSR related to the environment and society as potential specific drivers of Intellectual and social Capital development. This study develops a complex theoretical literature review investigating the interrelationships among social capital, innovation activities, intellectual capital, and social corporate responsibility. Even though the study believe that the review is sound, there is realization that it is not free of some limitations. The reviewed literature on intellectual, social capitals and corporate social responsibility is too general. It would be illuminating to repeat this research in a different specific organizations and compare the outcomes. While we have three mediators – intellectual capital, social capital and corporate Social Responsibility, it would be to strengthen the explanatory power of the review if additional mediators (like organizational learning and knowledge sharing) between innovation activities and intellectual capital were included in the model. This would have shed some additional light on the way intellectual capital, social capital and corporate social responsibility informs each other in organization management.

CONCLUSION

In this chapter social and intellectual capitals with particular emphasis on corporations has been reviewed, the argument that social and intellectual capitals are likely to contribute substantially to firm value has been extended. Without social capital, the returns on other forms of capital, such as physical, intellectual, and human capital, are likely to be lower. Social capital is important because it builds trust among the firm's stakeholders, thus enhancing the productivity of the firm. Firms are endowed with some of their social capital, simply because they are headquartered or operate in regions where the population is more willing to trust; the only way a firm can alter this is by changing location. However, social capital can also be built through specific investments in networks, and in CSR activities. There is clear evidence that CSR investments pay off, but it would be wrong to conclude that this necessarily implies that firms are not doing enough since the costs associated with building stronger networks and improving the well-being of stakeholders are likely substantial. Even if these intangible benefits are not fully incorporated in stock prices, this does not imply that managers are not making the necessary investments. There is clearly ample need for further research on the importance of social capital and its role in enhancing firm value. First, we need a better understanding of the various ways in which firms can build social capital. While studying CSR expenditures is clearly useful, focusing on the networks of firms, executives, and other employees may also yield further insights. This should also allow us to distinguish between the social capital of the firm and that of individuals within the firm. Second, the view that 'one size fits all' is clearly too simplistic. Social capital may be more important for some firms than others; there is a need for a better understanding of how social capital affects product market competition. Third, if some firms are not doing enough, while other firms are doing too much, we need to better understand what agency problems or other frictions lead to such sub optimal behavior and what the costs of fixing it are. Fourth, if there is a lack of CSR investment due to short-dated incentives, such a relation should manifest itself in the data. Addressing these questions will be fruitful areas for future research as the study of social capital becomes more mainstream in finance and economic

REFERENCES

Adler, P. S., & Kwon, S. (2002). Social capital: Prospects for a new concept. *Academy of Management Review*, *27*(1), 17–40. doi:10.2307/4134367

Afrazeh, A. (2005). *Knowledge management (concepts, models, measurement and implementation)*. Amirkabir University of Technology Publication Center.

Andriessen, D. (2001). Weightless Wealth: Four Modifications to Standard IC Theory. *Journal of Intellectual Capital*, *2*(3), 204–214. doi:10.1108/14691930110399941

Aramburu, N., & Sáenz, J. (2011). Structural capital, innovation capability, and size effect: An empirical study. *Journal of Management & Organization, 17*(3), 307–325. doi:10.5172/jmo.2011.17.3.307

Asonitis, S., & Kostagiolas, P. A. (2010). An analytic hierarchy approach for intellectual capital: Evidence for the Greek central public libraries. *Library Management, 31*(3), 145–161. doi:10.1108/01435121011027327

Avishek, B., & David, J. (2017). Corporate social responsibility and capital allocation efficiency. *Journal of Corporate Finance, 43*(3), 354–377.

Avishek, B., & Javakhadze, D. (2017) Corporate Social Responsibility and Capital Allocation Efficiency. *Journal of Corporate Finance, 43*, 354-377. https://ssrn.com/abstract=3054236 or doi:10.2139/ssrn.3054236

Azimi, M., Hemati, A (2018). Impact of voluntary disclosure of different dimensions of intellectual capital on disclosure level of social responsibility. *Quarterly of management, accounting and economic, 2* (1), 55-69.

Baker, R. J. (2008). *Mind Over Matter: why intellectual capital is the chief source of wealth.* John Wiley & Sons Publication.

Bartlett, M. S. (1954). A note on the multiplying factors for various $\chi 2$ approximations. *Journal of the Royal Statistical Society. Series B. Methodological, 16*(2), 296–298. doi:10.1111/j.2517-6161.1954.tb00174.x

Bassett, E., & Moore, S. (2013). Social capital and depressive symptoms: The association of psychosocial and network dimensions of social capital with depressive symptoms in Montreal, Canada. *Social Science & Medicine, 86*, 96–102. doi:10.1016/j.socscimed.2013.03.005 PMID:23608098

Bontis, N. (1996). There's a price on your head: managing intellectual capital strategically. Business Quarterly, 60, 40-78. doi:10.1108/00251749810204142

Bontis, N. (1998). Intellectual capital: An exploratory study that develops measures and models. *Management Decision, 36*(2), 63–76. doi:10.1108/00251749810204142

Bontis, N. (1998). Intellectual capital: An exploratory study that develops measures and models. *Management Decision, 36*(2), 63–76. doi:10.1108/00251749810204142

Bontis, N. (2003). Intellectual capital disclosure in Canadian corporations. *Journal of Human Resource Costing & Accounting, 7*(1), 9–20. doi:10.1108/eb029076

Bozbura, F. T., Beskese, A., & Kahraman, C. (2007). Prioritization of human capital measurement indicators using fuzzy AHP. *Expert Systems with Applications, 32*(4), 1100–1112. doi:10.1016/j.eswa.2006.02.006

Bradley, K. (1997). Intellectual capital and the new wealth of nations. *Business Strategy Review, 8*(1), 53–62. doi:10.1111/1467-8616.00007

Brooking, A. (1996). *Intellectual capital.* Cengage Learning EMEA.

Brown, J. R., Fazzari, S. M., & Petersen, B. C. (2009). Financing Innovation and Growth: Cash Flow, External Equity, and the 1990s R&D Boom. *The Journal of Finance, 64*(1), 151–185. doi:10.1111/j.1540-6261.2008.01431.x

Bryman, A., & Bell, E. (2011). *Business Research Methods* (3rd ed.). Oxford University Press.

Bueno, E., Arrién, M., & Rodríguez, O. (2003). Model for the measurement and management of Intellectual Capital. *Intellectus Model. Intellectus Documents*, *5*(2), 181–192.

Burt, R. (2005). *Brokerage and Closure: An Introduction to Social Capital*. Oxford University Press.

Cabello-Medina, C., López-Cabrales, A., & Valle-Cabrera, R. (2011). Leveraging theinnovative performance of human capital through HRM and social capital in Spanish firms. *International Journal of Human Resource Management*, *22*(4), 807–828. doi:10.1080/09585192.2011.555125

Carmona-Lavado, A., Cuevas-Rodríguez, G., & Cabello-Medina, C. (2010). Social andorganizational capital: Building the context for innovation. *Industrial Marketing Management*, *39*(4), 681–690. doi:10.1016/j.indmarman.2009.09.003

Carmona-Lavado, A., Cuevas-Rodríguez, G., & Cabello-Medina, C. (2013). Service Innovativeness and Innovation Success in Technology-based Knowledge-Intensive Business Services: An Intellectual Capital Approach. *Industry and Innovation*, *20*(2), 133–156. doi:10.1080/13662716.2013.771482

Castro, G. M., Delgado-Verde, M., Amores-Salvadó, J., & Navas-López, J. E. (2013). Linkinghuman, technological, and relational assets to technological innovation: Exploring a newapproach. *Knowledge Management Research and Practice*, *11*(2), 123–132. doi:10.1057/kmrp.2013.8

Chahal, H., & Bakshi, P. (2015). Examining intellectual capital and competitive advantagerelationship: Role of innovation and organizational learning. *International Journal of Bank Marketing*, *33*(3), 376–399. doi:10.1108/IJBM-07-2013-0069

Chen, C. -., Huang, J.-. and Hsiao, Y.-. (2010). Knowledge management and innovativeness: Therole of organizational climate and structure. International Journal of Manpower, 31(8), 848–870. doi:10.1108/01437721011088548

Chen, C. J., Liu, T. C., Chu, M. A., & Hsiao, Y. C. (2014). Intellectual capital and new productdevelopment. *Journal of Engineering and Technology Management*, *33*, 154–173. doi:10.1016/j.jengtecman.2014.06.003

Chen, H., & Chen, S. (2010). Investment-cash flow sensitivity cannot be a good measure of financial constraints: Evidence from the time series. *Journal of Financial Economics*, *103*(2), 393–410. doi:10.1016/j.jfineco.2011.08.009

Chen, J., Zhao, X. and Wang, Y. (2015). A new measurement of intellectual capital and its impact on innovation performance in an open innovation paradigm. *International Journal of Technology Management,* 67(1), 1-25.

Chen, J., Zhu, Z., & Yuan Xie, H. (2004). Measuring intellectual capital: A new model and empirical study. *Journal of Intellectual Capital*, *5*(1), 195–212. doi:10.1108/14691930410513003

Chen, Y. S., James Lin, M. J., & Chang, C. H. (2006). The influence of intellectual capital onnew product development performance–the manufacturing companies of Taiwan as an example. Total Quality Management and Business Excellence, 17(10), 1323-1339. doi:10.1108/01437721011088548

Chien, S. H. (2010). Market orientation and new product success: A mediator model based onintellectual capital. *Asia Pacific Management Review*, *15*(3), 377–390.

Chien, S. H., & Chao, M. C. (2011). Intellectual capital and new product sale performance ofthe financial services industry in Taiwan. The Service Industries Journal, 31(16), 2641-2659.

Cho, CH.(2007). *Organizations Legitimacy and the Strategic use of accounting information Three Studies Related to social and environmental disclosure.* [Thesis, University of Central Florida, USA].

Cohen, S., & Kaimenakis, N. (2007). Intellectual capital and corporate performance inknowledge-intensive SMEs. *The Learning Organization*, *14*(3), 241–262.

Cohen, S., & Kaimenakis, N. (2007). Intellectual capital and corporate performance in knowledge-intensive SMEs. *The Learning Organization*, *14*(3), 241–262. doi:10.1108/09696470710739417

Coleman, J. S. (1988), Social capital in the creation of human capital. *American Journal of Sociology*, *94*, 95.

Costa, R. V., Fernández, C. F. J., & Dorrego, P. F. (2014). Critical elements for productinnovation at Portuguese innovative SMEs: An intellectual capital perspective. *Knowledge Management Research and Practice*, *12*(3), 322–338. doi:10.1057/kmrp.2014.15

Costa, R. V., & Ramos, A. P. (2015). Designing an AHP methodology to prioritize critical elements for product innovation: An intellectual capital perspective. *Int. Journal of Business Science and Applied Management*, *10*(1).

Crossan, M. M., & Apaydin, M. (2010). A multi-dimensional framework of organizationalinnovation: A systematic review of the literature. Journal of management studies, 47(6), 1154-1191.

Curado, C., Henriques, L., & Bontis, N. (2011). Intellectual capital disclosure payback. *Man. Dec.*, *49*(7), 1080-1098.

De Carolis, D. M. (2010). Technological Characteristics of Industries. In V. K. Narayanan & G. Colarelli-O'Connor (Eds.), *Encyclopedia of Technology and Innovation Management* (pp. 77–79). Wiley.

Degli Antoni, G., & Sacconi, L. (2011a). *Social Capital, Corporate Responsibility, Economic Behaviour and Performance.* Palgrave MacMillan.

Degli Antoni, G., & Sacconi, L. (2011b). Modeling Cognitive Social Capital and Corporate Social Responsibility as Preconditions for Sustainable Networks of Relations. In L. Sacconi & G. Degli Antoni (Eds.), *Social Capital, Corporate Responsibility, Economic Behaviour and Performance.* Palgrave MacMillan. doi:10.1057/9780230306189_8

Di Giuli, A., & Kostovetsky, L. (2014). Are Red or Blue Companies More Likely to Go Green? Politics and Corporate Social Responsibility. *Journal of Financial Economics*, *111*(1), 158–180. doi:10.1016/j.jfineco.2013.10.002

Diekmann, A. (2004). The Power of Reciprocity: Fairness, Reciprocity, and Stakes in Variants of the Dictator Game. *The Journal of Conflict Resolution*, *48*(4), 487–505. doi:10.1177/0022002704265948

Dumay, J., Guthrie, J., & Puntillo, P. (2015). IC and public sector: A structured literaturereview. *Journal of Intellectual Capital*, *16*(2), 267–284. doi:10.1108/JIC-02-2015-0014

Dumay, J., Rooney, J., & Marini, L. (2013). An intellectual capital-based differentiation theory of innovation practice. *Journal of Intellectual Capital*, *14*(4), 608–633. doi:10.1108/JIC-02-2013-0024

Edmans, A., & Gabaix, X. (2016). Executive Compensation: A Modern Primer. *Journal of Economic Literature*, *54*(4), 1232–1287. doi:10.1257/jel.20161153

Edvinsson, L., & Malone, M. S. (1997). *Intellectual Capital: Realizing Your Company\'s TrueValue by Finding Its Hidden Brainpower*. Harper Collins.

Elsetouhi, A., Elbeltagi, I. and Haddoud, M.Y. (2015). Intellectual Capital And Innovations: IsOrganisational Capital A Missing Link In The Service Sector? *International Journal of Innovation Management*, *19*(2), 1-29.

Fan, I. Y., & Lee, R. W. (2012). Design of a weighted and informed NK model for intellectualcapital-based innovation planning. *Expert Systems with Applications*, *39*(10), 9222–9229. doi:10.1016/j.eswa.2012.02.083

Ferenhof, H. A., Durst, S., Zaniboni Bialecki, M., & Selig, P. M. (2015). Intellectual capitaldimensions: State of the art in 2014. *Journal of Intellectual Capital*, *16*(1), 58–100. doi:10.1108/JIC-02-2014-0021

Field, J. (2003). *Social Capital*. Routledge.

Granovetter, M. (1985), Economic action and social structure: the problem of embeddedness. *American Journal of Sociology*, *91*(3), 481–510.

Gu, Q., Wang, G. G., & Wang, L. (2013). Social capital and innovation in R&D teams: The mediating roles of psychological safety and learning from mistakes. *R & D Management*, *43*(2), 89–102. doi:10.1111/radm.12002

Hall, B. H., Jaffe, A., & Trajtenberg, M. (2005). Market Value and Patent Citations. *The RAND Journal of Economics*, *36*, 16–38.

Ibarra, H., & Andrews, S. B. (1993). Power, social influ- ence, and sense making: Effects of network centrality and proximity on employee perceptions. *Administrative Science Quarterly*, *38*(2), 277–303. doi:10.2307/2393414

Kaplan, S. N., & Zingales, L. (1997). Do Investment-cash Flow Sensitivities Provide Useful Measures of Financing Constraints. *The Quarterly Journal of Economics*, *112*(1), 169–215. doi:10.1162/003355397555163

López, M., Cabrales, G., & Schmal, R. (2005) Gestion del conocimiento: una revisión teórica y sus asosiación con la universidad. *Panorama Socioeconómico*, (30).

Massimo, M., & Corey, M. (2012). Everybody Needs Somebody: The Infuence of Team Network Structure on Information Technology Use. *Journal of Management Information Systems*, *29*(3), 9–42. doi:10.2753/MIS0742-1222290301

Mishra, D. R., & Sodok, E. (2011). Does corporate social responsibility affect the cost of capital? *Journal of Banking & Finance*, *35*(9), 2388–2406. doi:10.1016/j.jbankfin.2011.02.007

Musibah, A. S., Bin, W. S., & Alfattani, W. Y. (2013). Impact of Intellectual Capital on Corporate Social Responsibility Evidence from Islamic Banking Sector in GCC. *International Journal of Finance and Accounting, 2*(6), 307–311. doi:10.5923/j.ijfa.20130206.02

Nahapiet, J., & Ghoshal, S. (1998). Social capital, intellectual capital, and the organizational advantage. *Academy of Management Review, 23*(2), 242–266. doi:10.2307/259373

Navarro, J. G. C., Reverte, C., Melero, E. G., & Wensley, A. K. P. (2016). Linking social and economic responsibilities with financial performance: The role of innovation. *European Management Journal, 34*(5), 530–539. doi:10.1016/j.emj.2016.02.006

Nekhili, M., Nagatib, H., & Tawhid, Ch. (2017). Claudia rebolledod corporate social responsibility disclosure and market value: Family versus nonfamily firms. *Journal of Business Research, 77*(C), 41–52. doi:10.1016/j.jbusres.2017.04.001

Nekhili, M., Nagatib, H., & Tawhid, Ch. (2017). Claudia rebolledod corporate social responsibility disclosure and market value: Family versus nonfamily firms. *Journal of Business Research, 77*(C), 41–52. doi:10.1016/j.jbusres.2017.04.001

(2015, November). Nuryaman. (2015). "The Influence of Intellectual Capital on The Firm's Value with The Financial Performance as Intervening Variable. *Procedia: Social and Behavioral Sciences, 211*(25), 292–298.

Oldroyd, J. B., & Morris, S. S. (2012). catching falling stars: A human resource response to social capital's detrimental effect of information overload on star employees. *Academy of Management Review, 37*(3), 396–418. doi:10.5465/amr.2010.0403

Olugu, E. U. & Wong Kuan. Y. (2012). An expert fuzzy rule-based system for closedloop supply chain performance assessment in the automotive industry. *Expert Systems with Applications, 39*(1), 375-384.

Podolny, J. M., & Baron, J. N. (1997). Resources and relationships: Social networks and mobility in the Putnam, R. D. (2000), Bowling Alone: The Collapse and Revival of American Community, Simon & Shuster.

Quinetta, M., Roberson, I., & Williamson, O. (2012). justice in self-managing teams: The role of social networks in the emergence of procedural justice climates. *Academy of Management Journal, 55*(3), 685–701. doi:10.5465/amj.2009.0491

Ramanathan, R., Ramanathan, U., & Bentley, Y. (2017). The debate on ßexibility of environmental regulations, innovation capabilities and Þnancial performance -A novel use of DEA. *Omega, 75*(5), 131–138.

Stulz, R. M. (1961). Managerial Discretion and Optimal Financing Policies. *Journal of Financial Economics, 26*(1), 3–27. doi:10.1016/0304-405X(90)90011-N

Trajtenberg, M. (1990). A Penny for Your Quotes: Patent Citations and the Value of Innovations. *The RAND Journal of Economics, 21*(1), 172–187. doi:10.2307/2555502

Uzzi, B., Amaral, L. A. N., & Reed-Tsochas, F. (2007). Small-world networks and management science research: A review. *European Management Review, 4*(2), 77–91. doi:10.1057/palgrave.emr.1500078

Wang, W.-Y., & Chang, C. (2005). Intellectual capital and performance in causal models: Evidence from the information technology industry in Taiwan. *Journal of Intellectual Capital, 6*(2), 222–236. doi:10.1108/14691930510592816

Wu, X. P., Xu, F. Y., & Zhou, Y. (2008). Analysis of Factors Affecting University Teachers' Job Performance. [Educational Sciences]. *Journal of East China Normal University, 24*, 30–37.

Xu, X. (2014). The Relation between Emerging Capital and Enterprise Performance. *Journal of Guangdong University of Finance and Economics, 1*, 22–34.

Yinyoung, R., Manisha, S., & Yoon, K. (2018). CSR and financia performance: The role of CSR awareness in the restaurant industry. *International Journal of Hospitality Management, 57*, 30–39.

Zhu, B., Watts, S., & Chen, H. (2010). Visualizing social network concepts. *Decision Support Systems, 49*(2), 151–161. doi:10.1016/j.dss.2010.02.001

ADDITIONAL READING

Adelman, S. (2010) Intellectual Capital: A Human Resources Perspective. *EIM Institute, 4*(5). http://www.eiminstitute.org/current-magazine/volumn-4-issue-5-october-2010/intellectual-capital-a-human-resources-perspective

Arthaud-Day, M. L. (2005). Transnational Corporate Social Responsibility: A Tri-Dimensional Approach to International CSR Research. *Business Ethics Quarterly, 15*(1), 1–22. doi:10.5840/beq20051515

Atashi, A., & Kharabi, H. (2012). Intellectual Capital Management, a Paradigm to Enhance the Human Resource Management in Knowledge-Based Economy. *Life Science Journal, 9*, 1336–1340.

Carroll, A. B., & Buchholtz, A. K. (2003). *Business and Society: Ethics and Stakeholder Management* (5th ed.). Thomson South-Western.

Garriga, E., & Mele, D. (2004). Corporate Social Responsibility Theories: Mapping the Territory. *Journal of Business Ethics, 53*(1/2), 51–71. doi:10.1023/B:BUSI.0000039399.90587.34

Jurczak, J. (2008) Intellectual Capital Measurement Methods.http://www.orgmasz.pl/wydawnictwo/files/Intellectual.pdfhttp://dx.doi.org/10.2478/v10061-008-0005-y

Kavida, V., & Sivakoumar, N. (2008) Corporate Governance in Knowledge Economy— The Relevance of Intellectual Capital. https://ssrn.com/abstract=1152892 doi:10.2139/ssrn.1152892

Marquez, A., & Fombrun, C. J. (2005). Measuring Corporate Social Responsibility. *Corporate Reputation Review, 7*(4), 304–308. doi:10.1057/palgrave.crr.1540228

Post, J.E., A.T. Lawrence, and J. Weber (200). *Business and Society* (10th ed.). McGraw-Hill.

KEY TERMS AND DEFINITIONS

Corporate Culture: Refers *the bast or proper way to behave within the organization. Culture consists of shared beliefs and values established by leaders and then communicated and reinforced through various methods, ultimately shaping employee perceptions, behaviors, and understanding.*"

Corporate Social Responsibility: Corporate social responsibility (CSR) refers to strategies that companies put into action as part of corporate governance that are designed to ensure the company's operations are ethical and beneficial for society

Intellectual Capital: Intellectual Capital is the knowledge of an organization's human resource that can be used for money-making or other useful purposes or any other information or knowledge that provides the organization with a competitive advantage. In other words, it is an asset of the company as it is the informational resource that the company can use at its disposal to make profits, attract customers, create a new product, enhance existing products, or improve business

Organization Performance: This is the organization's actual output or results as measured against its intended outputs (or goals and objectives).

Social Capital: In financial terms, social capital basically comprises the value of social relationships and networks that complement the economic capital for economic growth of an organization.

Trust: At its simplest, organizational trust is the confidence of your workforce in the actions of your company. While this may include confidence in managers or individual team members, it also extends to organizational factors like: The company's mission, Senior leadership's vision, The organization's culture and values, Workplace diversity, inclusion, and equality, Ethics and fairness of processes.

Chapter 3
An Integrated Approach to Records Management and Information Governance in South Africa for Sustainability

Nkholedzeni Sidney Netshakhuma
ⓘ https://orcid.org/0000-0003-0673-7137
University of South Africa, South Africa

ABSTRACT

The purpose of this book chapter is to assess information governance in South African organizations. The book chapter assess corporate governance, data privacy, legislation, information security, big data, access, and training. The success of corporate governance is dependent on executive management buy in, the alignment of organisational strategy with mission, and the vision of the organisation. Organisations are to implement systematic disposal of records, effective retention of records, and quality assurance should be proven.

INTRODUCTION

An information governance framework is an integrated approach to implementing information governance to improve decision rights and an accountability framework to encourage desirable behavior in the valuation, creation, storage, use, archival, and deletion of information. It includes the processes, roles, standards, and metrics that ensure the effective and efficient use of information in enabling an organization to achieve its goals.

The purpose of this book chapter is to assess information governance in South African organizations. This implies both public and non-public organizations design information governance. Organizations develop an information governance framework that demonstrates information flow from records creation until records disposal. This implies that organizations develop strategies to ensure compliance with a

DOI: 10.4018/978-1-6684-6815-9.ch003

regulatory framework. Various regulatory frameworks determine the management of records in South Africa. It starts with the Constitution of the Republic of South Africa of 1996, the Promotion of Access to Information Act of 2000, and the Protection of Personal Information Act of 2013. Despite several legislations which require information to be managed in a coordinated manner, South Africa still lacks to ensure effective governance of information. South Africa's governance system is not coordinated by the national department of South Africa (Mullon & Ngoepe 2019, p.113). There is ineffective coordination of information management at the national level or governance structure of South Africa (Matlala, Ncube, & Parbanath 2022, p. 204).

It seems that little has been done since South Africa gained independence in 1994 to address coordination of information from various spheres of government. This increased when there was the development of electronic records in South Africa. There is ineffective organizational structure established by both national and provincial departments to coordinate government information. There was an over-arching structure responsible for overall information governance in South Africa as the elements are fragmented in oversight mechanisms and institutions (Mullon & Ngoepe, 2019). This implies that information within the government is managed piecemeal without full coordination from various government departments.

Most staff are not aware of information governance systems to ensure the effective flow of information. This lack of effective governance was caused by a lack of training and awareness on records and archives management systems was conducted in South Africa. Hence efforts need to be made to ensure that all government departments structured their information according to information management systems. The lack of adequate training for staff officials on information systems was also reported in Malawi (Tough & Lihoma 2018). It was against this background that I conducted this research. This study attempted to fill the gaps by examining how organizations in South Africa develop and implement information governance.

METHODOLOGY

This study is constructed from a literature review. The literature reviewed includes regulatory body reports, articles referenced in peer-reviewed journals. The drive of information governance in South Africa is King IV Corporate governance, data privacy, information communication technology, records management, access to information, strategy, standards and best practices, transparency and accountability and transparency

CORPORATE GOVERNANCE (KING IV)

Corporate governance should be viewed as a holistic set of provisions that must be executed in an integrated manner (Esser & Delport, 2018). The King IV report give a holistic approach to governance for public and private sector organization (Ferguson, 2019). This considers a holistic approach to developing information governance in an organization. integration of information management systems is critical to improve compliance with a regulatory framework within an organization (Ngoepe & Mello, 2020).

Corporate governance in any organization is dependent on leadership commitment. The executive management set strategic direction for governance, approving policies, and oversee and monitoring policies (Swartz, Da Veiga, & Martins, 2021). Most organizations adopt top-down decisions to manage information from various divisions (Mourad, 2017). The organizational leadership provide finance, human resource, and information communication technology. Management is responsible to approve and amending policies with the view to minimizing risks to organizations' engagement with stakeholders.

An oversight and review plan must be developed and implemented by an organization. This oversight and review plan ensured that organizations met the target set on their plan. Organizations are to ensure the development of integrated risk management to ensure that issues related to risk matters are addressed. An integrated methodology for facilitating organization specify appropriate security and privacy-preserving measures for the information system is to be developed and implemented (Makri, Georgiopoulou, & Lambrinoudakis 2020).

Challenges of ineffective governance addressed through interinstitutional cooperation. Cooperation enabled information professionals to ensure the utilization of resources. There is a need for interrelation links to promote cooperation in an organization. Stakeholders involved in the development and implementation of governance strategy. For example, auditors play a role to ensure that organizations comply with regulatory framework and processes set in their strategic documents. This statement is alluded to by La Torre, Dumay, & Odendaal (2021) who state that auditors need to align their task to the privacy protection practices. Furthermore, auditors have the responsibility to keep interested parties informed about data security and privacy risks. Auditors corroborate evidence from external sources (Torres, Botes, Dumay, & Odendaal 2021). Engaging the community is necessary for an organization to get buy-in from management (Cook, 2011). Communities are key stakeholders to improve the management system. This was demonstrated by Vetter (2014) who stated that research across disciplines demonstrated several benefits associated with community engagement

Organizations work towards integrating information governance policies overall while allowing information management program staff and procedures to remain local to organizations. Integration of information management programs requires an organization to allocate resources. This will enhance organizations to comply with King IV Code of Corporate Governance, develop processes and King committees, ensuring disclosure and transparency.

King IV corporate governance is applied both to public and private sector in South Africa. This implied organization to develop systems and processes to ensure compliance with the king IV corporate governance. Organization should govern risk that supports the organization in setting and achieving its strategic objectives. King IV stresses the significance of business continuity for compliance. King IV is used by most organization to ensure compliance with corporate governance. Ethical and effective leadership is important for organization to execute corporate governance (Chauke, 2021). Organization should manage risk in their environment. Organization leadership should ensure that they have ethical culture, good performance, effective control, and legitimacy to achieve its objectives. Corporate governance promotes transparency and accountability in organization. Organizations are to develop systems to survive complex global economics for sustainability. Organization strategies and operations are directed by responsible leaders who aim to meet their organization's social and environmental responsibilities (King 111 Report, 2009). Organizations ensured that are complying with corporate governance to ensure flow of information systems. The model adopted by organizations is to ensure their sustainability for their future.

Quality of service provided to various stakeholders is necessary. The quality of information is dependent on the collection by the organization. Data collected by organizations are to be completed, accurately (Al- Abdullah, Alsmadi, Abdullah, & Farkas 2020). A study conducted by Mourad (2017) states that organizations develop internal and external control to ensure information quality. Mourad stated that the quality of information systems is possible through the collection and evaluation of information systems and by minimizing the risk of poor performance of individuals. Providing information to organizations improves brand in international organizations. The growth of organizations is mainly based on information about their quality components. Quality assurance provides opportunities for an organization to transform. Organizations will improve on their service renders to various organizations. Stakeholders are involved in decision-making.

DATA PRIVACY

Previous research identified the significance of privacy policies to ensure trust (Guo, Wang, & Wang 2022). Designing a privacy policy is essential for organizations to ensure privacy information. A lack of policy signifies a lack of accountability and awareness of the management of records within an organization (Makwae, 2021). The lack of privacy policy in most South African organizations shows a lack of accountability and awareness of records management standards. The staff is not aware of the significance of establishing POPIA action plan. The action plan provides opportunities for organization to prioritize activities.

Privacy is recognized as a fundamental human right (Solove, 2008). Worldwide, most countries enacted privacy legislation to protect the rights of individuals and organizations from any misuse. This implies that the privacy of information needs to be managed as a form of human rights. The literature shows that organizations have a concern about privacy and how Information communication technologies enable or hinder individual abilities to safeguard information (Earp & Payton, 2001). It seems most South African organizations are not yet developed effective records management systems, processes, and procedures to manage personal information. This despite that privacy concerns and data security are some of the risks faced by businesses (La Torre, Botes, Dumay, & Odendaal, 2021; Coss & Dhillon 2019). In South Africa, privacy is protected by the Constitution of the Republic of South Africa (Makulilo 2012). The Constitution of South Africa makes provisions for the protection of privacy.

Legislations play an essential role for organizations to build corporate governance. Organizations create records that need to be managed in compliance with the national legislation and the regulatory instrument (Skatuu & Ngoepe, 2015). Organization is established through the enactment of the legislation which enables organizations to develop structures, processes, and procedures. There is a relationship between information governance and compliance with the legislature. Individuals or organizations are to adhere to Constitution and relevant legislation (Li & Hu, 2022). Acts such as Protection of Personal Information Act No 13 of 2013, Promotion of Access to Information Act No 2 of 2002. This legislation has a direct impact on how government, organizations, and individuals manage their information (Makwae, 2021). The government ensures legislation to ensure that organizations keep records. The research pre-findings show that South Africa has various legislations that support the management of records.

Organizations align their procedures and processes in line with the Protection of Personal Information Act No 4 of 2013 to protect the privacy and confidentiality of information. Privacy principles such as purpose specification, collection limitation, data quality, use limitation, openness, Individual participation, accountability, and security safeguards must be adhered to (Makri, Georgiopoulou, & Lambrinoudakis, 2020). A privacy impact assessment conducted to determine the organization's level of compliance with information privacy requirements and the safety of personal information (Swartz, Da Veiga, & Martins 2021). Organizations concerned with the protection of private information. Most organizations develop policies to control the confidentiality of various types of records and understand the protective actions of the employees. The study adds to privacy policy literature.

Most organizations and individual does not trust that their information is effectively protected in their systems. This may be because South Africa emerged from the apartheid system where privacy was the order of the day. The lack of trust in the public sector was a course of concern (Baloyi & Kotze, 2017). This means that for any organization to be successful requires the confidence of ordinary people within their platform. Organizations ensure the integrity of information collected, stored, and disseminated. Information integrity is essential to protect information from unauthorized modification (Coss and Dhillon 2019).

Organizations assign a division responsible for information security. For example, the Information Communication Technology (ICT) division is mostly assigned to provide information communication technology services. To advise other divisions on the type of ICT to be purchased by organizations in compliance with appropriate legislation. The Operation division which includes the Security Management section is responsible for physical security management. Records Management is responsible for the management of physical records in the custody of the organization. The review of the literature shows a lack of integration of security clusters of the organization. Cybersecurity is one of the sections of information within an organization threatening the security of information. It is necessary to ensure that information security is managed in an integrated manner. Security manager responsible

In South Africa, security classification has been dealt with the protection of the State Information bill. This bill protects information from the government from alteration or deletion of records. Minimum Information Security Standards (MISS). MISS is a national policy approved by the South African National cabinet with the view to classifying information according to different security levels, For example, Restricted, Confidential information, secret, and Top Secret. Security measures are of utmost significance for archives repositories (Nengomasha & Nyanga 2012). MISS has implications for the management of records and archives management in South Africa and another part of the world. An Archives management system should be built to protect records from both internal and external threats. Records preserved in the archives should be protected from unauthorized access.

INFORMATION COMMUNICATION TECHNOLOGY GOVERNANCE

The information communication technology (ICT) developed across the world in the twentieth century has brought benefits to information-generating and organizing institutions (Dzandza, 2020). Most organizations adopted ICT to provide service to their community. Most South African governments adopted and implemented information communication technology (ICT) with the view to improve service delivery by providing access to information. ICT was essential to promote sharing of information.

The South African government expands ICT as enabler services across public institutions. No single government department is responsible for the information governance management system in South Africa . As a result, there was a generation of electronic records across all government institutions. The review of the literature showed that South Africa's ICT systems are not integrated. There is no national department coordinating the ICT. The National Archives and Records Services of South Africa is only responsible to control its records management system. Despite that, the Department of Science and Technology established the State Information Technology Agency (SETA) as a State Enterprise to coordinate government information technology systems. SETAS was established to coordinate all ICT of government for both public and non-public organizations. Seta's role is to advise organizations on the type of ICT infrastructure for organizations. The lack of a clear framework for managing electronic records poses a risk to the sustainability, stability, and quality of services offered through electronic records management systems as alluded to by (Ambira, Kemoni, & Ngulube, 2019). ICT applied to carry out business activities and for transmitting information (Matlala, Ncube, & Parbanath, 2022). This implies that SETA takes a lead role to develop ICT specifications and functional requirements for digital records systems within the South African context to ensure that all software is acquired for managing all types of electronic records. ICT provides businesses with a means to nurture trust with their customers regarding collected data (Al-Abdullah, Alsmadi, Aiabdullah, & Farkas, 2020).

South African government departments inherited paper-based records management systems through the years. The growing volume of paper-based records was a challenge to improve information management (Phillips 2011). The disadvantage of paper-based records is that physical records cannot be disseminated to various communities at the same time compared to digital records. To improve service delivery and provide access to information to communities, the government embarked on digitization projects. The digitization project was conducted as part of organization moving form paper based records to digital platform. The digitization projects provide opportunities for the preservation of records such as audiovisual materials (Assmann, 2009). Privacy concerns are also compounded in the cloud computing environment due to the pervasive nature of how personal information is collected and processed and used within the scope of business activities (Coss & Dhillon, 2019).

Institutional repositories were established to preserve digital records. They are significant since they support access to research, learning, and teaching (Chisita & Chiparausha 2021). These are systems aimed at managing digital content (Yakel, Rieh, Jean, Markey, & Kim, 2008). Trusted digital repositories are significant because of the Trusted Repositories Audit and Certification: Criteria and Checklist.

Despite the South African government's investment in an electronic environment, not all records created by organizations stored in established records management systems. Most of the records created by organizations reside in email systems, enterprise content management systems, electronic document and records management systems, and a variety of cloud systems. Most government institutions adopted cloud services to increase operational efficiencies, accessibility, collaboration, security, reliability, and opportunities for innovation (Franks, 2015).

South Africa lacks infrastructure in information communication structure. On the management of the digital platform. Funding for digitization projects remains a challenge for an organization (Dzandza 2020). The issue of lack of funding was also raised by (Matla, Ncube & Parbanath 2022, and Rakemane & Mosweu 2021). The management and preservation of records need to be continually funded. Lack of funding threatened sustainability of such systems and may contribute to technological obsolescence as the management would not continue to fund the system. ICT may not be able to dispose of records regularly.

Organizations establish a training program to develop staff on records and archives management systems. With the fourth industrial revolution and its demands to use new technologies, organizations may recruit, and train staff on disruptive ICT (Lim, 2001). Staff development and training are integral cornerstones to information management systems. African staff is not yet re-develop in terms of the ICT (Brown, Crocamo, Bielskas, Ransom, Vanti & Wilfong, 2017). The review of literature shows that organizations ensure that systems are in place. Staff are to be trained in an information management system.

The fourth Industrial Revolution forces an organization to create big data. Organizations develop processes, and procedures to manage big data without compromising quality. The concept of big data has been established because of the development of data and data processing (Blakesley & Yallop, 2019).

Organizations collect, store and process a huge amount of information on customers to understand behaviors and preferences (Guo, Wang Wang, 2022). The big data will enable an organization to analyze the systems. Organizations develop systems to ensure the preservation of big data. Big data is developed to improve the decision-making of the organization (La Torre, Botes, Dumay, & Odendaal, 2021).

Big data enable an organization to improve on business decision–making. Organizations required to ensure that a data governance framework was put in place. Organizations are to ensure that privacy governance is put in place to ensure the management of information. Several measures are to be put in place to ensure that staff trust data on the information management system without violating privacy. There should be staff awareness of the creation and awareness of big data created by various organizations.

RECORDS MANAGEMENT

A records management system is the process to manage the creation, maintenance, use, and disposal of records. The review of the literature shows that records management systems in South Africa are not effective. The lack of effective records management program was non-conformity with the requirement and guidelines issued by the National Archives of South Africa for systematic disposal of records, thus leading to a lot of caution on how could the organizations ensure effective records management system (Makwae, 2021). Good records management commences with putting records structure in place. Management and establishment of policies and guidelines to regulate preservation of records and management of records lifecycle (Matlala, Ncube, & Parbanath, 2022). A good records management framework consists of information-related laws policies and programs, records management standards, and qualified staff to drive records and archives management programs. This statement is alluded to by Ipinge and Nengomasha (2018).

The review of literate indicated that records management in South Africa operates under the framework and guidance of the National Archives and Records Services Act 43 of 1996. This act gave the National Archives and Records Services of South Africa oversight of records and archives management in South Africa. The Department of Arts and Culture is responsible for Archives and Records Management chief directorate under the Chief Directorate the necessity of transferring records to the records center in Pretoria (Nengomasha & Nyanga, 2012). Any decision about records management in the South African public sector is subject to approval by the National Archivists of South Africa (Marutha, 2019). Similar to the archives of the Republic of Namibia, The National Archives of South Africa decentralized its services on the preservation of archives materials. The National Archives and Records Service Act 43 of 1996 provides for the establishment of the nine provincial Archives in South Africa. This implies that each South African province establishes a provincial archive to preserve archives materials. It is meant to be used alongside other existing laws and legislation governing records management.

Despite the development of records management systems in South Africa, there is still a lack of uniformity among South African public institutions. This challenge of uniformity was also reported by Shepherd, Stevenson, and Flinn (2011). Despite lack of uniformity, it is the role of records management professionals to ensure effective and efficient records management systems of organizations.

Lack of records management training was cited as a challenge to implement South African public services. Institutions offering archives management course from basic to Ph.D. level is the University of South Africa, the University of Limpopo, University of Fort Hare offers a program in Information science. The University of Witwatersrand and University of Cape Town offered Cultural heritage normally at the postgraduate level from Postgraduate level, Masters's to Ph.D. in information sciences. Records Management programs or courses must be based on market-related issues (Tsabedze & Ngoepe, 2021). By late 2004, formal education in records and archives had finally expanded to were over fifteen universities in South Africa offered qualifications in records and archives management.

The information governance approach recognized record management as a governance function. This implies that records management must be viewed as a strategic function of any organization. It should be managed as part of risk management in an organization. Records are to be viewed and managed at the organization's strategic level (Phiri & Tough, 2018).

Organizations need to develop a strategy, processes, and procedures to control the lifecycle of records. Organizations advise, and use guidelines, mandates, and regulations for managing the lifecycle of their records (Noonan, 2016). There is no single legislation ensuring the retention schedule of records in South Africa (Mullon & Ngoepe, 2020). There are various legislation such as the National Archives and Records Services Act 43 of 1996, The Public Finance Management Act responsible for the management of records management systems. Classification and assessment of the records inventory contribute to the development of the records schedule (Peltz 2006 p. 194). An appraisal is the first step in determining the retention of records. Archivists and records managers in the twentieth century recognized the need for systematic analysis of records because of the records management system and technologies (Convery, 2014). There is a need to refine criteria and techniques for records selection in their organization. Organizations are to develop procedures to appraise, retain and dispose of terminates (Mojapelo, 2022). Inactive records need to be periodic reviews to ensure that records with enduring value are preserved. The records retention procedure should be put in place to ensure that records containing confidential information are burned or shredded. An organization needs to adjust the transferability of the appraisal strategies and criteria to determine the retention of organizational records (Vellino & Alberts 2016). The National Archives of South Africa recommends public entities retain five percentage records with historical, cultural, and scientific significance (Ngoepe & Nkwe 2018). The survey conducted at public entities demonstrates the difficulty both of assessing state performance in records retention. This implies that the implementation of a records retention system requires a statement both of mandatory standards and voluntary best practices (Peltz, 2006). However, the appraisal strategy of organizations differs concerning how the organization retains some of the organization records. This is so because the implementation of a records retention schedule requires a decision on the part of the implementation of the organization's strategy.

Records need to be disposed of on regular basis in terms of regulatory requirements and organizational retention schedule. Records managers play an important role in the management of the lifecycle of records until the disposal of records. Records managers are guided by rules, regulations, and policies to dispose of records that are no longer required for administrative processes. These rules and guidelines and processes are to be informed by a national policy and legislation. Organizations develop a system to enable the automated disposal of records. In the electronic environment, the system must be able to define disposition classes, ensuring the definition of each class includes a disposition trigger, a retention period, and a disposition action. The system allowed the system for retention periods to be defined from one day to an indefinite length of time (Franks, 2015).

The success of the records and archives management program depends on the support provided by the government. This means that there should be a government framework supporting records and archives management programs.

ACCESS

Organizations are to ensure that information is disseminated to various stakeholders' platforms. Democratizing access to knowledge is among the drivers of open access to publications and research data (Borgman, 2018). Open access expands readership. The advent of electronic records management systems ensure that organizations share information through various platforms such as emails. Some organizations outsource electronic records management system to manage all forms of records in their environment. This provides opportunities to share information with various stakeholders. Information professionals' services are tasks with the responsibility of providing access to information to the public (Segaetsho, 2014). This implies that systems are to be developed to ensure that information is provided to relevant stakeholders. This implies that organizations are to develop processes, and procedures to ensure the management of information from various platforms. Archivists have a responsibility to promote access to archives (Nengomasha & Nyanga, 2015). It seems that most people in South Africa access records without authorization. Records should be protected against unauthorized users.

Records arranged and described according to records and archives management principles such as provenance and principles of original order. This implies that the physical condition of the archives materials determines the level of access (Nengomasha & Nyanga, 2015). The more archives are properly arranged and described accordingly.

Strategy

Organizations operate within its strategy to achieve their objectives. However, most South African organizations lack a strategy to implement information management systems (Matlala, Ncube, & Parbanath, 2021). It seems that most organizations invested resources in electronic records management systems without a proper strategy. Therefore, you cannot expect organizations to develop a strategy if their staff are not aware of records and archives management systems. The coordinated departmental program requires planning and program phasing. The Executive management should develop an organizational structure to ensure effective management of resources. The flat organizational structure promotes the flow of information from executive management to all administrative staff. The flow of information within an organization will ensure sharing of information from various departments. Adoption of organizational strategy influence the degree of transparency and accountability. Strategy is derived from the long-term objectives of the organization which are informed by its mission and vision. An organization determine what needs to be measured, establish standards of performance, and compare the actual performance with the established standard and correction action (Gcaza & Solms, 2017). Organizations develop risk management strategies to mitigate any challenges faces by organizations.

Information management strategy should be viewed by all organizational stakeholders to improve compliance with the regulatory framework. The review of the literature shows that most South African organizations are not complying with the statutory regulations. Most organizations are not punished for not complying with legislation. Expectations are necessary for organizations to comply with a regulatory framework.

Standards and Best Practices Guidelines

Various records management standards established to assist organization to comply with. Records management professions are guided by the standards developed by the International Council on Archives (ICA), International Organization for Standardization (ISO)(Katuu, 2016). The standards developed by these organizational bodies had an impact on the preservation of archives materials. ISO is an international standard.

The application of records management standards established a professional environment of best practices. The use of records management standards is essential in organizational development. ISO 15489 is viewed as the lens of records management. This standard is significant to manage all types of records created (Stuart, 2017). ISO 15489 was adopted by organizations to improve records management systems all over the world (Shepherd, Stevenson, & Flinn 2011)

ARMA International identified Generally Accepted Recordkeeping Principles that could be applied to records embedded in the cloud (Franks, 2015). This principle requires organizations to manage records in line with its strategic objectives. Organizations are to establish principles to manage all types of records created. This implies that records to be managed from the creatin stage until disposal stage.

The review of the literature showed that most research applied the records readiness assessment tool developed by the International Records Management Trust and the World Bank in 2004 (Asogwa, Ezeani & Asogwa, 2021). The model classified records into the three risk areas such as high risk, moderate risk, and low risk. However, it is not easy to measure performance evaluation criteria of privacy protection. Staff may use appropriate privacy protection technology according to their requirement (Li & Hu, 2022).

Change management is at the center of corporate governance because South Africa emerges from the apartheid system where information governance was not an issue. The communication management division plays a role to inform staff of the governance. Change management to implement an information management system is necessary. An organization needs to justify the adoption of information governance.

The information governance framework used in the literature may be used as a benchmark information and records management systems. It may also be used for the formulation of policy development and improvement and implementation of records management strategies. Organizations may be able to improve their standards and processes. To measure the degree of security and privacy requirements that have been addressed by an organization, it is necessary to used metrics for the quantification of the requirements (Makri, Georgopoulos, & Lambrinoudakis, 2020). The sensitivity of data checked against governance standards. The outcome of any risk analysis will be a numeric value known as a risk factor. The risk facts determined by the risk that occurred in the organization during the evaluation period.

ACCOUNTABILITY AND TRANSPARENCY

Heads of departments are responsible for effective decision-making. Records Management is viewed as the main source of accountability (Makwae, 2021). Records enable individuals to monitor and evaluate the program on any project embarked on by an organization. Accountability is the principle relating to the processing of personal data under the GDPR (Dove, 2018). Effective records management is the basis for organization planning, accountability, and transparency (Mojapelo 2022). Accountability is dependent on well-organized records. Organizations are to develop systems, processes, and procedures to ensure an effective management system. Effective records management should de be developed by organizations to facilitate the accessibility of records management. Information should be available to various stakeholders.

An organization should ensure that security measures are in place. Organization are to develop archives Centre and archive repository to preserve both physical and electronic records. The physical cabinets should include lockable cabinets, and strong rooms to ensure that records are protected against any threat. Archives repository should back up on a regular basis to ensure that records are preserved on continuous basis.

CONCLUSION

This study provided an insight into the legal framework in South Africa. Governance framework is the foundation of any organization's program and activities to facilitate effective decision-making and actions. Records management used as a catalyst to implement sound information governance. Records management program cannot be separated from information governance. A multi-staged approach is needed to address the vast amount of digital data that needs to be appraised for permanent retention.

Areas for Further Research

Future research may be conducted by applying the foundation of this study. There is a need for further research to determine responsible for overall corporate governance as a driver to implementing effective records management programs.

REFERENCES

Al-Abdullah, M., Alsmadi, I., Aiabdullah, R., & Farkas, B. (2020). Designing Privacy-Friendly data repositories: A framework for a blockchain that follows the GDPR. *Digital Policy. Regulation & Governance*, *22*(5/6), 389–411. doi:10.1108/DPRG-04-2020-0050

Ambirar, M. C., Kemoni, N. H., & Ngulube, P. (2019). A framework for electronic records management in support of e-government in Kenya. Electronic records. *Records Management Journal*, *29*(3), 305–319. doi:10.1108/RMJ-03-2018-0006

Assmann, I. (2009). Digital Audiovisual archives; Unlocking our Audio and Audiovisual heritage Potential. *ESARBICA Journal*, *28*(1), 230–237. doi:10.4314/esarjo.v28i1.44406

Baloyi, N., & Kotze, P. (2017). Are Organisations in South Africa Ready to Comply with Personal Data Protection or Privacy Legislation and Regulations? *IST- Africa Conference Proceedings*. IST.

Blakesley, I. R., & Yallop, A. C. (2019). What do you know about me? Digital privacy and online data sharing in the UK insurance sector. Journal of Information *Communication and Ethics in Society*, *18*(2), 281–303. doi:10.1108/JICES-04-2019-0046

Borgman, L. C. (2018). Open Data, Grey Data, and Stewardship. *Universities at the Privacy Frontier*, *33*, 365.

Brown, J., Crocamo, T. J., Bielskas, A., Ransom, E., Vanti, B. W., & Wilfong, K. (2017). Evolving skills for emerging technologies: A collaborative approach. *Library Hi Tech*, *35*(3), 346–359. doi:10.1108/LHT-12-2016-0156

Chauke, R. (2021). King IV municipal supplements: The impact on the municipal's approach to governance. *Technium. The Social Science Journal*, *26*, 54–64.

Chisita, T. C., & Chiparausha, B. (2021). An Institutional Repository in a Developing Country: Security and Ethical Encounters at the Bindura University of Science Education, Zimbabwe. *New Review of Academic Librarianship*, *27*(1), 130–143. doi:10.1080/13614533.2020.1824925

Convery, N. (2014). From reactive to proactive appraisal. *Archives and Manuscripts*, *42*(2), 158–160. doi:10.1080/01576895.2014.911676

Cook, T. (2011). We are What We Keep; We keep What We are: Archival Appraisal Past, Present and Future. *Journal of the Society of Archivists*, *32*(2), 173–189. doi:10.1080/00379816.2011.619688

Coss, L. D., & Dhillon, G. (2019). Cloud Privacy objectives a value-based approach. *Information & Computer Security*, *27*(2), 189–220. doi:10.1108/ICS-05-2017-0034

Dove, S. E. (2018). The EU General Data Protection Regulation: Implications for International Scientific Research in the Digital Era. *The Journal of Law, Medicine & Ethics*, *46*(4), 1013–1030. doi:10.1177/1073110518822003

Dzandza, E. P. (2020). Digitizing the intellectual output of Ghanaian universities. *Collection and Curation*, *39*(3), 69–75. doi:10.1108/CC-05-2019-0012

Earp, B. J., & Payton, C. F. (2001) Data Protection in the University Setting: Employee Perceptions of Student Privacy. *Proceedings of the 34th Hawaii International Conference on System Sciences*. 10.1109/HICSS.2001.927152

Esser, I.M and Delport, P.A (2018). The South African King IV Report on Corporate Governance: Is the crown shiny enough? *Company lawyer, 39*(11), 378 – 384.

Ferguson, C. S. (2019). Assessing the King IV Corporate Governance Report in relation to business continuity and resilience. *Journal of Business Continuity & Emergency Planning*, *13*(2), 1–13. PMID:31779744

Franks, C. P. (2015). New Technologies, New Challenges: Records Retention and Disposition in a Cloud Environment. *Canadian Journal of Information and Library Science*, *39*(2), 192–209. doi:10.1353/ils.2015.0011

Gcaza, N., & Solms, V. R. (2017). A strategy for a Cybersecurity Culture: A South African Perspective. *The Electronic Journal of Information Systems in Developing Countries. EJISDC*, *80*(6), 1–17.

Guo, Y., Wang, X., & Wang, C. (2022). Impact of privacy policy content on perceived effectiveness of privacy policy: The role of vulnerability, benevolence and privacy concern. *Journal of Enterprise Information Management*, *35*(3), 774–795. doi:10.1108/JEIM-12-2020-0481

Ipinge, A., & Nengomasha, T. C. (2018). An investigation into the records management profession in the public service of Namibia. Records in Namibian Public Service. *Information and Learning Science*, *119*(7/8), 377–388. doi:10.1108/ILS-11-2017-0123

Katuu, S. (2016). Managing digital records in a global environment. A review of the landscape of international standards and good practice guidelines. Managing digital records. *The Electronic Library*, *34*(5), 869–894. doi:10.1108/EL-04-2015-0064

Katuu, S., & Ngoepe, M. (2015). Managing digital heritage an analysis of the education and training curriculum for Africa's archives and records professionals. *Archives and Manuscripts*, *43*(2), 96–119. doi:10.1080/01576895.2015.1050677

King III Report (2009). King code of governance for South Africa 2009, Institute of Directors in Southern Africa. www.ngopulse.org/sites/default/files/king_code_of_governance_for _sa_2009 _updated _june_2012.pdf

La Torre, M., Botes, L. V., Dumay, J., & Odendaal, E. (2021). Protecting a new Achilles heel: The role of auditors within the practice of data protection. *Managerial Auditing Journal*, *36*(2), 218–239. doi:10.1108/MAJ-03-2018-1836

Li, Y., & Hu, X. (2022). Social network analysis of law information privacy protection of cybersecurity based on rough set theory. Law information privacy protection. *Library Hi Tech*, *40*(1), 133–15. doi:10.1108/LHT-11-2018-0166

Li, Y., & Hu, X. (2022). Social Network analysis of law information privacy protection of cybersecurity based on rough set theory. *Library Hi Tech*, *40*(1), 133–151. doi:10.1108/LHT-11-2018-0166

Lim, K. S. (2001). Transforming centres of excellence- the National Heritage Board experience. *Library Review*, *50*(7/8), 366–373. doi:10.1108/00242530110405364

Makri, L. E., Georgiopoulou, Z., & Lambrinoudakis, C. (2020). Utilizing a privacy impact assessment method using metrics in the healthcare sector. *Information & Computer Security*, *28*(4), 503–529. doi:10.1108/ICS-01-2020-0007

Makulilo, B. A. (2012). Privacy and data protection in Africa: A state of the Art. *International Data Privacy Law*, *2*(3), 163–178. doi:10.1093/idpl/ips014

Makwae, N. E. (2021). Legal frameworks for personnel records management in support of accountability in devolved governments: A case of Garissa County Government. *Records Management Journal*, *31*(2), 109–133. doi:10.1108/RMJ-05-2019-0024

Marutha, N. (2019). The application of legislative frameworks for the management of medical records in Limpopo Province, South Africa. *Information Development*, *35*(4), 551–563. doi:10.1177/0266666918772006

Matlala, E. M., Ncube, R. T., & Parbanath, S. (2022). The State of digital records preservation in South Africa's public sector in the 21st century: A literature review. *Records Management Journal*, *32*(2), 198–212. doi:10.1108/RMJ-02-2021-0004

Mojapelo, M. S. (2022). Records Management in government schools in South Africa: A case study in Limpopo province. Records management in government schools. *Records Management Journal, 32*(1), 21–42. doi:10.1108/RMJ-04-2020-0012

Mourad, M. (2017). Quality Assurance as a driver of information management Strategy Stakeholders perspectives in Higher education. Stakeholders' perspectives in HE. Stakeholders' perspectives in HE. *Journal of Enterprise Information Management, 30*(5), 779–795. doi:10.1108/JEIM-06-2016-0104

Mullon, A., & Ngoepe, M. (2019). An integrated framework to elevate information governance to a national level in South Africa. *Records Management Journal, 29*(1/2), 103–116. doi:10.1108/RMJ-09-2018-0030

Nengomasha, C. T., & Nyanga, H. E. (2012). Managing Semi current records: A case for records centers for the public services of Namibia. *Journal for Studies in Humanities and Social Sciences, 1*(2), 231–245.

Nengomasha, T. C., & Nyanga, H. E. (2015). Access to Archives at the National Archives of Namibia. *ESARBICA Journal, 34*, 88–103.

Ngoepe, M and Mello, V (2020) Integration of records management systems at a South African Water Utility Company. *Integration of records management system.*

Ngoepe, M., & Nkwe, M. (2018). Separating the Wheat from the Chaff with the winnowing fork. The eeny meeny miny mo appraisal approach of digital records in South Africa. *Records Management Journal, 28*(2), 130–142. doi:10.1108/RMJ-09-2017-0027

Noonan, W. D. (2016). Column: Technology Matters in Archives, Email: an appraisal approach. *Journal of Archival Organization, 13*(3-4), 16–151. doi:10.1080/15332748.2018.1445607

Peltz, J.R (2006). Arkansas's Public Records Retention Program: Records Retention as a Cornerstone of Citizenship and Self- Government. *University of Arkansas at Little Rock Law Review, 28*(2), 175 – 249.

Phillips, T. J. (2011). *Mergers, Acquisitions, Diverstitures and Closures Records and Information Management Checklists. AMRMA International Education Foundation.* ARMA International Educational Foundation. Pittsburgh, Rakemane, D and Mosweu, O (2021). Challenges of managing and Preserving audio-visual archives in archival institutions in Sub Saharan Africa: A Literature review. *Collection and Curation, 40*(2), 42–50.

Phiri, J. M., & Tough, G. A. (2018). Managing university records in the world of governance. Managing university records. *Records Management Journal, 28*(1), 47–61. doi:10.1108/RMJ-11-2016-0042

Segaetsho, T. (2014). Preservation Risk Assessment Survey of the University of Botswana Library. *African Journal of Library Archives and Information Science, 24*(2), 176–186.

Shepherd, E., Stevenson, A., & Flinn, A. (2011). Freedom of Information and Records Management in local government: Help or Hindrance? *Information Polity, 16*(2), 111–121. doi:10.3233/IP-2011-0229

Solove, J. D. (2008). *Understanding Privacy.* Harvard Unversity Press.

Stuart, K. (2017). Methods, methodology and madness: Digital records management in the Australian government. *Records Management Journal, 27*(2), 223–232. doi:10.1108/RMJ-05-2017-0012

Swartz, P., Da Veiga, A., & Martins, N. (2021). Validating an information privacy governance questionnaire to measure the perception of employees. *Information & Computer Security*, *29*(5), 761–786. doi:10.1108/ICS-08-2020-0135

Torre, L. M., Botes, L. V., Dumay, J., & Odendaal, E. (2021). Protecting a new Achilles heel: The role of auditors within the practice of data protection. *Managerial Auditing Journal*, *36*(2), 218–239. doi:10.1108/MAJ-03-2018-1836

Tough, G. A., & Lihoma, P. (2018). Medical record-keeping systems in Malawi. Is there a case for hybrid systems and intermediate technologies? Medical records keeping systems. *Records Management Journal*, *28*(3), 265–277. doi:10.1108/RMJ-02-2018-0004

Tsabetse, V., & Ngoepe, M. (2021). A Framework for quality assurance for archives and records management education in an open distance e-learning environment in Eswatini. A Framework for quality assurance for ARM. *The International Journal of Information and Learning Technology*, *38*(1), 91–102. doi:10.1108/IJILT-03-2020-0033

Vetter, A. M. (2014). Archive 2.0: What Composition Students and Academic Libraries Can Gian From Digital- Collaborative Pedagogies. *Composition Studies*, *42*(1), 35–53.

Yallop, C. A., Gică, O. A., Moisescu, O. I., Coroş, M. M., & Séraphin, H. (2021). The digital traveler: Implications for data ethics and data governance in tourism and hospitality. *Journal of Consumer Marketing*. Advance online publication. doi:10.1108/JCM-12-2020-4278

KEY TERMS AND DEFINITIONS

Information Governance: This is a framework that defines the creation, valuation, use, sharing, storage, archiving, and deletion of records .

Records Disposal: This is a process of identification of records with historical, cultural, and scientific value for permanent preservation hence records witch administration value expired are permanently destroyed.

Records Management Standards: These are standards use to direct and manage records management systems in an organization.

Records Management: It is the process of management of records from creation to disposal stage of records.

Records Retention: This is a process of determining the period to keep records.

Chapter 4
Analysis of Business Ethics and Social Responsibility Practices in Government Agencies in South Africa

Tlou Maggie Masenya

Durban University of Technology, South Africa

ABSTRACT

Government agencies are important due to their contributions to the growth of economy and the benefits they bring to the society. However, there is an increasing need for these agencies to be ethical, especially in the 21st century, an era full of competitors, and also characterized by an increasingly globalized business world and a cascade of corporate corruption and fraud in both developed and developing countries. Government agencies thus require the enforcement of business ethics for long-term business success and sustainability. Although the main objective of business is to earn the money and profit, government agencies should take initiative for the welfare of the society and perform their activities within the framework of environmental norms and social responsibility. These agencies should provide goods and services legally, and profitably to the society and operate responsibly to address social and environmental issues. The study utilised literature review to critically analyse business ethics and social responsibility practices in government agencies in South Africa.

INTRODUCTION

The earlier you create ethical culture and apply business ethics in your organization the better as the proverbs say: A man without ethics is a wild beast loosed upon this world. – **Albert Camus**

As noted by Mohammed (2012) organizations that are committed to long-term success realize that creating a culture where ethical behaviours are rewarded and encouraged is the ultimate key to survival today and growth in the future. Government agencies are important due to the benefits they bring to the

DOI: 10.4018/978-1-6684-6815-9.ch004

people who are the consumers of goods and services. These agencies should thus run their operations in the most economical, efficient and effective manner possible to increase performance and focus on creating an ethical culture for business sustainability. The interest in business ethics that began in the 1970s, was in realization that businesses could be tempted to act immorally and unethically whenever necessary in pursuit of profit. This interest grew rapidly in recent years when it became evident that many heavy global businesses like Enron collapsed due to breaches in good corporate governance and business ethics (Ugoani, 2019). Business ethics thus become an international issue as the globalization process takes hold and the world begins to resemble a global village.

Sexty (2011) described ethics as codes of values and principles that govern the action of a person, or a group of people regarding what is right versus what is wrong. In the business setting, being ethical means applying principles of honesty and fairness to relationships with co-workers and customers (Daft, 2001). Sahin (2018) define business ethics as ethically the right way to run business and similarly as to apply ethical principles and values to business practices. Brimmer (2007) also described business ethics as a set of moral principles, values and standards that guides business practices to reflect a concern for society as a whole while pursuing profit (Brimmer, 2007). Furthermore, Albdour (2017) described business ethics as the ability and willingness to reflect on values in the course of organizational decision-making process, and thus to determine how value, and decision affect the various stakeholder groups are fundamental to organizational performance and sustainability. It is the behaviour that a business adheres to in its daily dealings with its stakeholders (i.e employees, customers, suppliers, immediate community and society in general (Dombin, 2012).

Employees in an organization are critical stakeholders, therefore when management considers business ethics in its actions they can be able to increase productivity (Ugoani, 2019). Business ethics are thus necessary to ensure ethical business decision-making and to this extent more than 90% of global sustainable organizations have code of ethics and huge regard to prevailing laws (Ugoani, 2019). On the other hand, ethical behaviour is defined as a practice that applies to everyone employed in the organization regardless of position, level of responsibility and range of responsibilities (Paliwal, 2006). It relates to actions which are characterized by honesty, integrity, morality and good management practices (Paliwal, 2006), while earning profits for the business organization. Business leaders are making decisions on a daily basis that could alter the likelihood of survival in today's market and are often forced to adopt a code of ethics or ethical codes and apply them in their daily business operations. Codes of ethics are formal standards and rules on beliefs about right or wrong that managers can use to help themselves in making appropriate decisions with regard to the interests of the stakeholders (Ezigbo, 2013). The decisions made within the organization forces business leaders to weigh pros and cons regarding benefiting the business, shareholder needs, legality issues, geographical concerns and other business matters.

However, when business people make decisions that are unethical, many people can be hurt, including employees, customers and members of the general population as well as the business itself (Mohammed, 2012). Organizations that choose not to do what is right, often do not survive for the long term and this may result in short term profit and also lead to eventual demise of the organization. However, ethics in business may be affected by many factors including the strength of legal, business regulation and human characteristics such as ethnicity, gender, level of education and socio-cultural environment (Wise, Ali, & Wise, 2010). As noted by Wise, Ali and Wise (2010) a low level of ethics adoption in the business sector is a part of wider socio-economic and political problems faced by many countries, such as loopholes in legal and business regulation often contribute to the corruption that can plague business operations. Brimmer (2007) further identified factors which inhibit ethical behavior including increasing competition, pressure for profits and return on investment political corruption, values and morals not considered important by younger generations, the expectancy of fast money and profits and disregard for social responsibility, honesty and integrity.

WHY BUSINESS ETHICS AND SOCIAL RESPONSIBILITY ARE IMPORTANT

*All the members of human society stand in need of each other's assistance, and are likewise exposed to mutual injuries. Where the necessary assistance is reciprocally afforded from love, from gratitude, from friendship and esteem, the society flourishes and is happy-***Adam Smith.**

There has been a proliferation of interest in corporate governance and business ethics, since the beginning of the 21st century, a period characterized by both an increasingly globalized business world and a cascade of corporate corruption and fraud in both developed and developing countries (Gold & Dienhart, 2007). In the contemporary business environment full of changes and competitors, each organization faces numerous challenges if their business plan is not based on business ethics. The purpose of business ethics is to guide the efforts of managers in discharging their duties to the satisfaction of various stakeholders, i.e. employees, owners, customers, suppliers and the general public. Business ethics or code of ethics is becoming increasingly important in any business organization because it allows them to efficiently respond to needs of all stakeholders, customers, employees, shareholders and society as a whole. It focuses on organizational culture, rules, regulations, procedures, laws and practices with regard to productivity, services and relationship with employees and other relevant stakeholders (Grigoropoulosi, 2019). Code of ethics is necessary for business owners and their employees to ensure every employee knows and understands which behavior is acceptable as right and wrong, as it pertains to the individuals and the business as a whole (Kim et al., 2010). Government agencies thus need to establish a formal code of ethics outlining the policies, regulations and expectations for all stakeholders. Good corporate governance and high ethical standards are thus essential for corporate long-term success, in any business organization (Robbins et al., 2010).

A growing number of government agencies is now focusing on the adoption of ethical values and standards as a fundamental component of business ethics. The effective management of the relationships among the many stakeholders involved in the organization and the attainment of its goals thus require that ethical standards be set, monitored and maintained (Albdour, 2017). The rights of employees, suppliers, customers, and the community at large cannot be protected and ensured in the long-term if the company's directors and executives act and allow others to act in ways that are unethical (Terblanche et al., 2008). There have been several corporate misconducts that includes a theft in the employees' pension fund, bribery and corruption, that have highlighted the need for organizations to impose and re-examine the role of corporate governance and business ethics in their day to day operations (Saidi, 2004). For example, failure to observe the principles of business ethics has led to the collapse of Enron, WorldCom and many banks in the 2000s and the misfortune of Cadbury Nigeria Plc border on management ineffectiveness and indiscipline (Grigoropoulosi, 2019). When reflecting on our changing times, one sees that the business ethics of each company as well as the implementation of those ethics at all company levels are prerequisites for securing the desired atmosphere of fairness (Takahashi, 1995).

Ethical business practice is regarded as a means for organizations to comply with relevant environmental rules and regulations necessary to enhance the prosperity of the business (Sharafa, 2014). Therefore, acting in an ethical way involves distinguishing between right and wrong, and then making the right choice. It is relatively easy to identify unethical business practices, for example, companies should not use child labor, should not unlawfully use copyrighted materials and processes and should not engage in bribery (Salleh, 2016). Government agencies will not adequately meet its goals and ensure sustainability where there are breeches in business ethics and standards. Business leaders thus observe that without ethical business practices, there would be irrationality, irresponsibility, illegality and corruption that would lead to the unsustainability of their businesses. The government as the supreme authority in the regulation of business in society also relies much on business ethical principles in the enactment and enforcement of legally established standards for business behavior and activities (Albdour, 2017). Any government agency must thus have a code of ethics outlining the mission, vision and common language shared across the organization that all employees need to understand. The code of ethics must be thoroughly communicated throughout the organization in a formal or informal way (written and oral communication), and ensure that there is provision for guidance and support in cases of dilemmas or insecurities.

Government agencies should have effective managers who are responsible for teaching employees and colleagues what ethics are and how important it is in the overall business activities of the organization. Business leaders are the most influential body in any institution greatly impacting the organizational culture, promoting principles and values in accordance to the objectives, mission and vision shared with employees (Senge, 2006). Businesses that are managed by leaders who conduct themselves in an ethical manner and who reward employees for doing what is right are much more likely to be characterized by a positive ethical culture (Bulog & Grancic, 2017). The role of business leaders is thus to create, install and nurture business cultures which are based on ethics, values and principles. Business leaders must instil shared core values, such as honesty, respect, responsibility, fairness and compassion among employees (Brimmer,2007), and these core values must be the ones driving decision-making within the organization.

Social responsibility means that businesses, in addition to maximising shareholder value, must act in a manner that benefits society and it is a duty of the corporate body to protect the interest of the society as well as the environment (Anderson, 2021). Social responsibility is also known as Corporate Social Responsibility (CSR) as it applies to business. Holme and Watts (2000) described Corporate Social Responsibility as the continuing commitment by business to behave ethically and contribute to economic development while improving the quality of life of the workforce and their families as well as of the local community and society. More investors and consumers are now factoring in a company's commitment to socially responsible practices before making an investment or purchase. The International Organization for Standardization (ISO) 26000 (2010) also emphasizes that a business's ability to maintain a balance between pursuing economic performance and adhering to societal and environmental issues is a critical factor in operating efficiently and effectively.

BUSINESS ETHICS PRACTICES IN GOVERNMENT AGENCIES

Ethical issues are usually debated in terms of corporate governance, environmental degradation and global warming, corporate social responsibility and corporate consciousness (Nakano, 2007). Twin, Drury and Perez (2021) describe business ethics as a study of proper business policies and practices regarding potentially controversial issues, such as corporate governance, insider trading, bribery, discrimination, corporate social responsibility and fiduciary responsibilities. Business ethics emphasizes moral values and stand on principles such as trust, honesty, loyalty, integrity, fairness or equality, transparency, accountability and responsibility to stakeholders and shareholders. The lack of accountability, unethical behaviour and corrupt practices have become so pervasive to the extent that one may conveniently speak of a crisis of ethics in government agencies.

There have been discussions regarding the applicability of business ethics in the modern business age, in the wake of unethical scandals and misconduct caused by outright bribery and corruption, patronage, favouritism and nepotism, use of one's position for self- enrichment, abuse of public property, leaking and abuse of government information are some of the common manifestation of this plight (Rasheed, 1995). These scandals have caused millions of dollars in losses, left behind damaged organizations, forced them to close their business and left thousands of employees jobless without any future guarantee or security. All these experiences have also led to more emphasis on business ethics considerations, and as a result, many government agencies are now focusing on how they are supposed to behave in their operations and how to incorporate these considerations in their frameworks. Some of the scholars and business school leaders are also asking themselves on what role they can play in tackling the unethical scandals or the realities of unethical behaviour. Business leaders and employees should thus act in the best interests of their organizations in a manner based on moral values and principles as discussed below.

Honesty, Loyalty and Trustworthiness

Carr (2004) observed that most of the executives are almost compelled in the interests of their companies or themselves, to practice some form of deception when negotiating with customers, dealers, labor unions, governmental officials, or even other departments of their own companies. As noted by Ahmed (2009) this is a moral hazard that arises when business managers or leaders are tempted to act in their own self-interest and not those of the principal (usually equity and debt investors). Unethical behavior and lack of loyalty involving customers and the business could result in lost sales, lack of referrals and cancelled accounts. Therefore, in any government agency the customers should be satisfied at every stage, as per the products and services. Velasquez (2014) stated that when business organizations have managers and employees behaving unethically or opposing behaviours that enjoin virtues of honesty, loyalty and trust, the resulting internal conflicts could cause disruption to the organizational culture and overall productivity. Conflicts among co-workers and trust issues with management could hamper work flow and communication. Leaders in government agencies thus have the moral obligation to create an environment where employees experience honesty, loyalty and trust. For example, the remuneration of employees should also comply with loyalty, fairness and honesty. It is also important that the loss of trust in leadership and employees be restored, while confidence, pride, trust, hope and optimism are enhanced. Government agencies may build trust by always acting with integrity, and maintaining a high standard of ethical, honest, safe and transparent business practice.

Leadership

South Africa is lacking in ethical leadership and key posts in government are compromised due to cadre deployment that illustrates a narrow-minded government that is willing to line the pockets of a few at the expense of the South African people. Burden of corruption and incompetence seems to be the order of the day and the existing government swindles money that is meant to save lives. There is a proverb by

Robert Noyce, that says "if ethics are poor at the top, that behaviour is copied down through the organization". During COVID 19 lockdown the ruling party, African National Congress (ANC) found their way to funds that were raised to cushion struggling citizens from a struggling economy that was forced to shut down. The case of the misappropriated R500-billion Covid-19 relief package and the minister of health's Digital Vibes is the evidence of corruption by members of the ANC, ruling party. In the case of eThekwini municipality, residents are squeezed to the core in the form of electricity hikes to the tune of 14.5% and the introduction of an irrational infrastructure levy of R1.50/kl that is effective from 1 July 2021 (Corruption Watch Report, 2021). The residents of eThekwini in Kwa Zulu Natal, South Africa, are expected to miraculously raise R1-billion over the next three years to fund infrastructure maintenance.

Corruption Watch report (2021) also revealed an alleged company to be owned by a relative of a provincial premier, which was said to have received a tender worth R200-million to supply vaccines. A whistle-blower also alleged that a private laboratory was falsifying Covid-19 test results at a price to enable individuals to travel and another alleged a covert operation for the sale of Covid-19 test kits outside a public clinic. The majority of complaints in the report came from Gauteng, where Corruption Watch is located, followed by KwaZulu-Natal (10%), the Western Cape (9%), and the Eastern Cape (7%) (Corruption Watch report, 2021). Corruption Watch report (2021) also cites complaints of instances where high school principals operated outside the regulations of their provincial departments by hiring unqualified teachers and soliciting sexual favours from those temporary teachers to safeguard their jobs. Whistle-blowers who reported cases to Corruption Watch were informed by their belief in a corruption-free South Africa.

Accountability and Responsibility

Accountability refers to the fact that every person is responsible or answerable to someone. Corporate accountability refers to the obligation and responsibility to give an explanation or reason for the company's actions and conduct (Grigoropoulosi, 2019). Government agencies are thus encouraged to be effective and accountable, while eliminating unethical behaviours. Once the culture of accountability is embedded in the organization and becomes an irreplaceable part of everyday work and performance, the whole organization in alignment with the objectives set and the goals aimed at (Rogers & Meehan, 2007). Any government agency should thus account for its ethical performance and duly communicate and report to relevant stakeholders at regular intervals. As also stated by Grigoropoulosi (2019) business organizations need to be accountable to their stakeholders and shareholder for ensuring prudence in the management of the organization and for demonstrating this through the highest standard of shareholder engagement, oversight and transparency. But how do government agencies ensure that they take responsibility for sustainable development and holistic improvement of society? For example, in any business organization including government agencies, the Board of Directors should be made accountable to the shareholders for the way in which the company has carried out its responsibilities. The Board of Directors are given authority to act on behalf of the organization and they should therefore accept full responsibility for the powers that it is given and the authority that it exercises. These directors are responsible for overseeing the management of the business, affairs of the organization, appointing the chief executive and monitoring the performance of the organization. Directors are required to act in the best interests of the company. As noted by Bulog and Grancic (2017) the directors need to respect the rights of shareholders and facilitates the effective exercise of those rights and they also have a responsibility for ensuring that a satisfactory dialogue with shareholders takes place by communicating effectively with them, giving them ready access to balanced and understandable information about the company and making it easier for them to participate in general meetings.

Government agencies thus need to recognizes the rights of all interested parties permitted by applicable principles and seeks to cooperate with such parties for their own development and financial stability. However, all the employees within the government agencies has the responsibility to ensure that they deliver prudent and superior results that align with their strategy and the needs of their shareholders. Gruning (2001) further stated that for an organization to be effective, it should behave ethically and be socially responsible, which means that an organization engages in quality relationship management with its publics. The goal of every business organization is to maintain viability through long-term profitability, and if the organization behaves responsibly, benefits accrue directly to the bottom line. Robinson (2003) also noted that when discussing business ethics, it is also important to emphasize Corporate Social Responsibility (CSR) because business does not function in a vacuum, but depends upon its environment, and cannot be separated from it and it thus has a responsibility to ensure its wellbeing. CSR need to be regarded as a crucial component in the decision-making process of management that must determine, among other goals, how to maximize profits and enhance organizational sustainability.

Law Abiding

The behaviour of any leader or manager has more impact within the organisation, and every individual and organisation in society should abide by certain moral codes in a way that there is no separate ethics of business. Therefore, every leader or manager should obey the laws even though he or she may personally believe them to be unjust or immoral. Government officials, law enforcement and any public servant who works in a position of authority and accepts a gift of monetary value can expect to be faced with questions regarding ethics. Financial gain seems to be one of the most prevalent ethical battles in our country and the world today. In a struggling economy where unemployment is quiet high it should not be a surprise that where ethical concerns exist, it usually revolves around money. Since 2019, the Corruption Watch reports highlighted what appears to be an unabated corruption problem in the government sector. Corruption Watch (2021) reported that the corruption by members of law (i.e South African Police Services and National Prosecuting Authority) is on the rise, sitting at 12% on the list. For example, in one incident, a woman in South Africa was arrested after pointing a firearm at her neighbour has, however, claimed that the police demanded a bribe to circumvent their failure to follow the right procedure and protocols during her arrest.

A detective employed in the South African Police Service (SAPS) has also been convicted for corruption by the Polokwane Specialised Commercial Crimes court. A detective was arrested by the Hawks' Serious Corruption Investigation members for extorting money from a person who had been arrested for dealing in drugs in order to make his docket disappear (Corruption Watch report, 2021). Corruption Watch report, 2021) further reported that a detective kept on pestering and demanding more money, although the victim paid R6 000 in the past until the matter was reported to the Hawks. A state vehicle was also spotted with 23 big bags containing cocaine with an estimated street value of R200 million, and the alleged victim was a warrant officer attached to Zonkezizwe police station, and was placed under arrest on the scene together with his three accomplices, another police warrant officer attached to National Investigative Unit, a Gauteng chief traffic officer and a civilian. A lawyer in Cape Town, South Africa was also arrested recently for drug possession that was meant for an accused he was representing. All these incidents indicated that efforts by the public and private sectors to seriously address the scourge of corruption in South Africa were woefully inadequate. The anti-corruption bodies thus need to tighten the leash on corruption, as looters come in all shapes and sizes to endanger even the most basic of human rights afforded by South African Constitution.

Equal Treatment or Fairness

Principle of equal treatment or fairness is closely related to concepts such as good faith, diligence, integrity and trust which are standards to define liability of directors as well. Mizuo (1998) stated that the string of business scandals also leads to the conclusion that fairness is an essential requirement for all business activities. Fairness or equal treatment, means that all shareholders should receive equal consideration for whatever shareholdings they hold. In addition to shareholders, there should also be fairness in the treatment of all stakeholders including employees, communities and public officials. The fairer the entity appears to stakeholders, the more likely it is that it can survive the pressure of interested parties. Equal treatment or fairness thus indicates that all stakeholders and shareholders including minorities should be treated equitably. For example, if consumers or customers believe they have been treated unfairly, such as being overcharged, they will no longer buy products from the company. Dissatisfied customers can quickly disseminate information about negative experiences with the company while the unethical dealings may also hurt the company's chances to obtain new customers.

Talented employees at all levels of an organization would also like to be compensated fairly for work and dedication. Government agencies who are fair and open in their dealings with employees thus have a better chance of retaining the most talented employees. These agencies need to ensure that the level and composition of remuneration is sufficient and reasonable and that its relationship to corporate and individual performance is defined. It is important that there is a clear relationship between performance and remuneration. In order to achieve this, government agencies need to adopt remuneration policies that attract and maintain talented and motivated employees so as to encourage enhanced performance of the company. However, employees must also have a responsibility to be ethical and be honest about their capabilities and experience. Center for Applied Ethics at Santa Clara University indicates that often customers who feel they are being treated unfairly or feel that businesses are withholding vital information and keeping secrets believe that unethical behavior is occurring. Justice approach may need to be applied to decision making based on treating all people fairly and consistently when making business decisions. An advantage of the justice approach is that it is more flexible than other ethical criteria because it recognizes that standards of fairness vary depending on the individuals involved in the decision (Gomez-Mejia & Balkin, 2002). There are two forms of justice approaches, namely: distributive justice approach and procedural justice approach. Distributive justice approach involves how an individual is treated and includes the fairness of rewards, punishments, and outcomes in an organization. This approach asks whether an employee received compensation equitable with performance or whether the employee was over paid or under paid. Procedural justice involves the fair and consistent application of rules and procedures. In case of a safety rule infraction, the procedural justice standard would be violated if other employees who broke the rule were not similarly disciplined.

However, some companies prefer to have a shareholder agreement, which can include more extensive and effective majority protection. Utilitarianism approach can also be applied for fairness whereby one would examine all the people who will be affected by a decision and choose the solution that would satisfy the most people. It is a means of making decisions based on what is good for the greatest number of people. This approach tries to minimize the pain and maximize the pleasure of the greatest number of people. Although utilitarianism strives to attain the ideal of democracy by promoting good for the majority, it may overlook the rights or needs of a minority of individuals, which one of the disadvantages of using this approach.

Integrity and Reputation

It takes 20 years to build a reputation and five minutes to ruin it. If you think about that, you'll do things differently - **Warren Buffett**

A positive public image can help an organization in maintaining competitive advantage, being ahead in profitability as well as sustaining good will and good reputation (Onsongo et al., 2017). Business organization should engage with its internal and external stakeholders to determine its current ethical reputation amongst the stakeholders, as well as what their ethical expectations are of that organisation (Rossouw, 2010). A company's reputation for ethical behavior can therefore help it create a more positive image in the marketplace, which can bring in new customers through word-of-mouth referrals. Business leaders who lead with purpose, values, integrity and motivate their employees to provide superior customer service, and create long-term value for shareholders (Avolio & Gardner, 2005). Integrity is regarded as an important ethical factor in business prosperity and continuity (Ezeh, 2019). It can be described as committing to accept and follow moral values of the organization. For example, whistle blowing in a company that an employee communicates its concerns about unlawful or unethical acts or transactions within the company serves to integrity (Sahin, 2018).

Integrity is an ethical issue and for sound corporate performance, and therefore the Board of Directors (BODs) should exercise leadership and judgment, with enterprise and integrity, so as to achieve continuing prosperity for the corporation (Ugoani, 2019). Corruption Watch (2021) reported that the widespread corruption is the main obstacle to economic growth in South Africa, and estimated that the country loses about $1.5 billion which is about 2% of its Gross Domestic Product (GDP) to corruption every year. World Bank and International Finance Corporation surveys have also indicated that 91.8% of firms in Bangladesh report having to pay bribes. The Analysis of Corruption Trends (ACT) report (2021) also reveals the large extent to which corruption has continued unabated during the first half of 2021 in South Africa. As a result, the Millennium Challenge Corporation, an organization providing the assistance for developing countries, has excluded other countries such as South Africa from the list of beneficiaries citing corruption as the reason (Analysis of Corruption Trends (ACT) report, 2021). To date, up to 1 964 whistle-blowers have reported acts of corruption in both the public and private sectors, from extortion by police through to sextortion by school principals. ACT report (2021) indicated that South Africans are desperate and deprived of much-needed protection due to corruption. Corruption Watch (2021) has noticed similar trends over the years where common types of corruption ranged from maladministration, dodgy procurement deals, fraud and abuse of authority. The negative publicity can cause long-range damage to the company's reputation that can even be most costly than paying the legal fees or fines.

Transparency

Transparency means openness, a willingness by the company to provide clear information to shareholders and other stakeholders. It refers to the openness and willingness to disclose financial performance figures which are truthful and accurate. Transparency ensures that stakeholders can have confidence in the decision-making and management processes of a company. As noted by Grigoropoulosi (2019), transparency and disclosure ensure timely, accurate disclosure on all business-related matters including the financial situation, performance, ownership and corporate governance. Business leaders must promote the transparency of the organization's business philosophy and the communication of company's practices, principles and values (Effron, 2017). According to the principle of transparency, there is a need to make effective means of communication with the internal and external persons as engaged with the business. The communication should be clear, open and be in a justified manner. A principle of transparency also include that stakeholders should be informed about business organization's activities, what it plans to do in the future and any risks involved in its business strategies. Disclosure of matters concerning the organisation's performance and activities should be timely and accurate to ensure that all investors have access to clear, factual information which accurately reflects the financial, social and environmental position of the organisation (Grigoropoulosi,2019). Government agencies thus need to provide timely, accurate disclosure of information about all material facts relating to its activities, including its financial situation, social and environmental indicators, performance, ownership structure and its governance as well as free access to such information for all stakeholders. Leaders or managers in government agencies thus need to listen effectively and convey messages with transparency.

Respect and Concern for Others

Government agencies need to master the art of being respectful by promoting an environment that is respectful, inclusive, and celebrates their diversity and minimizes perceived and real barriers. It is required that every leader within government agencies should follow the human values, human decorum and human aspects within their policies, programmes and different working areas. Concern or respect for others may determine the path of humanity. For example, ruining occupations of age-old inhabitants in a particular locality and their ethical way of life, by using advanced technology, is an ethical dilemma. Technology should by all means be used to uplift and make better the lives of human beings all over the world. However, consideration should also be given to see whether alternative means of arrangements can be made so that people are not unduly disturbed or that their upheaval is kept at a minimum.

Another example of concern or respect to others is the Life Healthcare Esidimeni Tragedy involved the deaths of 144 people at psychiatric facilities in the Gauteng province of South Africa due to starvation and neglect. In October 2015, MEC for Health in Gauteng announced the end of a contract between the Gauteng Department of Health (GDOH) and Life Esidimeni, a long-term psychiatric care hospital, which provided highly-specialised chronic care to approximately 2000 mental health care users. Cruel and inhumane decisions of the Gauteng Department of Health resulted in the death of 144 patients with mental health problems who died in undignified conditions. Over 1,400 surviving patients were exposed to torture, trauma and severe violations of their human rights. The GDOH planned to transfer these mental health care users to NGOs and other psychiatric hospitals in an attempt to deinstitutionalise mental healthcare and to save costs. However, at the beginning, civil society was concerned about the safety, health and dignity of the mental healthcare users that would be transferred. The South African Society of Psychiatrists (SASOP) wrote to the MEC detailing serious risks about the premature cancellation of the agreement with Life Esidimeni facilities. The South African Depression and Anxiety Group (SADAG), SASOP, the SA Federation for Mental Health (SA Fed) and families of Life Esidimeni residents also met with the Department asking it to slow down and follow fair processes to ensure comprehensive care for their loved ones. However, the GDOH ignored these warnings and went ahead, without consulting the families of mental healthcare users or following due procedure. Against all expert advice and contrary to their constitutional obligations, the GDOH went ahead with a plan that resulted in deaths, trauma and torture of some of the most vulnerable members of society and the residents of Life Esidimeni since the transfer out of the facility. The evidence later showed that at the time, 144 patients had passed away because of the inhumane move from Life Esidimeni to other Non-Profit Government Organizations (NGOs). Rights approach was supposed to be applied in respect and concern for others principle. This approach means making decisions based on the belief that each person has fundamental human rights that should be respected. People have a right to a safe and healthy environment. People have the rights of freedom of speech, privacy, and due process when charged with a crime or rule infraction. These rights make it possible for them to act in their own best interests, and this benefits society. Therefore, a decision is unethical if it deprives an individual of fundamental human rights. The United Nations (UN, 2003) has also produced a document proclaiming code of conduct that cover general obligations to promote human rights as well as recognizing international and national law, including the rights of indigenous peoples and other vulnerable groups such as consumers and workers, and also have regard to environmental protection.

SOCIAL RESPONSIBILITY PRACTICES IN GOVERNMENT AGENCIES

It is easy to dodge our responsibilities, but we cannot dodge the consequences of dodging our responsibilities – **Josiah Charles Stamp**

It was accorded in literature review that investors and consumers are more likely to support and purchase from business organization that fosters a social cause they believe in or practices social responsibility in other ways, such as engaging in environmentally friendly activities. Government agencies that practice corporate social responsibility aim to improve communities, the economy or the environment. The majority of government agencies have become more eager to practice corporate social responsibility after realizing that it can increase their revenues and profits. Social responsibility refers to business practices of engaging in ethical behaviour and in taking actions aimed at benefiting the society that the business operates in (Schooley, 2021), while corporate social responsibility is a type of business self-regulation with the aim of being socially accountable. In European countries, corporate social responsibility is understood as the mechanism for companies to contribute to sustainable development, and specifically to the strategic objectives adopted by member governments and heads of state. In today's socially conscious environment, employees and customers place a premium on working for and spending their money with businesses that prioritize corporate social responsibility. Socially responsible business practices refer to those corporate activities whose main purpose is to benefit individuals, a community or the environment (Schooley, 2021). As noted by Schooley (2021) nearly 90% of the consumers surveyed mentioned they would purchase a product because a company supported an issue they care about whereas 75% said they would refuse to buy from a company if they learned the company supported an issue contrary to their own beliefs.

The practice of social responsibility by government agencies has become more widespread, and some best practices have been recognized. Governments have joined other stakeholders in assuming a relevant role as drivers of social responsibility and adopting public sector roles in strengthening initiatives, in the past few decades. An increasing number of government agencies have taken policy initiatives in promoting corporate social responsibility, and they have been pressured by various social agents to adopt these initiatives. For example, in the European political debate on corporate social responsibility, governments have come under strong pressure from corporate and business associations for not introducing legislation and making corporate social responsibility policies mandatory. On the other hand, civil society in general and NGOs in particular have demanded that government increase its regulation of and control over business organizations in social and environmental fields. The framework provided by social responsibility initiatives provides society with a way to learn what successful collaboration looks like among corporations, governments, and society, in this modern world that has become inherently globalized with its economies and political challenges. Most of government agencies are implementing socially responsible practices in different ways, and the area of social responsibility that the government agencies focuses heavily on is social marketing, which is a marketing concept that works to develop and integrate marketing tactics with other approaches to influence behaviours that benefit individuals and communities for the greater social good. Government agencies are able to better disseminate important health information to key publics and target audiences through this type of integrated marketing communication. The United States Centers for Disease Control and Prevention (CDC) is an example of a key agency within the U.S. federal government that successfully integrates public health initiatives with communication and social marketing practices. This agency has dedicated gateway page on their website, providing resources to help partners build health communication or social marketing campaigns and programs. The CDC and many other health-focused and social change agencies use social media channels as a vital way of communicating with their key audiences. A report analyzing the CDC's social media practices found that the centre's efforts were timely, important, and science-and-evidence based and shared pertinent messages of prevention, individual responsibility, safety, and community collaboration (Austin, 2012). The report further stated that the governments who actively use of social media have the potential to influence public health initiatives and beyond on a large scale and garner support for positive social change efforts among policymakers and regulators.

Other government agencies also choose to practice social responsibility simply by contributing to the communities where they are located, such as by providing fitness facilities or housing subsidies to their employees. However, many government agencies are focusing on corporate social responsibility activities in recognizing how important socially responsible efforts are to the society, employees and stakeholders, including:

- **Social sponsorship:** this is a form of sponsorship whereby the audiences are invited to engage and experience the products.
- **Cash donations:** it is a way of granting financial support and it is historically the most popular way government agencies and other business organizations have contributed to social causes. Government agencies can practice social responsibility by donating money, products or services to social causes and non-profits. Larger business organizations tend to have plentiful resources that can benefit charities and local community programs, however, efforts by small businesses can also make a big difference. Government agencies should thus reach out to the society and ask about their specific needs, whether a donation of money, time or see if their products can best help them.
- **Gift in-kind:** it is a form of corporate giving through donating goods and services to help non-profits pursue their goals in a more efficient way.

- **Corporate volunteering:** many government agencies offer employees the possibility to volunteer extra-time for non-profits, school or other institutions. Participating in local causes or volunteering time in community events says a lot about a company's sincerity. Government agencies can therefore express their concern and support for specific issues and social causes by doing good deeds without expecting anything in return.
- **Community engagement:** it is a way of giving back to the community, which is a powerful strategy to enhance reputation.

However, when the organization's socially responsible practices are incorporated or integrated into their core business operations, they tend to be easier to implement, sustain and will garner a better public response.

THE IMPACT OF CORRUPTION ON ECONOMIC GROWTH AND INVESTMENT

Graycar (2015) described corruption as the unauthorised trading of one's entrusted authority, dishonest or illegal behaviour especially by powerful people, the abuse of entrusted power for private gain and an act done with intent to give some advantage inconsistent with official duty and the rights of others. Corruption has an indirect effect on a country's economic performance by affecting many factors fuelling economic growth such as investment, taxation, level, composition and effectiveness of public expenditure, as noted by Mauro (1997). At the company level, corruption raises costs, introduces uncertainties, reputational risks and vulnerability to extortion. It depresses a company's valuations, makes access to capital more expensive and undermines fair competition (Transparency International, 2009). In the presence of corruption, businessmen are often made aware that an up-front bribe is required before an enterprise can be started and that afterwards corrupt officials may lay claim to part of the proceeds from the investment. The study by Rothstein and Holmberg (2011), using country-level data to explore cross-country variations in both governance and economic indicators, have consistently found that corruption significantly decreases economic growth and development, and it is correlated with lower growth rates, GDP per capita, economic equality, as well as lower levels of human development. Similar study by Ugur and Dasgupta (2011) on the effect of corruption on economic growth reveals that corruption has a direct and negative effect on growth in low income countries, and it also has indirect effects through transmission channels such as investment, human capital and public finance or expenditure.

However, the detrimental impact of corruption on growth may be context specific and associated with factors such as the country's legal and institutional framework, quality of governance, political regime etc. The study by Méndez and Sepúlveda (2006) further indicate that the impact of corruption on growth and development may also be regime specific and that the type of political regime is an important determinant in the relationship between corruption and economic growth. Although corruption may help to reduce the costs induced by cumbersome administrative processes in some contexts in the short term, however, as noted by Dreher and Gassebner (2011) it has a long-term detrimental effect on the operations of companies and a corrosive impact on a country's overall governance environment, eroding the efficiency and legitimacy of state institutions and ultimately undermining sustainable development and the rule of law. Several economists have identified a number of channels through which corruption may affect economic growth (Mauro 1995; Tanzi, 1997; Gyimah-Brempong, 2001) including:

- It distorts incentives and market forces, leading to misallocation of resources.
- It diverts talent and resources, including human resources, towards "lucrative" rent-seeking activities, such as defence, rather than productive activities.
- It acts as an inefficient tax on business, ultimately raising production costs and reducing the profitability of investments.
- It may also decrease the productivity of investments by reducing the quality of resources, for example, by undermining the quality and quantity of health and education services, corruption decreases a country's human capital.
- Rent-seeking behaviour is also likely to create inefficiencies, fuelling waste of resources and undermining the efficiency of public expenditure.

Similarly, Tanzi (1997) have identified four channels through which corruption affects economic growth, including: higher public investments, lower government revenues, lower expenditures on other categories of public spending such as health and education and lower quality of public infrastructure. Corruption also discourages investment and acts as an additional cost of doing business and reducing the profitability of investment projects. Regression analysis also indicates that the amount of corruption is negatively linked to the level of investment and economic growth, and therefore, the more corruption, the less investment and the less economic growth (Mauro, 1997). Analysis further shows that if the corruption index improves by one standard deviation, the investment rate increases by more than 4 percentage points and the annual growth rate of per capita Gross Domestic Product (GDP) increases by over a half percentage point. For example, a country that improves its standing on the corruption index from 6 to 8 (recall that 0 is most corrupt, 10 least), will enjoy the benefits of an increase of 4 percentage points of investment, with consequent improvement in employment and economic growth (Mauro,1997). Mauro (1997) further noted that corruption reduces the ratio of investment to GDP, lowers investment and retards economic growth to a significant extent. It is also known to distort the decision-making process associated with public investment and affects the composition of government expenditure. In addition, Lambsdorff (2003) provided empirical evidence that corruption lowers capital productivity and constitutes an important element of investors' decision-making processes. Therefore, under the assumption that effective investments enhance capital productivity, the corruption spoils the quality of infrastructures, thus depressing growth (Tanzi, 1997). As stated by Tanzi (1997), corruption may lead public officials to allocate public resources less on the basis of public welfare than on the opportunity they provide for extorting bribes such as large infrastructure or defence projects. Zurawicki and Habib (2010) also identified corruption as a significant factor in reducing Foreign Direct Investment (FDI) in the host country. Corruption deters foreign direct investment because major investors are subject to anti-corruption codes at various governmental and international levels (Centro de Integridade Pública, 2016). The study by Gani (2007) also confirmed FDI to be positively correlated with governance indicators such as rule of law, control of corruption, regulatory quality, etc. Corruption is also perceived to increase the costs of investment. A survey carried out by Control Risks and Simmons & Simmons (2006) reveals that a quarter of its respondents claimed that corruption increased their costs of international investment by up to five (5) per cent and nearly eight (8) per cent of respondents claimed that it increased their costs by fifty (50) per cent. However, Meon and Sekkat (2005) argued that corruption may be economically justified as it provides opportunities to bypass inefficient regulations and red tape, and it allows the private sector to correct government failures and inefficiency. It may "grease the wheels", thus enhancing or promoting economic growth by removing bureaucratic barriers to entry and lowering business' transaction costs when trying to comply with excessive regulations. Other studies indicate that while corruption is consistently detrimental in countries where institutions are effective, it can potentially increase productivity and entrepreneurship in highly regulated countries that do not have effective government institutions and governance systems (Houston, 2007, Méon & Weill, 2008).

THE EFFECT OF CORRUPTION ON TAX REVENUES

It is widely agreed that the presence of tax evasion and corruption of public officials is a social phenomenon that can significantly reduce tax revenue and seriously hurt economic growth and development (Ajaz & Ahmad, 2010). Although corruption and outright tax evasion are distinct concepts, various studies show that they are interrelated and together bring about lower tax revenues and compliance levels and a range of economic and fiscal distortions (Fjeldstad & Tungodden, 2003; Attila, 2008). Gupta (2007) finds that several structural factors like per capita GDP, share of agriculture in GDP, trade openness foreign aid, foreign debt and some new institutional variables such as corruption and political stability are statistically significant and strong determinants of revenue performance. Imam and Jacobs (2007) consider corruption as a potential institutional variable that can affect tax revenues. The collection of tax revenue is thus one of the important areas where corruption is most likely to arise. Tanzi (1997) have provided evidence that countries with high level of corruption tend to have lower collection of tax revenues in relation to GDP. Therefore, when corruption takes the form of tax evasion or claiming improper tax exemptions, it may lead to a significant loss in tax revenue collected in a country, which in turn is likely to have adverse budgetary consequences (Nawaz, 2010).

However, corruption not only lowers the tax to GDP ratio but also causes long-term damage to the economy by increasing the size of the underground economy, distorting the tax structure and corroding the tax morality of taxpayers which is likely to further reduce the tax revenue base of a country (Attila, 2008; Nawaz, 2010). Attila (2008) describes three mechanisms that link corruption and tax evasion, namely: corruption decreases public revenues available for productive public investments in areas such as roads, health and education, it reduces growth through distortions in the tax structure and an indirect positive effect growth may be found if the unpaid revenue is utilised in productive investment spending. Centro de Integridade Pública (2016) has however noted that corruption also imposes costs on the private sector by weakening competitiveness and crowding out local small and medium sized companies in favour of the state-owned sector leading to the imposition of higher rates of tax under an eroded tax base. Ajaz and Ahmad (2010) identified some of the factors that contribute to corruption in tax system, namely:

- A complex and fragmented tax system increases the demand for corruption.
- Tax auditors and tax payers get advantages through complex rule, unclear laws, regulations and procedures of tax system.
- Complexity of regulation allows to the official to use their flexible powers and mount corruption in the system.
- Complexity in paying tax leads to corruption (tax payer saves their time and reduce uncertainty).
- High tax rates increase the incentive for tax payer to evade tax.
- Individuals compare their benefits with the risk of detection and punishment, to indulge in corrupt behaviour, and engage in corrupt activities if they feel that the expected punishment is low.
- Low wages of tax administrator and tax payers also foster corruption.

As stated by Fuest, Maffini and Riedel (2010) public sector corruption has a large negative impact on corporate tax payments, and therefore the reduction in public sector corruption could have a significant impact on a country's tax capacity. The World Bank (2016) also found that countries with high levels of corruption tend to collect less tax revenues, suggesting that only relatively incorrupt governments can sustain high tax rates. Companies also lose significant business opportunities because of corruption risks. Price Waterhouse Coopers (2008)'s report based on a survey of 390 senior executives in 14 countries, confirms the high costs that businesses pay for corruption in terms of market distortion, reputational damages, legal risks and deterioration of the company's internal structure.

Strategies to Prevent and Combat Corruption in Developing Countries

Corruption is a threat to good governance, socio-economic development, political stability and to any positive progress, nation building and national prosperity. Poor governance, bribery and corruption are thus key drivers of the growing inequality, persistent poverty and the exclusion of the most vulnerable from the gains of economic growth in developing countries, particularly South Africa. As reported by Global Corruption Barometer (GCB) for Africa (2019) one in four people in African countries pay bribe for essential public services to access basic services such as health or education. Government agencies and other relevant stakeholders in developing countries should encourage good governance and administration, improve transparency, promote ethical values and prevent conflicts of interest among public workers. These agencies need to design, implement and adopt anti-corruption strategies to prevent and combat corruption (National Anti-Corruption Strategy 2020-2030; Anti-Corruption Commission, 2003 & Global Corruption Barometer (GCB) for Africa, 2019), including:

- Formulating anti-corruption policies, procedures and regulations.
- Promoting zero tolerance for corruption society by educate public or the nation on the consequences of corruption.
- Establishing accountability and transparent decision-making.
- Investigate, prosecute and sanction all reported cases of corruption in all public sectors with no exception.
- Develop ethical standards and promote business ethics and ethical behaviour among employees.
- Communicate the organization's policies and code of conduct clearly to the employees.
- Develop principles of equal treatment or fairness in the workplace.
- Create mechanisms to collect citizens' complaints and strengthen whistle blower protection to ensure that they can report instances of corruption without fear of reprisal.
- Enable media and civil society to hold governments accountable.
- Allow cross border cooperation to prevent and combat corruption.

CONCLUSION AND RECOMMENDATIONS

The principles of business ethics and social responsibility practices have been analysed in this study in order to understand its application in various government agencies. Considerable debates and efforts have been made regarding the applicability of business ethics in the modern business age. Yet, some substantial challenges remain due to unethical scandals, corruption and misconduct by business leaders and employees within the government agencies. It is therefore recommended that the appropriate regulatory structures and processes cognizant of the nature of organizations and considering the perspective of the country where the business process occurs be developed and be properly implemented if acceptable ethical standards in business are to be achieved (Wise, Ali & Wise, 2010). Government agencies need to provide training program in order to increase employee ethical awareness and to define the policies and criteria for ethical decision-making within the organization. Business schools or institutions need to also design and develop ethical practices courses and programs, and also integrate business and entrepreneurship learning with ethical conduct. These institutions need to produce entrepreneurs and ethical leaders who cater for the needs of the labour market. Leaders or managers in government agencies also need to design a system that promotes ethical culture within their organizations and increase cross-sector social responsibility efforts while also establishing culture of accountability. The vulnerability of whistle blowers in South Africa also need to be addressed as a matter of urgency, in order to eradicate corruption that has shut down the economy.

FUTURE RESEARCH DIRECTIONS

We dream into government of the future with effective good governance principles, rearticulated by corruption free and law-abiding citizens, not for self-promotion, personal gain and greed but for community well-being and the respect and concern for others. Sustainable Development Goals (SDG)16 also includes key elements on building effective, accountable and inclusive institutions and reducing bribery and corruption. Government agencies, communities, citizens and political leaders need to work together in dismantling corruption and implementing anti-corruption policies and strategies for the prevention and eradication of corruption. Future research should thus focus on:

- Good governance to promote ethical values among employees in government sectors.
- Developing, implementing and monitoring anti-corruption strategies in government agencies cooperation with a wide range of stakeholders in business and civil society.
- developing government agencies' capacities to improve and deliver good or quality services, for example in key areas such as health, education etc.
- Identifying, managing and mitigating organizational integrity risks.
- Promoting transparency, responsibility and accountability within government agencies.

REFERENCES

Adda, G., Azigwe, J. B., & Awuni, A. R. (2016). Business ethics and corporate social responsibility for business success and growth. *European Journal of Business and Innovation Research*, *6*(4), 26–4.

Ajaz, T., & Ahmad, E. (2010). The effect of corruption and governance on tax revenues. *Pakistan Development Review*, *49*(4II), 405–417. doi:10.30541/v49i4IIpp.405-417

Albdour, L.R.M. (2017). Principles of Corporate Governance and Ethics for Sustainable Business. *International Journal of Business and Management Invention*, *6*(4), 01-07.

Anti-Corruption Commission Bill. (2003). Republic of South Africa.

Attila, G. (2008). Corruption, Taxation and Economic Growth: Theory and Evidence. *Centre d'Etudes et de Recherches sur le Development International working paper 2008/29*, Clermon: Ferrand.

Austin, L. L. (2012). Government's use of social media to frame health information: A review of the U.S. Centers for Disease Control and Prevention's social media practices. In S. C. Duhe (Ed.), *New Media and Public Relations* (2nd ed., pp. 209–217). Peter Lang Publishing Inc.

Brimmer, S. E. (2007). The role of ethics in 21st century organizations. *Leadership advance online, 11*.

Bulog, I., & Grancic, I. (2017). The Benefits of Business Ethics-Ethical Behavior of Decision Makers: The Empirical Findings from Croatia. *Mediterranean Journal of Social Sciences, 8*(4), 9–14. doi:10.2478/mjss-2018-0067

Carr, A. (2004). Is Business Bluffing Ethical? in Ethical Theory and Business (7th ed), Beauchamp, T. & Bowie, N. (Eds.). Prentice Hall.

Centro de Integridade Pública. (2016). The Costs of Corruption to the Mozambican Economy. *Centro de Integridade Pública Policy Brief, 24/2016*.

Davoodi, H. R., & Tanzi, V. (1997). Corruption, public investment and growth. *In IMF Working Paper. WP/97/139*. Washington: International Monetary Fund.

Dombin, A.N. (2012). Role of Corporate Governance in Attracting Foreign Investments in Nigeria. *Journal of Educational and Social Research, 19*. doi:. v3n9p35. doi:10.5901/jesr.2013

Dreher, A., & Gassebner, M. (2011). *Greasing the Wheels? The Impact of Regulations and Corruption on Firm Entry*. http://corruptionresearchnetwork.org/resources/articl es/greasing-the-wheels-the-impact-of-regulations

Drucker, P. F. (1981). What is business ethic? *The Public Interest*, (63), 18.

Ezigbo, C. A. (2013). Assessing Enforcement of Ethical Principles in the Work Place. *International Journal of Business and Social Science, 3*(22).

Ferrell, O. C. (2016). A framework for understanding organizational ethics. In *Business ethics: New challenges for business schools and corporate leaders* (pp. 15–29). Routledge.

Fjeldstad, 0. H., & Tungodden, B. (2001). *Fiscal Corruption: A Vice or a Virtue?* (CMI Working Papers WP 2001:13).

Fuest, C., Maffini, G., & Riedel, N. (2010). *How Does Corruption in Developing Countries Affect Investment and Tax Compliance?* https://editorialexpress.bin/conference/?

Gani, A. (2007). *Governance and Foreign Direct Investment Links: Evidence from Panel Data Estimations*. http://ideas.repec.org/a/taf/apeclt/v14y2007i10p753- 756.html

Graycar, A. (2015). Corruption: Classification and Analysis'. *Policy and Society, 34*(2), 87–96. doi:10.1016/j.polsoc.2015.04.001

Grigoropoulosi, J. E. (2019). The Role of Ethics in 21st Century Organizations. *International Journal of Progressive Education*, *15*(2), 167–175. doi:10.29329/ijpe.2019.189.12

Gupta, S. A. (2007) Determinants of Tax Revenue Efforts in Developing Countries. Washington, DC: *The International Monetary Fund*. (IMF Working Paper No.07/184).

Gyimah-Brempong, K. (2001). *Corruption, Economic Growth and Income Inequality in Africa*. https://link.springer.com/article/10.1007/s101010200

Houston, D. (2007). *Can Corruption Ever Improve an Economy?* http://object.cato.org/sites/cato.org/files/serials/files/ cato-journal/2007/11/cj27n3-2.pdf

Imam, P. A., & Jacobs, D. F. (2007). Effect of Corruption on Tax Revenues in the Middle East. *IMF Institute and Fiscal Affairs Department*. (IMF Working Paper No.07 /270).

Lambsdorff, J. (2003). How Corruption Affects Economic Development. http://www.wiwi.unipassau.de/fileadmin/dokumente/lehrstuehle/lambsdorff/Papers/C_Development.pd

Mauro, P. (1997). *Why worry about corruption? Economic Issues*. International Monetary Fund.

Méndez, F., & Sepúlveda, F. (2006). *Corruption, Growth and Political Regimes: Cross Country Evidence*. http://ideas.repec.org/a/eee/poleco/v22y2006i1p82- 98.html

Méon, P., & Sekkat, K. (2005). Does corruption grease or sand the wheels of corruption? *Public Choice*, *122*(1-2), 69–97. doi:10.100711127-005-3988-0

Méon, P., & Weill, L. (2010). Is Corruption an Efficient Grease? *World Development*, *38*(3), 244–259. doi:10.1016/j.worlddev.2009.06.004

Mohammed, F. (2012). *Business ethics: A case study in Gavle in Sweden*. Akademin for Utbildning Och Ekonomi.

Nakano, C. (2007). The Significance and Limitations of Corporate Governance from the Perspective of Business Ethics: Towards the Creation of an Ethical Organizational Culture. *Asian Business & Management*, *6*(2), 163–178. doi:10.1057/palgrave.abm.9200216

Nawaz, F. (2010). *Exploring the Relationships between Corruption and Tax Revenue*. https://www.u4.no/publications/exploring-therelationships-between-corruption-and-tax-revenue/

Paliwal, M. (2006). *Business ethics*. New Age International. https://ebookcentral/proquest-com.acg.idm.oclc.org

Pillay, K. (2021). *Corruption, dodgy Covid-19 procurement deals and sextortion at schools are on the rise*. Corruption Watch.

PricewaterhouseCoopers. (2008). *Confronting Corruption: The Business Case for an Effective Anti-Corruption Programme*. http://www.pwc.com/gx/en/forensic-accounting dispute-consulting-services/business-case-anti-corruption-programme.jhtml

Rothstein, B., & Holberg, S. (2011). *Correlates of Corruption*. http://www.qog.pol.gu.se/digitalAssets/1357/135784 0_2011_12_rothstein_holmberg.pdf

Sahin, A. (2018). How Principles of Business Ethics Relates to Corporate Governance and Directors? *European Journal of Economics and Business Studies*, *4*(3), 22–27. doi:10.2478/ejes-2018-0056

Salleh, M. F. (2016). *Business Ethics and Entrepreneurship Education*. Conference: 3rd. International Conference of Business, Economics and Social Sciences (ICBESS), Bali, Indonesia.

Schooley, S. (2021). *What is Corporate Social Responsibility?* Business News Daily Staff.

Sexty, R. (2011). *Canadian business and society: Ethics and responsibilities* (2nd ed.). McGraw-Hill Ryerson.

Tanzi, V. (1998). Corruption around the World: Causes Consequences, Scope and Cures. *IMF Fiscal Affairs Department*, Washington, DC: International Monetary Fund (Working Paper No. 98/63).

Transparency International. (2009). *Global Corruption Report: Corrupt. Ion and the Private Sector.* http://www.cgu.gov.br/conferenciabrocde/arquivos/English-Global-Corruption-Report 2009.pd.

Twin, A., Drury., & Perez, Y. (2021). *Business ethics.* Business Essentials.

Ugoani, J. N. N. (2019). Business ethics and its effect on organizational sustainability. *Global Journal of Social Sciences Studies*, *5*(2), 119–131. doi:10.20448/807.5.2.119.131

Ugur, M., & Dasgupta, N. (2011). Evidence on the Economic Growth Impacts of Corruption in Low Income Countries and Beyond. Available at: http://eppi.ioe.ac.uk/cms/LinkClick.aspx

Velasquez, M. G. (2014). *Business Ethics Concepts and Cases*. Pearson Education Limited.

Wise, V., Ali, M. M., & Wise, T. (2010). Ethical conduct in business: A case study analysis using Bangladesh experiences. *Problems and Perspectives in Management*, *8*, 4–1.

World Bank. (2016). *Doing Business 2016: Measuring Regulatory Quality and Efficiency*. Washington, DC.

Zurawicki, L., & Habib, M. (2010). Corruption and Foreign Direct Investment: What Have We Learned? *International Business & Economics Research Journal (IBER), 9*(7).

KEY TERMS AND DEFINITIONS

Business Ethics: The rules, standards, codes or principles that applies to all aspects of business conduct and provide guidance for morally appropriate behaviour relating to the operations of the organization or business relationship with the society.

Corruption: Abuse of public resources, fraudulent conduct or a form of criminal offense which is undertaken by a person or an organization which is entrusted in a position of authority in order to acquire illicit benefits or personal gain.

Ethical Behaviour: Being in accordance with the accepted standards of behaviour, values and moral principles regarding proper conduct in the workplace including honesty, transparency, integrity, trustworthiness, diligence, respect, responsibility and accountability.

Ethics: Set of standards and moral principles that govern a person's behaviour or conduct with respect to what is right or wrong.

Government Agency: A permanent or semi-permanent organization within a national or state government responsible for oversight or administration of specific functions or activities for a specific sector.

Social Responsibility: An ethical theory refers to an individual or organization's accountability to fulfil their civic duty and take actions that will benefit the community and society at large.

Chapter 5
Analyzing the Evolution From Intellectual Capital to Green Intellectual Capital:
A Literature Review

Javier Martínez Falcó

https://orcid.org/0000-0001-9004-5816
University of Alicante, Spain

Bartolomé Marco Lajara

https://orcid.org/0000-0001-8811-9118
University of Alicante, Spain

Patrocino Zaragoza-Sáez
University of Alicante, Spain

ABSTRACT

Knowledge plays a fundamental role in the achievement of business success. This has led to the intensification of the study of the set of intangible assets of the organization called intellectual capital (IC) as well as its impact on the achievement of sustainable competitive advantages over time. Moreover, IC that incorporates sustainable aspects (i.e., green intellectual capital [GIC]) was only recently introduced in the academic literature and has since become an emerging field of study. The lack of consistency in the terminologies used has made it difficult to establish clear measurements of intangibles, especially of the dimensions of IC, which have posed an additional difficulty in advancing this area of knowledge. To overcome this research problem, the authors analyze the origins and conceptualization of IC and GIC, trying to shed light on the field of study by answering the following questions: (1) What are the origins of IC? (2) How is IC defined? (3) What are the origins of GIC? (4) How is GIC defined?

DOI: 10.4018/978-1-6684-6815-9.ch005

INTRODUCTION

In this new millennium, information and knowledge play a preponderant role in society. This has led to substantial changes in the way we understand reality. Strategic management is also facing the challenge of managing knowledge in organizations, which is why research in this area has taken an important turn towards the study of intangibles and their impact on obtaining sustained competitive advantage, because although it has long been recognized that economic prosperity rests on knowledge and its useful application, the emphasis on the latter is relatively new (Alvino et al., 2020).

The interest in studying intangibles, also known as Intellectual Capital (IC), arises from their strategic value, which has been emphasized in the work of various academics. This recognition of intangibles is not new, if we consider that Penrose (1959) had already pointed out that the capacity to make assets perform better (he refers to management capacity) is the cause of a better competitive position and this capacity is an intangible resource. The fact of calling it "capital" refers to its economic roots, as it was described in 1969 by the economist Galbraith, as a process of value creation and an asset at the same time; a definition that highlights the dynamic aspect of IC, as he refers to it as a "process" (Galbraith, 1969).

In general terms, IC reflects intangible assets, such as: a company's ability to learn and adapt to new trends in market economics and management, with an emphasis on Knowledge Management (KM) as the most significant act of value creation. This fact has had a special impact on economic organizations, as their success is increasingly related to the investment and management of their IC; hence the need to specify the specific role of knowledge and skills in the value creation process (Martín-de Castro et al., 2019). Additionally, IC that incorporates environmental aspects, Green Intellectual Capital (GIC), was introduced by Chen (2008), becoming an emerging field of study today (Yong et al., 2019). This concept emerged in the academic literature with the aim of emphasizing the importance of the environmental intangibles possessed by the organization in order to improve the organization's competitive position.

However, as this is a relatively new field of research, there are still diverse views and no accepted or agreed position within the scientific and business community has yet been identified (Bellucci et al., 2020). Correspondingly, interest in these issues is growing in the business community and definitions of IC and GIC have been developed to serve as a basis for future research related to their identification and measurement (Demartini & Beretta, 2020). Two of the most important problems in intangibles research are the lack of a common terminology and the underdevelopment of measurement scales for the constructs associated with intangibles (Garanina et al., 2021). It is quite common for each author to try to build a theory of intangibles from scratch, creating new definitions, introducing new dimensions of intangibles and intellectual capital, and trying to impose their own terminology (Bontis, 2001). This fact hinders the accumulation of knowledge, and justifies the little progress that has been made in the last twenty years in building a theory of intangibles in organizations (Gallego et al., 2020). The lack of consistency in the terminologies used has made it difficult to establish clear measurements of intangibles, especially of the dimensions of intellectual capital, which has posed an additional difficulty to progress in this area of knowledge. The objective of the present research is therefore to analyze the origin and conceptualization of IC and GIC, trying to answer the following four research questions: (1) What are the origins of IC? (2) How is IC defined? (3) What are the origins of GIC? (4) How is GIC defined?

In order to answer the following research questions, the study is structured as follows. After this brief introduction, Section 2 presents the research methodology, Section 3 the results, and finally, Section 4 the main conclusions, limitations and future lines of research.

METHODOLOGY

In this research, a narrative literature review was conducted to analyze the origins and conceptualization of IC and GIC. A literature review is considered a detailed study that aims to gather information on a given topic through the analysis of published literature (Oliver, 2012).

The aim of the narrative literature review is to synthesize fragmented knowledge from previous research on IC and GIC. The research is therefore descriptive in scope, as there are no hypotheses to test, but rather to describe and make sense of the information collected. Furthermore, the present review follows more flexible and less restrictive procedures than systematic reviews (Ferrari, 2015). Therefore, the present review does not aim to generalize the results obtained to the population (Tranfield et al., 2003), but to offer an interpretation of the literature that allows for a better understanding of the field of study of IC and GIC. To conduct the literature review, the phases proposed by Wee & Banister (2016) were followed, which are: selection of the topic, selection and reading of sources, and writing of the topic. First, the selected topic is the analysis of the origin and conceptualization of IC and GIC. Second, handbooks, readings, books, chapters and articles focusing on the evolution and conceptualization of IC and GIC were included for the research, excluding colloquium reports, seminars, doctoral theses and working papers. The time period of the publications spans from the beginnings of the IC concept in the 1990s to the present day. The Scopus and Web of Science databases were used for the selection of the publications, as they are prestigious databases containing articles published in high impact journals, which ensures that the information obtained is accurate and of high value, legitimizing reliable results. A total of 95 academic articles were reviewed and read in depth, this being the scientific production that allowed us to reflect on the concepts analyzed. Thirdly, once the article and sources had been selected and the publications had been read, the bibliographic review was carried out.

RESULTS

The results are then structured in the following three blocks: (1) origins of IC, (2) its dimensions and (3) GIC.

The Origins of Intellectual Capital

The Intellectual Capital View (ICV) is the academic framework under which IC has traditionally been analyzed. Said approach, which emerged at the end of the 90s of the last century, derives from the Resource-Based View (RBV) and aims to overcome the deficiencies of the latter vision, given that, although in the RBV approach, business intangible assets are considered as strategic resources to achieve a high profitability, the arguments used are excessively general and the mechanisms through which intangibles allow obtaining a superior relative position are not clarified (Priem & Butler, 2001).

The ICV is considered as complementary to the Knowledge-Based View (KBV). However, although both theories (KBV and ICV) argue the value of the company through hidden knowledge, they differ in their approach. Thus, while the KBV theory focuses on the effective use of KM through knowledge creation tools, such as organizational culture, human resource policy and Information and Communication Technologies (ICT) (Nonaka et al., 2005), the ICV theory focuses on the evaluation and measurement of intangible assets (Reed et al., 2006). Thus, while the main focus of the KBV is to "assess the effectiveness of a company's use of knowledge management tools as knowledge-generating mechanisms, such as its information technology systems and information management systems, information" (Reed et al., 2006, p. 869).

From a historical point of view, organizations have always considered as assets those tangible elements that appeared in traditional financial statements, clearly identified and valued. However, very few times other elements that did not have a dimension were conceived as assets. The term IC intends to value precisely the intangible assets, since it refers to all those assets that, even though they do not have a physical presence, contribute to generating value for the organization and achieving its objectives.

To understand the concept of IC, it is interesting to analyze the definition of the term used by Edvinsson & Malone (1999). These authors used the following simile: "A corporation is like a tree. There is a visible part (the fruits) and a part that is hidden (the roots). If we only care about the fruits, the tree may die. For the tree to grow and continue to bear fruit, the roots must be healthy and nourished." In other words, if organizations focus exclusively on the fruits (financial results) and ignore their roots (intangible assets), the company will not survive in the long term.

Two fundamental ideas can be extracted from the definition: (1) the IC is a non-financial capital and (2) it represents the gap between the market value and the book value of a company. Therefore, for the cited authors, IC refers to the set of knowledge, experiences and relationships that give the organization a competitive advantage that is sustainable over time.

According to Euroforum (1998), it is possible to define IC as the set of assets of a company that, despite not being reflected in the financial statements, produce or will produce value for the organization in the future. In this regard, derived from this accounting vision of the concept, there is a very subtle formula to calculate the value of the intangible assets of a company: the value of the IC = the market value of the organization (stock market value) - the value of the tangible assets (book value).

Bueno (2000, 2003) based on the main characteristics of the concept, proposes the following integrating proposal: "accumulation of knowledge that creates value or cognitive wealth possessed by an organization composed of a set of intangible (intellectual) assets or resources and capabilities based on knowledge, which when put into action, according to a certain strategy, in combination with physical or tangible capital, is capable of producing goods and services and of generating competitive advantages or essential competencies in the market for the organization." Likewise, the same author identifies a series of characteristics that his definition gathers:

1. It is a concept that indicates the value of accumulated wealth derived from a set of assets of an intangible nature.
2. The combination of intangible assets generates new knowledge that is transformed into business skills or the creation of a competitive advantage.
3. It is capital of an intellectual nature that represents the new source of wealth for organizations.
4. It is a capital that integrates different intangible assets, generated through a strategy based on intellectual assets.

Table 1 offers a summary of the definitions made by different authors around the concept of IC. From it two ideas emerge fundamentally. In the first place, there is a certain convergence in all the definitions when pointing out that the intangible assets derived from knowledge add value to the company and, secondly, there is an emphasis on the idea that said assets do not appear in the financial statements of the companies, generating informative asymmetries for the groups interested in them.

Table 1. IC definitions

Author	Definition
Galbraith (1969)	The difference between the market value and book value of an organization.
Bontis (1996)	The capture, coding and dissemination of information to acquire new skills.
Brooking (1997)	Set of intangible assets that allows the company to function.
Sveiby (1997)	The difference between the market value and the book value of the company.
Stewart (1998)	Intellectual components that can be harnessed to create wealth in the organization.
Euroforum (1998)	Set of assets that, despite not being reflected in the financial statements of the company, generate or will generate value for it.
Roos (1998)	The IC is the sum of the Human Capital (HC) and the Structural Capital (SC). The HC represents the skills and experiences of the employees, and the SC the extension and manifestation of the HC in innovations, business processes and relationships with third parties.
Sullivan (1999)	The knowledge that can become future benefits.
Edvinson & Malone (1999)	The non-financial capital that justifies the difference between the market value and the book value.
Harrison & Sullivan (2000)	Knowledge that can be turned into profit.
Viedma (2001)	The IC is made up of all those intangible assets formed by tacit or explicit knowledge that generate economic value for the company.
Heisig et al. (2001)	An intangible asset is a future collection right that has no physical or financial presence.
Ordoñez de Pablos (2003)	It is the difference between the company's market value and its book value, which contributes to the company's sustained competitive advantage.
Rastogi (2003)	IC can be thought of as a company's holistic ability to coordinate, orchestrate, and deploy its knowledge resources toward value creation in pursuit of its future vision.
Youndt et al. (2004)	IC is the sum of all the knowledge that the company uses to obtain a competitive advantage
IASB (2004)	A non-monetary, non-physical asset held for use in the production or supply of goods or services, for rental to third parties, or for administrative purposes.
García-Meca & Martinez (2005)	The knowledge, information, intellectual property and experience that can be used to create wealth.
Mavridis & Kyrmizoglou (2005)	An intangible asset with the potential to create value for the company and society itself.
Martinez-Torres (2006)	It includes the intangible assets of an organization that are not recorded in the financial statements but that may constitute 80% of the organization's market value.
Reed et al. (2006)	Core competencies of an intangible nature that enable the creation and maintenance of a competitive advantage.
Chang et al. (2008)	It represents the intangible assets related to knowledge integrated in an organization.
Hsu & Fang (2009)	The set of capabilities, knowledge, culture, strategy, processes, intellectual property and relational networks of a company that create value or competitive advantages and help the company achieve its objectives.
Mondal & Ghosh (2012)	IC can be interpreted as the set of intangible assets that do not appear explicitly in the balance sheets of a company, but that have a positive impact on the results and success of the same.
Mehralian et al. (2012)	IC is an implicit value for the company that aims to achieve a competitive advantage.
Dumay (2016)	IC is the intellectual material, knowledge, experience, intellectual property and information that can be used to create value.

Source: own elaboration from the cited authors

Based on the above definitions and the main ideas that emanate from them, we propose the following comprehensive definition:

"Intellectual capital represents a set of intangibles that justify the difference in value between the market value and the book value of the organization, and although they are increasingly recognized by the stock market, they are often omitted from the financial statements."

Dimensions of Intellectual Capital

There are several contributions, both theoretical and practical, to classify the different elements that make up the IC. However, there is a certain consensus in dividing the IC into three dimensions: the HC, the SC and the Relational Capital (RC) (Bontis, 2001; Ordóñez de Pablos, 2003; Sánchez-Medina et al., 2007). Next, we analyze in detail how each of these three dimensions has been conceived.

In today's globalized world, organizations require workers with values, attitudes and skills that allow them to obtain critical and systematic thinking within a changing environment (Bontis, 2001). For this reason, one of the most reiterated dimensions in the different IC models is that related to HC, as it is an essential factor for the organization (Sveiby, 1997; Becker et al., 2001), whose lack negatively conditions the rest of the organization. activities that generate value for it (Edvinsson & Malone, 1999).

The HC is defined as the main source of value and innovation in the company, since the ideas of the organization emanate from it (Viedma, 2001). That is, the HC refers to the knowledge, both tacit and explicit, that the workers have, as well as their ability to put it into practice in the organization.

It is possible to classify three components within the HC: (1) competencies, made up of knowledge, skills and talent; (2) the attitude, which translates into the motivation, action and behavior of people; and (3) intellectual agility, which generates value when new knowledge is applied to transform ideas into products and services (Roos et al., 2001). Therefore, the motivation of the employees, their mental agility, their tacit and explicit knowledge, their institutional commitment or their degree of satisfaction are clear examples of HC.

Petrash (1996), Euroforum (1998) and Bontis et al. (2002) conceive HC as the stock of knowledge possessed by the members of a company. Consequently, part of the HC represents the accumulated value of the investments that organizations have made to train their employees (Skandia, 1996). Thus, although the true owner of HC is not the company, but the employees themselves (Sveiby, 1997; 2001), this is one of the main elements that make up the value of the company and, as a consequence, it must be considered as capital for the same.

From another perspective, HC has been defined as the knowledge that the organization loses when its employees decide to leave it (Sullivan, 2000; Sveiby, 2001). For this reason, organizations must try to retain the most valuable employees (Roos et al., 2001), adequately remunerating those workers who provide the greatest value to the organization (Sveiby, 2001).

Brooking (1997) conceives this dimension with the name of assets centered on the individual and incorporates assets such as: creativity, the ability to solve problems or leadership. In this same line of thought, Edvisson & Mallone (1999) and Nevado-Peña & López-Ruiz (2002) consider that the HC is made up of a set of knowledge, individual capacities, skills and experiences of the members that make up the organization.

Another of the most common dimensions within IC models is that of SC. This capital is described as that knowledge that the organization internalizes and that, therefore, remains in it despite the fact that its employees leave it (Bontis et al., 2001). Consequently, this dimension includes all the non-human intangibles of the organization, ranging from culture or internal processes to databases or information systems (Bontis et al., 2000). In addition, unlike what happens with the HC, the SC is owned by the company (Euroforum, 1998).

According to Edvinsson & Malone (1999) and Roos et al. (2001), SC can be broken down into three dimensions, these are: organizational capital, renewal and development capital, and RC. However, it is necessary to clarify that in various models these subdivisions make up their own dimensions and are not included in the SC. This happens with the renovation and development capital dimension in the Nova model (Camisón et al., 2000) and with the RC in models such as Brooking (1997), Intelect (Euroforum, 1998), the monitor of intangible assets (Sveiby, 2001).

On the one hand, organizational capital includes the value produced by the internal structure of the company and the way in which the operations and processes that take place within it are developed. Consequently, all intangibles related to culture and values, organizational structure, routines, capabilities and policies are part of said capital. On the other hand, renewal and development capital, also called technological capital, refers to those aspects that can generate future value in the organization through improvements in products and/or processes. This capital therefore includes all intangibles related to Innovation, Development and Research activities and policies (patents, copyrights, licenses, etc.).

Brooking (1997) subdivides SC into intellectual property assets and infrastructure assets. The former is related to the legal protection exercised by the organization over those assets that it considers to have a special value for it, among which can be found: manufacturing secrets, patents, copyright or design rights. As for the latter, they provide order, security and quality to the organization, such as corporate culture, databases or methodologies. Social capital is based on the consideration that organizations are not isolated systems, since they maintain relationships with their environment. In this way, the intangibles derived from the company's network of relationships are what should be considered RC.

This type of capital includes the value generated by the company's relationships with its environment, not only with its shareholders, customers and suppliers, but also with all its stakeholders (Bontis, 1996, Stewart, 1998; Ordóñez de Pablos, 2003). That is, the RC represents the knowledge that is incorporated in the links of the organization with its environment (Bontis, 1999). Customer loyalty and satisfaction, strategic alliances or the list of suppliers and distributors are clear examples of this type of intangible assets.

In the academic literature, there are numerous ways of naming this capital. Sveiby (2001), in his model *Intangible assets monitor*, designates this external component dimension, including relationships with customers and suppliers, trademarks, reputation or image. In this way, some of these elements may have legal protection, while, in others, said protection is complex. Kaplan & Norton (1997), in their model *Store card*, call the customer perspective RC and it analyzes the sources of value for the customer. Along these same lines, Edvinsson (1997) and Edvisson & Malone (1999) consider that RC is mainly made up of the value generated by the organization's relationships with its customers. However, although the Kaplan & Norton (1997) model explicitly limits this dimension to customers, it can be extrapolated to all the relationships that the company has with its environment (Olve et al., 2000).

On the other hand, Brookings (1997), in its Technology Broker model, it calls this dimension market assets, defining it as those intangible assets derived from the organization's relationship with the market. Caminsion et al. (2000), on the other hand, call it social capital, defining it as the set of knowledge-based assets from the company's relationships with customers.

Finally, it is important to note that, although each of the dimensions that make up the IC has been presented in isolation, the existence of links between them is of special importance for its proper management (Bontis, 2001).

Green Intellectual Capital

The qualifier green has gained the attention of both academics and professionals in recent decades. The academic literature shows an incipient interest in green business, characterized by: green purchasing (Zhang et al., 2018), green supply chain management (Kazancoglu et al., 2018; Zaid et al., 2018), green innovation (Li et al., 2018), green finance (Ng, 2018), green management (Mustapha et al., 2017), green information technologies (Przychodzen et al., 2018) and green human resource management (Renwick et al., 2013; Zaid et al., 2018).

In this context, Chen (2008) introduced the concept of GIC with the aim of incorporating environmental concepts into IC. The GIC allows organizations to apply strict international regulations, comply with the growing environmental awareness of consumers and create value for the organization (Huang & Kung, 2011). For this reason, their role is essential to guarantee the success of the Sustainable Development Goals (SDGs) promoted by the United Nations (Yadiati, 2019; Marco-Lajara et al., 2021a; Marco-Lajara et al., 2021b; Marco-Lajara et al., 2022a; Marco-Lajara et al., 2022b; Marco-Lajara et al., 2022c; Marco-Lajara et al., 2022d; Marco-Lajara et al., 2022e; Marco-Lajara et al., 2022f; Marco-Lajara et al., 2022g; Marco-Lajara et al., 2022h; Marco-Lajara et al., 2022i; Marco-Lajara et al., 2022j, Marco-Lajara et al., 2022k;Marco-Lajara et al., 2022l, Marco-Lajara et al., 2022m, Marco-Lajara et al., 2022n; Marco-Lajara et al., 2023a; Marco-Lajara et al., 2023b; Marco-Lajara et al., 2023c; Martínez-Falcó et al., 2023a; Martínez-Falcó et al., 2023b; Martínez-Falcó et al., 2023c; Martínez-Falcó et al., 2023d; Millan-Tudela et al., 2022a; Millan-Tudela et al., 2022b; Seva-Larrosa et al., 2022). However, GIC has only recently emerged as a major field of study (Yong et al., 2019; Yusoff et al., 2019).

Definitions of GIC are scarce in the management literature. On the one hand, Chen (2008) defined it as the total set of intangible assets, knowledge and skills related to environmental protection or ecological innovation at the individual and organizational level within an organization. Liu (2010), on the other hand, defined it as the integration of green and environmental knowledge sources in the organization to improve its competitive advantage. In the same way, López-Gamero et al. (2011) conceived it as the sum of all the knowledge that an organization is capable of taking advantage of in the environmental management process to obtain a competitive advantage. Next, each of the dimensions that make up the GIC is analyzed in detail, which, according to Chen (2008), are: Green Human Capital (GHC).

As explained in previous sections, the RBV highlights the importance of HC in the performance of the organization to obtain a competitive advantage among competitors (Barney, 2001). Chen (2008) points out the distinctive value of the GHC by defining it as the set of knowledge, skills, abilities, experiences and commitments of the employees about the protection of the environment and/or green innovation that are integrated in the employees and not in organizations.

The GHC allows an organization to recognize its intangible assets related to the environment, helping to apply green strategies in a given competitive environment. For this reason, the GHC has been considered one of the main strategic resources to obtain sustainable competitive advantages in the current dynamic organizational environment (Yusoff et al., 2019). Likewise, a higher GHC contributes more to the development of a green organization, since environmental knowledge and skills are embedded in it (Yong et al., 2019).

The scientific production related to the GHC focuses its interest on the relationship existing between the GHC and corporate sustainability. Yong et al. (2019) prove that the GHC has a positive effect on the management of green human resources. For their part, Chen & Chang (2013), through their research, confirm the link between the GHC and green innovation performance. Furthermore, Akhtar et al. (2018) affirm the importance of the GHC to achieve business sustainability.

The SC is conceived as the set of knowledge that houses the non-human assets of an organization, among which we can highlight: organization charts, databases, technology or process instructions (Jardon & Martos, 2012). Chen (2008), on the other hand, defined the Green Structural Capital (GSC) as the organizational assets that showed concern for the protection of the environment or green innovation within the company.

Jardon & Dasilva (2017) suggest that the organization's concern for environmental aspects is not only modified by HC, since the support of the organizational culture and systems is required to increase the level of environmental awareness in the organization. Widener (2006) states that an organization with poor systems and procedures cannot achieve its full performance. In contrast, an organization with a strong SC has a strong supportive environment that motivates its employees to generate new knowledge (Florin et al., 2003).

ICTs play a fundamental role in the development of the GSC. In fact, previous studies verify the effect of ICT on ecological practices (Yusliza et al., 2017) and green information systems for supply chain activities (Giménez et al., 2015). Likewise, Chen (2008) and Chen & Chang (2013) state that ecological innovation is essential for achieving sustainable performance. Lee & Min (2015), for their part, highlight that an organization that invests in Research and Development (R&D) activities, together with eco-innovation, tends to reduce its costs and environmental impacts.

Likewise, numerous investigations address the positive effect of GSC on business performance and environmental awareness. Chen (2008) affirmed the existence of a positive relationship between GSC and competitive advantage. Similarly, Erinos & Rahmawati (2017) demonstrated the positive impact of GSC on financial performance. On the other hand, while Huang & Kung (2011) revealed the positive effect of GSC on environmental competence and activities related to environmental commitment, Delgado-Verde et al. (2014) found a positive relationship between GSC and green product innovation.

Chen (2008) defined Green Relational Capital (GRC) as the set of intangible assets based on existing relationships between the organization and suppliers, customers, network members and partners to improve the company's environmental management and thus achieve a competitive advantage. As already described in the previous section, RC refers to an intangible asset focused on nurturing and preserving relationships with any organization, individual or group that can influence a company's position in the market. Therefore, it is essential that organizations align their interests with those of their stakeholders in order to survive and remain competitive.

Longoni & Cagliano (2018) state that the needs of different stakeholders can be addressed through the management of ecological supply chains. Likewise, other research also highlights green supply chains and the environmental perspective as powerful tools to meet the needs of stakeholders (Zhu et al., 2013; Luthra et al., 2016; Jabbour et al., 2019). Therefore, the GRC plays an important role in building strong and lasting relationships between suppliers and organizations. As far as customers are concerned, their expectations have started to focus on sustainable environmental behaviors, rather than just product, price or service (Dangelico & Pujari, 2010; Eweje, 2014). Furthermore, most of the previous studies have revealed a positive and significant effect between GRC and business results. Chen (2008) and Firmansyah (2017) demonstrated the positive link between GRC and competitive advantage. Similarly, Huang

& Kung (2011) revealed the positive influence of GRC on competition and environmental commitment. Likewise, Delgado-Verde et al. (2014) found that for an organization to be successful in environmental product innovation, it must have a GRC that encourages cooperation among its employees.

CONCLUSION

Historically, organizations have always considered as assets those tangible items that appeared in traditional accounting statements, clearly identified and valued. However, other elements that did not have a spatio-temporal dimension were rarely conceived as assets. The term IC is intended to highlight intangible assets, since it refers to all those assets that, although they do not have a physical presence, contribute to generating value for the organization and to achieving its objectives.

From the definitions of IC analyzed, the idea emerges that IC represents a set of intangibles that justify the difference in value between the market value and the book value of the organization, and although they are increasingly recognized by the stock market, they are often omitted from the accounting statements. Furthermore, four fundamental characteristics are identified in the definitions studied: (1) it is a concept that indicates the value of the accumulated wealth derived from a set of assets of an intangible nature, (2) the combination of intangible assets generates new knowledge that is transformed into business competences or in the creation of a competitive advantage, (3) it is a capital of an intellectual nature that represents the new source of wealth of organizations, (4) it is a capital that integrates different intangible assets, generated through a strategy based on intellectual assets.

Concern for environmental management has gained the attention of both academics and practitioners in recent decades. In this context, Chen (2008) introduced the concept of GIC with the aim of incorporating environmental concepts into IC. GIC enables organizations to implement stringent international regulations, meet the growing environmental awareness of consumers and create value for the organization. For this reason, its role is critical to ensure the success of the SDGs promoted by the United Nations. However, GIC has only recently emerged as a major field of study. Definitions of GIC are scarce in the management literature. However, based on the conceptual review of the term, it can be considered as the sum of all the knowledge that an organization is able to leverage in the environmental management process to gain a competitive advantage. The following is a detailed analysis of each of the dimensions that make up GIC, which Chen (2008) suggests are: GHC, GSC and GRC.

This research presents several theoretical and practical contributions. On the one hand, as far as theoretical contributions are concerned, this research helps to bring clarity to an emerging field of study such as GIC. Likewise, to the best of our knowledge, there are no narrative reviews that have addressed this topic. On the other hand, the study serves as a reference guide for those professionals who are thinking of enhancing their intangible assets, since it improves the understanding of the terms, as well as the characteristics that determine each type of intangible. In such a way that the greater understanding by managers of the subject matter of the study can serve as a catalyst for improving practices that enhance the development of intangible assets.

FUTURE RESEARCH DIRECTIONS

Despite the important contributions of the study, it is important to note that the research suffers from certain limitations. The fundamental limitation of the study is methodological in nature, given that narrative reviews are dominated by the subjective criteria of the authors and do not quantitatively synthesize the data found in the different publications. To overcome these limitations of narrative reviews, a systematic review of GIC is proposed as a line of future research to increase the reproducibility of the research and increase the validity of the results obtained.

REFERENCES

Akhtar, P., Khan, Z., Frynas, J., Tse, Y., & Rao-Nicholson, R. (2018). Essential micro-foundations for contemporary business operations: Top management tangible competencies, relationship-based business networks and environmental sustainability. *British Journal of Management*, *29*(1), 43–62. doi:10.1111/1467-8551.12233

Alvino, F., Di Vaio, A., Hassan, R., & Palladino, R. (2020). Intellectual capital and sustainable development: A systematic literature review. *Journal of Intellectual Capital*, *22*(1), 76–94. doi:10.1108/JIC-11-2019-0259

Barney, J. (2001). Is the resource-based "view" a useful perspective for strategic management research? Yes. *Academy of Management Review*, *26*(1), 41–56.

Becker, B., Huselid, M., & Ulrich, D. (2001). *The HR scorecard: Linking people, strategy, and performance*. Harvard Business Press.

Bellucci, M., Marzi, G., Orlando, B., & Ciampi, F. (2020). Journal of Intellectual Capital: A review of emerging themes and future trends. *Journal of Intellectual Capital*, *22*(4), 744–767. doi:10.1108/JIC-10-2019-0239

Bontis, N. (1996). There is a price on your head: Managing intellectual capital strategically. *Business Quarterly*, *60*(4), 41–47.

Bontis, N. (2001). CKO wanted - Evangelical skills necessary: A review of the chief knowledge officer position. *Knowledge and Process Management*, *8*(1), 29–38. doi:10.1002/kpm.100

Bontis, N., Crossan, M., & Hulland, J. (2002). Managing an organizational learning system by aligning stocks and flows. *Journal of Management Studies*, *39*(4), 437–469. doi:10.1111/1467-6486.t01-1-00299

Brooking, A. (1997). The management of intellectual capital. *Long Range Planning*, *30*(3), 364–365. doi:10.1016/S0024-6301(97)80911-9

Bueno, E. (2000). De la sociedad de la información a la del conocimiento y el aprendizaje: La necesidad de programas de dirección del conocimiento y aprendizaje [From the information society to the knowledge and learning society: The need for knowledge and learning management programs]. *Jornadas Españolas de Documentación*, *7*, 647–657.

Bueno, E. (2003). Enfoques principales y tendencias en dirección del conocimiento (knowledge management). In *Dirección del conocimiento: Desarrollos teóricos y aplicaciones*. Ediciones La Coria.

Camisón, C., Palacios, D., & Devece, C. (2000). *Un modelo para la medición del capital intelectual en la empresa: el modelo Nova* [A model for measuring intelectual capital in the cmopany: The Nova Model]. Disponible en: http://www. gestiondelconocimiento.com

Chang, S., Chen, C., & Lai, J. (2008). The Effect of Alliance Experience and Intellectual Capital on the Value Creation of International Strategic Alliances. *Omega, 36*(2), 298–316. doi:10.1016/j.omega.2006.06.010

Chen, Y. (2008). The positive effect of green intellectual capital on competitive advantages of firms. *Journal of Business Ethics, 77*(3), 271–286. doi:10.100710551-006-9349-1

Chen, Y., & Chang, C. (2013). Utilize structural equation modeling (SEM) to explore the influence of corporate environmental ethics: The mediation effect of green human capital. *Quality & Quantity, 47*(1), 79–95. doi:10.100711135-011-9504-3

Dangelico, R., & Pujari, D. (2010). Mainstreaming green product innovation: Why and how companies integrate environmental sustainability. *Journal of Business Ethics, 95*(3), 471–486. doi:10.100710551-010-0434-0

Delgado-Verde, M., Amores-Salvadó, J., Martín-de Castro, G., & Navas-López, J. (2014). Green intellectual capital and environmental product innovation: The mediating role of green social capital. *Knowledge Management Research and Practice, 12*(3), 261–275. doi:10.1057/kmrp.2014.1

Demartini, M. C., & Beretta, V. (2020). Intellectual capital and SMEs' performance: A structured literature review. *Journal of Small Business Management, 58*(2), 288–332. doi:10.1080/00472778.2019.1659680

Dumay, J. (2016). A critical reflection on the future of intellectual capital: From reporting to disclosure. *Journal of Intellectual Capital, 17*(1), 168–184. doi:10.1108/JIC-08-2015-0072

Edvinsson, L., & Malone, M. (1999). El capital intelectual [Intellectual Capital]. *Gestion*.

Erinos, N., & Yurniwati, Y. (2018). Green intellectual capital and financial performance of manufacturing companies in Indonesia. In *First Padang International Conference On Economics Education, Economics, Business and Management, Accounting and Entrepreneurship* (pp. 613-618). Atlantis Press.

Eweje, G. (2014). *Introduction: trends in corporate social responsibility and sustainability in emerging economies*. Emerald Group Publishing Limited.

Ferrari, R. (2015). Writing narrative style literature reviews. *Medical Writing, 24*(4), 230–235. doi:10.1179/2047480615Z.000000000329

Firmansyah, A. (2017). Pengaruh green intellectual capital dan manajemen lingkungan organisasi terhadap green organizational identity dan dampaknya terhadap green competitive advantage. *Substansi: Sumber Artikel Akuntansi Auditing dan Keuangan Vokasi, 1*(1), 183-219.

Galbraith, J. (1969). The Consequences of Technology. *Journal of Accountancy, 127*, 44–56.

Gallego, C., Mejía, G. M., & Calderón, G. (2020). Strategic design: Origins and contributions to intellectual capital in organizations. *Journal of Intellectual Capital, 21*(6), 873–891. doi:10.1108/JIC-10-2019-0234

Garanina, T., Hussinki, H., & Dumay, J. (2021). Accounting for intangibles and intellectual capital: A literature review from 2000 to 2020. *Accounting and Finance*, *61*(4), 5111–5140. doi:10.1111/acfi.12751

García-Meca, E., & Martínez, I. (2005). Assessing the quality of disclosure on intangibles in the Spanish capital market. *European Business Review*, *17*(4), 305–313. doi:10.1108/09555340510607352

Giménez, F., Ciurana, J., Borras, F., & Pastor, D. (2013). Efficiency analysis of the designations of origin in the Spanish wine sector. *Spanish Journal of Agricultural Research*, *2*, 294–304.

Harrison, S., & Sullivan, P. Sr. (2000). Profiting from intellectual capital - learning from leading companies. *Journal of Intellectual Capital*, *1*(1), 33–46. doi:10.1108/14691930010324124

Heisig, P., Vorbeck, J., & Niebubr, J. (2001). *Intellectual capital. Knowledge Management - Best Practices in Europe*. Springer.

Hsu, Y., & Fang, W. (2009). Intellectual Capital and New Product Development Performance: The Mediating Role of Organizational Learning Capability. *Technological Forecasting and Social Change*, *76*(5), 664–677. doi:10.1016/j.techfore.2008.03.012

Huang, C., & Kung, F. (2011). Environmental consciousness and intellectual capital management: Evidence from Taiwan's manufacturing industry. *Management Decision*, *49*(9), 1405–1425. doi:10.1108/00251741111173916

IASB. (2004). Intangible Assets, International Accounting Standard. International Accounting Standards Board.

Jabbour, C., De Sousa Jabbour, A., & Sarkis, J. (2019). Unlocking effective multi-tier supply chain management for sustainability through quantitative modeling: Lessons learned and discoveries to be made. *International Journal of Production Economics*, *217*, 11–30. doi:10.1016/j.ijpe.2018.08.029

Jardon, C., & Dasilva, A. (2017). Intellectual capital and environmental concern in subsistence small businesses. *Management of Environmental Quality*, *28*(2), 214–230. doi:10.1108/MEQ-05-2015-0085

Jardon, C., & Martos, M. (2012). Intellectual capital as competitive advantage in emerging clusters in Latin America. *Journal of Intellectual Capital*, *13*(4), 462–481. doi:10.1108/14691931211276098

Kaplan, R., & Norton, D. (1997). Cuadro de mando integral [The Balance Scorecard]. *Gestion*.

Kazancoglu, Y., Kazancoglu, I., & Sagnak, M. (2018). A new holistic conceptual framework for green supply chain management performance assessment based on circular economy. *Journal of Cleaner Production*, *195*, 1282–1299. doi:10.1016/j.jclepro.2018.06.015

Lee, K., & Min, B. (2015). Green R&D for eco-innovation and its impact on carbon emissions and firm performance. *Journal of Cleaner Production*, *108*, 534–542. doi:10.1016/j.jclepro.2015.05.114

Li, T., Liang, L., & Han, D. (2018). Research on the efficiency of green technology innovation in China's provincial high-end manufacturing industry based on the RAGA-PP-SFA model. *Mathematical Problems in Engineering*, *2018*, 1–13. doi:10.1155/2018/9463707

Longoni, A., & Cagliano, R. (2018). Inclusive environmental disclosure practices and firm performance. *International Journal of Operations & Production Management*, *38*(9), 1815–1835. doi:10.1108/IJOPM-12-2016-0728

López-Gamero, M., Zaragoza-Sáez, P., Claver-Cortés, E., & Molina-Azorín, J. (2011). Sustainable development and intangibles: Building sustainable intellectual capital. *Business Strategy and the Environment*, *20*(1), 18–37. doi:10.1002/bse.666

Luthra, S., Garg, D., & Haleem, A. (2016). The impacts of critical success factors for implementing green supply chain management towards sustainability: An empirical investigation of Indian automobile industry. *Journal of Cleaner Production*, *121*, 142–158. doi:10.1016/j.jclepro.2016.01.095

Marco-Lajara, B., Falcó, J. M., Fernández, L. R., & Larrosa, P. S. (2022k). Evolución del pensamiento en la disciplina de dirección estratégica: la visión de la empresa basada en las capacidades dinámicas y en el conocimiento. [Evolution of thinking in the discipline of strategic management: the vision of the company based on dynamic capabilities and knowledge.] In *Investigación y transferencia de las ciencias sociales frente a un mundo en crisis* (pp. 1801–1826). Dykinson.

Marco-Lajara, B., García, E. S., Larrosa, P. S., & Falcó, J. M. (2022m). Knowledge creation and diffusion inspecialized environments: What are the factors involved? In *Empresa, economía y derecho. Oportunidades ante un entorno global y disruptivo* (pp. 432–459). Dykinson.

Marco-Lajara, B., Sáez, P. D. C. Z., Falcó, J. M., & García, E. S. (2022l). Las rutas del vino de España: el impacto económico derivado de las visitas a bodegas y museos. [Las rutas del vino de España: el impacto económico derivado de las visitas a bodegas y museos] In *Investigación y transferencia de las ciencias sociales frente a un mundo en crisis* (pp. 1774–1800). Dykinson.

Marco-Lajara, B., Sánchez-García, E., Martínez-Falcó, J., & Poveda-Pareja, E. (2022j). Regional Specialization, Competitive Pressure, and Cooperation: The Cocktail for Innovation. *Energies*, *15*(15), 5346.

Marco-Lajara, B., Seva-Larrosa, P., Martínez-Falcó, J., & García-Lillo, F. (2022i). Wine clusters and Protected Designations of Origin (PDOs) in Spain: An exploratory analysis. *Journal of Wine Research*, *33*(3), 1–22. doi:10.1080/09571264.2022.2110051

Marco-Lajara, B., Seva-Larrosa, P., Martinez-Falco, J., & Sanchez-Garcia, E. (2021a). How Has COVID- 19 Affected The Spanish Wine Industry? An Exploratory Analysis. *Natural Volatiles & Essential Oils Journal*, *8*(6), 2722–2731.

Marco-Lajara, B., Seva-Larrosa, P., Ruiz-Fernandez, L., & Martinez-Falco, J. (2021b). The Effect of COVID- 19 on the Spanish Wine Industry. In *Impact of Global Issues on International Trade* (pp. 211–232). IGI Global. doi:10.4018/978-1-7998-8314-2.ch012

Marco-Lajara, B., Zaragoza-Saez, P., Falcó, J. M., & Millan-Tudela, L. A. (2022a). Analysing the Relationship Between Green Intellectual Capital and the Achievement of the Sustainable Development Goals. In *Handbook of Research on Building Inclusive Global Knowledge Societies for Sustainable Development* (pp. 111–129). IGI Global. doi:10.4018/978-1-6684-5109-0.ch005

Marco-Lajara, B., Zaragoza-Sáez, P., Falcó, J. M., & Millan-Tudela, L. A. (2022f). Corporate Social Responsibility: A Narrative Literature Review. *Frameworks for Sustainable Development Goals to Manage Economic, Social, and Environmental Shocks and Disasters*, 16-34.

Marco-Lajara, B., Zaragoza-Saez, P., Falcó, J. M., & Sánchez-García, E. (2022b). COVID-19 and Wine Tourism: A Story of Heartbreak. In Handbook of Research on SDGs for Economic Development, Social Development, and Environmental Protection (pp. 90-112). IGI Global.

Marco-Lajara, B., Zaragoza-Saez, P., & Martínez-Falcó, J. (2022e). Green Innovation: Balancing Economic Efficiency With Environmental Protection. In Frameworks for Sustainable Development Goals to Manage Economic, Social, and Environmental Shocks and Disasters (pp. 239-254). IGI Global.

Marco-Lajara, B., Zaragoza-Sáez, P., Martínez-Falcó, J., & Millan-Tudela, L. A. (2023). The Export Intensity of Spain's Autonomous Communities in Terms of the Marketing of Wine and Their Geographical Destinations. In *The Transformation of Global Trade in a New World* (pp. 1–21). IGI Global.

Marco-Lajara, B., Zaragoza-Sáez, P., Martínez-Falcó, J., & Millan-Tudela, L. A. (2023a). The Export Intensity of Spain's Autonomous Communities in Terms of the Marketing of Wine and Their Geographical Destinations. In *The Transformation of Global Trade in a New World* (pp. 1–21). IGI Global.

Marco-Lajara, B., Zaragoza-Sáez, P., Martínez-Falcó, J., & Ruiz-Fernández, L. (2022g). The Effect of Green Intellectual Capital on Green Performance in the Spanish Wine Industry: A Structural Equation Modeling Approach. *Complexity*, *2022*, 2022. doi:10.1155/2022/6024077

Marco-Lajara, B., Zaragoza-Sáez, P., Martínez-Falcó, J., & Sánchez-García, E. (2022c). Green Intellectual Capital in the Spanish Wine Industry. In Innovative Economic, Social, and Environmental Practices for Progressing Future Sustainability (pp. 102-120). IGI Global. doi:10.4018/978-1-7998-9590-9.ch006

Marco-Lajara, B., Zaragoza-Sáez, P., Martínez-Falcó, J., & Sánchez-García, E. (2022d). El capital intelectual verde como hoja de ruta para la sostenibilidad: El caso de bodegas Luzón. *GeoGraphos: Revista Digital para Estudiantes de Geografía y Ciencias Sociales*, *13*(147), 137–146.

Marco-Lajara, B., Zaragoza-Sáez, P., Martínez-Falcó, J., & Sánchez-García, E. (2023b). The Internationalization of the Spanish Wine Industry: An Analysis of Trade Flows and Their Degree of Concentration. In *The Transformation of Global Trade in a New World* (pp. 22–46). IGI Global.

Marco-Lajara, B., Zaragoza-Sáez, P. C., Martínez-Falcó, J., & Sánchez-García, E. (2022h). Does green intellectual capital affect green innovation performance? Evidence from the Spanish wine industry. *British Food Journal*.

Marco-Lajara, B., Zaragoza Sáez, P. D. C., & Martínez-Falcó, J. (2022n). Does Green Intellectual Capital Affect Green Performance? The Mediation of Green Innovation. *Telematiquie*, *21*(1), 4594–4602.

Martín-de Castro, G., Díez-Vial, I., & Delgado-Verde, M. (2019). Intellectual capital and the firm: Evolution and research trends. *Journal of Intellectual Capital*, *20*(4), 555–580. doi:10.1108/JIC-12-2018-0221

Martínez-Falcó, J., Marco-Lajara, B., & Zaragoza-Sáez, P. (2023b). Corporate Social Responsibility: A Comprehensive Analysis. In Positive and Constructive Contributions for Sustainable Development Goals (pp. 131-160). IGI Global.

Martínez-Falcó, J., Marco-Lajara, B., & Zaragoza-Saez, P. (2023c). Corporate Social Responsibility vs. Corporate Sustainability: Different Concepts for a Common Goal. In Positive and Constructive Contributions for Sustainable Development Goals (pp. 76-87). IGI Global.

Martínez-Falcó, J., Marco-Lajara, B., & Zaragoza-Saez, P. (2023d). Theoretical Perspectives on Corporate Social Responsibility: A Narrative Review. *Positive and Constructive Contributions for Sustainable Development Goals*, 96-113.

Martínez-Falcó, J., Marco-Lajara, B. M., Zaragoza-Sáez, P., & Ruiz-Fernández, L. (2023a). Green Intellectual Capital as a Catalyst for the Sustainable Development Goals: Evidence From the Spanish Wine Industry. In Climate Change, World Consequences, and the Sustainable Development Goals for 2030 (pp. 163-182). IGI Global.

Martínez-Torres, A. (2006). Procedure to Design a Structural and Measurement Model of Intellectual Capital: An Exploratory Study. *Information & Management*, *43*(5), 617–626. doi:10.1016/j.im.2006.03.002

Mavridis, D., & Kyrmizoglou, P. (2005). Intellectual capital performance drivers in the Greek banking sector. *Management Research News*, *28*(5), 43–62. doi:10.1108/01409170510629032

Mehralian, G., Rajabzadeh, A., Sadeh, M., & Rasekh, H. (2012). Intellectual capital and corporate performance in Iranian pharmaceutical industry. *Journal of Intellectual Capital*, *13*(1), 138–158. doi:10.1108/14691931211196259

Millan-Tudela, L. A., Marco-Lajara, B., Martínez-Falcó, J., & Sánchez-García, E. (2022b). Pursuing Business Longevity: Ways to Enhance Sustainable Development. In Frameworks for Sustainable Development Goals to Manage Economic, Social, and Environmental Shocks and Disasters (pp. 79-95). IGI Global.

Millan-Tudela, L. A. M., Marco-Lajara, B., Falcó, J. M., & Pareja, E. P. (2022a). Longevidad empresarial: revisión bibliométrica sobre la supervivencia y caída de las compañías [Corporate longevity: a bibliometric review of company survival and decline]. In Leveraging new business technology for a sustainable economic recovery (p. 170). Escuela Superior de Gestión Comercial y Marketing, ESIC.

Mondal, A., & Ghosh, S. (2012). Intellectual capital and financial performance of Indian banks. *Journal of Intellectual Capital*, *13*(4), 515–530. doi:10.1108/14691931211276115

Mustapha, M., Manan, Z., & Alwi, S. (2017). Sustainable Green Management System (SGMS)-An integrated approach towards organisational sustainability. *Journal of Cleaner Production*, *146*, 158–172. doi:10.1016/j.jclepro.2016.06.033

Nevado-Peña, D., & López-Ruiz, V. (2002). Un modelo e informe contable para la medición del capital intelectual desarrollo y aplicaciones [A model and accounting report for the measurement of intelectual capital deveopment and applications]. *Revista de Contabilidad y Tributación*, *229*, 161–206.

Ng, A. (2018). From sustainability accounting to a green financing system: Institutional legitimacy and market heterogeneity in a global financial centre. *Journal of Cleaner Production*, *195*, 585–592. doi:10.1016/j.jclepro.2018.05.250

Nonaka, I., Peltokorpi, V., & Tomae, H. (2005). Strategic knowledge creation: The case of Hamamatsu Photonics. *International Journal of Technology Management, 30*(3-4), 248–264. doi:10.1504/IJTM.2005.006709

Oliver, P. (2012). *Succeeding with your literature review. A handbook for students*. McGraw-Hill, Open University Press.

Olve, N., Roy, J., & Wetter, M. (2000). Implantando y gestionando el cuadro de mando integral [Implementing and managning the balanced scorecard]. *Gestion*.

Ordoñez de Pablos, P. (2001). La gestión del conocimiento como base para el logro de una ventaja competitiva sostenible: La organización occidental versus japonesa [Knowledge management as a basis for achieving a sustainable competitve advantage: The Western versus Japenese organization]. *Investigaciones Europeas de Dirección y Economía de la Empresa, 7*(3), 91–108.

Penrose, E. T. (1959). *The Theory of the Growth of the Firm*. John Wiley.

Petrash, G. (1996). Dow's Journey to a knowledge value management culture. *European Management Journal, 14*(4), 365–373. doi:10.1016/0263-2373(96)00023-0

Priem, R., & Butler, J. (2001). Is the resource-based "view" a useful perspective for strategic management research? *Academy of Management Review, 26*(1), 22–40.

Przychodzen, W., Gómez-Bezares, F., & Przychodzen, J. (2018). Green information technologies practices and financial performance-the empirical evidence from German publicly traded companies. *Journal of Cleaner Production, 201*, 570–579. doi:10.1016/j.jclepro.2018.08.081

Rastogi, P. (2003). The nature and role of IC - rethinking the process of value creation and sustained enterprise growth. *Journal of Intellectual Capital, 4*(2), 227–248. doi:10.1108/14691930310472848

Reed, K., Lubatkin, M., & Srinivasa, N. (2006). Proposing and Testing an Intellectual Capital-Based View of the Firm. *Journal of Management Studies, 43*(4), 867–893. doi:10.1111/j.1467-6486.2006.00614.x

Renwick, D., Redman, T., & Maguire, S. (2013). Green human resource management: A review and research agenda. *International Journal of Management Reviews, 15*(1), 1–14. doi:10.1111/j.1468-2370.2011.00328.x

Roos, G. (2017). Knowledge management, intellectual capital, structural holes, economic complexity and national prosperity. *Journal of Intellectual Capital, 18*(4), 745–770. doi:10.1108/JIC-07-2016-0072

Sánchez-Medina, A., Melián-González, A., & García-Falcón, J. (2007). El concepto del capital intelectual y sus dimensiones. *Investigaciones Europeas de Dirección y Economía de la Empresa, 13*(2), 97–111.

Seva-Larrosa, P., Falcó, J. M., & Fernández, L. R. (2022). Analizando las principales variables empresariales en los clusters vinícolas españoles teniendo en cuenta la localización de las empresas y su pertenencia a una marca colectiva. [Analyzing the main business variables in Spanish wine clusters taking into account the location of the companies and their membership in a collective brand.] In *Miradas sobre el emprendimiento ante la crisis del coronavirus* (pp. 629–634). Dykinson.

Skandia. (1996). *Customer Value*. Supplement to the Annual Report. Author.

Stewart, T. (1998). *La nueva riqueza de las organizaciones: el capital intelectual.* Granica.

Sullivan, P. (1999). Profiting from intellectual capital. *Journal of Knowledge Management, 3*(2), 132–142. doi:10.1108/13673279910275585

Sullivan, P. (2000). *Value driven intellectual capital: how to convert intangible corporate assets into market value.* John Wiley & Sons, Inc.

Sveiby, K. (1997). *The new organizational wealth. Managing and measuring knowledge-based assets.* Berret-Koehler Publishers, Inc.

Sveiby, K. (2001). A knowledge-based theory of the firm to guide in strategy formulation. *Journal of Intellectual Capital, 2*(4), 344–358. doi:10.1108/14691930110409651

Viedma, J. (2001). ICBS - Intellectual Capital Benchmarking System. *Journal of Intellectual Capital, 2*(2), 148–165. doi:10.1108/14691930110385937

Wee, B. V., & Banister, D. (2016). How to write a literature review paper? *Transport Reviews, 36*(2), 278–288. doi:10.1080/01441647.2015.1065456

Yadiati, W., Nissa, N., Paulus, S., Suharman, H., & Meiryani, M. (2019). The role of green intellectual capital and organizational reputation in influencing environmental performance. *International Journal of Energy Economics and Policy, 9*(3), 261–268. doi:10.32479/ijeep.7752

Yong, J., Yusliza, M., Ramayah, T., & Fawehinmi, O. (2019). Nexus between green intellectual capital and green human resource management. *Journal of Cleaner Production, 215*, 364–374. doi:10.1016/j.jclepro.2018.12.306

Youndt, M., Subramaniam, M., & Snell, S. (2004). Intellectual capital profiles: An examination of investments and returns. *Journal of Management Studies, 41*(2), 335–361. doi:10.1111/j.1467-6486.2004.00435.x

Yusliza, M., Othman, N., & Jabbour, C. (2017). Deciphering the implementation of green human resource management in an emerging economy. *Journal of Management Development, 36*(10), 1230–1246. doi:10.1108/JMD-01-2017-0027

Yusoff, Y., Omar, M., Zaman, M., & Samad, S. (2019). Do all elements of green intellectual capital contribute toward business sustainability? Evidence from the Malaysian context using the Partial Least Squares method. *Journal of Cleaner Production, 234*, 626–637. doi:10.1016/j.jclepro.2019.06.153

Zaid, A., Jaaron, A., & Bon, A. (2018). The impact of green human resource management and green supply chain management practices on sustainable performance: An empirical study. *Journal of Cleaner Production, 204*, 965–979. doi:10.1016/j.jclepro.2018.09.062

Zhang, L., Li, D., Cao, C., & Huang, S. (2018). The influence of greenwashing perception on green purchasing intentions: The mediating role of green word-of-mouth and moderating role of green concern. *Journal of Cleaner Production, 187*, 740–750. doi:10.1016/j.jclepro.2018.03.201

Zhu, Q., Sarkis, J., & Lai, K. (2013). Institutional-based antecedents and performance outcomes of internal and external green supply chain management practices. *Journal of Purchasing and Supply Management, 19*(2), 106–117. doi:10.1016/j.pursup.2012.12.001

ADDITIONAL READING

Benevene, P., Buonomo, I., Kong, E., Pansini, M., & Farnese, M. L. (2021). Management of Green Intellectual Capital: Evidence-Based Literature Review and Future Directions. *Sustainability*, *13*(15), 8349. doi:10.3390u13158349

Haldorai, K., Kim, W. G., & Garcia, R. F. (2022). Top management green commitment and green intellectual capital as enablers of hotel environmental performance: The mediating role of green human resource management. *Tourism Management*, *88*, 104431. doi:10.1016/j.tourman.2021.104431

Mansoor, A., Jahan, S., & Riaz, M. (2021). Does green intellectual capital spur corporate environmental performance through green workforce? *Journal of Intellectual Capital*, *22*(5), 823–839. doi:10.1108/JIC-06-2020-0181

Nisar, Q. A., Haider, S., Ali, F., Jamshed, S., Ryu, K., & Gill, S. S. (2021). Green human resource management practices and environmental performance in Malaysian green hotels: The role of green intellectual capital and pro-environmental behavior. *Journal of Cleaner Production*, *311*, 127504. doi:10.1016/j.jclepro.2021.127504

Ullah, H., Wang, Z., Mohsin, M., Jiang, W., & Abbas, H. (2022). Multidimensional perspective of green financial innovation between green intellectual capital on sustainable business: The case of Pakistan. *Environmental Science and Pollution Research International*, *29*(4), 5552–5568. doi:10.100711356-021-15919-7 PMID:34424468

KEY TERMS AND DEFINITIONS

Green Intellectual Capital: A set of human, structural, and relational intangibles that the organization possesses and whose purpose is the preservation of the environment.

Human Capital: The body of knowledge that people possess.

Intangible Asset: A business asset that cannot be physically perceived.

Intellectual Capital: A set of human, structural, and relational intangibles owned by the organization.

Relational Capital: Set of knowledge that derives from the network of relationships that the organization possesses.

Structural Capital: The body of knowledge possessed by the organization.

Chapter 6
Conceptual–Theoretical Approaches to the Ecology of Organizations

José G. Vargas-Hernández
https://orcid.org/0000-0003-0938-4197
Posgraduate and Research Department, Tecnológico Mario Molina Unidad Zapopan, Mexico

Omar C. Vargas-González
https://orcid.org/0000-0002-6089-956X
Tecnológico Nacional de México, Ciudad Guzmán, Mexico

ABSTRACT

This study aims to analyze the conceptual and theoretical approaches to ecology of organizations from the assumption that the unit of analysis of the ecology of organizations can be described, analyzed, and explained from different frameworks of reference. The method employed is the analytically referential and reflective of the main characteristics of the different perspectives already systematized in the theoretical and empirical research literature. It is concluded that the unit of analysis of the ecology of organizations in both the internal and external environments can be approached to be systematized from the perspectives of the open systems, the evolutionary theory, institutional and functionalist, and structural and community theories.

INTRODUCTION

The ecology of organizations contributes to the analysis of external environment and the structures that fit. The organization is an organism associated with systems theory, contingency theory and the organizational ecology approach, complexity paradigm and theory of chaos. There are various conceptual and theoretical debates focusing organizational ecology and organizational determinants; general and specific strategies, the liabilities of newness and smallness; organizational demographics and competitive industrial structures and modelling of organizational processes (Wholey & Brittain,1986).

DOI: 10.4018/978-1-6684-6815-9.ch006

The ecology of organizations has the elements of the industrial economy (Porter, 1980) and the population ecology approach (Hannan & Freeman, 1977, the adaptive capacity (Beinocker, 2006; Reeves & Deimler, 2011; Bernardes & Sá, 2009). The population ecology, from Hannan and Freeman (1977), through Wholey & Brittain (1986), the balance between ecological variation and selection process and the choices strategies (Wholey & Brittain, 1986 For Hannan & Freeman (1977).

Postmodern ontology tries to give a conceptual and technical response to the postmodern era and offers notions and concepts of the different theoretical-methodological versions and characteristics of postmodern organizational ecological theory that replace individual rationality, questions the stable, emphasizes the organizational procedural constitution. for communal and social construction (Rueda, 2022).

The biological ecology models describe changes in organisms not depending on the ontology of the involved populations. Direction and speed of social change of modern and dynamic constituent organizations and their diversity of organizational populations are responsive to the changing conditions of the society (Hannan & Freeman, 1989). The theoretical approach to the ecology of organizational populations can be done if it is taken as the unit of analysis and the second in the selection of adaptation. Ecological theory perspective is not prescriptive with an emphasis placed on population dynamics considering the variety of event types, structures, services, and strategies.

Social organizations are analysed using the organizational ecology and sociological perspectives framework, in their emergence, change, growth and decline of organizations, economic, social, and political conditions shaping organizational changes over time, organizations dealing with their environments through tactics and imitation, adaptation, interactions with competitors and other environmental actors.

The theoretical framework of organizational ecology drawn from ecology and environmental factors surrounding the organization, including the competition from other similar organizations, the target niche, and the organizational fitness to have access to the environmental resources. In religious ecology of organizations, the framework applies to voluntary organizations (McPherson, 1983; Ammerman, 1997; Eiesland & Warner 1998).

Organizational ecology theory supports the analysis of variables on the characteristics of organizational populations, institutional characteristics, environmental conditions, individual and specific to organizations, such as mortality, survival of created organizations, etc. (Bruderl et al. 1992). Organizational ecology theory and research is studied through change and mortality.

Ecological pressures on organizations have implications for unsustainable practices and strategies that they cannot cope with, such as decreased population density, mortality, and increased survival (Salimath & Jones, 2011). Eco-efficiency is the conception about the organizational ecology including the social demand on the organizations beyond the internal limits and that have influence in the human being in the climate and the natural environment.

The empirical research of the ecology of organizations undergoes changes. Research in population ecology of organizations with its different theoretical approaches of ecological population, provides a critique of the foundations of sustainability (Salimath & Jones, 2011).

This study intends to contribute to the analysis of the ecology of organizations by systematizing the theoretical and empirical literature review. It begins analyzing the systemic approach, to continue with the evolutionary perspective, the institutional and functional perspectives, followed by structural analysis and community theory. Finally, the analysis presents the conclusions.

A SYSTEMIC APPROACH OF ORGANIZATIONAL ECOLOGY

Organizational ecology is a concept that considers the workplace related to interdependent organizational systems with social and physical-environmental factors that design and are designed by work processes, organizational culture, demographic characteristics of workers and information technologies. Organizational ecology studies the life cycle of organizations supported by the background biology and sociology with concepts such as revolutionary innovation and creative destruction. Evolutionary ecology relates defined niches in terms of patterns of processes and resource use to competition and growth.

The organizational ecological perspective deals with coevolution processes. Ecological coevolution with demography and non-linear evolution of populations. There is a wide range of models on the co-adaptation and coevolution of the ecology of organizations. Ecology is a system of organisms interrelated with their natural environment framed by biology and life sciences. The interrelationships between and among organisms in their environment necessary for the sustainability of the system (Weaver-Hightower 2008).

Organizational ecology is complex and interactive with often unintended consequences recognizing that there is not design like in evolutionary theories able to manipulate situations to reach the desired and intended outcomes and results, instead of local decisions made by different agents

The organization as ecological systems are moved by contingent situations and the changing interaction of its unpredictable agents. The intra-organizational ecological perspective directs the elaboration of the strategic evolution of organizations for organizational adaptation. The inter-population dynamics of organizations active internationally are structurally constrained by density depending on the stage in the evolution of population, initial emergence, short-term growth, and long-term development.

Differentiated systems based on ecological principles comprise various parts in a complementary form that work together. There is a diversity of typologies to study and analyze organizations such as for example the ones focusing on organizational adjustment (Mintzberg, 1978), as a complete system (Miles and Snow, 1978), on strictly strategic approach (Porter, 1980; 1985), a typology of configurations to integrate the theoretical contribution (Zammuto, 1988).

The type of impact, the elements of the system and the intensity of use, determine the ecological, physical, social, and economic capacity. For example, given a systemic shock, the challenges posed to intergovernmental organizations have different reactions while some endure others may falter. This emergent organizational ecology may be biased in favor of business and counterfactual of intergovernmental organizations which represent the interests of consumers, labor, social actors, and stakeholders modelled in private governance systems with normative implications.

The surviving intergovernmental organizations are stronger by design and operations and more adaptable to environmental and ecological exogenous shocks. There have been identified systemic changes causing an organizational ecological decline in population of the intergovernmental organizations between 1982 and 1991 (Shanks et al. 1996).

A model of ecological dynamics of organizations characterizes ecosystems in parallel between the population model and the global e-commerce environment. A dynamic socio-ecological system supports the organizational transformations. The organizational behavior as biotic systems occur between similar ecological populations and the environments. Ecosystem analyzes include controlled species experiments in micro ecologies that show that low diversity systems are more stable (Hannan, 2005).

The study of the organization was carried out in a limited concept of closed systems. The concept of open system is a comprehensive interdisciplinary approach and presupposing influence and exchange interrelationships between them. The ecological framework proposed by Hawley (1950) considers that systemic technologies in uniform, standardized and differentiated elemental systems.

THE EVOLUTIONARY THEORY OF ORGANIZATIONAL ECOLOGY

Organizational ecology is a reference of the processes of change and organizational evolution. Evolutionary organizational theory is supported by the assumptions that organizations descend from past organizations and the diversity and differences have arisen gradually from changes processes. The theory of organizational ecology as organizational theory relates organizations with behavior, based on evolution and natural selection as adaptability resources (Vàsquez Garcìa, 2011). The evolutionary theory of economic change has its origin in the evolutionary behavior of economic systems (Holzl, 2005). The evolutionary economy is characterized by disequilibrium processes that economic agent create and adapt through learning.

The evolution based on cumulative processes does not necessarily guarantee the survival of the fittest, but by a selection process based on structures (Hölzl, 2005). The theory of the evolution of the firm focuses on the technological aspects of production and the cognitive nature of the organizational structure (Nelson and Winter, 1082). The theory of the evolution of the firm is like the culture of neoclassical economics that studies evolutionary dynamics.

The evolutionary theory of organizational ecology is one of the components of the population analysis (McKelvey 1979) calling for systematic and evolutionary analysis and explains the organizational structures and forms (Mackinley, 1982). The population ecology of organizations links the vital manifestations between populations (Hannan and Freeman, 1989) with results that validate the theory with dissimilar populations and the theory expands under conditions of competition.

The population ecology of organizations considered as spaces of social interaction in interdependent spaces where intra and interorganizational elements converge (Vàsquez Garcìa, 2011). The population analysis arises from ecological models to include the diversity forms, populations change, and limits of growth over time. The ecological analysis organizational uses the elements and principles of ecology laid out by Hannan and Freeman (1977, 1993) and Carroll (1984) which focus on the behavior growth of organizational populations.

The evolutionary approach to organizations explains adaptive behavior through the tensions between innovation and selection mechanisms. The theory of the evolution of the firm provides a theoretical framework for the analysis of changes in organizations (Hölz, 2005). The theory of organizational ecology is intricately linked to evolution and therefore does not remain inert. The organizational ecology approach points out the inertia organizational structure as a change element in search of attractive market niches to fit the competencies, organizational systems, structural skills, routines. Ecology assumes that the inertia despite the attempts at transformation introducing the complexity of the conceptual organizational analysis.

Ecological organizational theory supports the concept of niche as an expression of environmental variations and competition that affects the growth of populations (Hannan & Freman, 1991). In organizational ecology, the population niche is defined as the set of environmental conditions with a growth rate. The population ecology of organizations defines the population niche that depend on the diversity of the niche structure, as the set of environmental conditions with their growth rate. Environmental variations and competition shape population dynamics and ecological segmentation (Vàzquez Garcìa, 2011).

The niche concept provides a reference framework for the analysis of environmental variations and competencies of population dynamics and its ecological segmentation. The approach to the theory of population ecology analyzes the selection and imitation that give rise to the growth and rational adaptation of the organization, considering that organizations are spaces of social interaction with interdependent scenarios, where intra and interorganizational dimensions converge (Vàzquez Garcìa, 2011). In the set of environmental conditions of a niche, in which the population can grow, the population growth is non-negative (Hannan & Freman,1991).

The population niche is the set of environmental conditions with a growth rate that provides a reference framework to analyze the environmental variations that shape population dynamics and ecological segmentation (Vàsquez Garcìa, 2011). An analysis of population dynamics concludes that the events had risen faster than population growth correlated with gross domestic product (Andersson, Getz, and Mykletun, 2013).

Jaeger and Mykletun (2009) pertaining to the region of Finnmark in northern Norway, they examined several demographics for an entire population of festivals, and raised issues regarding definition of a festival population. Subsequently, Andersson, Getz, and Mykletun (2013) reported on population dynamics in three Norwegian Counties, including Finnmark, concluding that the number of events in each county had risen faster than population growth before levelling off, and changes were correlated with the gross domestic product.

Organizational ecology studies organizational diversity and analyzes the social conditions that have effects on the dynamic evolutions of selection processes that affect organizational development (Singh & Lumsden, 1990). Population ecology is supported by the long-term changes in organizational diversity as the result of the accumulation of short-term effects and differences in net mortality population rates facing environments with limited resources.

The ecological analysis focuses on organizational founding and mortality processes of organizational populations while lagging the understanding of organizational growth (Harrison, 2004). Ecology models the development of organizations through the analysis of dependency and mortality based on the segmentation of organizational populations. The growth of organizational population depends on its intrinsic features such as the resilience of public organizations and the agility of private organizations

Population ecology is an evolutionary organizational and population changes, slow and continuous, descending from previously existing organizations and organizational forms. However, unlike evolution based on natural selection, organizational evolution does not lead to optimization depending on the coupling between the intents and the outcomes Hannan, and Freeman, 1989).

Population ecology studies the dynamic long-term changes in terms of birth, mortality, and diversity of organizational forms occurring through selection within a set of organizations, using population as the level of analysis over extended periods. The population ecology approach is based on the theory of species selection of Darwin considered as the structural elements of ecosystems influenced by the choice of strategic logics of an environmental uncertainty and complexity. This argument extends that it is the structural characteristics of ecosystems that select the influence of environmental uncertainty in the choice of strategic logics. Strategy formulation and implementation are an intra-organizational ecological process that establishes internal selection processes for the growth and survival of the organization (Burgelman, 1991).

Ecological organizations theory takes advantage of the ecological and ethnographic analysis of the population to analyze organizational life cycles with a biological and sociological approach, through concepts such as creative destruction and revolutionary innovation. The density dependence theory sustains that the object of study of organizational ecology has developed a theoretical body since its appearance, although subject to criticism such as the biological analogy because organizations are not organisms that are born, grow, develop, reproduce, age, die and leave offspring, as concepts they cannot be operationalized (Gómez Cumpa, 2003). The density dependence in organizational ecology theory demonstrates the growth in festival populations, which may be no sustainable when resources diminish.

The conceptual framework of population ecology is methodological rigorous approach for research. The analysis of population ecology is facilitated by statistical analyses and model building based on accessibility large databases and datasets from public and governmental institutions, agencies, commercial and civil organizations at resource cost. Research control improves with governmental database in relation to the uncertainties on returns and codification of questionnaire and structured interviews.

The organizational ecological concept of a population of organisms makes difficult to identify the several types of existing organizations in the same environment and the most appropriate to the same context. The organizational population concept in the context of ecology and population genetics, is focused by biologists and philosophers (Berryman, 2002; Camus & Lima, 2002; Baguette & Stevens, 2003; Krebs, 2001; Gannett, 2003). Organizational ecology analyzes ignored phenomena such as the birth and death of organizations, evolutionary patterns of populations, and the imitations of managers in maintaining adaptive capacities, and is also considered an anti-management theory (Pina, Cunha & & Kamoche 2003; Donaldson, 1995).

The perspective of the evolutionary theory of organizational ecology considers it a mistake to seek the best organizational form, considering that uncertain volatile environments are supported in many ways depending on the conditions (Burgelman, 1991). Organizational ecology incorporates population structure and spatial distribution to understand evolutionary organizational dynamics. The ecological organization that incorporates information from the different environments and spatial components of its organizational populations affects its evolutionary dynamics of growth and development (Lomi, 1995).

Under the principles of universal Darwinism, the social evolution of complex and changing social systems conforms to inheritance, selection, variation and conforms to the acquired inheritance of characters as a Lamarckian characteristic (Hogdson, 2001). In biological theories and social, economic, and cultural life must be consistent where social evolution is Lamarckian must be consistent with Darwinian principles. However, from the biological perspective, Lamarck's theoretical inconsistency with the social, economic, and cultural sciences is raised (Hogdson, 2001). Lamarckism proposes the acquisition of hereditary characters with variations acquired through adaptations rather than mutations. Thus, social evolution remains Lamarckian is a methodological theoretical challenge for modern Darwinists (Hogdson, 2001).

Organizational ecology questions the basic premise of Darwinian evolution under the argument that population changes are carried out by the replacement of organizations that do not continue to exist under different environmental conditions (Gómez Cumpa, 2003). Ecology postulates Darwinian evolution without excluding the Lamarckian, making possible a synthesis of both on applicability (Baum, 1996).

Organizational ecology analyzes the propositions that apply at the level of organizational populations to propose dominant models, based on the adaptationist and Lamarckian theory of evolution and population changes that are explained from organizational adaptation to environmental variations. Standard traditional models include constant parameters over time because of the underlying assumption of two-scale dynamics between ecological and evolutionary processes (Sole & Bascompte, 1995).

The concept of depreciation refers to the behavior of the interactions of a biological and ecological population. Ecological depreciation is identified in types based on their interactions and degrees of intimacy and lethality of the actions. The concept of organizational predation is associated with the deterioration of the organizational means. The construct schema of organizational predation bridges the ecological theory and the field of organizations, the relations between organisms and the ecological affinities derived from the evolutionary history for the perpetuation of species and to satisfy the sustenance of life (Kormondy, 1994, p. 17). Some events in ecology of organizations may engage in predation or parasitism making pertinent to consider some ecological concepts.

A second stream is the organizational systematics which has a minor role on the study of population ecology organizations. (McKelvey & Aldrich, 1883; Aldrich, 1979; 1999; Aldrich & Pfeffer, 1976; McKelvey, 1978; 1982). A good example is the socio ecological sustainability of agroecosystems and farming systems. Two relevant camps in the agronomical field are the farming systems, the ecology, biotechnology, and physiology. Molecular biology and genetic engineering are very respected from the agroecological point of view, not considered as imperil sustainability but are steps toward ecologically sound agriculture. Genetic engineering has not been considered legitimate field of agroecology for its reductiveness and inability to capture the complexity of agricultural ecosystems and its association with industrialized oriented agriculture.

Between the holistic and reductionist perspectives can be instantiated agroecology with its complex interconnections of ecosystems in juxtaposition with the tendency of molecular biology to reduce organisms into mechanisms (Galison, 1996; Gerson, 1998). The complexity of ecological food webs has consequences at the species level in ecosystems. Each country must produce the food it consumes is the notion different that the genetic engineering and industrialized agriculture market-oriented (Lacey, 2000).

The contradiction between agroecology and molecular biology is tangible and the conflict fuelled the local tensions. Agroecology and traditional agronomy tend to be pushed out by the growth of molecular biology. A clash between agroecology and biotechnology concerning the social consequences of the biotechnology business, centers on issues related to the robbery of genetic resources from indigenous and domestic agricultural systems by multinational companies, led to serious antagonisms. Agroecology is critical of monopolization of seed production and modified crop varieties leading to the control of agricultural production systems.

Sustainable agriculture is enhanced using molecular biological techniques and genetic engineering, with diversity limited results and with the socio-ecosystemic chaos. The ecosystem-oriented perspective on agricultural production uses the sustainable development of food production systems (Vereijken, 1992).

Integrated farming systems research has been challenged from practicality and ecological sustainability. Farming systems research empirically oriented mix practices and theories of farm management with an ecological perspective (Bawden, 1991). The integrated production systems in agroecologically oriented farming integrates the economic, ecological, and social dimensions into a mutually compatible relationship (Vereijken, 1992).

INSTITUTIONAL AND FUNCTIONALIST ANALYSES OF ORGANIZATIONAL ECOLOGY

The organizational field is the set of organizations that, in the aggregate, constitute a recognized area of institutional life (DiMaggio & Powell, 1983). Organizational ecology is an autonomous perspective that has established theoretical-methodological relationships through complementary links with institutionalism. Institutionalism provides the contextualization that facilitates ecological analyzes (Baum, 1996).

The theories of organizational and institutional ecology are demarcated from the ecological perspective and the institutional criteria of policy and institutional culture that derive in organizational selection processes. In this sense, ecology can be emphasized at the levels of analysis of institutional theory. However, ecological theory has incorporated institutional theory despite the differences in the roles of competition and institutional constraints that determine organizational vitality (Amburgey, 1996).

Organizational ecology as a theoretical framework for research in population of events can be complemented by the theories of the firm, resources, and knowledge-based and institutional theory. Institutional and ecological research converge in issues of legitimacy in population dynamics, institutional variables, and vital rates. The theory of organizational ecology develops processes of institutional isomorphism due to the forms of organization of organizational populations. Organizational ecology in its niche exploitation theory identifies structural isomorphism or polymorphism applicable to organizations (Hannan and Freeman, 1977). The niche of any organizational form consists of economic, social, and political conditions of organizational functioning.

The principle of isomorphism implies that the organizational diversity of the social system depends on the diversity of agents that control the flows of the system's resources (Hannan & Freman,1991). Resource partitioning in the organizational population suggested by ecological work in generalist subpopulations, the functional niches may contract, and the specialists may grow. The resource partitioned taking place in the population by most of the ecological work, the functional niches may contract, and specialists may grow.

The ecological and institutional characteristics of the niches have population effects Organizational economics encompasses economic transaction costs, agency theory, and selection processes that determine the growth and development of organizational forms. Organizational ecology theory states that efficiency levels affect the change of institutional processes in organizations, in situations such as legitimacy in organizational fluctuations (Amburgey, 1996).

The institutional analysis has been relevant in conservation (Barrett et al., 2001)], supported by conservation science and socio-ecological systems analysis (Anderies et al., 2004; Ostrom, 1990). The concept of relational density in organizational ecology is the number of formal relationships between the members of populations and institutions in the environment (Baum and Oliver, 1992), which corresponds to an operationalization of embeddedness in institutional theory. The perspective of the organizational ecology theory pays attention to the environment with its changes that determine the factors of the survival of the institutions that create opportunities and restrictions.

A more complex model of analysis incorporates neo institutionalism theory and ecological population theory under the assumption that founder rates are proportional to legitimacy that increases with density. The organizational population density affects the growth of another population which should be applied to international organizations. The density dependence of organizational ecology assumes that vital rates are the function of the entities and events in an area (Hannan & Freeman, 1977). The ecological argument assumes that the founding rates are inversely proportional to the population competition as a function of the acceleration of its density.

Population ecology applied to international growth dynamics is related to the long-term differentiation and survival strategies. The ecological process in its organizational dimension identifies changes and internal dynamics that adapt and respond to self-direction, functioning and adaptability. The intra-organizational ecological process requires self-induced innovation and adaptability by the organization in interaction with exogenous factors (Vázquez García, 2011).

The intra-organizational dimension of the ecological process generates changes and dynamics that respond to self-driving adaptability and functioning the intra-organizational ecological process leads to innovation and adaptability in interaction with external factors (Vázquez García, 2011). The perspective of organizational ecology considers the external forces of the environment outside the organizational limits such as economic, social, political, natural, technological forces, etc., which interfere in the functions and activities that are substantial to organizations (Aldrich, 2008; Hannan y Freeman, 1977).

The growth rate of international organizations populations in climate change, private transnational, and intergovernmental organizations, are observed by the analysis of Abbott, Green & Keohane (2016). Organizational ecology converges with the legitimacy of dynamic ecological populations with effects on institutions on vital rates. The relationship prey-predator is a functional classification which is proposed by population ecology as part of the knowledge available in ecology to facilitate the organizational management styles.

Institutional factors are exogenous to the population and include economic, social, political, technological factors, etc. A category of factors makes difficult to elaborate theory based on environmental changes and conditions to influence the carrying capacity of institutional ecology. The features of membership and flexibility of institutional and organizational ecological design of intergovernmental organizations and classified by a rationalist perspective (Koremenos et al., 2001). The attributes of institutional design are independent variables which has an influence on the organizational robustness.

The organizational ecology of the foundation considers the population as a unit of events and identifies segments of the population that respond competitively in a heterogeneous way to institutional processes (Lomi, 1995). The associational institutional structure followed by a population ecology is subdivided into core that refers to identities, procedures and routines, and periphery consisting of subunits and organizational maps. The core tends to institutional inertia and periphery is a buffer against environmental influences.

Human ecology has developed in a micro-ecology many statements that indicate interests in functional relations concerned with spatial patterns. The interest to human ecology influences the organizational and spatial sustenance relevant to human ecology. An organizational ecological approach may be open to the system dynamics complexity ruled by functionalist approaches to governance, comprising populations of organizations performing governance functions. Populations occupy ecological niches defined by the set of resources in terms of economic, social, and political conditions to sustain the functioning of organizational forms.

The ecology of the organizational governance and political system has different governance organizations, intergovernmental organizations and private governance organizations that set, monitor, and enforce the rules subject to domestic systems and defined spheres, including the states as the primary actors. The emergence and growth of private governance organizations are enhanced by organizational ecology.

For example, the private land conservation areas are not a function of ecological attributes, biophysical and socioeconomic characteristics including affordability, accessibility, and available facilities (Bayliss et al., 2014; De Vos et al., 2016). The interdependencies between the socio ecological systems and the private land conservation areas are considered in their biodiversity (Berkes et al., 2000) and incorporate the management and governance of natural resources.

Governance organizations ecology sustains limited government in determined minorities, and it is not a guarantee of the system stability. To achieve more stable government a balanced ecology is necessary. Ecology of global governance supports changes of the organizational forms supported by flexibility in the increasing governance institutions. Governance organizations and state structures is concerned with the ecology of states and their arrays of organizations in and institutional arrangements of checks and balances from and organizational ecology perspective and other alternatives of organizational ecologies of the ecology of global governance. At global and national levels, there are not any inventory of governance organizations and the global ecology growths in diversity.

Economic, political, and environmental integration is leading towards demands for global governance giving place to the creation of new organizations and governance niches to meet the demand for regulations of new organizations, national organizations, and transnational organizations. International governance organizations grew rapidly during the 1970s. In the early 21st century, international governance organizations are in stagnation and the private governance organizations are growing.

The institutions of global governance are changing to include in new organizational forms the trans governmental networks, private transnational regulatory organizations, and informal institutions. The analysis level of governance organizations drawing on principles of organizational ecology to analyze the governance systems. Models of global governance has moved from the focus on states to intergovernmental organizations and to private governance organizations.

STRUCTURAL PERSPECTIVE

Organizational ecology is in line of thought on the structural paradigm-strategy. Contingency theory, structural and Marxist theories, resource dependence theories, hold that organizations adopt and adapt strategies to fit organizational structures to environmental demands. Organizational sociology is related to historical and social transformations of the roles of organizational diversity, core structures leading to create and shape new organizational forms and social change to become more suitable to environmental demands. Organizational diversity has consequences for social structure and individuals (Carroll & Hannan 2000). Economic, social, and political conditions affect the abundance and diversity of organizational forms (Baum & Shipilov, 2006).

The theory of organizational ecology is based on a theoretical assumption of the ability of organizations to adapt to its environment, as it is assumed by the structural and neoclassical contingency theories. Organizational ecology is identified with many theoretical fragments including population and organizational forms, structural inertia and change, diversity in organizations, social movements dynamics, age and density dependence, resource partitioning, niche structure, etc. Organizational ecology assumes that the structural nuclei of organizations are subject to pressure from inertia and efforts.

The theory of organizational ecology is constituted by the economic theory of the firm and the Darwinian principle of natural selection. The firm is an actor with a limited rationale interacting with organizational structural inertia in a competitive environment that determines the environmental variations restricting the organizational populations and selecting the most apt for surviving and eliminating the weakest organizations (Hannan; Freeman, 1977, 1989; Baum, 2001).

Local ecology in organizational population arena is constrained by the multiplicity of social worlds and dimensions of formal organizational structures (Dingwall and Strong, 1985). The principles raised by population ecology are the structural inertia, density dependence, age, and size. A controversial principle of organizational ecology theory is the fatalistic nature of structural inertia that negates adaptation and any possibility of change. Heterogeneity in population ecology is problematic because homogeneity analyzes organizing populations with not always observable factors that relate to their location affecting structure (Lomi, 1995). Selection theories in organizational ecology support the variability of organizational structures that occurs with the creation of new organizational forms and the disappearance of old ones (Burgelman, 1991).

Structural inertia may be selectively favorable for the organizational populations resulting in evolutionary processes (Hannan, Pólos, & Carroll, 2007; Hannan et al., 1995; Carroll & Hannan 2000). Organizations develop structural inertia to the environmental changes that hinders the adaptation leading to selection (Hannan, and Freeman, 1989). The structural inertia theory proposes that organizations are unable to adapt to emerging environmental challenges and changing conditions which may undermine the organizational accountability and reliability (Hannan et al., 2004; Stieglitz et al., 2016). The theory of structural inertia exposes a growing vulnerability of organizations and denies the possibilities of organizational change. The theory of structural inertia proposes the impossibility of adaptive organizational change. Structural inertia theory does not add to organizational ecology (Hannan and Freeman, 1984, 1989).

The organizational ecology theory is based on the principles based on the theory of structural inertia, age and size and density dependency theory. The structural inertia theory assumes the existence of a rigidity that makes impossible the changes due to managerial decisions not implemented into appropriate actions. The structural inertia does not prevent individual organizations from changing their basic form, contrary to an assumption of organizational ecology from migrating populations and species. The assumption that organizations can adjust to environmental changes is a breaking point structure (Hannan and Freeman, 1978, 1989) in organizational ecology responsible for growth and disappearance of organizations.

The interdependence between the organization and the ecology of populations from organizational sociology is related to power, direction, and organizational leadership. The population ecology approach centers on the relationships between the organizational actors interacting with the power, intimacy, and lethality of their performance. Population ecology is the blueprint organizational DNA, an organizational form inferred from the formal organizational structure, forms of authority, patterns of activity (Hannan and Freeman, 1977).

In different contexts, emerging ecological networks share universal properties. Population structures can match the similarities and differences of the most relevant statistical characteristics of ecological networks (Hannan, 2005). Ecological complexity includes structural robustness, species richness and fragility. The biological and ecological context does not specify the concept of power present in the strategic behavior of groups. The trophic levels of ecological communities are determined by energy constraints. The ecological efficiencies with their trophic interactions do not determine their structure.

The political factors have access to the sectoral regulation of structures. Terminations of intergovernmental organizations increase during the periods of geopolitical instability, and many survive during periods of turmoil, while others buckle during periods of geopolitical tranquility (Eilstrup-Sangiovanni, 2020).

Agroecology is apoliticized line of research no concentrated in solving scientific problems but in achieving political goals. Agroecology is represented sociologically (Gieryn, 1999). The organizational ecology related to competition between governance organizations determine the rule and policy making, practices and the political outcomes, all as products of organizational ecology.

Ecological predation is influenced by the power of the organizational agent and depends on the levels of intimacy of the agents and the degree of lethality of their actions. Varying types of governance organizations in ecological approach is a way to limit the power of the state. The diverse types of ecological depredation identify the soft or hard degree of power, consequence of the hierarchy of the organization.

New niches in the state power are likely to be filled by adapting private governance organizations ensuring organizational ecology.

COMMUNITY ECOLOGY THEORY

Social ecology analysis draws from a diversity of scientific disciplines and research traditions that interact in communities of practices (Clarke and Star, 2004; Strauss, 1991b). Communities and populations of organizations are the elements necessary for an ecological analysis of organizations. Population ecology is the origin of the term community, but nothing in common with interorganizational community. Populations affecting the resources of others form a co-evolving ecological community within the shared environment. Organizational populations in an ecological community are mutually affecting each other resources besides the co-evolving resources within their shared environment.

The population of the organizations is developed in similar communities as in the organizations of power as agents of change (Singh & Lumsden, 1990).

Ecological theory analyzes life cycles throughout the community. The organizational ecological construct supports the analysis of characteristics of organisms withing their environment in a community such as purpose, ownership organization, life cycle, age dependence, etc. The ecological theory is presented as a perspective that explains the factors that affect the life cycles of organizations in each population of existing community and organizations. Ecological theory is one of the branches of organizational theory that analyzes the organization and its life cycles, birth, life, and independent death of the population.

The levels of analysis of organizational ecology are organizational, population and community characterized by selection, development, and evolution (Singh & Lumsden, 1990). The levels of the analysis of population are birth and death rates within an organizational population, the vital-rate interaction between populations and the communities of populations that share similar environments. A higher level of complexity used in organizational ecological approach implies the competing organizational populations in the ecological community. The dependent variable may be the diversity in the entire international organizational ecological community

The new ecological approach based on the concept of organizational community as the bounded set of forms with interrelated identities (Ruef, 2000). Organizational ecology is a concept that is used for the analysis of civil society organizations (CSOs), which have gone from hand of the process of political democratization (Soto & Viveros, 2016).

Organizational mortality approaches are the fitness set theory, density dependence liability of newness, resource partitioning, effects of founding and liability of smallness. The heterogeneity in the context of mortality processes have not determined the consequences of the founding of the organization (Lomi, 1995). Organizational mortality varies as the function of age in large populations (Freeman, Carroll, & Hannan, 1983; Carroll, 1983). Organizational mortality under conditions of systemic technological change after proliferation, growth and failure of firms drawing on community ecology theory, such as the case in the telephone industry, Barnett, (1990) has concluded that technological change not always favor advanced organizations.

CONCLUSION

This study on the different perspectives of theoretical and empirical of ecology of organizations as the unit of analysis in both the internal and external environments can be systematized from the perspectives of the open systems, the evolutionary theory, institutional and functionalist, structural and community theories.

The theory of organizational ecology has relevant contributions based on the assumptions and ideas related with the structures of the model to determine the key organizational factors of survival, and to detect any environmental alteration by the introduction of these concepts into the theory and their relationships with the structural inertia, age, size, and density dependence. The organizational ecology theory offers a metaphor that provides perceptions and conceptualize strategies.

The sustainability of organizational practices and strategies are selected by ecological pressures that allow increased population density, reduced mortality, and survival of organizational populations. Some outcomes of organizational strategies are recursive affecting the stability and growth of different organizational forms. The ecology-based perspective evaluates the access, availability and use of natural resources focusing on changes that have an impact on international B2B growth strategy.

The conception of organizational ecology with the implementation of environmental measures will improve the internal organizational climate that influences the environment and surroundings.

The new forms of organizations develop and evolve to become more suitable to face the competitive and environmental variables, relations, and challenges. The emergence of organizational ecology questions the premise of Darwinian evolution. The evolutionary theory of organizations has questioned practical consequences such as voluntary strategies for organizational intervention. Organizational evolution theory adjusts to environmental pressures by supporting the generation of organizational inertial forces that drive changes powered by Darwinian selection. The evolutionary theory of organizations considers the contributions of organizational ecology in synthesis with other evolutionary perspectives.

The population ecology of organizations constitutes an influential perspective in organizational analysis, while organizational sustainability is a competitor in the organizational literature (Salimath, & Jones, 2011). However, there are convergences between the population ecology of organizations and the construction of levels of analysis, dimensions, and results of sustainability. Organizational memory has as elements within organizations, the organizational structures, organizational culture and transformations, organization, organizational ecology, external archives and in individuals (Walsh & Ungson 1991). These elements contribute the implementation of organizational memory is analyzed by the information and knowledge.

Organizational strategies ecologically oriented are conditional to the power and opportunities characteristics for strategic flexibility and adaptation on organizational forms. Organizational legitimation in ecology theory is a non-observed variable making difficult to assess its explanatory power.

More research is needed on the interrelationships that result from the intersection of the population ecology of organizations and sustainability. The future research of populations in ecology with links to sustainability, in such a way that the sustainability of organizations is analyzed.

REFERENCES

Abbott, K., Green, J., & Keohane, R. (2016). Organizational Ecology and Institutional Change in Global Governance. *International Organization, 70*(2), 247–277. doi:10.1017/S0020818315000338

Aldrich, H. (2008). *Organizations and Environments*. Stanford University Press.

Aldrich, H. E. (1979). *Organizations and environments*. Prentice-Hall.

Aldrich, H. E. (1999). *Organizations evolving*. Sage.

Aldrich, H. E., & Pfeffer, J. (1976). Environments of organizations. *Annual Review of Sociology, 2*(1), 79–105. doi:10.1146/annurev.so.02.080176.000455

Amburgey, T., & Hayagreeva, R. (1996). Organizational Ecology: Past, Present, and Future Directions. *Academy of Management Journal, 39*(5), 1265–1286. doi:10.2307/256999

Ammerman, N. T. (1997). *Congregation and community*. Rutgers University Press.

Anderies, J. M., Janssen, M. A., & Ostrom, E. (2004). A framework to analyze the robustness of social–ecological systems from an institutional perspective. *Ecology and Society, 9*(1), 18. doi:10.5751/ES-00610-090118

Andersson, T., Getz, D., & Mykletun, R. (2013). Sustainable festival populations: An application of organizational ecology. *Tourism Analysis, 18*(6), 621–634. doi:10.3727/108354213X13824558188505

Baguette, M., & Stevens, V. M. (2003). Local populations and metapopulations are both natural and operational categories. *Oikos, 101*(3), 661–663. doi:10.1034/j.1600-0706.2003.12539.x

Barnett, W. P. (1990). The Organizational Ecology of a Technological System. *Administrative Science Quarterly, 35*(1), 31–60. doi:10.2307/2393550

Barrett, C. B., Brandon, K., Gibson, C., & Gjersten, H. (2001). Conserving tropical biodiversity amid weak institutions. *Bioscience, 51*(6), 497–502. doi:10.1641/0006-3568(2001)051[0497:CTBAWI]2.0.CO;2

Baum, J. (1996). Organizational ecology. In S. Clegg, C. Hardy, & W. Nord (Eds.), *Handbook of organizational study* (pp. 77–115). Sage.

Baum, J., & Oliver, C. (1992). Institutional embededdness and the dynamics of organizational populations. *American Sociological Review, 57*(4), 540–559. doi:10.2307/2096100

Baum, J. A., & Shipilov, A. V. (2006). 1.2 Ecological Approaches to Organizations. The Sage handbook of organization studies, 55.

Baum, J. A. C. (2001). Ecologia organizacional. In S. R. Clegg (Ed.), *Hardy, C.; Nord, W. R. (orgs). Handbook de Estudos Organizacionais*. Atlas.

Bawden, R. J. (1991). Systems Thinking and Practice in Agriculture. *Journal of Dairy Science, 74*(7), 2362–2373. doi:10.3168/jds.S0022-0302(91)78410-5

Bayliss, J., Schaafsma, M., Balmford, A., Burgess, N. D., Green, J. M. H., Madoffe, S. S., Okayasu, S., Peh, K. S. H., Platts, P. J., & Yu, D. W. (2014). The current and future value of nature-based tourism in the Eastern Arc Mountains of Tanzania. *Ecosystem Services*, *8*, 75–83. doi:10.1016/j.ecoser.2014.02.006

Beinhocker, E. D. (2006). The adaptable corporation. *The McKinsey Quarterly*, (2), 76–87.

Berkes, F., Colding, J., & Folke, C. (2000). Rediscovery of traditional ecological knowledge as adaptive management. *Ecological Applications*, *10*(5), 1251–1262. doi:10.1890/1051-0761(2000)010[1251:ROTEKA]2.0.CO;2

Bernardes, M. E. B. SÁ, F. S. (2009). Voluntarismo e determinismo em implementação de estratégias colectivas de PME: uma análise de dois processos em arranjos produtivos moveleiros [Voluntarism and determinism in implementation of collective SME strategies: An análisis of two processes in productive furniture arrangements]. In Encontro de estudos de estratégia, IV, Recife, 2009 - IV Encontro de Estudos de Estratégia. Recife: ANPAD.

Berryman, A. A. (2002). Population: A central concept for ecology? *Oikos*, *97*(3), 439–442. doi:10.1034/j.1600-0706.2002.970314.x

Bruderl, J., Preisendorfer, P., & Ziegler, R. (1992). Survival Chances of Newly Founded Business Organizations. *American Sociological Review*, *57*(2), 227–242. doi:10.2307/2096207

Burgelman, R. A. (1991). Intraorganizational Ecology of Strategy Making and Organizational Adaptation: Theory and Field Research. *Organization Science*, 239 – 262.

Camus, P. A., & Lima, M. (2002). Populations, metapopulations, and the open-closed dilemma: The conflict between operational and natural population concepts. *Oikos*, *97*(3), 433–438. doi:10.1034/j.1600-0706.2002.970313.x

Carroll, G. (1984). Organizational ecology. *Annual Review of Sociology*, *10*(1), 71–93. doi:10.1146/annurev.so.10.080184.000443

Carroll, G. R. (1983). A stochastic model of organizational mortality: Review and reanalysis. *Social Science Research*, *12*(4), 303–329. doi:10.1016/0049-089X(83)90022-4

Carroll, G. R., & Hannan, M. T. (2000). *The Demography of corporations and industries*. Princeton University Press. doi:10.1515/9780691186795

Clarke, A. E., & Star, S. L. (2004). Symbolic Interactionist Science, Technology, Information and Biomedicine Studies. In L. T. Reynolds & N. J. Herman-Kinney (Eds.), *Handbook of Symbolic Interactionism*. Rowman & Littlefield.

De Vos, A., Cumming, G. S., Moore, C. A., Maciejewski, K., & Duckworth, G. (2016). The relevance of spatial variation in ecotourism attributes for the economic sustainability of protected areas. *Ecosphere*, *7*(2), e01207. doi:10.1002/ecs2.1207

DiMaggio, P., & Powell, W. W. (1983). The iron cage revisited: Collective rationality and institutional isomorphism in organizational fields. *American Sociological Review*, *48*(2), 147–160. doi:10.2307/2095101

Dingwall, R., & Strong, P. M. (1985). The Interactional Study of Organizations: A Critique and Reformulation. *Urban Life*, *14*(2), 205–231. doi:10.1177/089124168501400204

Donaldson, L. (1995). *American Anti-Management Theories of Organization: A Critique of Paradigm Proliferation*. Cambridge University Press.

Eiesland, N., & Warner, R. S. (1998). Ecology: Seeing the congregation in Contest. In N. Ammerman, J. Carroll, C. Dudley, & W. McKinney (Eds.), *Studying congregations: A new handbook* (pp. 40–77). Abingdon Press.

Eilstrup-Sangiovanni, M. (2020). Death of international organizations. The organizational ecology of intergovernmental organizations, 1815–2015. *The Review of International Organizations*, *15*(2), 339–370. doi:10.100711558-018-9340-5

Freeman, J., Carrol, G. R., & Hannan, M. T. (1983). The Liability of Newness: Age Dependence in Organizational Death Rates. *American Sociological Review*, *48*(5), 692–710. doi:10.2307/2094928

Galison, P. (1996). Introduction: The Context of Disunity. In P. Galison & D. J. Stump (Eds.), *The Disunity of Science: Boundaries, Contexts, and Power* (pp. 1–33). Stanford University Press.

Gannett, L. (2003). Making populations: Bounding genes in space and time. *Philosophy of Science*, *70*(5), 989–1001. doi:10.1086/377383

Gerson, M. P. R. (1998). *The impact of fiscal policy variables on output growth*. Google Books.

Getz, G., & Andersson, T. (2016). Analyzing whole populations of festivals and events: An application of organizational ecology. *Journal of Policy Research in Tourism, Leisure & Events*, *8*(3), 249–273. doi:10.1080/19407963.2016.1158522

Gieryn, T. F. (1999). *Cultural Boundaries of Science: Credibility on the Line*. University of Chicago Press.

Gómez Cumpa, J. (2003). *Dossier del curso Sociología de la organización1* [Dossier of the Sociology of Organization course 1]. Escuela Profesional de Sociología Facultad de Ciencias Histórico-Sociales y Educación.

Hannan, M., & Freeman, J. (1993). *Organizational Ecology*. Harvard University Press.

Hannan, M. T. (2005). Ecologies of organizations: Diversity and identity. *The Journal of Economic Perspectives*, *19*(1), 51–70. doi:10.1257/0895330053147985

Hannan, M. T., Carroll, G. R., Dundon, E. A., & Torres, J. C. (1995). Organizational evolution in a multinational context: Entries of automobile manufacturers in Belgium, Britain, France, Germany, and Italy. *American Sociological Review*, *60*(4), 509–528. doi:10.2307/2096291

Hannan, M. T., & Freeman, J. (1977). The population ecology of organizations. *American Journal of Sociology*, *82*(5), 929–964. doi:10.1086/226424

Hannan, M. T., & Freeman, J. (1978). Internal politics of growth and decline. In M. Meyer (Ed.), *Environments and organizations*. Jossey-Bass.

Hannan, M. T., & Freeman, J. (1984). Structural inertia and organizational change. *American Sociological Review*, *49*(2), 149–164. doi:10.2307/2095567

Hannan, M. T., & Freeman, J. (1989). Organizations and social structure. In Organizational Ecology. Harvard U. Press.

Hannan, M. T. & Freman, J. (1991). Organizations and social structure. In *Organizational Ecology*. Harvard U. Press.

Hannan, M. T., Pólos, L., & Carroll, G. R. (2004). The evolution of inertia. *Industrial and Corporate Change*, *13*(1), 213–242. doi:10.1093/icc/13.1.213

Hannan, M. T., Pólos, L., & Carroll, G. R. (2007). *Logics of organization theory: Audiences, codes, and ecologies*. Princeton University Press.

Harrison, J. R. (2004, February). Models of growth in organizational ecology: A simulation assessment. *Industrial and Corporate Change*, *13*(1), 243–261. doi:10.1093/icc/13.1.243

Hawley, A. (1950). *Human ecology*. Roland.

Hogdson, G. M. (2001). Is Social Evolution Lamarckian or Darwinian? In J. Laurent & J. Nightingale (Eds.), *Darwinism and Evolutionary Economics* (pp. 87–118). Edward Elgar.

Hölzl, W. (2005). The Evolutionary Theory of The Firm: Routines, Complexity and Changes, Growth and Employment in Europe. Sustainability and Competitiveness, 2-18.

Jaeger, K., & Mykletun, R. (2009). The festivalscape of Finnmark. *Scandinavian Journal of Hospitality and Tourism*, *9*(2/3), 327–348. doi:10.1080/15022250903119520

Koremenos, B., Lipson, C., & Snidal, D. (2001). The rational design of international institutions. *International Organization*, *55*(4), 761–799. doi:10.1162/002081801317193592

Kormondy, E. (1994). *Conceptos de ecología*. Alianza.

Krebs, C. J. (2001). *Ecology: The experimental analysis of distribution and abundance* (5th ed.). Benjamin Cummings.

Lacey, H. (2000). Seeds and the Knowledge They Embody. *Peace Review*, *12*(4), 563–569. doi:10.1080/10402650020014654

Lomi, A. (1995). The Population Ecology of Organizational Founding: Location Dependence and Unobserved Heterogeneity. *Administrative Science Quarterly*, *40*(1), 111–144. doi:10.2307/2393702

McKelvey, B. (1978, September). Organizational Systematics: Taxonomic Lessons from Biology. *Management Science*, *24*(13), 1428–1440. doi:10.1287/mnsc.24.13.1428

McKelvey, B. (1982). *Organizational systematics: Taxonomy, evolution, classification*. University of California Press. doi:10.1525/9780520314696

McKelvey, B., & Aldrich, H. E. (1983). Populations, natural selection, and applied organizational science. *Administrative Science Quarterly*, *28*(1), 101–128. doi:10.2307/2392389

McPherson, M. (1983). An ecology of affiliations. *American Sociological Review*, *48*(4), 519–532. doi:10.2307/2117719

Miles, R. E. & Snow, C. C. (1978). *Organizational Strategy, Structure and Process*. McGraw-Hill.

Mintzberg, H. (1978). Patterns in strategy formation. *Management Science*, *24*(9), 934–948. doi:10.1287/mnsc.24.9.934

Nelson, R., & Winter, S. (1982). *An Evolutionary Theory of Economic Change*. Harvard University Press.

Ostrom, E. (1990). *Governing the Commons: The Evolution of Institutions for Collective Action*. Cambridge University Press. doi:10.1017/CBO9780511807763

Pina e Cunha, M., Vieira da Cunha, J., & Kamoche, K. (2003). Organizational Improvisation: What, When How and Why. *International Journal of Management Reviews*, *1*(3), 299–341. Advance online publication. doi:10.1111/1468-2370.00017

Porter, M. (1980). *Competitive strategy*. The Free Press.

Porter, M. (1985). *Competitive advantage*. The Free Press.

Reeves, M., & Deimler, M. (2011). *Adaptability: The new competitive advantage*. Harvard.

Rueda, L. I. (2022). *Teoria(s) Organizacional(es) Postmoderna(s) y la Gest(ac)ión del sujeto Postmoderno* [Tesis Doctoral]. Universidad Autónoma de Barcelona.

Ruef, M. (2000). The Emergence of Organizational Forms: A Community Ecology Approach. *American Journal of Sociology*, *106*(3), 3. doi:10.1086/318963

Salimath, M. S., & Jones, R. (2011). *Population ecology theory: Implications for sustainability*. Emerald Group Publishing Limited.

Shanks, C., Jacobson, H. K., & Kaplan, J. H. (1996). Inertia and change in the constellation of IGOs, 1981-1992. *International Organization*, *50*(4), 593–627. doi:10.1017/S002081830003352X

Singh, J. V., & Lumsden, Ch. J. (1990). Ecology Organizations: Theory and Investigate. *Annual Review of Sociology*, *16*, 161–195. doi:10.1146/annurev.so.16.080190.001113

Sole, R. V., & Bascompte, J. (1995). Spatial Self Organization Self-Organization in complex Ecosystems. Princeton University Press.

Soto Barrientos, F., & Viveros Caviedes, F. (2016). Organizaciones de la sociedad civil en Chile: Propuesta para financiamiento público y fortalecimiento institucional. *Polis*, *15*(45), 429–454. doi:10.4067/S0718-65682016000300021

Stieglitz, N., Knudsen, T., & Becker, M. C. (2016). Adaptation and inertia in dynamic environments. *Strategic Management Journal*, *37*(9), 1854–1864. doi:10.1002mj.2433

Strauss, A. L. (1991b). A Social World Perspective. In A. L. Strauss (Ed.), *Creating Sociological Awareness: Collective Images and Symbolic Representations* (pp. 233–244). Transaction Publishers.

Vázquez García, Á. W. (2022). Teorías del cambio organización: una síntesis [Theories of organization change: a synthesis]. *Revista Gestión Y Estrategia*, (39), 93-96.

Vereijken, P. (1992). A Methodic Way to More Sustainable Farming Systems. *Netherlands Journal of Agricultural Science*, *40*(3), 209–223. doi:10.18174/njas.v40i3.16507

Walsh, J. P., & Ungson, G. R. (1991). Organizational Memory. *Academy of Management Review*, *16*(1), 57–91. doi:10.2307/258607

Weaver-Hightower, M. (2008). An ecology metaphor for educational policy analysis: A call to complexity. *Educational Researcher*, *37*(3), 153–167. doi:10.3102/0013189X08318050

Wholey, D. R., & Brittain, J. W. (1986). Organizational ecology: Findings and implications. *Academy of Management Review*, *11*(3). Advance online publication. doi:10.5465/amr.1986.57140723

Zammuto, R. F. (1988). Organizational Adaptation: Some Implications of Organizational Ecology for Strategic Choice. *Journal of Management Studies*, *25*(2), 105–112. doi:10.1111/j.1467-6486.1988.tb00026.x

Chapter 7
Green Knowledge in Urban Green Innovation Spaces and Green Roofs

José G. Vargas-Hernandez

Posgraduate and Research Department, Tecnológico Mario Molina Unidad Zapopan, Mexico

Omar C. Vargas-González
ⓘ https://orcid.org/0000-0002-6089-956X
Tecnológico Nacional de México, Ciudad Guzmán, Mexico

ABSTRACT

This study aims to analyze the implications of green knowledge and technology in organizational green innovation, urban green innovation, and green roofs. The analysis is supported by the assumption that green sharing knowledge and technology is basic to organizational green innovation and urban green innovation areas practices, operations, and activities. The methods employed are based on the analytical-reflective and descriptive supported with the review of theoretical and empirical literature. The analysis concludes that green knowledge sharing is relevant to create and develop the green technology with positive implications for organizational green innovation, urban green innovation areas, and green roofs.

INTRODUCTION

The COVID-19 pandemic is a sanitary crisis that questions many activities to become greener and more sustainable. Sustainable and green are two concepts increasingly used to mean the same, however, sustainability refers to the persistence and indefinite future of necessary and desired characteristics of the human subsystem within and the ecosystem (Hodge, 1997).

Organizational environmental and green knowledge learning is linked to green technology for the environmental protection to stimulate organizational green innovation, urban green innovation areas and green roofs. Sustainable development is related to decision making in the economic and social effects (Wiering, Liefferink, Boezeman, Kaufmann, Crabbé, & Kurstjens, 2020). Sustainable development

DOI: 10.4018/978-1-6684-6815-9.ch007

meets the needs of the present without compromising the ability of future generations to meet their own needs (Brundtland, 1987).

Urban sustainability including social and economic has been highlighted as one of the leading features of cities (VisitBerlin (Ed.) 2017). Some green trends are proposed as smart city, sustainable city, and so forth. Use of green and ecofriendly technology offers more sustainability environment with zero gas emissions to the environment and some other opportunities and challenges.

People living in dense communities tend to use public urban green innovation spaces and public parks more frequently to have more relaxation time and may travel more to the countryside for leisure. Experimenting and testing new greener ways of conducting organizations concentrated on environmental sustainability, enable to introduce green innovations (Anderson et al., 2010; Stubbs and Cocklin, 2008). Organizations embracing the concept of saving money, by creating recycling programs and monitoring thermostats, focusing on environmental sustainability. Organizations may contribute to support nongovernmental agencies involved in environmental troublesome areas.

The frequency of use of a green space living environment support individuals to be satisfied with public spaces and improves the social space and the mental health (Hadavi, 2017). People using public and private urban green innovation spaces attach meanings, identity, and psychological experiences to diverse types of green spaces, as described in the Place identity integrated model and environmental representation (Bernardini and Irvine 2007). Research on green organization identity has focused on individual level (Chen, Chang, 2013; Chen, 2011). Green organizational identity supports individual tasks of organizational members related to the organizational environmental activities and strengthens the ability to cope with organizational green oriented conditions. Landscape connectivity has some differences between urban green innovation roofs and urban open space management.

Organizations are facing challenges regarding the compliance with green sustainability strategy. The deployment of a green strategy to face the negative effects that industrialization has on the environment. Organizational business sustainability considers the green growth, green branding, and green sustainable reporting. Branding sustainability enhance the ability of the organization to appeal customers concerned about the environment.

Green sustainable development combined with economic growth, social justice and progress and environmental security concepts are relevant issues in research such as green entrepreneurship in organic farming (Gupta, and Vegelin, 2016; Mohd, and Norhidayah, 2016; Savickiene, and Miceikiene, 2018; Ihnatenko, and Novak, 2018; Kucher, 2019; Shevchenko, and Petrenko, 2020, Skydan, Nykolyuk, Pyvovar, and Martynchuk, 2020). Not much research has addressed the integration of green roofs and urban green innovation space.

Organizations engage in green initiatives to develop sustainable competitive advantages and competitiveness (Wysocki, 2021; Galdeano-Gómez, Céspedes-Lorente, & Martínez-del-Río, 2008; López-Gamero, Claver-Cortés, & Molina-Azorín, 2008). Sustainable components of organizations and business achieve competitive advantage (Namkung and Jang, 2012; Chang and Fong 2010; Bansal, 2005 and Barnet, 2007). Organizational business systems are the foundation for any sustainable organizational business. Organizations are formulating and implementing green initiatives to attain sustainability and competitiveness (Chuang & Huang, 2015). The ecological partnership between organizations and society provides sustainable competitiveness.

The organizational ecological and sustainable procedures follow a strategic orientation (Fernandes & Solimun, 2017). Sustainability has been considered and an added cost, but nowadays is viewed as a sustainability strategy and tool to derive value and leads to innovation (Van Holt et al., 2020). An organizational shared vision enables development of green behaviors, making meaningful contributios (Larwood, Falbe, Kriger, Miesing, 1995; Tsai, Ghoshal, 1998; Oswald, Mossholder, Harris,1994).

BACKGROUND

Green Knowledge and Technology

New knowledge in green organizational and business models are uncertain and volatility in business ecosystem conditions, challenging risk management and decision making. Technological knowledge of economic, social, and environmental benefits of constructing green roofs enhances the good construction of green roofs without any problems of maintaining the roof vegetation. Organizational green knowledge shares issues adopting a multilevel framework to make contributions to green technology. Organizational management must formulate green knowledge and green technology.

Knowledge management of environmental issues is a source for learning, solving problems and creating competitiveness (Liao, Chang, Cheng, Kuo, 2004). Green knowledge management is an effective tool for organizational improvement in transformation environment (Raudeli ¯ unien˙ e, Davidavi˘cien ˙ e, Jakubavi˘cius, 2018). The dynamic complexity of organizational green innovation requires environmental knowledge learning (Li et al., 2019) and green technology. Organizational environmental green knowledge learning drives green innovation. Organizational environmental knowledge learning is linked to green technology for the environmental protection to stimulate green innovation (Redman, 2014).

Knowledge sharing is the basis for knowledge management (Zhang, Sundaresan, 2010). Green knowledge sharing in terms of sustainable development goals such as eliminating pollution, environmental protection, and SDGs, etc.) with other organizational members is good (Bock, Zmud, Kim, Lee, 2005). Green knowledge sharing is the behavior of organizational members who pass information, data and knowledge about green concerns and issues to other members and create new knowledge and learning opportunities to encourage others (Norton, Parker, Zacher, Ashkanasy, 2015; Chen, Chang, 2013).

Green Knowledge Sharing. GKS is the organizational members behavior which is keen to pass on personal information and new knowledge learning opportunities about green issues to other members (Bock, Zmud, Kim, Lee, 2005). Green property psychological ownership and green knowledge sharing are influenced by green organizational identity. Knowledge sharing of people under pressure of time is reduced (Chang, Chen, Yeh, Li, 2020).

Organizational knowledge sharing focuses on creating an atmosphere of environmental protection to create green knowledge sharing related to green issues. Green technology is a socio-environmental healing technology capable to reduce environmental damages and degradation while conserving natural resources. Sustainable green technologies used in processes and applications do not create footprint (Aithal & Aithal Shubhrajyotsna, 2016).

Urban green innovation technology can be transferred by public government and confidential business pursuing inclusive green growth and ensuring social integration by eradicating poverty of vulnerable groups and maintaining the footprint of humanity within the ecological boundaries. Building an inclusive and green organization of available and retained talent is an arduous task (Goulden, Mason & Frasch 2011; Pell, 1996; Brands & Fernandez-Mateo, 2017). Green roof technology is used to tackle social and environmental concerns to enhance climate resilience. Green plant based green chemistry principles are used for green synthesis, nanomaterials, and nanoparticles (Maas, and Hox, 2005). Green and eco-friendly nanotechnology based on green chemistry techniques tends to decrease the risks associated to industrial applications

Green eco-friendly nanotechnology solutions used in sustainable development goals reduces the technification threat. Environmental degradation and climate pose a threat to global sustainable development and the Sustainable Development Goals. The concept of achieving sustainable development goals by means of using and developing proven green ecofriendly nanotechnology processes further accelerates the spread and growth of many other systems and devices. Green nanotechnology solutions are critical in realizing sustainable development goals by eliminating the threat technification development processes.

Green nanotechnology treats with environmentally friendly processes of manufacturing and industrial use of nanomaterials able to minimize potential risks of environmental degradation and reduce health hazards. Green nanotechnology and nanomaterials solve many socio economic and environmental problems and improve the quality of life supporting the United Nations sustainable development goals which ca be realized by using green nanotechnology.

Green nanotechnology is based in miniature sized communication and computation devices and nano sensor devices, high density, and memory chips. Ensuring ecological communication among the stakeholders disclose the relevance of environmental concerns (Abimbola, Lim, Hillestad, Xie, & Haugland, 2010). Sustainable green nanotechnology principles and processes in the primary sector of the economy is related to the extraction of raw materials from nature but also in manufacturing and services. Green nanotechnology is used for renewable energy management systems in generation, transmission, and storage.

Long-term effects of human food are required by green manufactured nanomaterials designed according to principles of green nanotechnology complemented with current regulations aimed to address sustainable development of green technology. Manufactured and processed inorganic food has increased the cases of illnesses leading to healthy food safety. Green design and development of health and environment using nanoscale materials is a concern to improve sustainable solutions. Green synthesis methods can be used to take care of adverse effects on nanomaterials on the environment and user health. Complementarity of mixed methods to detect contradictions, improve the results of one method using the results of the other method and enhance the scope and breath for different components of research (Greene et al. 1989).

Manufacturing green nanoelectronics devices involves complexity in the shifting from silico-based to molecular nanomaterials-based devices. Green nanomaterials enable the network for smart city communications. Green nanotechnology develops miniaturized drones and bots equipped with artificial intelligence and bees, nanosatellites, and nano sensors to provide more visibility and nano-nuclear biological and chemical weapons. Adding nanoparticles to sustainable green nanotechnology improves the properties of construction materials. Green nanotechnology provides some special effect paints changing their color at different spaces and times. Green nanotechnology supports the design in multiple properties of the fashion industry.

Green nanotechnology in the service industry is intangible in nature and affected directly and indirectly. Green nanotechnology innovates in educational technology through higher quality and low-cost and ubiquitous online education. ICCT technologies working with green nanotechnology provide intelligent services in artificial intelligence, internet of things, cloud and quantum computing, 3D printing, etc. Green nanotechnology supports ICCT technologies to develop super-intelligent machines and human beings. Green nanotechnology improves the durability, speed, and reachability of digital entertainment instruments (Aithal & Aithal Shubhrajyotsna, 2018).

Organizational Green Innovation

Organizational green business innovations follow the principles, values and norms of economic concern, societal parity, and ecological accountability (Alawattage & Fernando, 2017). New green organizational innovations are created either in-house or external. Organizational green innovation activities are stimulated by green contexts-oriented factors. Organizations have attached more relevance to environmental issues based on green organizational identity that enhances organizational green innovation and competitiveness and ensures organizational competitive advantages (Geraie, Rad, 2015). Organizational identity theory and psychological ownership theory are combined to integrate a conceptual model.

Organizational green process innovation is friendly to the environment through developing processes of manufacturing goods according to their cycle (Chiou, Chan, Lettice, Chung, 2011; Kam-Sing Wong, 2012). Organizational green innovation and actions are designed to reduce adverse environmental consequences. There is a relationship between organizational green innovation strategy and actions because the green innovation behaviors conducted under a strategy.

Motivational mechanisms stimulate innovation to facilitate organizational green innovation. Motivated organizational stakeholders to pursue collective efforts towards green innovative outcomes with their teammates lead with values of organizational green innovation Norton, Parker, Zacher, Ashkanasy, 2015; Jabbour, Santos, Fonseca, Nagano, 2013). Meta-analytical research contends that prosocial motivation is a mechanism to link contextual factors and innovative and creative outcomes (Liu, Jiang, Shalley, Keem, Zhou, 2016).

Organizational green innovation addresses the potential risks and challenges of implementing innovative resources and inputs supported by green efficacy (Liu, Chen, Tao, 2015). Green organizational innovation is related to individual tasks of organizational environmental activities to strengthen the organization. Some demographic variables are related to green organizational innovation behaviors such as age. Older people are less likely to perform employee green behaviors using more innovative technologies and involving changing habits and interacting with others.

Sustainable green organizations encourage employees to participate in social and environmental. This often means encouraging employees to participate and get involved in the social and environmental initiatives such as promoting to refuse, reduce, repair, reuse, and recycle. Society gives relevance to environmental issues and concerns where green organizational identity enhancing organizational creativity and innovation and ensuring sustainable competitive advantages (Geraie, Rad, 2015). Social acceptance enables the organization to attain and develop sustainable organizational green competitiveness capability.

The green competitive advantage is the concept describing the conditions to hold a position in sustainable and ecological management and innovation of the firm which cannot be imitated by others (Lin & Chen, 2017). Resources and capabilities that are not imitable provide sustainable competitive advantage (Barney, 1991). The resource-based view of organizational research focuses on the characterization of organizations (Pereira & Vence, 2012) and organizational resources and capabilities (Fong & Chang, 2012; Marchi, 2012) such as organizational redundancy, innovation capabilities, network, embedding, strategy orientation and green innovation strategy as the drivers of green innovation practices.

Organizations depend on intangible resources to enhance environmental sustainability (Singh, Del Giudice, Chierici, & Graziano, 2020). In a resource intensive sector, a green pioneer organization must have an organizational model (Elkington,1994) with a social and environmental impact.

Human resources green management deals with valuable organizational resources and assets considered based on environmental sustainability. There is evidence that the workforce engages strongly about the environmental sustainability development and become more organizational committed and satisfied. Human resource green management is engaged in organizational environmental sustainability management (Wirtenberg, Harmon, Russell, & Fairfield, 2007; Shoeb and Nisar 2015).

Green dynamic capability is in the nature within the organization processes. The green dynamic capabilities are permanently dependable in the organizations (Chen, 2008).

URBAN GREEN INNOVATION SPACES AND GREEN ROOFS

The rapid growth of the urban population and the low rate of economic development due to the pandemic, are leading to serious civilization problems, among others the lack of urban greener innovations spaces, pollution, and lack of health. Smart growth is supported by sustainable growth based on adoption of greener, efficient technologies, inclusive growth, fostering employment and social cohesion (Gunn, & Mintrom, 2016). Organizations must take an approach to stay in inclusive green organizations embracing elements such as equity and social justice needed to create goals, formulate, and implement strategies and develop public commitment (Johnson, 2017).

Organizational green innovation refers to the innovation that emphasizes the implementation of organizational green culture, environmental prevention of pollution and waste reduction to enhance organizational sustainability. Urban green innovation areas are increasing in green metropolis driven by the preservation and expansion of sustainable environmental development (Kalandides, Grésillon, 2021).

Urban green innovation spaces must be defined by the limits of construction and protection. The interactions of people and urban green innovation spaces are divided in public and private (Vijayaraghavan, 2016). Public and private urban green innovation spaces co-exist and can be incorporated green roofs as open green spaces aimed to use multi-functionality framed in an effective landscape management. Public and private green spaces have differences in perception (Coolen & Meesters, 2012) although they should co-exist (Mesimaki, et al. 2017).

People have different perceptions on private and green urban spaces with social identity and environmental sustainability. Green behaviors are defined as the actions and behaviors on which employees engage linked with and contribute to environmental sustainability (Ones & Dilchert, 2012). This concept includes voluntary green behaviors beyond the job tasks referred as organizational citizenship, also considered as task-related environmental behavior (Boiral & Paillé, 2012; Bissing-Olson, Iyer, Fielding, & Zacher, 2013). Sustainable development and green jobs guidelines are adopted by the international labor organization (ILO) for a transition towards environmentally sustainable societies and economies (ILO, 2015).

Public parks contribute to develop more community social interactions and livability while private gardens are paces for freedom and enjoying life (Coolen & Meesters, 2012). Residents attach to open and green spaces removed from urban plans of the sustainable, green, and intelligent city. The minimum green urban areas should be fifty m2 per urban resident (Russo & Cirella, 2018).

The disappearance of green urban areas due to residential and commercial purposes, enhanced by the urban sprawl, leads to loss of habitats, biodiversity, and recreation areas, and decrease of natural resources and elements (Burszta-Adamiak, Fiałkiewicza, 2019). Urban green spaces with high social and environmental vulnerability are the most urbanized areas with high land temperature might be prioritized for the implementation of urban green innovation areas and green roofs.

Traditional streets can be transformed into green urban connecting areas considered as an open space system and park lands. An urban green innovation belt prevents urban expansion and urban sprawl by merging with nearby settlements. Greenbelt conserves accessibility of open spaces along roadways and connect to a regional trail. Nevertheless, greenbelt was not successful to prevent urban expansion and sprawl but facilitates the access to open spaces (Maruani and Amit-Cohen 2007).

Intensification of investments to develop accessible green spaces conceived to cover economic, social and leisure needs, and activities contribute to create the sense of community and respond to the pressures of construction. Urban green innovation areas are open to enhance urban green innovation space networks and extend the green infrastructure with the functions of green roofs (Fung, 2018). Green infrastructure is the urban physical environment in a network of green open spaces that brings economic, social, and environmental benefits to residents of communities in cities, towns, and villages (TEP 2005, 1).

Green infrastructure is a way to create an attractive environment, increase the urban resilience benefits by better managing stormwater, mitigating the urban heat island effect, purifying air. Green roofs are considered passive open green spaces that have environmental benefits and provide open spaces for more urban livability (Mesimaki, et al. 2017). Eco roofs are required for new city infrastructures and facilities. Multi-functional urban green innovation infrastructure should allocate funding for green initiatives of development.

The benefits of urban green innovation infrastructure include multiple socio-ecological, and economic benefits. Green roofs have environmental and social benefits used as multidimensional green infrastructure. Green roofs have some comprehensive benefits. Green roofs environmental benefits are the measure to enhance climate resilience and energy efficiency and provide development opportunities. Development of urban green innovation roofs is driven on aesthetic reasons, climate resilience and to increase property values of buildings. Green building plays a critical role in dealing with socioenvironmental issues serving as an organizational platform for financial savings. Suitable buildings for green roofs could be improved by including roof decks and courtyards. Urban green innovation roofs developments mismatch in some places and areas where are needed to be prioritized.

Scholars have applied quantitative and qualitative analysis to address the needs and perceptions of people on green roofs. The environmental effectiveness of green roofs should improve public health and connect the social needs of vulnerable people (Vijayaraghavan 2016). Green roofs and solar and living roofs considered a multi-benefit asset bringing significant economic benefits beyond stormwater management, energy efficiency for cooling, improving air quality, reducing urban heat island. Loss of green spaces intensify heat island effect and storm water runoffs. The development of urban green innovation spaces and roofs are required to comply with regulations on stormwater control. A motivation program for the installation of eco roofs provides incentives to better management of the stormwater.

Green roofs have historically evolved from the hanging gardens in Babylon embracing the aesthetic values and facilitating the human interactions and increase the insulation. Le Corbusier applied green roofs to modern architecture. (Berardi, GhaffarianHoseini and GhaffarianHoseini 2014). In Germany followed by France and Switzerland occurred the research and implementation of green roofs. In Portland, USA in 2005 requires the city-owned buildings to build green roof while Toronto passed a bylaw requiring all the new developed buildings. In Tokyo, the new constructed buildings must have green roofs (Vijayaraghavan 2016).

Urban green innovation areas should provide spaces for green infrastructure solutions such as the building green roofs, which have beneficial influence on the urban environment. The stage of operation of green infrastructure is the maintenance solutions. The green infrastructure is single function derived from the ability to effectively manage stormwater and focusing on ecological landscape conservation than social and economic benefits (Mell 2010). Urban green innovation roofs integrated into open space management have multifunctional opportunities to develop green infrastructure and benefits in urban communities and neighborhoods. Private and public green roofs as open spaces a multi-functional green infrastructure and should accommodate the urban open space needs of residents (Meerow and Newell 2017)

Well-developed urban green innovation infrastructure needs to be supported by a multi-faceted approach. The increasing awareness of green roofs to alleviate global and local environmental impacts. Vegetated green roofs reduce CO_2 in the atmosphere naturally sequestered through the photosynthesis processes (Rowe 2011). It has been confirmed the capacity of green roofs to retain rainwater, reduce air pollutants and improve microclimate that have a positive influence in urban heat island effect (Shafi que, Kim & Rafi q, 2018; Burszta-Adamiak, Stańczyk & Łomotowski, 2019).

There are diverse types of intensive and extensive green roofs which include vegetation with different soil depth and weight, irrigation, plant species and maintenance. Urban green innovation projects include urban gardening, permaculture, guerrilla gardening, smart city and building architecture. Productive urban green innovation combines urban agriculture, allotment gardens and self-sufficiency culture ecologically motivated (Plattform produktives Stadtgrün 2020; Chen, Lin, Lin, Hung, Chang, Huang, 2020).

Mitigation of greenhouse gas emission technique to improve the environmental impact of agriculture needs to consider animal welfare the largest anthropogenic contributor (Llonch, Haskell; Dewhurst; Turner, 2017; Reisinger, Clark, 2018; Kucher, Heldak, and Orlenko, 2018). Wasteland spaces can be converted into a place of productive greenery and developed into natural and green innovation areas that preserve and increase the ecological value and be used also as place for joint creation and learning, (Nachhaltiges Berlin, 2020; Green Berlin, 2020).

Rehabilitation of buildings using energy optimization should consider the creation of new alternative green spaces transformed into green innovation areas for free recreational purposes. Green roofs provide leisure spaces and enhance aesthetical values of buildings (Sutton, 2014) reduce carbon footprint in urban areas (Ugai, 2016) and direct water footprint (Fialkiewicz et al., 2018). Matching urban places needing urban green innovation areas and green roofs in suitable buildings to determine opportunities to implement in communities and neighborhood

Administrative and technical support are necessary in designing, constructing, developing, and maintaining urban green innovation areas and green roofs. This task recommendation enhances the allocation of urban green innovation areas based on the structural design of buildings and the surrounding environmental characteristics in the community. The design and construction of green roofs need to consider the plant species and the development of small fauna.

The construction and application of green roofs can be achieved in large urban areas are located near another urban constructed areas and should not be single investments. Stovin, Vesuviano & Kasmin (2012) calculate that the surface of roofs accounts for almost 50% of the sealed urban areas with the potential for urban green innovation roofs. Green roofs decrease the costs for discharging snowmelt and stormwater. The infrastructure of green storm water initiative reduces greenhouse gas emissions and improves the air quality. The development initiatives of green roofs are linked with storm water management to meet the flood management control required

Some studies evaluate the functionality and usefulness of constructing green roofs, such as the Forschungsanstalt Landschaftsentwicklung Landschaftsbau (FLL) guidelines (FLL, 2002). The FLL guidelines are used as the basis for the construction of green roofs. Vegetation on green roof infiltration reduces the stormwater runoff. Vegetated surfaces may utilize public facilities to demonstrate a mandate of a green buffer surrounded by parking facilities that may also function as a stormwater infiltration. Green stormwater infrastructure reduces the demand of grey stormwater infrastructure, enhancing the climate resilience.

Investments in green roofs increases the biologically active areas in urban areas and towns to mitigate heat island, reduce carbon emissions, and improve the flood control. Cities have created incentives and regulatory programs to encourage implementation of urban green innovation areas and green roofs. The incentive programs for green roofs focus on the local level should be tied to storm water management and combined sewers overflow control, improve water quality and quantity. Local government uses green roofs as infrastructure to control stormwater and reduce water pollution.

Local building codes must allow green roofs exempted from the building floor area and related to open spaces. The incentives for zoning to encourage the implementation of the urban green innovation roof should include the development of parking landscapes as one measure adopted in a stormwater management plan that may provide solutions (Murray 2017).

The development of green roofs value investments as an additional incentive for potential customers. Meeting the ecological needs of customers (Jain and Kaur 2004). There is a trend of organizations to shift operations towards the direction of environment-friendly processes despite the challenges of customer cynicism regarding organizational green actions (Kumar & Christodoulopoulou, 2014). Co-financing and local legal regulations for the construction of green roofs are most often used incentives. Green development finance has been assigned to Multilateral Development Banks, alongside public-private partnerships (PPPs) and new forms of finance, blended finance, bond instruments, green bonds, social impact bonds and development impact bonds. Urban green innovation roofs are the result of the implementation of motivational tools and other incentives for the different stakeholders.

The implementation of tools to motivate public and private investors to construct green roofs requires a program to gather information to identify future incentives and to formulate recommendations for the construction of green roofs in green urban areas. The results of reasonable investments in urban green innovation areas and green roof should be to receive the return on investment within certain period in relation with regulations. Efficiency of operations in cost-savings are the concern of green investments.

The growing interest in green roofs in urban areas comes with the introduction of incentives. However, the limited incentives for green roof investments rise the construction costs. Introducing incentives for green roofs may increase biologically active areas by introducing nature-based solutions. The implementation of incentives is leading to the realization of green roofs in local spatial development plans.

Documenting the existing locations of urban green innovation areas and green roofs and compiling to determine spatial development patterns including details of purposes, types, size, locations, etc., focusing more on the comparison of social and environmental vulnerability among the various places. Local governments are relevant actors in promoting environmentally friendly solutions by granting financial and non-financial subsidies, regulate eligibility and increasing the surface area of urban green innovation roof spaces.

The existence of types of barriers encourages local authorities to improve the use of incentives for the creation and functioning of urban green innovation areas and urban green innovation roofs. The most commonly use of incentives are the direct ones and legal regulations for the construction of regulations (Mentens, Raes & Hermy, 2006). Incentives must be translated from sufficient interest into motivation for the excessively strict requirements for the construction of green roofs such as the minimum surface area, to become eligible for co-financing and tax allowance.

Market demand-related incentives such as promotional instruments, are tools to determine demand for buildings with greenery in comparison to traditional. The implementation of financial and non-financial incentives is a crucial factor for the green roofs as a relevant element of urban environment (Brudermann & Sangkakool, 2017). Financial incentives include subsidies or donations granted to reimburse costs of investments that are aimed to support potential investors.

The non-financial incentives include instruments of gratification. Other financial incentives are real property tax allowances to green roofs constructed depending on the surface area of buildings. The financial and non-financial incentive programs must be complementary and flexibility in terms of the different options of greenery design as the determining the subsidy amount of creating surfaces that are water-permeable along with incentives in tax allowances in snowmelt and stormwater.

The development of urban green innovation areas and green roofs are limited to regulations in local spatial development plans on incentives not only limited to co-financing. Some indicators to measure the adaptability of urban green innovation areas and green roofs are more effective to tackle environmental concerns such as the land temperature and stormwater. Environmental vulnerability indicators in stormwater flow, air quality and pollution are considered in the analysis to acknowledge the priorities of all actors and stakeholders in any urban community.

The development of rural and urban green innovation tourism close to nature and based on settlements is becoming more relevant for the impact on green economy and ecology, with the self-employment of residents to provide environmentally accommodation and food to the visitors (Tomashuk, Baldynyuk, 2021, Kolomiets, Tomashuk, 2021, Mazur, Tomashuk, 2019). The green economy development and the pursuit of environmental protection is bringing profits to the organizations (Chen, Lai, Wen, 2006).

CONCLUSION

This study analyzes the organizational environmental and green knowledge learning is linked to green technology for the environmental protection to stimulate organizational green innovation, urban green innovation areas and green roofs.

Organizations transform to mitigate and neutralize the environmental impact and to adapt environmental sustainability. Green transformation is a multifaceted process incorporating interconnected and overlapping processes posing several managerial challenges. Environmental community involvement promotes and improve the natural environment aiming to sustainable growth of society, inspiring for voluntary participation in social activities. The green government should make and secure access to affordable sustainable housing in urban green innovation spaces and open buildings to create an urban social cohesion process consolidated in urban social movements.

Organizational networks are vital to connecting each other in the space of a green movement. The environmental movements along the nongovernment organizations and environmental foundations lack of racial diversity despite the efforts to increase diversity and inclusion (Johnson, 2019) Residents also express their intentions to be involved in discussions and debates to develop a green urban framework.

Adding green components to technology can become sustainable green technologies able to avoid degradation and provide clean environment. Green roof technology is used to tackle social and environmental concerns to enhance climate resilience. Green roof is related to be linked to resilience, restorative, and accessible. Green nanotechnology represents opportunities and challenges in industry to encourage growth by supporting nanotechnology usage.

Gain competitive advantage through the implementation of a sustainable organizational strategy is relevant for the survival. The organizational green shared vision should involve sustainable business goals. Long-term organizational green innovation strategy must stimulate followers to implement green operations. Organizational socio ecological strategies are formulated an implemented to achieve green competitiveness (Wang, Hu, Dai, & Burns, 2021).

FUTURE RESEARCH DIRECTION

This research contributes to a valuable input for both decision making and research in the field of green knowledge in urban innovation spaces and green roofs to explore these issues in greater depth in further research.

Further research must be conducted on the implications of green knowledge creation and technology development in organizational green innovation, urban green areas of innovation, and urban green roofs.

Further research related to supported programs for the distribution and estimated benefits of urban green roofs suggesting optimal siting in urban green areas, seeking to capture high-level trends in infrastructure filters, which should be deeply examined in future research.

REFERENCES

Abimbola, T., Lim, M., Hillestad, T., Xie, C., & Haugland, S. A. (2010). Innovative corporate social responsibility: The founder's role in creating a trustworthy corporate brand through "green innovation." *Journal of Product and Brand Management*, *19*(6), 440–451. doi:10.1108/10610421011085758

Aithal, P. S., & Aithal, Shubhrajyotsna (2016). Nanotechnology Innovations and Commercialization – Opportunities, Challenges & Reasons for Delay. *Proceedings of National Conference on Changing Perspectives of Management, IT, and Social Sciences in Contemporary Environment*, 14, 1-12. 10.5815/ijem.2016.06.02

Aithal, P. S. & Aithal, S. (2018). Nanotechnology based Innovations and Human Life Comfortability –Are we Marching towards Immortality? *International Journal of Applied Engineering and Management Letters*, *2*(2), 71–86.

Alawattage, C., & Fernando, S. (2017). Postcoloniality in corporate social and environmental accountability. *Accounting, Organizations and Society*, *60*, 1–20. doi:10.1016/j.aos.2017.07.002

Anderson, R., Amodeo, M., & Harzfeld, J. (2010). Changing business cultures from within. The World Watch Institute. W.W. Norton.

Bansal, P. (2005). Evolving sustainably: A longitudinal study of corporate sustainable development. *Strategic Management Journal*, *26*(3), 197–218. doi:10.1002mj.441

Barnet, M. L. (2007). Stakeholder influence capacity and the variability of financial returns to corporate social responsibility. *Academy of Management Review*, *33*(3), 794–816. doi:10.5465/amr.2007.25275520

Barney, J. (1991). Firm Resources and Sustained Competitive Advantage. *Journal of Management, 17*(1), 99–120. doi:10.1177/014920639101700108

Berardi, U., GhaffarianHoseini, A. H., & GhaffarianHoseini, A. (2014). State-of-the-art analysis of the environmental benefits of green roofs. *Applied Energy, 115*, 411–428. doi:10.1016/j.apenergy.2013.10.047

Berlin, N. (2020). *Stadt der grünen Trends-Wie Berlin den Weg der urbanen Nachhaltigkeit geht.* Available online: https://about.visitberlin.de/nachhaltiges-berlin

Bernardini & Irvine. (2007). The 'nature' of urban sustainability: private or public greenspaces? *Transactions on Ecology and the Environment,* 661-673.

Bissing-Olson, M. J., Iyer, A., Fielding, K. S., & Zacher, H. (2013). Relationships between daily affect and pro-environmental behavior at work: The moderating role of pro-environmental attitude. *Journal of Organizational Behavior, 175*(2), 156–175. doi:10.1002/job.1788

Bock, G. W., Zmud, R. W., Kim, Y. G., & Lee, J. N. (2005). Behavioral intention formation in knowledge sharing: Examining the roles of extrinsic motivators, social-psychological forces, and organizational climate. *Management Information Systems Quarterly, 2005*(29), 87–112. doi:10.2307/25148669

Boiral, O., & Paillé, P. (2012). Organizational citizenship behaviour for the environment: Measurement and validation. *Journal of Business Ethics, 109*(4), 431–445. doi:10.100710551-011-1138-9

Brands, R. A., & Fernandez-Mateo, I. (2017). Leaning out: How negative recruitment experiences shape women's decisions to compete for executive roles. *Administrative Science Quarterly, 62*(3), 405–442. doi:10.1177/0001839216682728

Brudermann, T., & Sangkakool, T. (2017). Green roofs in temperate climate cities in Europe - An analysis of key decision factors. *Urban Forestry & Urban Greening, 21*, 224–234. doi:10.1016/j.ufug.2016.12.008

Brundtland, G. (1987). *Our Common Future: The World Commission on Environment and Development.* Oxford University Press.

Burszta-Adamiak, E., & Fiałkiewicza, W. (2019). Review of green roof incentives as motivators for the expansion of green infrastructure in European cities. *Scientific Review – Engineering and Environmental Sciences, 28*(4), 641–652. DOI doi:10.22630/PNIKS.2019.28.4.5

Burszta-Adamiak, E., Stańczyk, J., & Łomotowski, J. (2019). Hydrological performance of green roofs in the context of the meteorological factors during the 5-year monitoring period. *Water and Environment Journal: the Journal / the Chartered Institution of Water and Environmental Management, 33*(1), 144–154. doi:10.1111/wej.12385

Chang, N. J., & Fong, C. M. (2010). Green product quality, green corporate image, green customer satisfaction, and green customer loyalty. *African Journal of Business Management, 4*(13), 2336–2344.

Chang, T. W., Chen, Y. S., Yeh, Y. L., & Li, H. X. (2020). Sustainable consumption models for customers: Investigating the significant antecedents of green purchase behavior from the perspective of information asymmetry. *Journal of Environmental Planning and Management, 2020*, 1–21.

Chen, Y. S. (2008). The driver of green innovation and green image–green core competence. *Journal of Business Ethics, 81*(3), 531–543. doi:10.100710551-007-9522-1

Chen, Y. S., & Chang, C. H. (2013). The determinants of green product development performance: Green dynamic capabilities, green transformational leadership, and green creativity. *Journal of Business Ethics, 2013*(116), 107–119. doi:10.100710551-012-1452-x

Chen, Y. S., Lai, S. B., & Wen, C. T. (2006). The influence of green innovation performance on corporate advantage in Taiwan. *Journal of Business Ethics, 2006*(67), 331–339. doi:10.100710551-006-9025-5

Chen, Y. S., Lin, S. H., Lin, C. Y., Hung, S. T., Chang, C. W., & Huang, C. W. (2020). Improving green product development performance from green vision and organizational culture perspectives. *Corporate Social Responsibility and Environmental Management, 2020*(27), 222–231. doi:10.1002/csr.1794

Chiou, T. Y., Chan, H. K., Lettice, F., & Chung, S. H. (2011). The influence of greening the suppliers and green innovation on environmental performance and competitive advantage in Taiwan. *Transp. Res. Logist. Transp. Rev, 2011*(47), 822–836. doi:10.1016/j.tre.2011.05.016

Coolen, H., & Meesters, J. (2012). Private and public green spaces: Meaningful but different settings. *Journal of Housing and the Built Environment, 27*(1), 49–67. doi:10.100710901-011-9246-5

Elkington, J. (1994). Towards the sustainable corporation: Win-win-win business strategies for sustainable development. *Cal. Manag. Rev., 36*(3), 90-100.

Fernandes, A. A. R., & Solimun. (2017). The mediating effect of strategic orientation and innovations on the effect of environmental uncertainties on the performance of business in the Indonesian aviation industry. *International Journal of Law and Management, 59*(6), 1269–1278. doi:10.1108/IJLMA-10-2016-0087

Fialkiewicz, W., Burszta-Adamiak, E., Kolonko-Wiercik, A., Manzardo, A., Loss, A., Mikovits, C., & Scipioni, A. (2018). Simplified direct water footprint model to support urban water management. *Water (Basel), 10*(5), 630. doi:10.3390/w10050630

Fong, C. M., & Chang, N. J. (2012). The impact of green learning orientation on proactive environmental innovation capability and firm performance. *African Journal of Business Management, 6*(32), 727–735.

Forschungsanstalt Landschaftsentwicklung Landschaftsbau. (2002). *Dachbegrünungsrichtlinie. Richtlinien für die Planung, Ausführung und Pfl ege von Dachbegrünungen* [Green roof policy. Guidelines for the planning, execution, and maintenance of green roofs]. Bonn: Forschungsanstalt Landschaftsentwicklung Landschaftsbau.

Fung, K. L. (2018). *Expanding the green network on rooftops: A study of integrating green roofs as a part of urban green innovation space planning* (Order No. 10932095). Available from ProQuest One Academic. (2124999351). Retrieved from http://wdg.biblio.udg.mx:2048/login?url=https://www.proquest.com/dissertations-theses/expanding-green-network-on-rooftops-study/docview/2124999351/se-2?accountid=28915 https://www.proquest.com/docview/2124999351?pqorigsite=gscholar&fromopenview=true

Galdeano-Gómez, E., Céspedes-Lorente, J., & Martínez-del-Río, J. (2008). Environmental performance and spillover effects on productivity: Evidence from horticultural firms. *Journal of Environmental Management*, *88*(4), 1552–1561. doi:10.1016/j.jenvman.2007.07.028 PMID:17825476

Geraie, M. S., & Rad, F. M. (2015). Mediator role of the organizational identity green in relationship between total quality management and perceived innovation with sustainable competitive advantage. *International Journal of Biology, Pharmacy and Allied Sciences*, *2015*(4), 266–276.

Goulden, M., Mason, M. A., & Frasch, K. (2011). Keeping women in the science pipeline. *The Annals of the American Academy of Political and Social Science*, *638*(1), 141–162. doi:10.1177/0002716211416925

Green Berlin. (2020). *Capital of Green Trends: How Berlin leads the Way in Urban Sustainability*. Available online: https://about. visitberlin.de/en/greenberlin

Greene, J. C., Caracelli, V. J., & Graham, W. F. (1989). Toward a conceptual framework for mixed-method evaluation designs. *Educational Evaluation and Policy Analysis*, *11*(3), 255–274. doi:10.3102/01623737011003255

Gunn, A., & Mintrom, M. (2016). Higher Education Policy Change in Europe: Academic Research Funding and the Impact Agenda. *European Education*, *48*(4), 241–257. doi:10.1080/10564934.2016.1237703

Gupta, J., & Vegelin, C. (2016). Sustainable development goals and inclusive development. *International Environmental Agreement: Politics, Law and Economics*, *16*(3), 433–448. doi:10.100710784-016-9323-z

Hadavi, S. (2017). Direct and indirect effects of the physical aspects of the environment on mental well-being. *Environment and Behavior*, *2017*(49), 1071–1104. doi:10.1177/0013916516679876

Hodge, T. (1997). Toward a conceptual framework for assessing progress toward sustainability. *Social Indicators Research*, *1997*(40), 5–98. doi:10.1023/A:1006847209030

Ihnatenko, M., & Novak, N. (2018). Development of regional programs for the development of agrarian enterprises with organic production based on the European and international experience. *Baltic Journal of Economic Studies*, *4*(4), 126–133. doi:10.30525/2256-0742/2018-4-4-126-133

ILO. (2015). *News*. https://www.ilo.org/global/topics/green-jobs/news/WCMS_422575/lang--en/index. htm

Jabbour, C. J. C., Santos, F. C. A., Fonseca, S. A., & Nagano, M. S. (2013). Green teams: Understanding their roles in the environmental management of companies located in Brazil. *Journal of Cleaner Production*, *2013*(46), 58–66. doi:10.1016/j.jclepro.2012.09.018

Jain, S. K., & Kaur, G. (2004). Green marketing: An Indian perspective. *Decision*, *31*(2), 161–209.

Johnson, S. K. (2017). What 11 CEOs have learned about championing diversity. *Harvard Business Review*.

Johnson, S. K. (2019). *Leaking Talent How People of Color are Pushed Out of Environmental Organizations*. www.diversegreen.org https://diversegreen.org/research/leaking-talent/

Kalandides, A., & Grésillon, B. (2021). The Ambiguities of "Sustainable" Berlin. *Sustainability*, *2021*(13), 1666. doi:10.3390u13041666

Kam-Sing Wong, S. (2012). The influence of green product competitiveness on the success of green product innovation: Empirical evidence from the Chinese electrical and electronics industry. *European Journal of Innovation Management, 2012*(15), 468–490. doi:10.1108/14601061211272385

Kolomiets, T.V., & Tomashuk, I.V. (2021). Entrepreneurship and development of rural areas in Ukraine. *Colloquium-Journal, 9*(96), 29-42.

Kucher, A. (2019), *Sustainable soil management in the formation of competitiveness of agricultural enterprises.* Academic Publishing House «Talent». . doi:10.13140/RG.2.2.19554.07366

Kucher, L., Heldak, M., & Orlenko, A. (2018). Project management in organic agricultural production. *Agricultural and Resource Economics, 4*(3), 104–128. doi:10.22004/ag.econ.281753

Kumar, V., & Christodoulopoulou, A. (2014). Sustainability and branding: An integrated perspective. *Industrial Marketing Management, 43*(1), 6–15. doi:10.1016/j.indmarman.2013.06.008

Larwood, L., Falbe, C. M., Kriger, M. P., & Miesing, P. (1995). Structure and meaning of organizational vision. *Academy of Management Journal, 1995*(38), 740–769. doi:10.2307/256744

Liao, S. H., Chang, J. C., Cheng, S. C., & Kuo, C. M. (2004). Employee relationship and knowledge sharing: A case study of a Taiwanese finance and securities firm. *Knowledge Management Research and Practice, 2004*(2), 24–34. doi:10.1057/palgrave.kmrp.8500016

Lin, Y. H., & Chen, Y. S. (2017). Determinants of green competitive advantage: The roles of green knowledge sharing, green dynamic capabilities, and green service innovation. *Quality & Quantity, 51*(4), 1663–1685. doi:10.100711135-016-0358-6

Liu, D., Jiang, K., Shalley, C. E., Keem, S., & Zhou, J. (2016). Motivational mechanisms of employee creativity: A meta-analytic examination and theoretical extension of the creativity literature. *Organizational Behavior and Human Decision Processes, 2016*(137), 236–263. doi:10.1016/j.obhdp.2016.08.001

Liu, J., Chen, J., & Tao, Y. (2015). Innovation Performance in New Product Development Teams in China's Technology Ventures: The Role of Behavioral Integration Dimensions and Collective Efficacy. *Journal of Product Innovation Management, 2015*(32), 29–44. doi:10.1111/jpim.12177

Llonch, P., Haskell, M. J., Dewhurst, R. J., & Turner, S. P. (2017). Current available strategies to mitigate greenhouse gas emissions in livestock systems: An animal welfare perspective. *Animal, 2017*(11), 274–284. doi:10.1017/S1751731116001440 PMID:27406001

López-Gamero, M. D., Claver-Cortés, E., & Molina-Azorín, J. F. (2008). Complementary resources and capabilities for an ethical and environmental management: A qual/quan study. *Journal of Business Ethics, 82*(3), 701–732. doi:10.100710551-007-9587-x

Maas, C. J., & Hox, J. J. (2005). Sufficient sample sizes for multilevel modeling. *Methodology, 2005*(1), 86–92. doi:10.1027/1614-2241.1.3.86

Marchi, V. D. (2012). Environmental innovation and R&D cooperation: Empirical evidence from Spanish manufacturing firms. *Research Policy, 41*(3), 614–623. doi:10.1016/j.respol.2011.10.002

Maruani, T., & Amit-Cohen, I. (2007). Open Space planning models: A review of approaches and methods. *Landscape and Urban Planning, 81*(1-2), 1–13. doi:10.1016/j.landurbplan.2007.01.003

Mazur, K. V., & Tomashuk, I. V. (2019). Governance, and regulation as an indispensable condition for developing the potential of rural areas. *Baltic Journal of Economic Studies, 5*(5), 67–78. doi:10.30525/2256-0742/2019-5-5-67-78

Meerow, S., & Newell, J. P. (2017). Detroit, Spatial planning for multifunctional green infrastructure: Growing resilience. *Landscape and Urban Planning, 62-75.*

Mell, I. C. (2010). *Green infrastructure: Concepts, perceptions, and its use in spatial planning* [Doctoral Thesis]. School of Architecture, Planning and Landscape Newcastle University.

Mentens, J., Raes, D., & Hermy, M. (2006). Green roofs as a tool for solving the rainwater runoff problem in the urbanized 21st century? *Landscape and Urban Planning, 77*(3), 217–226. doi:10.1016/j.landurbplan.2005.02.010

Mesimaki, M., Hauru, K., Kotze, D. J., & Lehvavirta, S. (2017). Neo-spaces for urban livability? Urbanities' versatile mental image of green roofs in the Helsinki metropolitan area, Finland. *Land Use Policy, 61*, 587–600. doi:10.1016/j.landusepol.2016.11.021

Mohd, H. A., & Norhidayah, S. (2016), Sustainable food production: insights of Malaysian halal small and medium sized enterprises. *International Journal of Production Economics, 181*(B), 303–314. . doi:10.1016/j.ijpe.2016.06.003

Murray, N. (2017). Urban disaster risk governance. A systemic review. PPI-Centre. UCL Institute of Education.

Namkung, Y., & Jang, S. (2013). Effects of restaurant green practices on brand equity formation: Do green practices really matter? *International Journal of Hospitality Management, 33*(2), 85–95. doi:10.1016/j.ijhm.2012.06.006

Norton, T. A., Parker, S. L., Zacher, H., & Ashkanasy, N. M. (2015). Employee green behavior: A theoretical framework, multilevel review, and future research agenda. *Organization & Environment, 2015*(28), 103–125. doi:10.1177/1086026615575773

Ones, D. S., & Dilchert, S. (2012). Employee green behaviors. In D. S. S. E. Jackson (Ed.), *Managing human resource for environmental sustainability* (pp. 85–116). Jossey-Bass.

Oswald, S. L., Mossholder, K. W., & Harris, S. G. (1994). Vision salience and strategic involvement: Implications for psychological attachment to organization and job. *Strategic Management Journal, 1994*(15), 477–489. doi:10.1002mj.4250150605

Pell, A. N. (1996). Fixing the leaky pipeline: Women scientists in academia. *Journal of Animal Science, 74*(11), 2843–2848. doi:10.2527/1996.74112843x PMID:8923199

Pereira, Á., & Vence, X. (2012). Key business factors for eco-innovation: An overview of recent firm-level empirical studies. *Cuadernos de Gestión, 12*, 73–103. doi:10.5295/cdg.110308ap

Plattform produktives Stadtgrün. (2020). Available online: https://www.berlin.de/gemeinschaftsgaertnern/

Raudeliuniene, J., Davidavičiene, V., & Jakubavičius, A. (2018). Knowledge management process model. *Entrep. Sustain. Issues*, *5*, 542–554.

Redman, C. (2014). Should sustainability and resilience be combined or remain distinct pursuits? *Ecology and Society*, *19*(2), 190–202. doi:10.5751/ES-06390-190237

Reisinger, A., & Clark, H. (2018). How much do direct livestock emissions contribute to global warming? *Global Change Biology*, *2018*(24), 1749–1761. doi:10.1111/gcb.13975 PMID:29105912

Rowe, D. B. (2011). Green Roofs as a means of pollution abatement. *Environmental Pollution*, *159*(8-9), 2100–2110. doi:10.1016/j.envpol.2010.10.029 PMID:21074914

Russo, A., & Cirella, G. (2018). Modern compact cities: How much greenery do we need? *International Journal of Environmental Research and Public Health*, *15*(10), 2180. doi:10.3390/ijerph15102180 PMID:30301177

Savickiene, J., & Miceikiene, A. (2018). *Sustainable economic development assessment model for family farms* (Vol. 64). Agricultural Economics. doi:10.17221/310/2017-AGRICECON

Shafique, M., Kim, R., & Rafiq, M. (2018). Green roof benefits, opportunities, and challenges– A review. *Renewable and Sustainable Energy Reviews, 90*, 757-773.

Shevchenko, A., & Petrenko, O. (2020). Current state of micro and small agribusiness in Ukraine. *Agricultural and Resource Economics*, *6*(1), 146–160. doi:10.51599/are.2020.06.01.10

Shoeb, A., & Nisar, T. (2015). Green Human Resource Management: Policies and practices. *Cogent Business & Management, 2*(1). https://www.tandfonline.com/doi/full/10.1080/23311975.2015.103081 7 doi:10.1080/23311975.2015.1030817

Singh, S. K., Del Giudice, M., Chierici, R., & Graziano, D. (2020). Green innovation and environmental performance: The role of green transformational leadership and green human resource management. *Technological Forecasting and Social Change, 150*, 119762. doi:10.1016/j.techfore.2019.119762

Skydan, O., Nykolyuk, O., Pyvovar, P., & Martynchuk, I. (2020). Methodological approach to the evaluation of agricultural business system flexibility. *Management Theory and Studies for Rural Business and Infrastructure Development*, *41*(4), 444–462. doi:10.15544/mts.2019.36

Stovin, V., Vesuviano, G., & Kasmin, H. (2012). The hydrological performance of a green roof test bed under UK climatic conditions. *Journal of Hydrology (Amsterdam)*, *414*, 148–161. doi:10.1016/j.jhydrol.2011.10.022

Stubbs, W., & Cocklin, C. (2008). Conceptualizing a sustainability business model. *Org. Env.*, *21*(2), 103-127.

Sutton, R. (2014). Aesthetics for green roofs and green walls. *The Journal of Living Architecture*, *1*(2), 1–20. doi:10.46534/jliv.2014.01.02.001

TEP. (2005). *Advancing the delivery of green infrastructure Targeting Issues in England's Northwest*. TEP.

Tomashuk, I.V., & Baldynyuk, V.M. (2021). Identification of problems and prospects of rural infrastructure development of Ukraine. *Colloquium-Journal, 13*(100). doi:10.24412/2520-6990-2021-13100-58-70

Tsai, W., & Ghoshal, S. (1998). Social capital and value creation: The role of intrafirm networks. *Academy of Management Journal, 1998*(41), 464–476. doi:10.2307/257085

Ugai, T. (2016). Evaluation of sustainable roof from various aspects and benefits of agriculture roofing in urban core. *Procedia: Social and Behavioral Sciences, 216*, 850–860. doi:10.1016/j.sbspro.2015.12.082

UNDP. (2020). *Environmentally Sustainable Operations.* https://www.undp.org/accountability/social-and-environmental-responsibility/sustainable-operations

Van Holt, T., Statler, M., Atz, U., Whelan, T., van Loggerenberg, M., & Cebulla, J. (2020). The cultural consensus of sustainability-driven innovation: Strategies for success. *Business Strategy and the Environment, 29*(8), 3399–3409. doi:10.1002/bse.2584

Vijayaraghavan, K. (2016). Green roofs: A critical review on the role of components, benefits, limitations, and trends. *Renewable & Sustainable Energy Reviews, 57*, 740–752. doi:10.1016/j.rser.2015.12.119

VisitBerlin. (Ed.). (2017). *12 mal Berliner Leben, 12 mal Berlin Erleben. Konzept für einen stadtverträglichen Berlin-Tourismus 2018+.* VisitBerlin. Available online: https://about.visitberlin.de/tourismuskonzept-2018

Wang, Y., Hu, H., Dai, W., & Burns, K. (2021). Evaluation of industrial green development and industrial green competitiveness: Evidence from Chinese urban agglomerations. *Ecological Indicators, 124*, 107371. doi:10.1016/j.ecolind.2021.107371

Wiering, M., Liefferink, D., Boezeman, D., Kaufmann, M., Crabbé, A., & Kurstjens, N. (2020). The Wicked Problem the Water Framework Directive Cannot Solve. The Governance Approach in Dealing with Pollution of Nutrients in Surface Water in the Netherlands, Flanders, Lower Saxony, Denmark, and Ireland. *Water (Basel), 12*(5), 1240. doi:10.3390/w12051240

Wirtenberg, J., Harmon, K. D., Russell, W. G., & Fairfield, K. D. (2007). HR's role in building a sustainable enterprise. *Human Resource Planning, 30*, 10–20.

Wysocki, J. (2021). Innovative green initiatives in the manufacturing SME sector in Poland. *Sustainability, 13*(4), 2386. doi:10.3390u13042386

Zhang, Z., & Sundaresan, S. (2010). Knowledge markets in firms: Knowledge sharing with trust and signalling. *Knowledge Management Research and Practice, 2010*(8), 322–339. doi:10.1057/kmrp.2010.22

KEY TERMS AND DEFINITIONS

Green Innovation: Form of innovation, including the creation and commercialization of environmentally better technologies, as well as the diffusion and adoption of these technologies.

Green Knowledge: Faculty of the human being to understand through reason the nature, sustainability, qualities, and relationships of natural resources to preserve the balance of the socio-ecological system.

Green Roof: A green roof is a vegetated roofing system functionally integrated onto a roof area.

Green Technology: Consists of a set of technology-related practices that focus on sustainability. The concept understands that, through technological innovations and the use of computing resources in a more responsible way, it is possible to contribute to the future of the planet.

Organizational Green Innovation: Is the introduction of organizational methods and systems of management to address environmental issues in production and products. Includes systems of pollution prevention, environmental auditing and management systems and supply chain management value (co-operation between companies to close the cycle of materials and avoid environmental damage to what along the entire value chain.

Urban Innovation Spaces: Urban areas that facilitate processes aimed at new and more efficient solutions to solve future and present complex problems.

Chapter 8
Impact of Environmental, Social, and Governance Practices on the Consumer Buying Decision

Hettiwattage Harshani Dedunu
Rajarata University, Sri Lanka

Darshana Sedara
Southern Cross University, Australia

ABSTRACT

The purpose of the study is to find out how consumer purchasing decisions affect environmental, social, and governance practices. Consumers with recent bachelor's degrees were given the questionnaire. Through smart pls, the survey questions were tested. The findings imply that consumers prioritize two factors, the environment and social. It was verified that the personal concerns regarding the recycling process, resource consumption, and environmentally friendly business practices. Further, customers' health and safety, organizations' healthy and good working environment, human right concentration have shown reasonable importance. However, governance factors consideration is very low in the customer decision-making process due to a low level of awareness about governing practices especially political involvement and fraud and corruption. Thus, the empirical findings of the study serve as a springboard for further investigation in this field and offer marketers and sellers of ESG practices strategic implications.

INTRODUCTION

Recent developments in the global environment, including Corporate Social Responsibility (CSR), Environment Social and Governance (ESG), Ethical AI Auditing (D'Amato et al., 2022) (Maniora, 2017), and Natural Ecosystem, have repeatedly warned the general public around the world about the need to reevaluate the impact of their practices on society and the environment. Global Sustainable Investment Alliance (2019) reports that ESG practices have improved in recent years in a number of countries, including the USA (by 38%), Canada (by 42%), Europe (by 11%), and Australia (by 46%). The latest

DOI: 10.4018/978-1-6684-6815-9.ch008

Nielsen Global Survey on CSR in 2017, revealed that 66% of customers globally and 73% of millennials worldwide are willing to pay more for sustainable offerings and brands respectively (Eliwa et al., 2021). Such pieces of evidence highlight the danger of doing business as usual, and the need for a new global mindset to meet the social and ecological demands of the world. In response to this global requirement, firms have started applying ESG practices to demonstrate how firms address the issue to the general public through accounting reporting. Previously, corporations functioned on a neo-liberal basis, therefore annual reports only featured information related to profit (Burawat, 2019), however, strategic priorities have shifted, and businesses are now primarily skewed away from a profit orientation (Huang, 2021). E.g., the following ESG practices are not mandatory but many firms practice them voluntarily because doing so increases stakeholders' confidence, and has a positive impact on customers purchasing decisions (Rodrigues & Borges, 2015a).

The stakeholder theory emphasizes that the success of the firm depends upon the degree to which firms meet stakeholder expectations (Barnett, 2007), accordingly meeting consumers' expectations and fulfilling their demands is always the top priority of the organization (Hassan et al., 2013). The theory also shows that consumers are interested in governance practices like board composition, audit committee structure, bribery and corruption, executive compensation, lobbying and political contribution (CFA Institute., 2018), in addition to various social factors like community relations, gender diversity, data privacy, fair remuneration, health and safety, and human rights (Bloomberg, 2013). The theory of planned behavior, another hand, emphasizes that consumers much-concerned the environment in their decisions, therefore they would like to purchase eco-friendly products (Leonidou & Leonidou, 2011; Paul et al., 2016), and organic products (Pino et al., 2012; Zhou et al., 2013). Based on the aforementioned theoretical foundations the study makes claims that a company's ESG policies have an impact on consumer purchasing decisions. Hence, exploring the impact of ESG practices on consumer buying decisions is timely and important.

With respect to the ESG practices, a number of studies have been conducted around the world to enrich and widen the depth and height of the existing stock of ESG literature. These studies discussed the concept from different perspectives. (Moon et al., 2022)clearly illustrated the antecedent and consequences of ESG practices. Bender et al., (2018) and Henriksson et al., (2019)explained why firms should consider ESG practices in portfolio designing and how it can be done. Brooks & Oikonomou, (2018) and Fuente et al., (2022) discussed ESG practices relating to firm value creation and value engagement, whereas Sila & Cek, (2017) and Tarmuji et al., (2016) highlighted how the firm can increase its economic performance through ESG implementation. Not only that, it was noticed from the existing literature that the majority of ESG research was discussed from the investors' side (Eccles et al., 2017; In et al., 2019a; Young-Ferris & Roberts, 2021) and the exploration of ESG from consumers' perspective has been significant unnoticed in recent literature. Further, it was noted in the buying behavior literature that this research had been done on consumer buying behavior and firm environment (Häubl & Trifts, 2000; Tasaki et al., 2013), and buying behavior and CSR (Bashar, 2012; Öberseder et al., 2011; Pradhan, 2018; Rodrigues & Borges, 2015b) as independent studies. Although understanding how these three behaviors interact and affect customer purchasing behavior is crucial for the accounting and marketing management literature, no single study relating to consumer purchasing behavior and business governance was produced by the extant literature. Further, it was noted in the literature that the exploration of firm environmental practices in developing countries is significantly low compared to developed nations. Consequently, it is still unclear how customers in developing countries that have different environmental concerns, beliefs, and attitudes, think of green products purchase, thus, more research is required to fill the existing literature gap. Also, the intention to be green is comparatively new and it happened with the sudden introduction of the organic fertilizer policy of the previous government, thus a largely unexplored research area in the Sri Lankan context (Ishar Ali & Siraji, 2021; Lee et al., 2019). Hence, the role of ESG practices in the consumer buying decision is not crystal clear. Therefore, the proposed study hopes to conduit ESG literature with marketing literature by exploring how a firm's ESG practices influence the consumer buying decision.

LITERATURE REVIEW

The business practices against CSR have been a focus of research on the place of business in society for a number of decades. However, with the advent of the triple bottom line concept (profit, planet, people) many changes have emerged in academic disclosure (Lin-Hi & Müller, 2013). As a result, researchers' attention has been drawn to studying the micro effects of CSR, namely how it affects company performance, as opposed to the macro-social implications of CSR. Additionally, the theoretical focus shifted from an ethics-focused approach to one that is performance-focused (Aguinis & Glavas, 2012). Subsequently, many researchers who were considered different perspectives ethical, legal, philanthropic and economic CSR (Visser, 2006), have shifted to ESG techniques. Although businesses are prepared to share their non-financial information with the public, the voluntary disclosure theory constantly underlined that the disclosures should help stakeholders foresee how long-term organizational value creation would occur (Suijs, 2005). ESG disclosure allegedly improves a company's reputation and stakeholders' trust, according to numerous recent studies (Twinamatsiko & Kumar, 2022). Consumers are more concerned than ever about companies' ESG policies because of the significant impact that ESG practices have on consumer choice.

Firm Environment Practices on the Consumer Buying Decision (E)

The E stands for environmental indicator, which examines how a business contributes to the environment with an emphasis on burning environmental issues like resource depletion, pollution, waste management, gas emissions, deforestation and etc. (Twinamatsiko & Kumar, 2022). Businessmen's eyes have been opened to environmental contamination as a strategy to increase customer loyalty and profits as a result of concurrently publicized ecological challenges and environmental problems by UNICEF and various media. Consequently, environmental concern has now become a lucrative source of competitive advantage (Twinamatsiko & Kumar, 2022), and thus many firms have turned toward more eco-friendly products (Su et al., 2021). We defined a green product for the study as a product that will not pollute the earth or deplore natural resources and can be recycled or conserved (Prem Shamdasani et al., 1993).

The Theory of Planned Behavior (TPB) and Theory of Reasoned Action (TRA) stated that individuals' decision to engage in a specific behavior such as purchasing an eco-friendly product can be predicated on their intention to engage in that behavior (Leonidou & Leonidou, 2011; Paul et al., 2016). As a result, customers who are more concerned about environmental issues are more likely to want to buy eco-friendly goods and find out what companies are doing to protect the environment. Therefore, businesses must take consumers' preferences into account when making decisions. This is because, according to the stakeholder theory (Ha & Janda, 2012), customer attitudes toward particular activities are a direct predictor of specific environmental actions, which are in turn predicted by environmental concern (Ajzen & Fishbein, 1977).

Customers' environment-friendly decisions are mainly based on several facts such as their environmental concerns levels (Kinnear & Taylor, 1973), perceived customer effectiveness, environmentally conscious behaviors (Do Paço & Raposo, 2009), and perceived ability of their efforts and actions to resolve environmental problems (Straughan & Roberts, 1999). Previous studies claimed that companies' environmental practices enhance customer purchasing intention (Ham & Han, 2013), customer loyalty (Molina-Azorín et al., 2009), consumers' decision-making process (Kim & Han, 2010), and the firm's financial performance. However, Kim & Han, (2010) further stated that hotel guests' decision to stay, was not significantly dependent on their hotel's environmentally friendly activities. On the other hand, many extant studies investigated customers' intentions (Molina-Azorín et al., 2009; Paul et al., 2016), satisfaction (Whitehouse et al., 2001), and preference (Aldanondo-Ochoa & Almansa-Sáez, 2009) on firm environmental practices. (Paul et al., 2016) believe that the country of origin may influence the degree of consumer concern for the environment. (N. Singh & Gupta, 2013) found that individuals in developed countries (61.5% of Australians, Scott & Suchard, 1992, 50% of Americans., Phillips. L, 1999) consume more environment-friendly products than people in developing countries. In addition, high media coverage was also found to be a significant pressure on government, organizations, and people to practice environmentalism and sustainable development (Sanjay Sharma & Harrie Vredenburg, 1998).

Based on the aforementioned theoretical underpinning the study believes that people are more concerned to purchase the eco-friendly product due to the fact that environmental awareness of people has swelled more dramatically than ever with noticed biological and environmental changes happening around the world, and that interests govern them to consume products that make the least impact to the environment. Accordingly, the study argues that a firm's environmental practices directly influence consumer decision-making behavior. Thus, the study hypothesis that

H_1: Firm environmental practices directly influence consumer decision-making behavior

Firm Social Practices on the Consumer Buying Decision (S)

The second pillar of ESG is the social factor (S) which discloses the organization's relationships with its stakeholders like employees, suppliers, customers, and the communities where it operates (Twinamatsiko & Kumar, 2022). This dimension of ESG is founded largely on the stakeholder theory. The theory emphasizes that firm should make an effort to treat all of these stakeholders fairly in order to succeed in the long run (Cordeiro & Tewari, 2015).This theory dramatically opposes the shareholder theory which holds that businesses are only driven to advance shareholder interests. According to the stakeholder theory a company cannot view any of its stakeholders if they like, in isolation (Mohr & Webb, 2005). As a result, social practices can be recognized as one of the strategic methods through which a corporation balances the interests of its diverse stakeholders. Firm social practices spread across many areas including firm administration: community relations, data protection, and privacy policies, employee concern; labor standards, employee diversity, employee equity, and employee inclusion, employee engagement and relations, social; health and safety, human rights, efforts to fund projects that help underserved communities, customer; customer satisfaction, customer loyalty (Collins & Clark, 2003) . At its inception, shareholder theory dominated business practices but later increased consumer bargaining power, and the consumer knowledge of business practices forced businesses to rethink diverse stakeholders' needs and disclose the social concern of their business operations (Mohr & Webb, 2005). The requirement became significant with the growing interconnection of world economies and the expansion of multinational enterprises (D. A. Singh & Gaur, 2009). Resulting, the firm disclosed its social practice through formal and informal channels to make stakeholders aware that the firm concerned on diverse social needs in business operations. The formal disclose includes annual reports, company documents, and websites whereas advertisements, social media campaigns and press release, speeches and all communication with stakeholders represented informal channels that communicate firms' social practices to the third party (Wendell H. Adair Jr et al., 1991)In 1999, more than two-thirds of consumers demanded businesses that were oriented toward social purposes (Isa, 2003). Later many studies found that a firm's social orientation increased consumer loyalty (Zdravkovic et al., 2010) and firm goodwill (Handelman & Arnold, 1999). (J. Singh et al., 2008) claimed that corporate image positively influences consumer product judgment and responses.

Further, many previous studies emphasized that a firm's ethical practices influence consumer purchasing decisions, and consumers are willing to pay a premium price for these ethical practices, and they would like to recommend the particular products to others (Bhattacharya & Sen, 2003). Further, (Kumar et al., 2006) states that supply chain flexibility, cross-functional integration, supply chain management practices significantly alter customer buying behaviour and their product or service preferences (Jääskeläinen & Heikkilä, 2019). Consequently, (Doyle et al., 2006) argues that suppliers and retailers should seriously concern consumers feedbacks so as to ensure firm's long term operational and financial sustainability. In addition to that many extents literature highlights why firm should care on its employees when ensuring sustainable consumers. In particular, (Lee & Lim, 2020) states that employees' behaviour and commitment directly link to product/service quality (Jones et al., 2017). Hence, treating employees beyond the requirements results high employee productivity, customer loyalty. Based on the aforementioned theoretical foundation, the study believes that consumers are more concerned about the external activities of firms that make a positive impact on society before the purchasing decision is taken place. Thus, the study hypothesis that

H$_2$: Firm social practices directly influence consumer decision-making behavior

Firm Governance Practices on the Consumer Buying Decision (G)

The third pillar of ESG practices, governance (G) stands for measuring how a firm is led and managed. Here more emphasis is given to company leadership, leadership incentives, stakeholder rights, tax strategies, board structure, and internal control exist to promote transparency & accountability (Twinamatsiko & Kumar, 2022). The governance principle is based on two main theories: agency and stakeholder. According to the agency theory principle and agent, the problem occurs when the interests of a principal and agent come into conflict (Kull & Heath, 2016). It is certain that not all agents will always act in the principal's best interests, consequently, miscommunication and disagreement may result in various problems in the business, therefore companies should seek to minimize these situations through solid corporate policy (Albareda, 2008). Corporate governance exists formally and informally. In contrast to informal governance, which is governed by executive leadership and evolves via values and culture, formal governance takes place through structure and process (Hemphill, 2013). The extant studies have thoroughly explored determinants of quality governing structure. In particular, (Wright & Martin, 2014) found that consumers' low participation, poor knowledge, and technical proficiency affect the quality of company governance practices. (Talesh, 2015) states that firm corporate governance influences customer ethics. However, (Béal & Sabadie, 2018) argue that consumers play a vital role in firm governance structure forcing them to disclose as much as possible information about the product and firm services. When consumers are closer to the firm, as emphasized in the psychological ownership theory, consumers' feelings of ownership highly influence consumers' attitudes toward purchasing decisions (Pierce et al., 2003).

Organization's governance practices also play a major role to change customers' buying decisions. According to Zhang & Zhang, (2018) state that government policy application, tax practices impact on consumer purchasing decision. Also, customers may include perceived indicators of ethical leadership into their decision-making process(van Quaquebeke et al., 2019), customer relationship leadership model improve business performance due to customers' positive feedback on organization products(Galbreath & Rogers, 1999). Based on the theoretical background the study believes that consumer buying decision is influenced by the existing governing mechanism of the firm. Accordingly, when the mechanism is open, transparent, and more accountable consumers tend to connect with firms more solidly than ever. Thus, study hypothesis that

H_3: Firm governance practices directly influence consumer decision-making behavior.

METHODOLOGY

The impact of ESG practices on consumer purchasing decisions was investigated in this quantitative study using the explanatory research method, developing causal hypotheses based on an extensive literature survey and an already-established theoretical foundation, particularly stakeholder theory and theory of plan behavior. The study primarily targeted consumers who are already familiar with ESG principles, then accounting graduates who learned ESG practices in their degree program, were prioritized. As Sri Lankan state universities follow fairly similar curricula compared to private universities most of which teach foreign curriculums, the study excluded all foreign university accounting graduates from the population. Further, the study excludes state university graduates who obtained their degrees more than five years ago as ESG was not one of the main considerable factors in state university curricula at that time. Accordingly, the study reached 300 graduates randomly. The sample size is fair enough as per the Morgan table which states 300 responses would be enough to represent around ten thousand population. A self-administrated questionnaire with 24 items, is used to collect data from respondents. Data collection started on 01st of April 2022, as at 5th August 2022 received 300 responses. The study applied Structural Equation Modelling (SEM) to analyse the data and used Smart-PLS software.

Measurement of Variables

The study operationalized the variables using the results of the literature review. Previously used and validated scales were employed, but most of the previous scales were developed in different contexts, and no scales were found that especially focused on Sri Lankan consumers. Considering the study background, and the target audience previous scales were amended and replaced with new items to make the scales easier for responders to understand. Accordingly, the study measured environmental, social and governance factors through 5 items, and 4 items are used to evaluate consumer decision-making behavior. The scales were mainly based on the Bloomberg Impact report 2022, Rodrigues & Borges, (2015) (Young In et al., 2019). All the items were rated on a ten-point scale ranging from 1, "strongly disagree", to 10, "strongly agree", by customers.

DATA ANALYSIS

Data

The model estimation draws on data from state university accounting graduates. A total of 304 respondents rated their preferences on a 10 Likert scale. As indicated in figure 1, the sample size is technically large enough to estimate the PLS model with the complex PLS path model. The data set included 19 patterned questions and 11 incomplete questions. Incomplete and patterned questionnaires were excluded from the analysis, whereas questionnaires with few missing values were considered. Missing values were treated with the mean of responses (Weerasinghe & Dedunu, 2020). Finally, the study ended up with 273 completed responses. The box plot diagnostics by means of IBM SPSS revealed no outlier observations. The skewness and the excess kurtosis values ranged between -1 and +1. This degree of non-normality of data in two indicators is not a critical issue (Sarstedt et al., 2017).

Table 1 shows the sample profile of the respondents. The highest number of respondents was from the Rajarata University of Sri Lanka (85 and 31%), followed by the University of Kelaniya (42 and 15%). The lowest response received from Jaffna university. In terms of gender, the majority was female and their representation was 53%. The statistics highlight that many respondents were recently graduated (35%, followed by respondents had learned ESG practices in their degree one years ago (25%). Around 50% of responses belong to the 25-30 age group. The majority of them (38%) received a monthly income of LKR 150,001 to LKR 200,000.

Table 1. Table sample profile

Gender	
Male	53%
Female	47%
Graduated Year	
2022	35%
2020	25%
2019	15%
Four Years Ago	16%
Five Years Ago	09%
Monthly Income	
LKR 50,000 to LKR 100,000	12%
LKR 100,001 to LKR 150,000	27%
LKR 150,001 to LKR 200,000	38%
LKR 200,001 to LKR 250,000	14%
Above 250,001	09%

Measurement Model

PLS algorithm steps were deployed to evaluate the measurement model in stage one. All the constructs were measured reflectively. The initial run detected some potentially problematic measures having low item loadings below 0.6 [E5-0.499, S5- 0.489 and S2- 0.577], but item loading of (S2) was very close to 0.6, therefore the study decided to remove the low power items except (S2). Accordingly, all items exhibit a sufficient level of reliability. The study assesses the internal consistency and reliability of the study using composite reliability and Cronbach's alpha of the constructs. The result of Cronbach's alpha indicates that all three variables: customer buying decisions (0.802), environment factors (0.788) social factors (0.813), meet the threshold Alpha value (0.7) except governance factors (0.640). As it was very close to the expected level, the study did not especially treat them. The composite reliability of all variables ranged between 0.6 and 0.8, which reflects collected data at an acceptable level for interpretation.

Next, the measurement model evaluates the convergent validity of variables to ensure the degree to which a measurement item correlates with measurement items of the same construct (Churchill, 1979). AVE values were well above the threshold level except for the social factor (0.474), which was the best value the study could obtain, and it was very close to the threshold level, therefore the study decided to keep the items as it is (table 2).

Table 2. Item loading, Cross Loading, convergent validity

Variable	Indicators	Descriptive		Convergent Validity		Internal Consistency	
		Mean	Overall Mean	Outer Loadings	AVE	Composite Reliability	Cronbach Alpha
	Range			>0.7	>0.5	>0.7	0.7 - 0.95
Environment Factors	E1	7.183	7.239	0.757	0.612	**0.819**	0.788
	E2	7.161		0.629			
	E3	7.256		0.864			
	E4	7.355		0.856			
Social Factor	S1	7.274	7.147	0.820	0.474	**0.692**	0.640
	S2	7.062		0.577			
	S3	7.124		0.637			
	S4	7.125		0.696			
Governess Factor	G1	6.615	6.971	0.727	0.563		0.813
	G2	6.846		0.719			
	G3	7.208		0.777		**0.820**	
	G4	7.044		0.782			
	G5	7.142		0.745			
Consumer buying decision	CBD1	8.110	8.533	0.672	0.629	**0.846**	0.802
	CBD2	8.571		0.735			
	CBD3	8.835		0.852			
	CBD4	8.615		0.894			

The study evaluated discriminant validity using cross-loadings (table 3), the Fornell-Larcker criterion and, Heterotrait-Monotrait Ratio (HTMT) test (table 4). According to table 3, the cross-loading results of all item's cross-loadings are greater than other constructs. Fornell-Larcker criterion states that the square root of each construct's AVE is greater than its highest correlation with any other construct (CBD - 0.793, E- 0.782, S- 0.688, and G-0.751). Not only that the findings of the HTMT ratio test results show that the data set did not have any discriminant validity issues (E-CBD – 0.620, G-CPD- 0.320, G-E- 0.480, S-CBD – 0.550, S-E -0.640 and S-G - 0.860). Accordingly, the study ensures the discriminant validity of the variables.

Table 3. Item loading and Cross Loading

	CBD	**E**	**G**	**S**
CBD1	**0.672**	0.308	0.144	0.278
CBD2	**0.735**	0.404	0.124	0.315
CBD3	**0.852**	0.362	0.263	0.357
CBD4	**0.894**	0.542	0.364	0.383
E1	0.483	**0.757**	0.382	0.433
E2	0.233	**0.629**	0.192	0.224
E3	0.440	**0.864**	0.312	0.340
E4	0.411	**0.856**	0.315	0.341
G1	0.196	0.336	**0.727**	0.291
G2	0.092	0.291	**0.719**	0.237
G3	0.257	0.248	**0.777**	0.371
G4	0.217	0.359	**0.782**	0.572
G5	0.274	0.285	**0.745**	0.654
S1	0.402	0.278	0.262	**0.820**
S2	0.182	0.320	0.659	**0.577**
S3	0.224	0.411	0.295	**0.637**
S4	0.295	0.287	0.631	**0.696**

Table 4. Fornell Larcker Criterion

	CPD	**E**	**G**	**S**
CPD	0.793			
E	0.523	0.782		
G	0.301	0.399	0.751	
S	0.424	0.443	0.610	0.688

Structural Model

PLS runs the structural model with 5000 bootstrapping. The structural model was assessed for its predictive capabilities of the model through the coefficient of determination, cross-validated redundancy, and path coefficients (Sarstedt et al., 2017). The first study checked the VIF values of the structural model to diagnose the collinearity problem, however, VIF values were well below the threshold value (5) and exhibited no collinearity problem in the model. We started the key target variable from the right-hand side of the model (consumer buying decision) in figure 1. The construct CBD has the strongest effect on E (0.421), followed by S (0.253), while the effect of G (-0.027) is very close to zero. The t-values of the hypothesized path of E and CBD is 9.145 which is above 2.57 and the p-value is 0.000 and both 2.5% and 97.5% intervals reflect positive results, therefore hypotheses path of CBD and E of the inner model is statistically significant. S and CBD model also emphasized statistically significant model according to the results (p= 0.000 and t-value= 4.309). However, CBD and G hypothesis model p value more than 0.05 and t value also less than 2.57 which support to conclude CBD and G of the inner model is statistically insignificant. The bootstrapping result substantiates that the effect of E and S is significant while G does not have a significant effect at a 95% confidence level. The study also found that the model explains 31.9% of CBD's variance (i.e., R^2 = 31.9), which is relatively high.

Figure 1. Structural Model

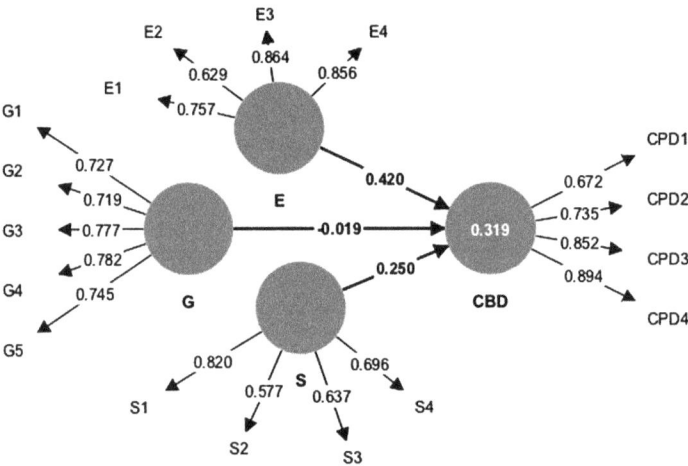

Table 5. Structural Model Evaluation Statistics

	Path Coefficient	95% CI	t-Values	p-Values
E -> CBD	0.421	[0.328, 0.506]	9.145	0.000
S -> CBD	0.253	[0.137, 0.369]	4.309	0.000
G -> CBD	-0.027	[-0.134, 0.110]	0.435	0.663

DISCUSSION OF RESULTS

The discussion part is presented in two sections; the evaluation of descriptive statistics and the interpretation of PLS-SEM analysis. First, with respect to the environmental factors, descriptive statistics state that consumers pay high attention to the recycling process (m- 7.355), resource consumption, and environmentally friendly business practices (m-7.256). This is largely due to the fact that it helps to reduce cost and time by reusing components, reduce pollution and manage wastage. Sri Lanka has implemented a number of regulatory measures to reduce environmental pollution at both the individual and national levels, and this awareness greatly influences people to buy goods that cause the least amount of environmental harm (mean=7.18). The findings suggest that the firm requires to disclose its practices and initiatives to safeguard the environment to the customers. Surprisingly, the survey discovered that consumers are less worried about harmful gas usage than other concerns (mean = 7.161). This is a little odd, but it might be caused by lax regulations regarding the release of harmful gases into the environment. Since Sri Lanka is not an industrialized nation and only has a few basic industries, academics and policymakers have paid little attention to air pollution. The study's conclusions were consistent with several earlier research. Mainieri et al., (1997) state that both males and females have an almost equal concern about environmental issues, Rodrigues & Borges, (2015) say that it is because recycling processes support conserving energy. (Howell & Laska, 1992) argue that green products price is very high and therefore unaffordable for the lower-income category.

Concerning the social factors, previous research suggested that older consumers pay close attention to health issues and only come across a few specific brands (Yoon et al., 2009), but more recent research indicates that there is no effect of age on the consumption of health products (Park et al., 1988). The findings of the current study demonstrate that young consumers valued an organization's commitment to customers' health and safety (mean =7.248) as a crucial social practice. In addition to the organizations' healthy and good working environment, human right concentration (mean= 7.098) have shown reasonable importance. Because a good working environment improves employees' well-being including quality of work and productivity therefore consumers experienced high satisfaction. Currently, organizations pay high attention to maintaining and developing customer-employee positive relationships (Anaza, 2015; Gremler & Gwinner, 2000). Further, the study noticed that peoples are highly concerned about child labour (mean = 7.036) utilization in production. Sri Lanka is always at top of the child labour protection, and child education compared to other Asian nations. Further, child labour is prohibited in Sri Lanka, therefore it is obvious that people refuse products that are from children's hands(Sharma, 2016)

Third, the study explores how governing factors influence consumer purchasing decisions. The light of study indicates that consumers have a low level of awareness about governing practices especially political involvement (mean = 6.821) and fraud and corruption (mean = 6.591). The findings are surprising and graduates are well aware of the repercussion of the firm bad practices, however, the study findings reviled that consumers do not care much about governing practices of firms when purchasing. This is due to the unavailability of information about such malpractices. Zhang & Zhang, (2018) states that consumers are highly concerned about organizational governance practices such as ethical practices, proper board structure, and transparency, but (Gerpott et al., 2019) mentioned consumers are always unaware of firm fraud and corruption, therefore influenceability of such practices on purchasing decision is very minimum. Deeper investigation on governance practices, the study found that governance practices have no significant impact on a consumer purchasing decision. The output of the study in line with many previous studies. (Carnini Pulino et al., 2022)states that the environmental and social pillars have a positive impact on firm performance. However, no significant impact has been found in relation to the governance pillar in Italy. reveals that, (Sultana et al., 2018)in investment decisions, investors prioritize governing practices such as the setting up of an effective board with allocated duties and responsibilities, adherence to financial reporting requirements, and the independence of auditors in Bangladesh. (Koh et al., 2022)states that governance practices has a positive significant effect on brand image, brand credibility, and the perceived quality of firm.

The Implication of the Study

The study contributes to the literature in several ways. First, the study examines the effect of a firm's ESG practices on consumer purchasing decisions which were largely untapped in the present literature. Most previous studies explored how firm investors' perspectives on firm performance (Nirino et al., 2021), corporate financial performance(Saygili et al., 2022), The result of current study shows that environment and social structures significantly influence consumer buying decision decisions. The Study result verified that consumers make a clear investigation of ecological and recycling dimensions under the environmental component and firm administration and employee concern dimensions in the social component. Further, company has to conduct and disclose their environment and social practices continuously to the public(Marin et al., 2009; Peloza & Shang, 2011). Otherwise, company will lose existing customers and difficult to attract new customers to the product. Another result seems to be that customers now consider corporate practices despite their friends' and siblings' purchasing power, lifestyle, motivation, personality, knowledge, and attitudes (Rodrigues & Borges, 2015). As a result, ESG practices considered as new marketing method in the future. Therefore, academics in the future can look into how ESG practices affect corporate branding. Finally, the study reveals that, not all ESG initiatives are evenly effective for consumer buying decision behaviour.

The findings of this research have important consequences for ESG practitioners in addition to its theoretical ramifications. First, the results suggest that environment and social factors have an impact on consumer buying decision. Hence, practitioners should concentrate heavily on these factors. Environmental factors produced the most significant impact on consumer buying decisions. Therefore, organizations can benefit from this aim by taking part in environmental activities including recycling, resource consumption, and environmentally friendly business practices. Further, the results demonstrate that consumer buying decisions were not significantly impacted by governance factors. According to the (Todt et al., 2009) customer knowledge is very low on governance factors and customers have poor experience and awareness on governance factors impact on society. Therefore, it is advised that practitioners carefully plan tactics to improve consumer awareness of governance practices and boost perceptions of these practices. Consumers can be made aware of governance initiatives through a variety of sources, including research reports, advertisements, company websites, and social media.

Overall, the study will provide a strong foundation for academics and practitioners to understand which ESG factors are highly considered by consumers in their buying decision process. Thus, the study support policymakers and practitioners to stimulate customer buying behaviors appropriate to redesign of firm ESG practices. Despite these implications, the study has numerous limitations which provide an avenue for future studies. First sample consist consumers' who has ESG knowledge but low level of experience in the market future studies can focus more experienced consumers in the market. Second conceptual model does not consider any mediator variables therefore future studies can consider brand name, brand experience as a mediator.

REFERENCES

Aguinis, H., & Glavas, A. (2012). What We Know and Don't Know About Corporate Social Responsibility. *Journal of Management, 38*(4), 932–968. doi:10.1177/0149206311436079

Ajzen, I., & Fishbein, M. (1977). Attitude-behavior relations: A theoretical analysis and review of empirical research. *Psychological Bulletin, 84*(5), 888–918. doi:10.1037/0033-2909.84.5.888

Albareda, L. (2008). Corporate responsibility, governance and accountability: From self-regulation to co-regulation. *Corporate Governance: The International Journal of Business in Society, 8*(4), 430–439. doi:10.1108/14720700810899176

Aldanondo-Ochoa, A. M., & Almansa-Sáez, C. (2009). The private provision of public environment: Consumer preferences for organic production systems. *Land Use Policy, 26*(3), 669–682. doi:10.1016/j.landusepol.2008.09.006

Anaza, N. A. (2015). Relations of fit and organizational identification to employee-customer identification. *Journal of Managerial Psychology, 30*(8), 925–939. doi:10.1108/JMP-12-2012-0389

Barnett, M. L. (2007). Stakeholder influence capacity and the variability of financial returns to corporate social responsibility. *Academy of Management Review, 32*(3), 794–816. doi:10.5465/amr.2007.25275520

Bashar, A. (2012). *The Impact of Perceived CSR Initiatives on Consumer's Buying Behaviour: An Empirical Study*. SSRN Electronic Journal. doi:10.2139srn.3924859

Béal, M., & Sabadie, W. (2018). The impact of customer inclusion in firm governance on customers' commitment and voice behaviors. *Journal of Business Research, 92*, 1–8. doi:10.1016/j.jbusres.2018.07.019

Bender, J., Bridges, T. A., & He, C., Lester, A., & Sun, X. (2018). A Blueprint for Integrating ESG into Equity Portfolios. *Journal of Investment Management, 16*(1).

Bhattacharya, C. B., & Sen, S. (2003). Consumer–Company Identification: A Framework for Understanding Consumers' Relationships with Companies. *Journal of Marketing, 67*(2), 76–88. doi:10.1509/jmkg.67.2.76.18609

Brooks, C., & Oikonomou, I. (2018). The effects of environmental, social and governance disclosures and performance on firm value: A review of the literature in accounting and finance. *The British Accounting Review, 50*(1), 1–15. doi:10.1016/j.bar.2017.11.005

Burawat, P. (2019). The relationships among transformational leadership, sustainable leadership, lean manufacturing and sustainability performance in Thai SMEs manufacturing industry. *International Journal of Quality & Reliability Management, 36*(6), 1014–1036. doi:10.1108/IJQRM-09-2017-0178

Carnini Pulino, S., Ciaburri, M., Magnanelli, B. S., & Nasta, L. (2022). Does ESG Disclosure Influence Firm Performance? *Sustainability, 14*(13), 7595. doi:10.3390u14137595

CFA Institute. (2018). *ESG Integration in the Americas: Markets*. Practices, and Data.

Collins, C. J., & Clark, K. D. (2003). Strategic Human Resource Practices, Top Management Team Social Networks, and Firm Performance: The Role of Human Resource Practices in Creating Organizational Competitive Advantage. *Academy of Management Journal*, *46*(6), 740–751. doi:10.2307/30040665

Cordeiro, J. J., & Tewari, M. (2015). Firm Characteristics, Industry Context, and Investor Reactions to Environmental CSR: A Stakeholder Theory Approach. *Journal of Business Ethics*, *130*(4), 833–849. doi:10.100710551-014-2115-x

D'Amato, V., D'Ecclesia, R., & Levantesi, S. (2022). ESG score prediction through random forest algorithm. *Computational Management Science*, *19*(2), 347–373. doi:10.100710287-021-00419-3

de la Fuente, G., Ortiz, M., & Velasco, P. (2022). The value of a firm's engagement in ESG practices: Are we looking at the right side? *Long Range Planning*, *55*(4), 102143. doi:10.1016/j.lrp.2021.102143

Doyle, S. A., Moore, C. M., & Morgan, L. (2006). Supplier management in fast moving fashion retailing. *Journal of Fashion Marketing and Management*, *10*(3), 272–281. doi:10.1108/13612020610679268

Eccles, R. G., Kastrapeli, M. D., & Potter, S. J. (2017). How to Integrate ESG into Investment Decision-Making: Results of a Global Survey of Institutional Investors. *Journal of Applied Corporate Finance*, *29*(4), 125–133. doi:10.1111/jacf.12267

Eliwa, Y., Aboud, A., & Saleh, A. (2021). ESG practices and the cost of debt: Evidence from EU countries. *Critical Perspectives on Accounting*, *79*, 102097. doi:10.1016/j.cpa.2019.102097

Galbreath, J., & Rogers, T. (1999). Customer relationship leadership: A leadership and motivation model for the twenty-first century business. *The TQM Magazine*, *11*(3), 161–171. doi:10.1108/09544789910262734

Gerpott, F. H., van Quaquebeke, N., Schlamp, S., & Voelpel, S. C. (2019). An Identity Perspective on Ethical Leadership to Explain Organizational Citizenship Behavior: The Interplay of Follower Moral Identity and Leader Group Prototypicality. *Journal of Business Ethics*, *156*(4), 1063–1078. doi:10.100710551-017-3625-0

Gremler, D. D., & Gwinner, K. P. (2000). Customer-Employee Rapport in Service Relationships. *Journal of Service Research*, *3*(1), 82–104. doi:10.1177/109467050031006

Ha, H., & Janda, S. (2012). Predicting consumer intentions to purchase energy-efficient products. *Journal of Consumer Marketing*, *29*(7), 461–469. doi:10.1108/07363761211274974

Ham, S., & Han, H. (2013). Role of Perceived Fit With Hotels' Green Practices in the Formation of Customer Loyalty: Impact of Environmental Concerns. *Asia Pacific Journal of Tourism Research*, *18*(7), 731–748. doi:10.1080/10941665.2012.695291

Handelman, J. M., & Arnold, S. J. (1999). The Role of Marketing Actions with a Social Dimension: Appeals to the Institutional Environment. *Journal of Marketing*, *63*(3), 33–48. doi:10.1177/002224299906300303

Hassan, L., Shaw, D., Shiu, E., Walsh, G., & Parry, S. (2013). Uncertainty in ethical consumer choice: A conceptual model. *Journal of Consumer Behaviour*, *12*(3), 182–193. doi:10.1002/cb.1409

Häubl, G., & Trifts, V. (2000). Consumer Decision Making in Online Shopping Environments: The Effects of Interactive Decision Aids. *Marketing Science*, *19*(1), 4–21. doi:10.1287/mksc.19.1.4.15178

Hemphill, T. (2013). The ISO 26000 guidance on social responsibility international standard: What are the business governance implications? *Corporate Governance: The International Journal of Business in Society, 13*(3), 305–317. doi:10.1108/CG-08-2011-0062

Henriksson, R., Livnat, J., Pfeifer, P., & Stumpp, M. (2019). Integrating ESG in Portfolio Construction. *Journal of Portfolio Management, 45*(4), 67–81. doi:10.3905/jpm.2019.45.4.067

Howell, S. E., & Laska, S. B. (1992). The Changing Face of the Environmental Coalition. *Environment and Behavior, 24*(1), 134–144. doi:10.1177/0013916592241006

Huang, D. Z. X. (2021). Environmental, social and governance (ESG) activity and firm performance: A review and consolidation. *Accounting and Finance, 61*(1), 335–360. doi:10.1111/acfi.12569

In, S. Y., Rook, D., & Monk, A. (2019b). Integrating Alternative Data (Also Known as ESG Data) in Investment Decision Making. *Global Economic Review, 48*(3), 237–260. doi:10.1080/1226508X.2019.1643059

Isa, M. K. M. (2003). *Applying the Triple Bottom Line Approach.* Business Times.

Ishar Ali, M. S., & Siraji, M. (2021). Marketing Stimulus and its Impact on Green Product Purchase Intention of Customer: With the Mediating Role of Customer Attitude. *International Journal on Economics. Finance and Sustainable Development, 3*(5), 36–46.

Jääskeläinen, A., & Heikkilä, J. (2019). Purchasing and supply management practices in customer value creation. *Supply Chain Management, 24*(3), 317–333. doi:10.1108/SCM-04-2018-0173

Jones, R. J. III, Reilly, T. M., Cox, M. Z., & Cole, B. M. (2017). Gender Makes a Difference: Investigating Consumer Purchasing Behavior and Attitudes Toward Corporate Social Responsibility Policies. *Corporate Social Responsibility and Environmental Management, 24*(2), 133–144. doi:10.1002/csr.1401

Kim, Y., & Han, H. (2010). Intention to pay conventional-hotel prices at a green hotel – a modification of the theory of planned behavior. *Journal of Sustainable Tourism, 18*(8), 997–1014. doi:10.1080/09669582.2010.490300

Kinnear, T. C., & Taylor, J. R. (1973). The Effect of Ecological Concern on Brand Perceptions. *JMR, Journal of Marketing Research, 10*(2), 191–197. doi:10.1177/002224377301000210

Koh, H.-K., Burnasheva, R., & Suh, Y. G. (2022). Perceived ESG (Environmental, Social, Governance) and Consumers' Responses: The Mediating Role of Brand Credibility, Brand Image, and Perceived Quality. *Sustainability, 14*(8), 4515. doi:10.3390u14084515

Kull, A. J., & Heath, T. B. (2016). You decide, we donate: Strengthening consumer–brand relationships through digitally co-created social responsibility. *International Journal of Research in Marketing, 33*(1), 78–92. doi:10.1016/j.ijresmar.2015.04.005

Kumar, V., Fantazy, K. A., Kumar, U., & Boyle, T. A. (2006). Implementation and management framework for supply chain flexibility. *Journal of Enterprise Information Management, 19*(3), 303–319. doi:10.1108/17410390610658487

LEE, C., & LIM, S.-Y. (2020). Impact of Environmental Concern on Image of Internal GSCM Practices and Consumer Purchasing Behavior. *The Journal of Asian Finance. Economics and Business*, *7*(6), 241–254. doi:10.13106/jafeb.2020.vol7.no6.241

Lee, K.-H., Lee, M., & Gunarathne, N. (2019). Do green awards and certifications matter? Consumers' perceptions, green behavioral intentions, and economic implications for the hotel industry: A Sri Lankan perspective. *Tourism Economics*, *25*(4), 593–612. doi:10.1177/1354816618810563

Leonidou, C. N., & Leonidou, L. C. (2011). Research into environmental marketing/management: A bibliographic analysis. *European Journal of Marketing*, *45*(1/2), 68–103. doi:10.1108/03090561111095603

Lin-Hi, N., & Müller, K. (2013). The CSR bottom line: Preventing corporate social irresponsibility. *Journal of Business Research*, *66*(10), 1928–1936. doi:10.1016/j.jbusres.2013.02.015

Mainieri, T., Barnett, E. G., Valdero, T. R., Unipan, J. B., & Oskamp, S. (1997). Green Buying: The Influence of Environmental Concern on Consumer Behavior. *The Journal of Social Psychology*, *137*(2), 189–204. doi:10.1080/00224549709595430

Maniora, J. (2017). Is Integrated Reporting Really the Superior Mechanism for the Integration of Ethics into the Core Business Model? An Empirical Analysis. *Journal of Business Ethics*, *140*(4), 755–786. doi:10.100710551-015-2874-z

Marin, L., Ruiz, S., & Rubio, A. (2009). The Role of Identity Salience in the Effects of Corporate Social Responsibility on Consumer Behavior. *Journal of Business Ethics*, *84*(1), 65–78. doi:10.100710551-008-9673-8

Mohr, L. A., & Webb, D. J. (2005). The effects of corporate social responsibility and price on consumer responses. *The Journal of Consumer Affairs*, *39*(1), 121–147. doi:10.1111/j.1745-6606.2005.00006.x

Molina-Azorín, J. F., Claver-Cortés, E., Pereira-Moliner, J., & Tarí, J. J. (2009). Environmental practices and firm performance: An empirical analysis in the Spanish hotel industry. *Journal of Cleaner Production*, *17*(5), 516–524. doi:10.1016/j.jclepro.2008.09.001

Moon, J., Tang, R., & Lee, W. S. (2022). Antecedents and consequences of Starbucks' environmental, social and governance (ESG) implementation. *Journal of Quality Assurance in Hospitality & Tourism*, 1–23. doi:10.1080/1528008X.2022.2070818

Nirino, N., Santoro, G., Miglietta, N., & Quaglia, R. (2021). Corporate controversies and company's financial performance: Exploring the moderating role of ESG practices. *Technological Forecasting and Social Change*, *162*, 120341. doi:10.1016/j.techfore.2020.120341

Öberseder, M., Schlegelmilch, B. B., & Gruber, V. (2011). "Why Don't Consumers Care About CSR?": A Qualitative Study Exploring the Role of CSR in Consumption Decisions. *Journal of Business Ethics*, *104*(4), 449–460. doi:10.100710551-011-0925-7

Paul, J., Modi, A., & Patel, J. (2016). Predicting green product consumption using theory of planned behavior and reasoned action. *Journal of Retailing and Consumer Services*, *29*, 123–134. doi:10.1016/j.jretconser.2015.11.006

Peloza, J., & Shang, J. (2011). How can corporate social responsibility activities create value for stakeholders? A systematic review. *Journal of the Academy of Marketing Science, 39*(1), 117–135. doi:10.100711747-010-0213-6

Phillips, L. (1999). Green Attitudes. *American Demographics, 21,* 46–47.

Pierce, J. L., Kostova, T., & Dirks, K. T. (2003). The State of Psychological Ownership: Integrating and Extending a Century of Research. *Review of General Psychology, 7*(1), 84–107. doi:10.1037/1089-2680.7.1.84

Pradhan, S. (2018). Role of CSR in the consumer decision making process – The case of India. *Social Responsibility Journal, 14*(1), 138–158. doi:10.1108/SRJ-06-2016-0109

Rodrigues, P., & Borges, A. P. (2015). Corporate social responsibility and its impact in consumer decision-making. *Social Responsibility Journal, 11*(4), 690–701. doi:10.1108/SRJ-02-2014-0026

Sarstedt, M., Ringle, C. M., & Hair, J. F. (2017). Partial Least Squares Structural Equation Modeling. In *Handbook of Market Research* (pp. 1–40). Springer International Publishing. doi:10.1007/978-3-319-05542-8_15-1

Saygili, E., Arslan, S., & Birkan, A. O. (2022). ESG practices and corporate financial performance: Evidence from Borsa Istanbul. *Borsa Istanbul Review, 22*(3), 525–533. doi:10.1016/j.bir.2021.07.001

Scott, D. R., & Suchard, H. T. (1992). Motivations for Australian Expenditure on Sponsorship—An Analysis. *International Journal of Advertising, 11*(4), 325–332. doi:10.1080/02650487.1992.11104508

Sharma, K. (2016). *Child Labour in South Asia* (G. Herath, Ed.). Routledge. doi:10.4324/9781315571454

Sharma, S., & Vredenburg, H. (1998). Proactive corporate environmental strategy and the development of competitively valuable organizational capabilities. *Strategic Management Journal, 19*(8), 729–753. doi:10.1002/(SICI)1097-0266(199808)19:8<729::AID-SMJ967>3.0.CO;2-4

Sila, I., & Cek, K. (2017). The Impact of Environmental, Social and Governance Dimensions of Corporate Social Responsibility on Economic Performance: Australian Evidence. *Procedia Computer Science, 120,* 797–804. doi:10.1016/j.procs.2017.11.310

Singh, D. A., & Gaur, A. S. (2009). Business Group Affiliation, Firm Governance, and Firm Performance: Evidence from China and India. *Corporate Governance, 17*(4), 411–425. doi:10.1111/j.1467-8683.2009.00750.x

Singh, J., de los Salmones Sanchez, M., & del Bosque, I. R. (2008). Understanding Corporate Social Responsibility and Product Perceptions in Consumer Markets: A Cross-cultural Evaluation. *Journal of Business Ethics, 80*(3), 597–611. doi:10.100710551-007-9457-6

Singh, N., & Gupta, K. (2013). Environmental Attitude and Ecological Behaviour of Indian consumers. *Social Responsibility Journal, 9*(1), 4–18. doi:10.1108/17471111311307787

Straughan, R. D., & Roberts, J. A. (1999). Environmental segmentation alternatives: A look at green consumer behavior in the new millennium. *Journal of Consumer Marketing, 16*(6), 558–575. doi:10.1108/07363769910297506

Su, X., Sun, B., & Liu, Y. (2021). Selection of cost-effective investment and output subsidies for eco-friendly products. *Journal of Cleaner Production, 286*, 124985. doi:10.1016/j.jclepro.2020.124985

Suijs, J. (2005). Voluntary Disclosure of Bad News. *Journal of Business Finance <html_ent Glyph="@amp;" Ascii="&"/>. Accounting, 32*(7–8), 1423–1435. doi:10.1111/j.0306-686X.2005.00634.x

Sultana, S., Zulkifli, N., & Zainal, D. (2018). Environmental, Social and Governance (ESG) and Investment Decision in Bangladesh. *Sustainability, 10*(6), 1831. doi:10.3390u10061831

Talesh, S. (2015). Rule-Intermediaries in Action: How State and Business Stakeholders Influence the Meaning of Consumer Rights in Regulatory Governance Arrangements. *Law & Policy, 37*(1–2), 1–31. doi:10.1111/lapo.12031

Tarmuji, I., Maelah, R., & Tarmuji, N. H. (2016). The Impact of Environmental, Social and Governance Practices (ESG) on Economic Performance: Evidence from ESG Score. *International Journal of Trade. Economics and Finance, 7*(3), 67–74. doi:10.18178/ijtef.2016.7.3.501

Tasaki, T., Motoshita, M., Uchida, H., & Suzuki, Y. (2013). Assessing the Replacement of Electrical Home Appliances for the Environment. *Journal of Industrial Ecology, 17*(2), 290–298. doi:10.1111/j.1530-9290.2012.00551.x

Todt, O., Muñoz, E., González, M., Ponce, G., & Estévez, B. (2009). Consumer attitudes and the governance of food safety. *Public Understanding of Science (Bristol, England), 18*(1), 103–114. doi:10.1177/0963662507078019 PMID:19579538

Twinamatsiko, E., & Kumar, D. (2022). Incorporating ESG in Decision Making for Responsible and Sustainable Investments using Machine Learning. *2022 International Conference on Electronics and Renewable Systems (ICEARS)*, 1328–1334. 10.1109/ICEARS53579.2022.9752343

Van Quaquebeke, N., Becker, J. U., Goretzki, N., & Barrot, C. (2019). Perceived Ethical Leadership Affects Customer Purchasing Intentions Beyond Ethical Marketing in Advertising Due to Moral Identity Self-Congruence Concerns. *Journal of Business Ethics, 156*(2), 357–376. doi:10.100710551-017-3577-4

Visser, W. (2006). Revisiting Carroll's CSR pyramid: An African perspective. In Corporate citizenship in developing countries: New partnership perspectives. Copenhagen Business School Press.

Weerasinghe, I. M. S., & Dedunu, H. H. (2020). Do demographic factors matter in university-industry knowledge exchange? A study based on Sri Lankan university system. *Journal of Knowledge Management, 25*(5), 973–988. doi:10.1108/JKM-02-2020-0092

Wendell, H. (1991). The 1990s: A new era of formal and informal corporate disclosure. *Journal of Corporate Accounting & Finance, 2*(3), 289–307. doi:10.1002/jcaf.3970020306

Wright, B., & Martin, G. P. (2014). Mission, Margin, and the Role of Consumer Governance in Decision-Making at Community Health Centers. *Journal of Health Care for the Poor and Underserved, 25*(2), 930–947. doi:10.1353/hpu.2014.0107 PMID:24858895

Young-Ferris, A., & Roberts, J. (2021). 'Looking for Something that Isn't There': A Case Study of an Early Attempt at ESG Integration in Investment Decision Making. *European Accounting Review*, 1–28. doi:10.1080/09638180.2021.2000458

Zdravkovic, S., Magnusson, P., & Stanley, S. M. (2010). Dimensions of fit between a brand and a social cause and their influence on attitudes. *International Journal of Research in Marketing*, *27*(2), 151–160. doi:10.1016/j.ijresmar.2010.01.005

Zhang, F., & Zhang, R. (2018). Trade-in Remanufacturing, Customer Purchasing Behavior, and Government Policy. *Manufacturing & Service Operations Management*, *20*(4), 601–616. doi:10.1287/msom.2017.0696

Zhou, Y., Thøgersen, J., Ruan, Y., & Huang, G. (2013). The moderating role of human values in planned behavior: The case of Chinese consumers' intention to buy organic food. *Journal of Consumer Marketing*, *30*(4), 335–344. doi:10.1108/JCM-02-2013-0482

Chapter 9
Intellectual Capital:
A New Process of Sustainable Value Creation for the Corporation

Deepak Kumar Nama

Devi Ahilya Vishwavidyalaya, India

Ranjana Kanungo

Sica College, India

ABSTRACT

Many businesses select business sustainability to satisfy the needs of the environment, society, and economy in order to be optimal in the long run. To do this, businesses must fully and efficiently utilize their resources. Intellectual capital, which increases market value and establishes long-lasting competitive advantages, is one of their most precious resources. This research advances the growth of two distinct but related fields of study: sustainability and intellectual capital. Purpose of the study is to comprehend the notion in its whole and how each component of intellectual capital contributes to a company's sustainable growth. The realization in an organization occurs at every level of management, whether on the basis of interactions with people, human resources, or effective life cycle processes or structures, as we have seen in all prior researches. A crucial or significant part of intellectual capital is played in the long-term sustainability of corporations. Intellectual capital boosts market value and solidifies long-lasting competitive advantages.

INTRODUCTION

The fundamental presumptions of how to point the way into the future are being rethought by a growing number of organizations today. The majority of Executives are already aware that metrics for the corporation's current state include profitability, market share, and even customer satisfaction. Simply said, current product-market pairings are poor indicators of where to make the most money in the future. Corporations must investigate the more subtle and less obvious drivers of future profits in order to determine the best guidelines for future action (Capital, T. I. 1998).Since the second half of the 1980s,

DOI: 10.4018/978-1-6684-6815-9.ch009

professionals and academics have been motivated by the successes of knowledge- and innovation-based enterprises to develop unique methods for measuring a company's worth and to understand the peculiarities of this novel value generation process. In order to explain the persistent creation of wealth and economic growth in organizations, endogenous and firm-specific factors have received primary responsibility (Barney, J. B., 2001; Dierickx et al., 1989; Grant, R. M., 1991). The development of the resource-based view theory and the knowledge-based view theory in the 1990s suggested that access to intangible assets, which are comparable to commodities, rather than just material resources, which are analogous to commodities, was what gave organizations a sustainable competitive advantage (Pedrini, M. 2007). Intangible resources are now considered to be a better "weapon" than actual resources for firms to achieve higher performance, allowing them to increase their competitive edge (Agostini et al., 2017; Yusoff et al., 2019). Intangible assets are becoming more important to businesses than ever before (Hansen, M. T. et al., 1999; Lev, 2001). According to a number of authors, businesses nowadays are more likely to focus on intangible assets than on tangible ones in order to gain a competitive advantage (Bontis, 1996; Martn de Castro et al., 2004). According to Edvinsson, L., and Malone, M. S. (1997), these intangible resources are assets that are not immediately visible on a standard accounting balance sheet but nevertheless boost the value of the firm. Intangible assets are all the components of a company firm that exist in addition to working capital and tangible assets, according to Smith et al. (1994). After working capital and tangible assets, these are the components that support the operation of the business and are frequently the main sources of the company's revenue. Their ability to survive depends on the availability or anticipation of income. Sullivan, P. H. (2000) Intangibles are described as "knowledge that can be transformed into profit". Businesses get value from the profit they make from the sale of their products or services. To assure recurring business, businesses rely on intangibles like reputation, customer loyalty, brand recognition, leadership, and standard-setting, all of which are critically dependent on human capital. In 1998 Nahapiet, J., & Ghoshal, S. refer IAs are described as "knowledge and knowing capabilities of a social collectivity, such as an organization, intellectual community, or professional practice". Hall, R. (1992) "Intangible assets are value generators that turn functional resources into assets with additional value". An intangible asset, according to Lev, B. (2001), "is a claim to future benefits... yet it does not have physical substance." Additionally, he offers a revised definition of assets that excludes financial assets like stocks and bonds from its purview. He claims that innovations, human capital, organizational capital, knowledge, etc. are all components of IAs.

Businesses that foster learning have switched their strategic focus from managing financial assets to managing intellectual capital, an intangible asset (Leliaert wt al., 2003; Rexhepi et al., 2013). One of these intangible resources that stands out is intellectual capital (IC) (Vale et al., 2022), and firms with high IC are more likely to survive (Hormiga et al., 2011).

On the other hand, "sustainable growth" is currently the most crucial worldwide concern. From the economic development model to the recently emerging paradigm of sustainable growth, sustainability is now being prioritized. This is increasingly elevating to the position of a top corporate priority. In today's highly competitive and dynamic environment, a mere concentration on growth maximisation would not lead to the beneficial and desired wealth maximization (Mukherjee, T., & Sen, S. S. 2019). Businesses that actively engage in sustainability (such as environmental management, green innovation, etc.) can not only increase productivity but also improve their corporate images and gain a competitive advantage given the trends of widespread consumer sustainability consciousness and strict international regulations (Chen at al., 2006; de Leaniz et al., 2013). According to Edvinsson, L. 1997 and Chen et al. (2005), intellectual capital (IC) is crucial for corporate sustainability since it offers companies a potential source of sustained competitive advantage (Mukherjee et al., 2019; de Leaniz et al., 2013). Intellectual capital is one of an organization's most valuable assets since it facilitates sustainable growth (Gross-Goacka et al., 2020).

METHODOLOGY

The study for this chapter, which was done using a qualitative technique, was built on the articles' considerations of intellectual intangible Asset, intellectual capital, and sustainable development. Following an examination of citations in famous publications, articles were located using a manual search technique on Google Scholar (GS). These publications, such as the Journal of Intellectual Capital, Journal of Knowledge Management, Sustainability, Journal of Business Ethics, etc., were chosen because they are renowned for publishing theoretical or empirical studies on topics related to IC, sustainable development. The research of Vale et al., 2022 on The Impact of Sustainable Intellectual Capital on Sustainable Performance: A Case Study, Digitalization and new technologies for sustainable business models at the ship-port interface: A bibliometric analysis, Del Giudice et al., 2022, Intellectual capital: A review and bibliometric study, Quintero-Quintero et al., 2021 for example, is included in this chapter, as are all the recent studies that are relevant to our field of study. Regarding the first part of the framework, the strategy is based on a review of the fundamental elements and definition of intellectual capital (IC), starting with a reexamination of the concept of an intangible asset and the question of where does intellectual capital originate in terms of long-term value generation.

Framework for the Context of IC

Intellectual Capital

Any stock's composition, whether material or immaterial, can qualify as capital as long as it is generates revenue. – Fisher 1906

The deepening of the impact of immaterial elements while simultaneously eliminating them from the traditional concept of organization is one of the traits of the modern economy. The reflection can be found in many different themes, such as "competing for the future," core competencies, and cutting-edge management thinking. The intellectual capital domain is made up of these components (Makarov, P. 2010). Tom Stewart's series of articles for Fortune magazine generated interest in intellectual capital. Stewart emphasized how companies build value through their "brain power" in his essays and most recent book, Intellectual Capital, the New Wealth of Organizations (Sullivan, P. H., 1999). When paired with organizational structure and stakeholder relationships, IC is a group of employee-related skills that can reasonably predict an organization's capacity to create value (joshi et al., 2013).

There are numerous definitions of intellectual capital, but most of them use it as an integrated term for the intangible components that support an organization's operations. For instance, A. Brooking, the author of a well-known book on these topics, defines intellectual capital as the "total intangible assets that enable the firm to function" (Brooking, 1996). Bontis, N. (2004) provides a rather general definition of the hidden values of people, enterprises, institutions, communities, and regions that are the current and potential drivers of wealth generation. The basis for sustaining and fostering future wellbeing is laid out by these silent ideals. According to Rastogi, P. N. (2003), knowledge management, the firm's people and social capital, and IC work together to create IC. In the sense that IC doesn't end on its own but is the result of the network effect, this definition is comparable to those of Lev (2001) and Daum, J. H. (2003). According to Mouritsen et al. (2004), IC mobilizes "things" including workers, clients, IT, administrative tasks, and knowledge. "IC cannot stand alone as it only provides a mechanism that permits the various assets to be tied together in the productive activity of the organization," they continue.

Intellectual capital can be considered as a combination of knowledge management ideas with the idea of human capital because it links knowledge and its parent, the individual. A model of intellectual capital that divides it into structural capital and human capital, as proposed by Edvinsson and Malone (1997), is based on such a perspective. Structural capital encompasses the calibre and scope of information technology systems, brand perception, databases, organizational structure, and paperwork. The latter also includes the skills of the workforce required to supply clients with solutions, innovate, and renew the business (Makarov, P. 2010). Intellectual capital is the whole store of knowledge, data, technology, skills, expertise, intellectual property, customer loyalty, and teamwork that may be used by a business to add value to its goods and services.

Emergence of IC

The fundamental framework for the creation of intellectual capital is the idea of organizational resources and capabilities. The notion that intangible assets in organizations ought to be valued served as the foundation for the development of the study of intellectual capital. In order to recognize the potential value of people in the financial accounts of enterprises, the term "human asset accounting" was originally coined in 1963. (Hermanson, R. H. 1963). Later, in 1967, economist J.K. Galbraith made the first formal mention of intellectual capital (Quintero-Quintero et al., 2021).

The historical development of the study of intellectual capital was consolidated in the 1990s and after (Quintero-Quintero et al., 2021). In the middle of the 1990s, four stages of intellectual capital were established. Considering the first phase, the creation of intellectual capital, and its importance in granting companies a competitive edge (Rooney, J., & Dumay, J. 2016; Guthrie, J., & Dumay, J. 2015). End of the 1990s endeavours to recognise intellectual capital as an area of study marked the beginning of the second stage. To increase businesses' competitiveness, numerous models were developed for its measurement (Dumay, J., & Garanina, T. 2013; Guthrie et al., 2017). The third stage was launched in 2004 with the goal of measuring intellectual capital, determining its measurement, and comparing theory and practice (Dumay, J., & Garanina, T. 2013; Guthrie et al., 2017). The fourth stage seeks to go beyond CI reports by expanding to more expansive open and collaborative ecosystems to understand the ramifications on the environment, society, and ethics. It is a complement to the previous stage and focuses on the research of intellectual capital's future (Giuliani et al., 2016).

Component of IC

It is necessary to describe intellectual capital's components in order to more fully comprehend and utilize it (Fidanbas et al., 2019). According to Reed et al. (2006), the intellectual capital approach enables specifying the intangible assets and capabilities that organizations need to have in order to obtain a competitive advantage.

Due to the fact that IC considers people and their abilities (human capital), organizational culture and technology (structural capital), and relationships (relational capital), organizations are able to achieve a competitive edge (kianto et al., 2014; Chen, Y. S. 2008). However, it is believed that the components of intellectual capital cannot all be categorized in the same way (Kozak, 2011; Yildiz et al., 2014). Human capital, customer capital, and structural capital, according to several scholars, are the three components that make up intellectual capital (Stewart, 1997; Brooking, A. 1997; Bontis, N. 1998; Chen, Zhu, & Xie, 2004; Rudez & Mihalic, 2007; Edvinsson, L. 1997; Li, Chen, Lui, & Chu, 2016; Orugun & Aduku, 2017; Stewart, T. A. 2010; Bontis, N. 2002; Kianto et al., 2014; Chen, Y. S. 2008; Brennan, N., & Connell, B. 2000; Marr, B., & Roos, G. 2012). Similarly, Sullivan, P. H. (2000) were also embraced the three categories of IC—human, organisational, and customer. Ramezan (2011) widened the perspective and added "Technological Capital" as an extra crucial component, contradicting Swart's (2005) belief that Social Capital, in addition to the aforementioned factors, is a significant part of IC. Khalique, Shaari, Isa, and Ageel (2011) supported the position, and Hashim, Osman, and Alhabshi (2015) added Spiritual Capital to the list of existing IC components.

Edvinsson, L., & Malone, M. S. (1997) Consider human capital (i.e., the knowledge, skills, and experience of employees) and structural capital as the two main components of intellectual capital (i.e. the supportive infrastructure of human capital). Organizational capital (i.e., the systems and tools) and customer capital are two ways that some authors split structural capital (i.e. relationships a firm has with its customers) As an enlarged definition of customer capital that takes into account the value of all relationships, including those with customers, Bontis (1996) presents the idea of relational capital. Gross-Goacka and colleagues, 2020 According to their research, human capital is the most important element of intellectual capital. Remember that structural and relational capital, two other elements of intellectual capital, is also used to increase a business's worth.

Taking into account the foregoing considerations, intellectual capital can be thought of as having three different subcategories: human, structural, and relational (Bontis, N., 1999; Johnson, W. H., 1999).

.Finally, by pointing out the three parts of intellectual capital, it offers more clarity, Intellectual capital comprises three components, just like physical capital does. The first is human capital, which has to do with employing skills. The second is structural capital, which is related to the internal component. The third category is relational capital, which includes the external element of an organization.

Figure 1. Three intellectual capital components
Source: Author

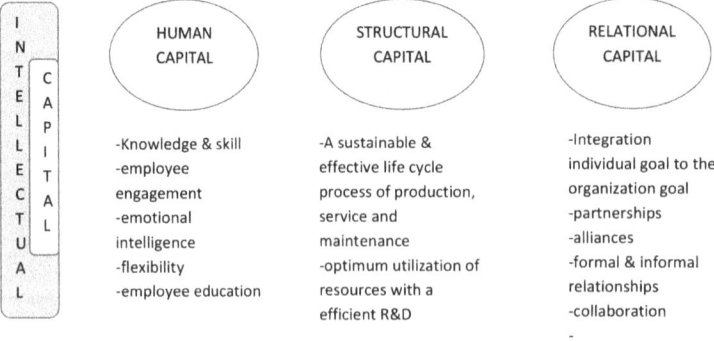

Human Capital

IC was seen as the sum of human and structural capital. Human capital was defined as the knowledge, skill and experience of employees (Capital, T. I. 1998). According to Bontis, N. et al. (1999), human capital is the organization's human aspect, or the intelligence, skills, and knowledge that collectively give the organization its unique personality. The organization's human resources are individuals who are capable of adapting, learning, innovating, and supplying the creative drive that, when appropriately motivated, can guarantee the organization's long-term survival. (Kucharčíková, A. 2011). Human capital, according to Armstrong (2006), is the information and abilities that people acquire, develop, and apply. People have innate skills, personality traits, and personal energy, which together make up the human capital they bring to their employment, according to Davenport, T. H., & Prusak (1998).Human capital, which is built on the abilities, competence, attitudes, knowledge, and intellectual agility of employees, is a significant source of value addition in firms.

Structural Capital

The intellectual resources that, unlike human capital, can be appropriated by the nation and exploited in economic transactions make up structural capital, according to Sanchez et al. The company's organizational procedures might be considered structural capital. It encompasses all the non-human knowledge reservoirs included in the systems, databases, structures, cultures, and programs that enhance productivity and enable the enterprise to create value. This information belongs to the organization even after individuals have left it (Bontis, N. 2000; Roos et al., 1997; Cabrita et al., 2008). As stated in Bontis, N. 2001 Structural capital is everything that an organization has that supports the productivity of its employees, such as its hardware, software, databases, organizational structure, patents, trademarks, and other intellectual property. In other words, structural capital is everything that remains at the office after employees leave for the day. Additionally, structural capital delivers customer capital in the form of the connections made with important clients. Structural capital is an intangible resource that may be shared, replicated, and traded across businesses. A business may be able to legally own certain structural capital assets under a separate title as legally protected intellectual property.

Relational Capital

Relational capital refers to all of the company's connections with external parties, including various stakeholders. It is frequently taken to mean the understanding that permeates interactions with customers, suppliers, investors, and others. It consists of the structural and human capital of the corporation that is connected to stakeholder relationships and perceptions of the business. All information flows that take place from the outside to the inside, as well as the other way around, is another definition of relational capital (Chen et al., 2006; Cabrita et al., 2008). It demonstrates how effectively a company can communicate with potential outside stakeholders (Mukherjee, T., & Sen, S. S. 2019). To put it another way, relational capital is the potential of an enterprise in relation to immaterial market assets like a company's name and reputation, customers' loyalty and contentment, licenses, concessions, and marketing strategies. In summarized way intellectual capital include three elements; human capital- the capabilities of the individuals required to provide solutions to customers, structural capital- the depth (penetration), width (coverage), attachment (loyalty), and profitability of customers, and relational or customer capital- the capabilities of the organization to meet market needs.

INVOLVEMENT OF IC IN SUSTAINABILITY

A business that upholds the philosophy of sustainable development actively incorporates social and environmental goals into its commercial endeavors and interactions with stakeholders. Intellectual capital is increasingly acknowledged as a crucial business strategic asset that can generate a long-lasting competitive advantage and enhanced financial performance, despite its often intangible nature (Chen et al., 2005).A regional institution's orientation toward attaining sustainable development might be seen as organizational capital (Makarov, P. 2010).

Human capital (HC) is the most crucial component in IC (Bontis, N. 1999). Businesses with higher human capital efficiency performed better financially or generally, according to numerous research (Khalique et al., 2011; Maditinos et al., 2011; Sumedrea, S. 2013, and Nassar, S. 2018). In other words, the efficient utilization of human capital contributes to greater financial or overall business success. According to Xu, J., and Wang (2018) Human capital (HC) significantly affects the sustainability of business growth (Mukherjee, T., & Sen, S. S. 2019). Wasiluk, K. L. (2013) and Rzempa et al. (2015) claim that human capital has a significant impact on an enterprise's capacity to grow sustainably. Most often, human resources are emphasized as being distinctive, valuable, challenging to imitate, and challenging to replace, which is a wonderful foundation for gaining long-term competitive advantage. They could function as a core competency (Rexhepi et al., 2013). According to Kusumawardhani, T. (2012), process capital efficiency (PCE) has a significant favorable effect on a company's profitability. Additionally, a high positive association between process capital efficiency and business sustainable growth is envisaged. Wasiluk, K. L. (2013) and Yusoff et al. (2019) both assert that structural capital has a significant impact on an enterprise's capacity to grow sustainably. Even though it is the third component of IC, relational capital is crucial for sustainable development. Relational capital, as defined by Marti, J. M. V. (2001), is an organization's ability to establish positive relationships with other members of the business community in order to stimulate the potential for wealth creation through enhancing human and structural capital. An organization's capacity for sustainable growth is significantly increased by relationship capital (De Leaniz et al., 2013; Wasiluk, K. L. 2013; Sokoowska, A. 2005). The sustainable growth of an enterprise and the image of a corporation, one of the elements of relational capital, are related (de Leaniz et al., 2013; Gross-Goacka et al., 2020). Furthermore, the research by Xu and Wang (2018) shows that relational capital also has a considerable favorable impact on the sustainable expansion of businesses.

The relationships between intellectual property and the long-term sustainability of firms were studied by researchers Massaro et al. (2018) and Dal Mas, F. (2019). In these studies, a perceptual measure based on the perspectives of practitioners was used. Sustainability and intellectual capital are linked, according to the conclusions of Omar et al. (2017), Chen et al. (2006), Chen et al. (2008), Akhtar et al. (2015), and Dal Mas, F. (2019). The competitiveness and sustainability of an organization are greatly improved by intellectual capital (Gross-Goacka et al., 2020). The knowledge-based economy's demands must currently be met by small and medium-sized firms. One of the most crucial assets for ensuring the company's sustainable growth and enabling the acquisition of a competitive advantage is intellectual capital (Gross-Goacka et al., 2020). Intellectual capital is a recognized strategic asset for long-term firm competitive advantages (Chen et al., 2005).

DISCUSSION

It is an interesting time to be active in the field of research into intellectual capital (IC) (Petty et al., 2000). Intellectual capital has gained popularity during the past twenty years. Numerous academics, researchers, and practitioners explored the idea and its significance in the knowledge-based economy (Akhavan et al., 2009). In the so-called modern knowledge economy, intellectual capital (IC) has played a crucial role in the commercial, institutional, and academic spheres, allowing the transition toward (vale et al., 2022). Organizations must continually update and apply the knowledge they receive, as well as develop their innovative potential, if they want to achieve long-term success (Liedtka, J., 1999; Bhatti et al., 2014). In this "Knowledge-based Economy," according to economists Augier and Teece (2005), "knowledge" and "intellectual capital" are two essential intangible assets that aid companies in producing value and profit. According to Drucker (1993), human knowledge fosters innovation and changes "Human Society" into a "Knowledge Society." It has been discovered that when intellectual capital influences the innovation capability and activities, the enterprise's learning, education, experience, and expertise factors, as well as its communication and interaction with internal and external stakeholders, quality management, and business performance are all positively impacted. It is encouraging to see that innovation activities are motivated appropriately and supported by appropriate tools and capabilities (Fidanbas et al., 2019). According to Kramer et al. (2011) and Vincent et al. (2004), an organization must be innovative in order to build a sustainable competitive advantage in the current context. According to Cheng et al. (2010), effectively managed innovation input improves customer interactions. The ability to innovate has a significant and favorable effect on sustainable consumer relationships.

According to Brooking, A. (1997), IC can be categorized as "market assets," "human-centered assets," "intellectual property assets," and "infrastructure assets" that, when combined with an organization's other productive resources, can ultimately result in value creation. According to Augier et al. (2012), organizations will experience negative effects if they don't have any plans for discovering and controlling their IC. Alcaniz et al. (2011) and Marr, B. (2012) concluded that the IC concept has emerged with various perspectives, including: Economic, Strategic, Accounting, Finance, Reporting, Marketing, Human resource, Information system, and the Legal perspective, based on a multidisciplinary previous studies of IC. According to Brown (2009) and Zschockelt (2009), IC and innovation are two essential resources that businesses must disclose and manage properly if they want to improve firm performance.

Starting with the analysis of our research's findings, the significance placed on intangible resources highlights the need to look into the cultural and social ramifications of the IC's role as an engine for long-term value creation and a guide for entrepreneurship in the direction of sustainable development (SD). The new economy is becoming increasingly significant in the corporate world of highly developed nations, demonstrating the critical role intellectual capital plays in enhancing the competitive edge of businesses. However, because it consists of the company's intangible resources, which cannot be valued using the financial instruments used to assess tangible assets, intellectual capital reflects the hidden portion of a company's value. Intangible assets and intellectual capital are necessary prerequisites for long-term growth and a competitive advantage that can be sustained. To attain competitiveness and convergence at the micro- and macroeconomic levels, the management of intangible assets and intellectual capital is crucial. (Todericiu, R., & Stăniţ, A. 2015). According to the International Integrated Reporting Council (IIRC), 2013 organizations derive value from a broad range of interactions, activities, linkages, causes, and effects. These interactions occur in the organization's operating environment and the regulatory, social, natural, and environmental contexts on which it depends. Consumers, employees, stakeholders, regulators, suppliers, and other people acting in the environment in which an organization performs commercial activities are involved in contacts with the organization. Limitations imposed by nature, the environment, and the planet have an impact on the context. For an organization to adapt and become more environmentally friendly, sustainably managed, and socially just, intellectual capital is essential.

The findings show that intellectual capital significantly contributes to improving sustainable corporate success. This general conclusion is consistent with the vast majority of empirical research on the relationship between intellectual capital and different firm performance outcomes, such as financial performance (Youndt et al. 2004), innovation performance (Carmona-Lavado et al. 2010; Subramanian and Youndt 2005; Wu et al. 2008), and new product development (Inkinen 2015). (Chen et al. 2006). Additionally, we discovered proof from the research of (Hussinki et al., 2019) that intellectual capital also has a good impact on a company's performance from the standpoint of internal sustainability. The sustainability perspective is a crucial approach to look at performance in the current global environment, since societies, employees, and investors have begun to favor businesses that can create outcomes in an ethical and sustainable way.

MANAGERIAL IMPLICATION

The discovery can be used to design an enterprise's strategy while identifying the resources that are particularly important and should be developed, created, and acquired. The research's findings are largely applicable to companies, which can use them to manage intellectual capital, track the results of business endeavors, allocate human, structural, and relational resources, and design systems that make the most use of each unit's resources. Employees can use this knowledge to establish their value and connection to the firm by figuring out their place and purpose within it. Additionally, managers and staff are becoming more aware of their role in influencing the sustainable development of businesses.

LIMITATIONS AND FUTURE RESEARCH

A few features of our study give it a unique advantage and influence the generalizability and precision of our conclusions. The more specific the field, however, the better, as it is stated that research with various objectives tend to be ambiguous. This study has some flaws, including the idea that intellectual capital, which includes intangible resources like employee knowledge, organization conviction, and a collection of data necessary for survival, reflects the hidden portion of a company's value. We have operated within the parameters of the sustainability and intellectual capital components..The chapter illustrates the connection between IC and sustainable value creation. The stock of knowledge that results from the organizational flow of knowledge generation through time is represented in this context by IC in terms of human capital, structural capital, and relational capital. Knowledge is entrenched and exploited to generate value for businesses, according to Grant, R. M. 1996; Lane, P. J. et al., 2001; Meier, M. 2011; and Garcia-Perez, A et al., 2020. In the context of knowledge management, this chapter can advance research by creating an alignment between the IC and two sources of knowledge: tacit knowledge (information gleaned from incidents, circumstances, patterns, and observations) and explicit knowledge (a structured set of information), as well as evaluate additional sources of knowledge.

CONCLUDING REMARKS

IC is frequently used to refer to a collection of potential intangible assets that could support profitable business expansion. It is crucial for a company's long-term worth as a strategic resource (Smriti, N., & Das, N. 2017). The knowledge, expertise, information, and intellectual property that a company can use to its benefit in the future are collectively referred to as its intellectual capital. According to Bontis (1999), organizational expertise (IC) provides a business with a competitive advantage (Mukherjee et al., 2019). It is the foundation for an organization's innovation and long-term viability (Bontis, N. 2000; Bontis, N. 2002; Bhatti et al., 2014). Intellectual capital is closely related to knowledge management, which can support organizational sustainability in a number of ways (social, economic, and environmental). It promotes the development of manufacturing methods that respect the natural and social balance of the entire ecosphere as a result (Del Giudice et al., 2022). Economic progress now is pushing humanity toward a stage of mental development when people seek more fulfillment from satisfying relationships, psychological gratification, and cultural enrichment than from ever-increasing material consumption. Thus, the ultimate determinant of sustainability is the steady development of human capital made possible by the ongoing evolution of human awareness (Laus et al., 2011). Superior financial performance is created by a sustainable competitive advantage and intellectual capital, which is acknowledged in all fields of study (Bollen et al., 2005; Bontis, N.1998; Firer, S., & Williams, S. M. 2003; Leliaert et al., 2003). As we have seen in all previous studies, the realization of intellectual capital occurs at every level of management, whether on the basis of interactions with people, human resources, or efficient life cycle processes or structures. Intellectual capital plays a major or important role in the long-term sustainability of corporations. Intellectual capital is one of their most important resources since it increases market value and solidifies enduring competitive advantages.

ACKNOWLEDGMENT

We are grateful to Dr. Disha Sharma of Amity University in Raipur, India. He introduced us to and has consistently supported the concept "Intellectual Capital as a "Precursor to Sustainable Corporate Social Responsibility." (https://orcid.org/0000-0003-2124-0970).

REFERENCES

Agostini, L., Nosella, A., & Filippini, R. (2017). Does intellectual capital allow improving innovation performance? A quantitative analysis in the SME context. *Journal of Intellectual Capital*, *18*(2), 400–418. doi:10.1108/JIC-05-2016-0056

Akhavan, P., Hosnavi, R., & Sanjaghi, M. E. (2009). Identification of knowledge management critical success factors in Iranian academic research centers. *Education, Business and Society*, *2*(4), 276–288. doi:10.1108/17537980911001107

Akhtar, C. S., Ismail, K., Ndaliman, M. A., Hussain, J., & Haider, M. (2015). Can intellectual capital of smes help in their sustainability efforts. *Journal of Management Research*, *7*(2), 82. doi:10.5296/jmr.v7i2.6930

Alcaniz, L., Gomez-Bezares, F., & Roslender, R. (2011, June). Theoretical perspectives on intellectual capital: A backward look and a proposal for going forward. *Accounting Forum*, *35*(2), 104–117. doi:10.1016/j.accfor.2011.03.004

Alvesson, M. (2002). *Understanding Organisational Culture*. Sage Publications.

Armstrong, M. (2006). *A handbook of human resource management practice*. Kogan Page Publishers.

Augier, M., & Teece, D. J. (2012). An Economics Perspective on Intellectual Capital1. In *Perspectives on intellectual capital* (pp. 3–27). Routledge.

Barney, J. B. (2001). Is the resource-based "view" a useful perspective for strategic management research? Yes. *Academy of Management Review*, *26*(1), 41–56.

Bhatti, W. A., & Zaheer, A. (2014). The role of intellectual capital in creating and adding value to organizational performance: A conceptual analysis. *Electronic Journal of Knowledge Management*, *12*(3), 185–192.

Bollen, L., Vergauwen, P., & Schnieders, S. (2005). Linking intellectual capital and intellectual property to company performance. *Management Decision*, *43*(9), 1161–1185. doi:10.1108/00251740510626254

Bontis, N. (1996). There is a price on your head: Managing intellectual capital strategically. *Business Quarterly*, *60*(4), 40–47.

Bontis, N. (1998). Intellectual capital: An exploratory study that develops measures and models. *Management Decision*, *36*(2), 63–76. doi:10.1108/00251749810204142

Bontis, N. (1999). Managing organizational knowledge by diagnosing intellectual capital: Framing and advancing the state of the field. *International Journal of Technology Management*, *18*(5-8), 433–462. doi:10.1504/IJTM.1999.002780

Bontis, N. (2000). *Managing organizational knowledge by diagnosing intellectual capital. In Knowledge Management: Classic and Contemporary Works*. MIT Press.

Bontis, N. (2001). Assessing knowledge assets: A review of the models used to measure intellectual capital. *International Journal of Management Reviews*, *3*(1), 41–60. doi:10.1111/1468-2370.00053

Bontis, N. (2002). *National intellectual capital index: Intellectual capital development in the Arab Region*. Institute for Intellectual Capital Research.

Bontis, N. (2004). National intellectual capital index: A United Nations initiative for the Arab region. *Journal of Intellectual Capital*, *5*(1), 13–39. doi:10.1108/14691930410512905

Bontis, N., Dragonetti, N. C., Jacobsen, K., & Roos, G. (1999). The knowledge toolbox: A review of the tools available to measure and manage intangible resources. *European Management Journal*, *17*(4), 391–402. doi:10.1016/S0263-2373(99)00019-5

Brennan, N., & Connell, B. (2000). Intellectual capital: Current issues and policy implications. *Journal of Intellectual Capital*, *1*(3), 206–240. doi:10.1108/14691930010350792

Brooking, A. (1996). *Intellectual Capital: Core Assets for the Third Millennium Enterprise*. Thomson Business Press.

Brooking, A. (1997). Intellectual capital. In Intellectual capital. International Thomson business press.

Brown, J. (2009). *Intellectual Capital and Innovation: Implications for New Service Development*. Cass Business School.

Cabrita, M. D. R., & Bontis, N. (2008). Intellectual capital and business performance in the Portuguese banking industry. *International Journal of Technology Management*, *43*(1-3), 212–237. doi:10.1504/IJTM.2008.019416

Capital, T. I. (1998). Exploring the concept of intellectual capital (IC). *Long Range Planning*, 31.

Chen, M. C., Cheng, S. J., & Hwang, Y. (2005). An empirical investigation of the relationship between intellectual capital and firms' market value and financial performance. *Journal of Intellectual Capital*, *6*(2), 159–176. doi:10.1108/14691930510592771

Chen, Y. S. (2008). The positive effect of green intellectual capital on competitive advantages of firms. *Journal of Business Ethics*, *77*(3), 271–286. doi:10.100710551-006-9349-1

Chen, Y. S., Lai, S. B., & Wen, C. T. (2006). The influence of green innovation performance on corporate advantage in Taiwan. *Journal of Business Ethics*, *67*(4), 331–339. doi:10.100710551-006-9025-5

Cheng, M. Y., Lin, J. Y., Hsiao, T. Y., & Lin, T. W. (2010). Invested resource, competitive intellectual capital, and corporate performance. *Journal of Intellectual Capital*, *11*(4), 433–450. doi:10.1108/14691931011085623

Dal Mas, F. (2019). The relationship between intellectual capital and sustainability: An analysis of practitioner's thought. In *Intellectual capital management as a driver of sustainability* (pp. 11–24). Springer. doi:10.1007/978-3-319-79051-0_2

Daum, J. H. (2003). *Intangible assets and value creation*. John Wiley & Sons.

Davenport, T. H., & Prusak, L. (1998). *Working Knowledge*. Harvard Business School Press.

de Castro, G. M., Sáez, P. L., & López, J. E. N. (2004). The role of corporate reputation in developing relational capital. *Journal of Intellectual Capital*.

De Leaniz, P. M. G., & del Bosque, I. R. (2013). Intellectual capital and relational capital: The role of sustainability in developing corporate reputation. *Intangible Capital*, *9*(1), 262–280.

Del Giudice, M., Di Vaio, A., Hassan, R., & Palladino, R. (2022). Digitalization and new technologies for sustainable business models at the ship–port interface: A bibliometric analysis. *Maritime Policy & Management*, *49*(3), 410–446. doi:10.1080/03088839.2021.1903600

Dierickx, I., & Cool, K. (1989). Asset stock accumulation and sustainability of competitive advantage. *Management Science*, *35*(12), 1504–1511. doi:10.1287/mnsc.35.12.1504

Dumay, J., & Garanina, T. (2013). Intellectual capital research: A critical examination of the third stage. *Journal of Intellectual Capital*, *14*(1), 10–25. doi:10.1108/14691931311288995

Edvinsson, L. (1997). Developing intellectual capital at Skandia. *Long Range Planning*, *30*(3), 366–373. doi:10.1016/S0024-6301(97)90248-X

Edvinsson, L., & Malone, M. S. (1997). *Intellectual Capital*. HarperBusiness.

Edvinsson, L., & Malone, M. S. (1997). *Intellectual capital: Realizing your company's true value by finding its hidden brainpower.* harperbusiness.

Fidanbas, O., & Irdan, G. (2019). The impact of intellectual capital on innovation: A literature study. *Business Management Dynamics*, *8*(12), 1.

Firer, S., & Williams, S. M. (2003). Intellectual capital and traditional measures of corporate performance. *Journal of Intellectual Capital*, *4*(3), 348–360. doi:10.1108/14691930310487806

Fisher, I. (1906). *The nature of capital and income*. Macmillan and Cie. doi:10.1515/9783112351369

Galbraith, J. K. (2007). *The new industrial state* (Vol. 9). Princeton University Press. doi:10.1515/9781400873180

Garcia-Perez, A., Ghio, A., Occhipinti, Z., & Verona, R. (2020). Knowledge management and intellectual capital in knowledge-based organisations: A review and theoretical perspectives. *Journal of Knowledge Management*, *24*(7), 1719–1754. doi:10.1108/JKM-12-2019-0703

Giuliani, M., Chiucchi, M. S., & Marasca, S. (2016). A history of intellectual capital measurements: From production to consumption. *Journal of Intellectual Capital*, *17*(3), 590–606. doi:10.1108/JIC-08-2015-0071

Grant, R. M. (1991). The resource-based theory of competitive advantage: Implications for strategy formulation. *California Management Review*, *33*(3), 114–135. doi:10.2307/41166664

Grant, R. M. (1996). Prospering in dynamically-competitive environments: Organizational capability as knowledge integration. *Organization Science*, *7*(4), 375–387. doi:10.1287/orsc.7.4.375

Gross-Gołacka, E., Kusterka-Jefmańska, M., & Jefmański, B. (2020). Can elements of intellectual capital improve business sustainability?—The perspective of managers of smes in Poland. *Sustainability*, *12*(4), 1545. doi:10.3390u12041545

Guthrie, J., & Dumay, J. (2015). New frontiers in the use of intellectual capital in the public sector. *Journal of Intellectual Capital*, *16*(2), 258–266. doi:10.1108/JIC-02-2015-0017

Guthrie, J., Dumay, J., Ricceri, F., & Nielsen, C. (Eds.). (2017). *The Routledge companion to intellectual capital*. Routledge. doi:10.4324/9781315393100

Hall, R. (1992, February). The Strategic Analysis of Intangible Resources. *Strategic Management Journal*, *13*(2), 135–144. doi:10.1002mj.4250130205

Hansen, M. T., Nohria, N., & Tierney, T. (1999). What's your strategy for managing knowledge? Response. *Harvard Business Review*, *77*(3), 196–196.

Hermanson, R. H. (1963). *A Method for recording all Assets and the Resulting Accounting and Economic Implications*. Michigan State University.

Hussinki, H., Kianto, A., Vanhala, M., & Ritala, P. (2019). Happy employees make happy customers: The role of intellectual capital in supporting sustainable value creation in organizations. In *Intellectual capital management as a driver of sustainability* (pp. 101–117). Springer. doi:10.1007/978-3-319-79051-0_6

International Integrated Reporting Council (IIRC). (2013). *Consultation draft of the international framework*. Author.

Johnson, W. H. (1999). An integrative taxonomy of intellectual capital: Measuring the stock and flow of intellectual capital components in the firm. *International Journal of Technology Management*, *18*(5), 562–575. doi:10.1504/IJTM.1999.002788

Joshi, M., Cahill, D., Sidhu, J., & Kansal, M. (2013). Intellectual capital and financial performance: An evaluation of the Australian financial sector. *Journal of Intellectual Capital*, *14*(2), 264–285. doi:10.1108/14691931311323887

Khalique, M., Nassir Shaari, J. A., Isa, A. H. B. M., & Ageel, A. (2011). Relationship of intellectual capital with the organizational performance of pharmaceutical companies in Pakistan. *Australian Journal of Basic and Applied Sciences*, *5*(12), 1964–1969.

Kianto, A., Ritala, P., Spender, J. C., & Vanhala, M. (2014). The interaction of intellectual capital assets and knowledge management practices in organizational value creation. *Journal of Intellectual Capital*, *15*(3), 362–375. doi:10.1108/JIC-05-2014-0059

Kramer, J. P., Marinelli, E., Iammarino, S., & Diez, J. R. (2011). Intangible assets as drivers of innovation: Empirical evidence on multinational enterprises in German and UK regional systems of innovation. *Technovation*, *31*(9), 447–458. doi:10.1016/j.technovation.2011.06.005

Kucharčíková, A. (2011). Human capital–definitions and approaches. *Human Resources Management & Ergonomics*, *5*(2), 60–70.

Kusumawardhani, T. (2012). Intellectual capital, financial profitability, and productivity: An exploratory study of the Indonesian pharmaceutical industry. *Asian Journal of Business and Accounting*, *5*(2).

Lane, P. J., Salk, J. E., & Lyles, M. A. (2001). Absorptive capacity, learning, and performance in international joint ventures. *Strategic Management Journal*, *22*(12), 1139–1161. doi:10.1002mj.206

Leliaert, P. J., Candries, W., & Tilmans, R. (2003). Identifying and managing IC: a new classification. *Journal of Intellectual Capital*.

Lev, B. (2001). *Intangibles: management. In Measurement, and Reporting*. Brookings Institution Press.

Liedtka, J. (1999). Linking competitive advantage with communities of practice. *Journal of Management Inquiry*, *8*(1), 5–16. doi:10.1177/105649269981002

Maditinos, D., Chatzoudes, D., Tsairidis, C., & Theriou, G. (2011). The impact of intellectual capital on firms' market value and financial performance. *Journal of Intellectual Capital*, *12*(1), 132–151. doi:10.1108/14691931111097944

Makarov, P. (2010). Intellectual capital as an indicator of a sustainable development. *Journal of Sustainable Development*, *3*(3), 85. doi:10.5539/jsd.v3n3p85

Marr, B. (2012). The evolution and convergence of intellectual capital as a theme. In *Perspectives on intellectual capital* (pp. 225–238). Routledge. doi:10.4324/9780080479934-24

Marr, B., & Roos, G. (2012). A strategy perspective on intellectual capital. In *Perspectives on intellectual capital* (pp. 28–41). Routledge.

Marti, J. M. V. (2001). ICBS–intellectual capital benchmarking system. *Journal of Intellectual Capital, 2*(2), 148–165. doi:10.1108/14691930110385937

Massaro, M., Dumay, J., Garlatti, A., & Dal Mas, F. (2018). Practitioners' views on intellectual capital and sustainability: From a performance-based to a worth-based perspective. *Journal of Intellectual Capital, 19*(2), 367–386. doi:10.1108/JIC-02-2017-0033

Meier, M. (2011). Knowledge management in strategic alliances: A review of empirical evidence. *International Journal of Management Reviews, 13*(1), 1–23. doi:10.1111/j.1468-2370.2010.00287.x

Mouritsen, J., Bukh, P. N., & Marr, B. (2004). Reporting on intellectual capital: Why, what and how? *Measuring Business Excellence, 8*(1), 46–54. doi:10.1108/13683040410524739

Mukherjee, T., & Sen, S. S. (2019). Intellectual capital and corporate sustainable growth: The Indian evidence. *Asian Journal of Business Environment, 9*(2), 5–15. doi:10.13106/jbees.2019.vol9.no2.5

Nahapiet, J., & Ghoshal, S. (1998). Social capital, intellectual capital, and the organizational advantage. *Academy of Management Review, 23*(2), 242–266. doi:10.2307/259373

Nassar, S. (2018). The impact of intellectual capital on corporate performance of IT companies: Evidence from bursa Istanbul. *Journal of Accounting and Applied Business Research, 1*(3), 1–10. doi:10.51325/ijbeg.v1i3.17

Omar, M. K., Yusoff, Y. M., & Zaman, M. D. K. (2017). The role of green intellectual capital on business sustainability. *World Applied Sciences Journal, 35*(12), 2558–2563.

Pedrini, M. (2007). Human capital convergences in intellectual capital and sustainability reports. *Journal of Intellectual Capital, 8*(2), 346–366. doi:10.1108/14691930710742880

Petty, R., & Guthrie, J. (2000). Intellectual capital literature review: Measurement, reporting and management. *Journal of Intellectual Capital, 1*(2), 155–176. doi:10.1108/14691930010348731

Quintero-Quintero, W., Blanco-Ariza, A. B., & Garzón-Castrillón, M. A. (2021). Intellectual capital: A review and bibliometric analysis. *Publications, 9*(4), 46. doi:10.3390/publications9040046

Rastogi, P. N. (2003). The nature and role of IC: Rethinking the process of value creation and sustained enterprise growth. *Journal of Intellectual Capital.*

Reed, K. K., Lubatkin, M., & Srinivasan, N. (2006). Proposing and testing an intellectual capital-based view of the firm. *Journal of Management Studies, 43*(4), 867–893. doi:10.1111/j.1467-6486.2006.00614.x

Rexhepi, G., Ibraimi, S., & Veseli, N. (2013). Role of intellectual capital in creating enterprise strategy. *Procedia: Social and Behavioral Sciences, 75*, 44–51. doi:10.1016/j.sbspro.2013.04.006

Rooney, J., & Dumay, J. (2016). Intellectual capital, calculability and qualculation. *The British Accounting Review*, *48*(1), 1–16. doi:10.1016/j.bar.2015.07.002

Roos, J., Edvinsson, L., & Dragonetti, N. C. (1997). *Intellectual capital: Navigating the new business landscape*. Springer. doi:10.1007/978-1-349-14494-5

Rzempała, J., & Rzempała, A. (2015). Analysis of SME companies' awareness of the value of intellectual capital. *Scientific Journals of the University of Szczecin. Finance, Financial Markets, Insurance*, (73), 483-495.

Sánchez Medina, A. J., Melián González, A., & Garcia Falcon, J. M. (2007). Intellectual capital and sustainable development on islands: An application to the case of Gran Canaria. *Regional Studies*, *41*(4), 473–487. doi:10.1080/00343400600928327

Simensky, M., & Bryer, L. G. (Eds.). (1994). *The new role of intellectual property in commercial transactions*. Wiley.

Šlaus, I., & Jacobs, G. (2011). Human capital and sustainability. *Sustainability*, *3*(1), 97–154. doi:10.3390u3010097

Smriti, N., & Das, N. (2017). Impact of intellectual capital on business performance: evidence from Indian pharmaceutical sector. *Polish Journal of Management Studies, 15*.

Sokołowska, A. (2005). Zarzadzanie kapitałem intelektualnym w małym przedsiebiorstwie. Polskie Towarzystwo Ekonomiczne.

Stewart, T. A. (2010). *Intellectual Capital: The new wealth of organization*. Currency.

Sullivan, P. H. (1999). Profiting from intellectual capital. *Journal of Knowledge Management*, *3*(2), 132–143. doi:10.1108/13673279910275585

Sullivan, P. H. (2000). *Value driven intellectual capital: how to convert intangible corporate assets into market value*. John Wiley & Sons, Inc.

Todericiu, R., & Stăniţ, A. (2015). Intellectual capital–The key for sustainable competitive advantage for the SME's sector. *Procedia Economics and Finance*, *27*, 676–681. doi:10.1016/S2212-5671(15)01048-5

Vale, J., Miranda, R., Azevedo, G., & Tavares, M. C. (2022). The Impact of Sustainable Intellectual Capital on Sustainable Performance: A Case Study. *Sustainability*, *14*(8), 4382. doi:10.3390u14084382

Vincent, L. H., Bharadwaj, S. G., & Challagalla, G. N. (2004). *Does innovation mediate firm performance? A meta-analysis of determinants and consequences of organizational innovation*. Academic Press.

Wasiluk, K. L. (2013). Beyond eco-efficiency: Understanding CS through the IC practice lens. *Journal of Intellectual Capital*, *14*(1), 102–126. doi:10.1108/14691931311289048

Xu, J., & Wang, B. (2018). Intellectual capital, financial performance and companies' sustainable growth: Evidence from the Korean manufacturing industry. *Sustainability*, *10*(12), 4651. doi:10.3390u10124651

Yusoff, Y. M., Omar, M. K., Zaman, M. D. K., & Samad, S. (2019). Do all elements of green intellectual capital contribute toward business sustainability? Evidence from the Malaysian context using the Partial Least Squares method. *Journal of Cleaner Production*, *234*, 626–637. doi:10.1016/j.jclepro.2019.06.153

Zschockelt, F. (2009). *The importance of developing intellectual capital for innovative organizations: contributions from a HRM-perspective* [Master's thesis]. University of Twente.

KEY TERMS AND DEFINITIONS

Human Capital: An organization's human capital is made up of competencies, knowledge, capacities, talents, and know-how as well as attitudes, ducts, motivation, performance, and ethics of the individuals as well as intellectual agility, dexterity, and experiences of employees and directors.

Intangible Assets: For organizations, intangible assets are sources of long-term competitive advantage. Additionally, they stress the significance of an approach to valuing intangible assets to assist with a number of administrative difficulties, including investment choices, discussions with lenders, and obtaining funds from investors.

Intellectual Capital: The capacity of a certain company to turn its knowledge and intangible assets into wealth as well as resource production is referred to as intellectual capital. The process of obtaining the value of knowledge is seen as the management of intellectual capital.

Relational Capital: Relational capital is a collection of talents that are ingrained in the organization and the people that make up its membership. Relationships with various market players and with society at large lead to the development of relational capital.

Structural Capital: Structural capital is what an organization can continue to use even after its personnel cease working there. It consists of a collection of knowledge and intangible assets produced by organizational processes that belong to the organization and endure even after an employee leaves.

APPENDIX

Table 1. Abbreviation

Abbreviation	Definition
IC	Intellectual Capital
IA	Intangible Asset
HC	Human Capital
SD	Sustainable Development
PCE	Process Capital Efficiency

Chapter 10

Investigation of Green Port Strategy in Sustainable Port Approach

Osman Arslan

https://orcid.org/0000-0003-4384-3510

Maritime Faculty, Kocaeli University, Turkey

ABSTRACT

The concept of "green port" reflects ecological practices aimed at protecting the environment during port activities. Green port practices are a long-term strategic approach in terms of ensuring the environmental sustainability of a port. The study focuses on the environmental dimension of sustainability, which is a popular concept today. By conducting a literature search on the green port strategy, important indicators were determined, and it was aimed to analyze these indicators. As a result of the study, important indicators such as air quality, climate change energy efficiency, noise pollution, relations with the local community, water quality and ship waste, dredging operations and port development, and garbage/port wastes have been reached.

INTRODUCTION

Ports are one of the most significant stakeholders of maritime transport, which is one of the modes of transport. Considering that maritime transport is at the center of global trade, ports contribute significantly to the region and country's economies. Ports connect the world through maritime transport and contribute to economic growth by supporting global trade. Ports, which have an important place in maritime transportation, are the gates of global trade that provide services such as loading, unloading and storage (Nagle, 2013; Pettit & Beresford, 2009). Nowadays, it has become a strategic factor for ports to follow sustainable policies due to their important role in the supply chain and economy. Carrying out activities related to sustainability is one of the biggest challenges facing countries today. In particular, people's use of natural resources without thinking and the emergence of environmental problems as a result of this threatens our world deeply. According to Organisation for Economic Co-operation and

DOI: 10.4018/978-1-6684-6815-9.ch010

Development (OECD) research, efficiently operated ports can contribute to economic development in their region; however, the negative effects of port activities on the environment should not be ignored (OECD, 2009). Maritime transport activities are recognized as the third largest source of air pollution after motor vehicles and industrial enterprises (Yılmaz, 2019). The increase in the amount of the goods to be transported has led to an increase in the tonnage of ships and an increase in the capacities of the ports serving the ships. As a result, more waste, more water pollution, more emissions and noise pollution have arisen. This situation has left the ports under more pressure due to their negative impact on the ecological environment. Therefore, in terms of maritime transport and ports, it is seen that environmental protection and sustainability issues are gaining importance day by day and becoming a competitive element (Sislian, Jaegler & Cariou, 2016).

Considering the future of the world, global problems such as ecosystem degradation and climate change have caused port activities to be questioned. As a result of port operations, ports have started to create various strategies in order to reduce the negative effects of regional pollution and greenhouse emissions from harbour field on the environment and people. Ports that have turned into logistics bases have focused on the concept of green ports in order to achieve environmental sustainability and to eliminate environmental pollution, especially from ship and port field operations.

The concept of sustainable development and green concept emerged as a solution to combat environmental pollution caused by the construction and operation of a port (Chiu et al., 2014). The green port approach focuses on the energy saving perspective, which is based on the continuity of operational processes without harming the environment. Green ports are also nature-friendly ports that care about human health and protect the ecosystem. The concept of green port can be achieved as a result of long-term strategies for ensuring the continuity of a port and its environmentally friendly development (Pavlic et al., 2014). In this context, the adoption of the green concept by the ports reflects the importance given by the countries to the people and the natural environment (Köseoğlu & Solmaz, 2019).

In the study, after an introduction to the subject was made, the subject was explained in the background and supported by a literature review. In the next section, the ports and the functions of the ports were explained. The concept of green port and environmental sustainability was explained and its importance today was emphasized. In the following sections, a legal framework was created by considering the international legislations related to the concept of green port. As a result of the literature research and especially the report published by European Sea Ports Organization (ESPO), the indicators and strategies regarding the green port practices in the world were revealed and solutions and suggestions were made. Finally, the conclusion was reached by including other future studies related to the study.

BACKGROUND

As in every sector, the concept of sustainability in the maritime sector has become an issue that is gaining importance every day in order to ensure the continuity of businesses. Sustainability has been defined as "development that meets the needs of the present without compromising the ability of future generations to meet their own needs" (WCED, 1987). The concept of sustainability, which covers economic, social and environmental issues in operational and managerial processes, becomes more important in terms of providing a better quality of life by using natural resources more efficiently. In sustainable development, the economic perspective considers not only the economic benefit, but also the environmental and social benefits that the business acquires by acting responsibly (Elkington, 1994). In the literature, it is seen that intensive studies are carried out on economic, environmental and social sustainability in various fields. In particular, studies on the damage to the ecosystem as a result of human activities and climate changes have begun to attract attention. Their significant role in transportation systems and their functions in the economy make ports important in ensuring sustainability (Özispa & Arabelen, 2021). With the increase in global trade volume, many port operators have started to follow sustainable policies in order to keep up with the demands of consumers and other stakeholders interacting with ports. Sustainability is regarding the adaptation of ports to economic and environmental changes (Wakeman, 1996). The main purpose of sustainability in ports can be expressed as reducing emissions by following environmentalist policies, providing more ecological services, saving energy, increasing the financial performance of ports and showing people-oriented approaches. It proposes an integrated framework aimed at green market development, stakeholder engagement, cost-effective environmental approach and development at the beginning of a sustainable port strategy (Özispa & Arabelen, 2021).

Studies on environmental problems concerned with harbours are quite various. A major concern for port operations in recent years has been the minimization of environmental impacts. Ports are trying to achieve a "greener" status by using new technologies and renewing their infrastructure, avoiding unnecessary energy use. The effects of ports on the environment are considered as a system consisting of several different parts. These can be divided into maritime activities, inland port operations and inland transport. As transport activity increases, so do undesirable side effects such as air pollution, noise pollution, emissions and traffic congestion (Chiu et al., 2014). Pollution and emissions originating from the port cause problems such as climate change. Ships handling cargo in ports also cause environmental effects. Examples of these effects are noise from vessel engines and cranes, emissions from ship engines, and particles and dust from handling bulk cargoes. Traffic due to the transportation network in the port causes additional environmental problems. Environmental effects from the port may be divided into three groups. These; problems arising from port operations; ship-related problems in ports; and emissions from vehicles operating in the port hinterland. In order to minimize the damage to the environment with the increase in operational activities, ports have focused on practices related to environmental sustainability. At the same time, the environmental sustainability of the ports, which operate as a logistics base and are important transit points in the world supply chain, has become the focus of the academic literature.

Ports are points where loading and unloading services are provided to ships and logistics services are provided by providing value-added services such as stowing and storage of cargo (Pettit ve Beresford 2009; Stopford, 2009; Esmer, 2019). Port authorities all over the world adopt the green concept to ensure their continuity and increase their competitiveness. Policies regarding the operation of the port indicate the strategy and performance of a port (Köseoğlu & Solmaz, 2019). The fact that environmental problems have reached the international dimension has revealed implementation plans in this direction by developing common policies between countries.

With the emphasis on the importance of sustainability in ports, the concept of "sustainable port" has started to attract the attention of port managers. In this context, "port sustainability" is defined in the literature as "operation strategies and activities that meet the present and future needs of ports and stakeholders while trying to protect and maintain people and natural resources (Tahazzud, Adams, & Walker, 2020). In ports, the concepts of "sustainability" and "green port" are separated from each other (Lu et al., 2016). While the concept of sustainability in ports takes into account social, economic and environmental problems, the concept of "Green Port" focuses only on environmental problems (Ashrafi et al., 2020). The objectives of the green port concept are the efficient use of resources, the ecological management of investments, the ecological conformance of technology and shift in the institutional behaviour of the port (Korucuk & Memiş, 2019). The concept of green port, which is included in environmental sustainability, is narrower than the concept of sustainable development. The important thing in green port implementations is that the port can carry out its operational activities without harming the environment and answer efficiently to the wants of stakeholders (Marzantowicz & Dembinska, 2018).

TRADE GATES OF THE MARITIME SECTOR: PORTS

Ports are one of the intersections of human actions and environmental problems (Köseoğlu & Solmaz, 2019). According to Stopford (2009), on the other hand, a port is a geographical area with a sheltered deep-water area, usually a cove or river mouth, where ships dock to load and unload cargo. Ports, which have a complex organizational structure, are considered as the nodal points of global trade and supply chains. Contributing to global and regional trade, ports are considered as an economic catalyst for generating income and employment (Ducruet & Lugo, 2013). With the advancement of technology and the expansion of international trade, new markets are emerging and freight movements are increasing. Parallel to this, modern and large-capacity ships are built, and ports are transformed into larger and more advanced facilities. Ports are increasingly becoming one of the important indicators in determining the economic development level of countries. The number and capacity of ports is an important criterion that shows the national power and competitive capacity of countries.

These facilities, which are very important in the economic development of countries, can be classified in many different ways. However, ports are commonly classified as follows according to their fields of activity, cargo types, ownership structures and the types of services provided by the ports (Esmer & Karataş Çetin, 2013).

Ports by field of activity:

- Intercontinental ports
- National ports
- Regional ports
- Local ports

Ports by cargo types:

- General cargo port: Bulk, Dry cargo, tracked, package, etc. it covers the loading, unloading and stacking operations of all kinds of dry cargo with the use of appropriate qualified tools and equipment.
- Container port: These are the ports where the cargoes placed in standard sized boxes used in sea and land cargo transportation are handled, customs procedures are carried out, and the ships dock and load and unload.
- Multi-purpose port: As the name suggests, these are the ports that allow more than one type of cargo to be handled.
- Ro-Ro port: With the understanding of door-to-door transportation prevailing in ship transportation, trailers and trucks, together with their cargoes, started to be transported by large ships called Ro-Ro. In this way, a vehicle loaded at one point provides the opportunity to be transported to the point where it needs to arrive without any loading or unloading. This provides a faster and

cheaper transfer opportunity. This large ports with large parking lots and maneuvering areas are called Ro-Ro ports.

- Bulk Cargo Port: Ports where dry bulk cargoes such as ore, cement, sand, grain, coal are handled.
- Liquid cargo port: Oil, natural gas, nitrogen, etc. Large ports where chemicals are transferred are called liquid cargo ports.

Ports by ownership structure

- Public ports: These are the ports where the ownership and operation of the port belongs to the state.
- Public-private ports: These are the ports whose land and ownership is owned by the state but operated by the private sector.
- Private ports: These are the ports where the land, ownership and management are private companies.
  Types of services provided by the ports:
- Home port: These ports have their own original regional cargoes that they import/export from backyards. They also provide the transfer of national or international cargoes from other ports to the feeding ports.
- Transshipping port: Generally, they are ports where cargoes are handled for international freight transfer and do not serve their own backyards.
- Port of call: International or intercontinental ships may visit this type of port periodically, but they do not handle transshipment cargoes.
- Feeding port: Container ships that stop at the main ports do not stop at these ports, they only serve their own back areas by handling cargo transferred from the main ports.

Ports perform a wide variety of functions. The most basic functions of ports are protecting ships from adverse conditions such as waves, currents and storms; providing loading and unloading services to the calling vessels; providing logistics services such as stowing, storing and transferring cargoes (Stopford, 2009; Esmer, 2019). The connection of ports with different transportation modes such as railway, highway and airway has gained importance in port competitiveness in order to deliver the cargo to the destination where the customers want. Ports develops new management and marketing strategies by focusing on customer-centered and market-oriented relationships. These strategies have come to the fore in recent years in order to survive in the competitive port industry (Çalıskan & Esmer, 2020). With the increase in ship tonnage in parallel with the increasing technology, larger ports that can serve these ships have been built or existing ports have been developed with dredging and infrastructure investments. Therefore, the renewal works will continue without stopping in order for the ports to adapt to these developments.

ENVIRONMENTAL SUSTAINABILITY AND THE GREEN PORT CONCEPT

The world is facing problems such as water pollution, air pollution, global warming, waste disposal and energy consumption due to very serious global environmental change. All these problems have been a factor in the emergence of the green approach. The emergence of 'green' as a concept has been adopted as a strategy after the establishment of environmental awareness. The green approach is considered as a process and in this process, it is expected that people's environmental awareness will be met by organizations. The green thinking system includes nature-related initiatives to make a sustainable environment possible and permanent (Aydın & Tufan, 2018). Today, the concept of sustainability has become a popular concept to make the Earth a more livable place and to reduce the ongoing destruction. The word "Sustainability" comes from the Latin *"sustinere", and means to "maintain","sustain", "support", "endure", and "to restrain"* (Caradonna, 2014; Katunian, 2019; Pal & Hazra, 2015). The adoption of the concept of sustainability in the report Our Common Future of the UN World Commission on Environment and Development in 1987 was welcomed. With the Burunland report, the concept has become a popular concept today. The Brundtland Report explains sustainability as "development that meets the needs of the present without compromising the ability of future generations to meet their own needs" (WCED, 1987). The Green Port concept is partially included in the definition of sustainability, creating the conditions for efficiency of resources, low gas emission and other harmful substances, low noise emission and optimum land use economy (Korucuk & Memiş, 2019). With the concept of sustainability, the need for effective and efficient use of resources at ports, taking into account the needs of future generations, minimizing the effects on the environment, and transparency and fairness of relations with stakeholders has created the need. Sustainable ports are described as ports that are safe, use energy resources efficiently, are environmentally friendly, have responsibilities towards society, and try to maximize their profitability while focusing on approaches that establish open communication with their internal and external stakeholders (AAPA, 2019). In another definition for the concept of green port, a port that uses sustainable strategies that are sensitive to the environment, climate and ecosystem in port activities can be expressed as a green port (Sanrı, 2021). As it can be understood from the definitions, it is concluded that being a sustainable port is possible not only economically and socially, but also with environmental sustainability. In order to provide green port activity; Many topics such as water quality, energy consumption, waste generation, air pollution, noise pollution, ship-sourced pollution, occupational health and safety are covered (Mataracı, 2016). The policies developed by the ports on these issues are the protection of nature, the reduction of pollution at the highest possible level, the increase in the use of renewable energy and the recycling of materials (Anastasopouos et al., 2011).

GREEN PORT EXAMPLES IN THE WORLD

In ports, which have an important place in the growth of Europe, the amount of cargo handled has increased significantly with the increase in ship tonnage. This situation also contributes to the environmental pollution caused by the ports. European ports, which take an environmentally friendly approach, contribute to decarbonisation efforts with the Paris Climate Agreement. In addition, Europe has taken important steps to reduce other pollutant emissions from maritime transport with the introduction of the IMO's Emission Control Areas. In particular, European ports are leading in the development of renewable energy sources by reducing the use of fossil fuels. At the beginning of these ports is the port of Rotterdam, which is the largest port in Europe. The port of Rotterdam is expected to be the port with the lowest ecological footprint per ton-kilometer in the world by 2030 (Satır & Sağlamtimur, 2018). Another important port in Europe is the port of Hamburg. The concept of sustainability plays a much more important role for the port of Hamburg, due to the proximity of the port of Hamburg to the city and the importance given to the Elbe river ecosystem. The port of Hamburg invests in renewable energy sources, especially in the development of wind energy (Satır & Sağlamtimur, 2018). Another exemplary port in the Ecoport initiatives in Europe is The Port Authority of Valencia (PAV), which consists of the ports of Valencia, Sagunto and Gandia, serving under the name Valenciaport. These ports are among the leading ports of Spain serving the heavy container traffic in the eastern Mediterranean. PAV, which follows environmentalist policies, contributes to many environmental projects and takes green initiatives. In particular, it is observed that it follows green policies such as air and water quality, waste management, prevention and control of spills, noise quality control network, and dredging. The water surface is cleaned with pelican-type craft regarding water quality. In addition, PAV has developed an emergency plan for possible pollution at sea. Developing a control network related to air quality, PAV provides air quality monitoring through particle collector and air stations. A noise quality control network has been developed with noise maps related to noise pollution, static port maps where empirical noise measurements can be made, and sound level meters installed in the port-city interface area. The Dredging activity carried out to increase the maneuverability and accessibility of the port aimed to minimize the impact on the marine ecosystem by using special equipment. Regarding waste management, it has reception and treatment facilities for garbage and oil wastes produced by ships. PAV has also been involved in projects such as Core Network Corridors and Liquefied Natural Gas, Implementing Fuel Cells and Hydrogen Technologies in Ports, Green and Connected Ports, Energy Efficiency in Container Port Terminals (HTTPS://WWW.VALENCIAPORT.COM/EN/ENVIRONMENTAL-POLICY/).

Examples of the greenest ports in the United States, which implement strategies to reduce emissions such as greenhouse gases, carbon monoxide and particulate matter, are Georgia Port, Port of Baltimore and Port of Long Beach. Ports that implement a green port strategy can be of different sizes. But what these ports have in common is that they take various initiatives to ensure that the ultimate returns to sustainability outweigh the costs. For example, the use of new photosensitive lights in the port of Georgia is estimated to reduce energy costs by $4.9 million over 10 years. The Port of Baltimore, which has taken serious initiatives regarding environmental management, has created a Dray Truck Replacement Program that allows them to exchange old model trucks used in port operations for new models with less emissions (HTTPS://WWW.INBOUNDLOGISTICS.COM/ARTICLES/10-GREENEST-PORTS-IN-AMERICA/).

In addition, Singapore port and Shanghai port in Asia can be given as examples of ports that give importance to green initiative. Green port, green ship, green technology and green awareness programs have been developed in Singapore port (HTTPS://WWW.MPA.GOV.SG/MARITIME-SINGAPORE/SUSTAINABILITY/MARITIME-SINGAPORE-GREEN-INITIATIVE).

Shanghai Port, on the other hand, created the world's first transpacific green shipping corridor with the Port of Los Angeles and other participants. A network of partnerships has been created by ports, shipping companies, cities and cargo owners to create a green shipping corridor in the transpacific, the world's busiest container line. With Trans-Pacific container ships, it is intended to gradually have low, ultra-low and zero-carbon fuel vessels, improving air quality by reducing emissions in the ports of Shanghai and Los Angeles and neighboring communities (HTTPS://WWW.C40.ORG/NEWS/LA-SHANGHAI-GREEN-SHIPPING-CORRIDOR/).

LEGISLATIONS RELATED TO THE CONCEPT OF GREEN PORT

Pollutions originating from ships and ports affect the region and the country and make an international impact. For this reason, local and international regulations have been developed to minimize possible damage to the environment and to protect the ecosystem. International Maritime Organization (IMO) is one of them. Many international conventions for the protection of the environment have been created by IMO, which has the largest participation in the world's maritime industry. Such international organizations contribute to the development of the Green Port concept with the legal regulations they publish. The most important convention on the subject adopted by IMO is the "International Convention for the Prevention of Pollution from Ships" (MARPOL 73/78). The contract consists of six annexes. The first 5 of them are rules for preventing oil pollution from ships; rules for controlling contamination by bulk noxious (toxic) liquid substances; rules on the prevention of pollution by harmful substances transported by sea in packaging; rules for the prevention of pollution by sewage from ships; and rules on the prevention of pollution by garbage originating from ships. Annex 6 contains rules for preventing air pollution from ships. This contract contributes to the formation of greener port facilities by preventing sea and air pollution caused by ships.

A wide variety of applications have been revealed around the world for the protection of the environment. For example, in 1990, the Environmental Protection Act (EPA) was published. The regulation within the EPA introduced regulations for better monitoring and control of pollution from industrial enterprises such as ports and for the disposal of waste from land, water and air, thus reducing pollution (EPA, 2007).

In Europe, the implementation and development of the green port concept is followed by the European Sea Ports Organization (ESPO). There is a structure that allows ports to interact with each other to implement ESPO's policies. With the green guide created by ESPO, the environmental targets of the sector are specified. The ESPO Environment Report is part of Eco Ports, the environmental flagship initiative of European Ports. The Environment Report provides ESPO and European policy makers with information on the environmental issues European ports are working on and informs about the initiatives taken by ESPO. Eco Ports, the main environmental initiative of the European port sector, has been working in full integration with ESPO since 2011. The main purpose of Eco Ports is to spread awareness of environmental protection among ports through cooperation and information sharing and to improve environmental management. ESPO provides ports with opportunities to address their Top 10 environmental priorities to enable greener shipping. When ESPO Environmental Reports are examined, it is seen that there are green approaches that attract attention. These are the supply of electricity network for ships in ports; the creation of facilities for LNG supply to ships in ports; and the implementation of a low wage policy for ships following environmental policies (ESPO, 2021).

ESPO offers strategic approaches for ports to interact with each other and the people of the region by following environmental policies. The Eco-Management and Audit Scheme (EMAS) and the Port Environmental Review System (PERS) have been instrumental in achieving the environmental management standards of the ports.

On the other hand, ISO 14001, one of the most important environmental standards, specifies certain environmental performance criteria. ISO 14001 specifies the requirements for an environmental management system that any organization, regardless of size or type, can use to improve its environmental performance. This system helps an organization to achieve specified environmental standards (ISO, 2015).

In Asia, a comprehensive code for ports, "Port Safety and Health and Environmental Management" (PSHEMS), is implemented by Partnerships in Environmental Management for the Seas of East Asia (PEMSEA), combining environmental, occupational health and safety and quality management.

Another important organization for ports is the International Association of Ports and Harbors (IAPH), which was established in 1955. Today, the member ports of the union, which represents 180 ports and approximately 140 port-related businesses from 90 countries, handle 60 percent of the world's maritime transport and about 80 percent of the world's container traffic. In 2017, IAPH decided to establish the World Ports Sustainability Programme (Sanrı, 2021).

The Association of American Port Authorities (AAPA) represents 130 port authorities in the Americas. It seeks to promote common interests in the fields of environmental management, trade, security and infrastructure management among member ports. For this purpose, AAPA member ports are developing joint projects such as the application of biofiltration systems to protect the environment, reduce diesel emissions, sustainable sediment practices and reduce pollutants from rainwater runoff (AAPA, 2019).

HIGHLIGHTED INDICATORS RELATED TO THE GREEN PORT CONCEPT

Ports play an important role among stakeholders in eliminating emissions from commercial and operational activities, improving air quality and achieving zero pollution targets. ESPO, which is an important guide in the implementation of green port policies of ports, is an important reference point. ESPO conducts surveys among its members to obtain useful information on the most important environmental issues in ports. According to the survey studies carried out by ESPO since 1996, the variables showing the environmental priorities of the ports have changed throughout history. Regarding ports, 99 ports from 21 countries participated in the 2021 Environmental Report survey. The 2021 results, presented in Figure 1, show the environmental priorities of European ports over the past three years. When the titles in the top 10 are examined, it is seen that they have been the same since 2017 and there has been no new indicator in the Top 10 in recent years. When Figure 1 is analyzed, it is seen that the first five indicators have not changed compared to the previous year. It is seen that there is a change in the ranking of the last five indicators within themselves.

The indicators related to the environmental priorities of the port sector in the Environmental Report are mentioned below (ESPO, 2021).

The first environmental priority for ports is undoubtedly environmental concern. Air pollution in port areas can be caused by ships, port operations and associated land traffic within the port area. Also, ports are often places of industrial activity and clusters, which adds to air quality problems. Since most of the ports are located close to urban areas, they also threaten human health.

Climate Change is seen as the second priority of the sector in 2021. Climate change entered the Top 10 in 2017 and has grown in importance since then. Addressing this issue has become a key issue for ports as ports face operational challenges as a result of climate change. At the same time, it has become a necessity to bring important approaches to reduce carbon emissions.

The third most important priority is Energy efficiency, which is critical for ports that want to reduce their energy consumption and, consequently, their emissions (Iris & Lam, 2019). Energy efficiency is a way to both reduce operating costs and contribute to greening efforts.

Noise is the fourth priority for the port sector. There are many potential sources of noise in ports. For example, noise from machinery and cranes used in cargo handling, as well as noise from the engines of ships in ports. Due to the fact that noise can disturb people and surrounding habitats, discussions about the negative effects of noise have gained importance in recent years.

Relations with the local community maintains fifth place in the Top 10 priorities. The vast majority of European ports are located in or very close to an urban area where ports tend to be perceived by the local population as representatives of the larger shipping industry. This means that ports need to address the general concerns of citizens and ensure that the port is seen as a positive force in the local community.

Figure 1. Environmental Priorities in the Port Sector (2017-2021).
Source: ESPO Environmental Report 2021.

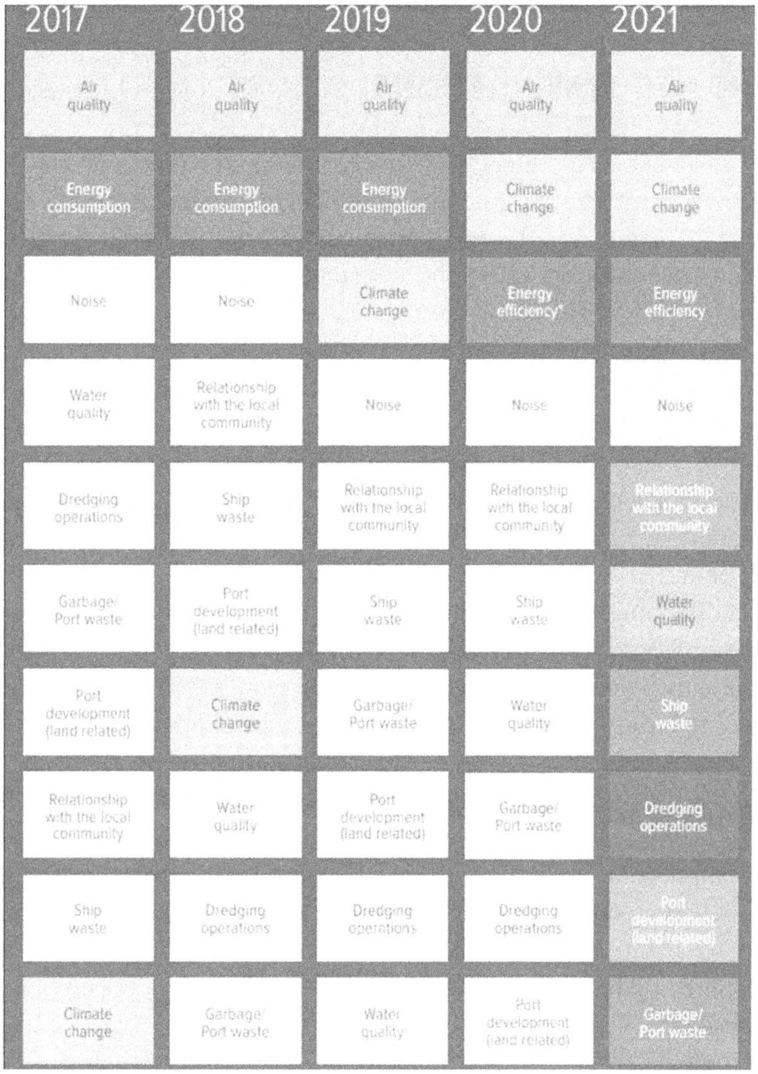

2017	2018	2019	2020	2021
Air quality	Air quality	Air quality	Air quality	Air quality
Energy consumption	Energy consumption	Energy consumption	Climate change	Climate change
Noise	Noise	Climate change	Energy efficiency*	Energy efficiency
Water quality	Relationship with the local community	Noise	Noise	Noise
Dredging operations	Ship waste	Relationship with the local community	Relationship with the local community	Relationship with the local community
Garbage/ Port waste	Port development (land related)	Ship waste	Ship waste	Water quality
Port development (land related)	Climate change	Garbage/ Port waste	Water quality	Ship waste
Relationship with the local community	Water quality	Port development (land related)	Garbage/ Port waste	Dredging operations
Ship waste	Dredging operations	Dredging operations	Dredging operations	Port development (land related)
Climate change	Garbage/ Port waste	Water quality	Port development (land related)	Garbage/ Port waste

Water quality and ship waste are seen as another important indicator. In 2021, water quality is the sixth priority and ship waste seventh priority. Water management and water quality issues are important for the environmental responsibilities of ports and the continuity of the business. There are two main sources of waste in ports: waste from port-based activities and waste from incoming ships.

Land-related port development and dredging operations rank eighth and ninth, respectively. The dredging process can affect the marine ecosystem. Port development is becoming a major priority in connection with the construction works carried out within the port area.

Garbage/port wastes are among the priority issues for the sector. Preventing waste generation and spread is key to handling waste from port-based activities. The more waste that can be reused and recycled, the better. Therefore, waste management is an important component of the positive contribution of ports to climate and environmental management. Port waste has consistently been the most watched indicator among Eco Ports members because of its importance.

SOLUTIONS AND RECOMMENDATIONS

Within the scope of sustainable environmental management, green practices are of vital importance in order to leave a livable environment for future generations. Increasing pollution, especially with industrialization, threatens the nature and the environment, as well as endanger the living spaces of future generations. Based on these facts, organizations leave material factors aside and turn to green practices. In recent years, one of the most important issues in many ports of the world, especially in European ports, has been to achieve environmental sustainability by following green policies. According to ESPO 2021 Port Sector Priorities, prominent points in the legislation implemented in ports within the framework of green ports are air quality, climate change, energy efficiency, noise pollution, relations with the local community, water quality and ship waste, dredging operations and port development, and garbage/port wastes. Based on these indicators, the strategies required for ports to become green ports can be reached.

The use of Onshore Power Supply (OPS) and alternative equivalent solutions in air quality strategies can help reduce air pollution and greenhouse gas emissions. Even if emissions at the dock are only a small fraction of total shipping emissions, they still need to be addressed. OPS is an important tool for many ports to reduce emissions from ships in port. With OPS, the energy needs of the ships are provided without the need to use their auxiliary engines while at the quay. OPS can be one of the important tools to achieve the goal of reducing greenhouse gas emissions, air pollution and noise. For this reason, it is necessary to increase the number of electricity supply points established in ports. In addition, the use of electricity or renewable energy sources by in-port transfer and handling vehicles will play an important role in improving air quality. In addition, ports providing LNG supply at ports will contribute significantly to the decarbonization of maritime transport. Because promoting the use of LNG as fuel will be another important strategy in order to reduce the sulphur content from ship fuels.

Another strategy related to the green concept is energy efficiency. In this regard, energy efficiency can be increased by the arrival planning of ships, the optimization of port operations and the use of new technologies. Collecting ship and port wastes, including them in reverse logistics processes and ensuring their recycling is a strategic approach that will contribute to energy efficiency.

In addition, discounts can be applied to environmentally friendly ships by the ports and incentives can be provided to meet the green port requirements. For example, separate charges may apply to ships that can demonstrate that they have reduced air emissions. In addition, encouraging the ports to adopt environmentally friendly legislation and regulations on a voluntary basis will facilitate their access to green port policies.

FUTURE RESEARCH DIRECTIONS

In this study, based on the sustainable port approach, the green port strategies of the ports in achieving environmental sustainability were revealed. In this study, all types of ports were discussed. The study may inspire studies to be carried out according to the types of ports in the future. And also, the study may inspire researchers to examine other dimensions of sustainability, economic and social, in order for ports to achieve sustainability. Finally, since the current study focuses only on the literature review of the green port concept, more contributions to the literature can be made with empirical studies to be conducted in the future.

CONCLUSION

With the increase in the world trade volume, the increasing operational activities in the ports have a negative impact on the environment. In particular, environmental improvement of cargo handling and transportation activities and infrastructures within the ship-shore and port area are elements that increase the financial development of ports and also contribute to the protection of the environment. In the green port approach, increasing environmental awareness, ensuring compliance with the legislation and integrating innovative technologies and sustainable practices into port operations are adopted. Thus, by adopting environmentalist approaches during the activities of the port, it is ensured that natural resources are protected and the negative impact of port operations on the environment is reduced.

Green ports are organizations with high environmental performance. There are many ports in Europe and other parts of the world that have adopted the green port concept. These ports aim to operate in a more livable environment by developing new strategies to be sustainable. One of the most important guides that ports refer to here is the "Green Guide" published by ESPO. This guide emphasizes an environmental management perspective that encompasses port authority, port field operations and transportation. ESPO, which enables ports to interact with each other, has enabled the implementation of the green concept with its initiatives and policies.

In the study, when the literature review and the results of the survey conducted by ESPO were examined, port-related environmental problems were identified and important green port strategies that could be developed against them were revealed. In the surveys of ESPO, which has been accepted worldwide, especially in European ports, the priority green port indicators are; Air Quality, Climate Change, Energy Efficiency, Noise, Relationship with the Local Community, Water Quality, Ship Waste, Dredging Operations, Port Development, Garbage and Port Waste. When the priorities were examined, it was seen that the strategies for improving air quality came first. Therefore, the operation of handling and transfer vehicles with electricity or alternative energy sources in port operations is one of the leading environmental policies. In addition, connecting the ships in the port to the electricity supply points to be established by the port facility instead of their own machines as an energy source will play an important role in reducing ship-sourced emissions. Other important green strategies are the disposal of all wastes originating from ships and ports in accordance with the legislation and even recycling these wastes, following policies to protect the marine ecosystem, and creating incentive activities by the states for ports and ships to follow green approaches.

REFERENCES

AAPA. (2019). *Environment and Energy*. Retrieved from https://aapa.files.cms-plus.com/PDFs/Environment%20and%20Energy%209-19.pdf

Anastasopouos, A., Kolios, S., & Styios, C. (2011). How Will Greek Ports Become Green Ports? Geo-Eco-Marina, 17, 73-80.

Ashrafi, M., Walker, T., Magnan, G., Adams, M., & Acciaro, M. (2020). A review of corporate sustainability drivers in maritime ports: A multi-stakeholder perspective. Maritime Policy & Management, 1–18.

Aydın, S. & Tufan, F. (2018). Purchasing Behaviors of Y Generation in the Context of Sustainability and Green Concepts. *Journal of Selcuk Communication, 11*(2), 397-420. DOI: doi:10.18094/josc.377009

Çalıskan, A., & Esmer, S. (2020). An assessment of port and shipping line relationships: The value of relationship marketing. *Maritime Policy & Management*, *47*(2), 240–257. Advance online publication. doi:10.1080/03088839.2019.1690172

Caradonna, J. L. (2014). Sustainability: A History. Oxford University Press.

Chiu, Lin, & Ting. (2014). Evaluation of Green Port Factors and Performance: A Fuzzy AHP Analysis. *Mathematical Problems in Engineering*. doi:10.1155/2014/802976

Ducruet, C., & Lugo, I. (2013). Cities and transport networks in shipping and logistics research. *The Asian Journal of Shipping and Logistics*, *29*(2), 145–166. doi:10.1016/j.ajsl.2013.08.002

Elkington, J. (1994). Towards the Sustainable Corporation: Win-Win-Win Business Strategies for Sustainable Development. *California Management Review*, *36*(2), 90–100. doi:10.2307/41165746

EPA (Environmental Protection Act). (2007). *Environmental Protection Act 1990, Chapter 43*. Retrieved January 25, 2022, from https://www.legislation.gov.uk/ukpga/1990/43/introduction

Esmer, S. (2019). *Liman ve Terminal Yönetimi* [Port and Terminal Management]. Anadolu Üniversitesi Açıköğretim Fakültesi Yayını.

Esmer, S., & Karataş Çetin, Ç. (2013). Liman İşletme Yönetimi. *Denizcilik İşletmeleri Yönetimi*.

ESPO. (2021). Environmental Report. Retrieved September 15, 2022, from https://www.espo.be/media/ESP-2844%20(Sustainability%20Report%202021)_WEB.pdf

Iris, Ç., & Lam, J. S. L. (2019). A review of energy efficiency in ports: Operational strategies, technologies and energy management systems. *Renewable and Sustainable Energy Reviews, Elsevier*, *112*(C), 170–182. doi:10.1016/j.rser.2019.04.069

ISO. (2015). ISO 14001:2015, Third Edition: Environmental Management Systems - Requirements with Guidance for Use. American National Standards Institute.

Katunian, A. (2019). Sustainability as a new approach for the human resource development in tourism sector. *Public Policy and Administration*, *18*(4), 405–417. doi:10.13165/VPA-19-18-4-03

Korucuk, S., & Memiş, S. (2019). Prioritizion of Green Port Applications Performance Criteria with Dematel Method: Case of Istanbul Province. *International Journal of Euroasian Research*, *7*(16), 134–148. doi:10.33692/avrasyad.543735

Köseoğlu, M. C., & Solmaz, M. S. (2019). Green Port Approach: A Comparative Assessment Criterion of Turkey and the World Green Port. *4th National Port Congress*. Doi: 10.18872/0.2019.2

Lu, C.-S., Shang, K.-C., & Lin, C.-C. (2016). Examining sustainability performance at ports: Port managers' perspectives on developing sustainable supply chains. *Maritime Policy & Management, 43*(8), 909–927. doi:10.1080/03088839.2016.1199918

Marzantowicz, Ł., & Dembinska, I. (2018). The Reasons for the Implementation of the Concept of Green Port in Sea Ports of China. *Logistics Infrastructure, 37*, 121–128.

Mataracı, G. D. (2016). *Green Port Approach and Sustainability in Port Authorities* [Master Thesis]. Istanbul Technical University.

Nagle, K. (2013). *Seaports: Essential to Our Economic Prosperity.* Retrieved from. http:// www.pnwa. net/wp-content/uploads/2013/03/Nagle-2013-Mission-Slides.pdf

OECD. (2009). *Environmental Impacts of International Shipping: A Case Study of the Port of Vancouver.* OECD Publishing.

Özispa, N., & Arabelen, G. (2021). Prioritizing the Sustainability Strategies of Ports via AHP. *Approach Journal of Yasar University, 16*(63), 1430-1453.

Pal, T., & Hazra, M. K. (2015). *Sustainable Development.* Yadava Publication.

Pavlic, B., Cepak, F., Sucic, B., Peckaj, M., & Kandus, M. (2014). Sustainable Port Infrastructure, Practical Implementation of The Green Port Concept. *Thermal Science, 18*(3), 935–948.

Pettit, S. J., & Beresford, A. K. C. (2009). Port development: From gateways to logistics hubs. *Maritime Policy & Management, 36*(3), 253–267. doi:10.1080/03088830902861144

Sanrı, Ö. (2021). A Content Analysis of Green Port, 2009-2020. *Beykoz Akademi Dergisi, 9*(2), 50-72. DOI: doi:10.14514/BYK.m.26515393.2021.9/2.50-72

Satır, T., & Doğan-Sağlamtimur, N. (2018). The protection of marine aquatic life: Green Port (EcoPort) model inspired by Green Port concept in selected ports from Turkey, Europe and the USA. *Periodicals of Engineering and Natural Sciences, 6*(1), 120–129. doi:10.21533/pen.v6i1.149

Sislian, L., Jaegler, A., & Cariou, P. (2016). A Literature Review on Port Sustainability and Ocean's Carrier Network Problem. *Research in Transportation Business & Management, 19*, 19–26. doi:10.1016/j.rtbm.2016.03.005

Stopford, M. (2009). *Maritime Economics.* Routledge.

Tahazzud, H., Adams, M., & Walker, T. R. (2020). Role of sustainability in global seaports. *Ocean and Coastal Management, 202*, 105435. doi:10.1016/j.ocecoaman.2020.105435

Wakeman, R. (1996). What is a Sustainable Port? The Relationship Between Ports and Their Regions. *Journal of Urban Technology, 3*(2), 65–79. doi:10.1080/10630739608724528

World Commission on Environment and Development (WCED). (1987). *"Our Common Future" report.* Retrieved January 19, 2020, from https://sustainabledevelopment.un.org/content/documents/5987our-common-future.pdf

Yılmaz, F. (2019). "Yeşil-Eko Liman Yaklaşımı"nın Deniz Ticareti ve Lojistik Sektörüne Katkıları: Türkiye ve AB'deki Uygulamaların Karşılaştırması [Contribution of Green-Eco Port Approach to Maritime Trade and Logistics Sector: Comparison of Practices in Turkey and EU]. *Journal of Transportation and Logistics*, 4(2), 65–78. doi:10.26650/JTL.2019.04.02.02

KEY TERMS AND DEFINITIONS

Biofiltration Systems: It is an environmental pollution control technique that uses a bioreactor containing living material to capture and biodegrade pollutants.

Environmental Sustainability: It is the protection of the environment and natural order, and the transfer and continuity of natural resources to future generations by using them correctly and appropriately.

Green Port Strategies: Actions to be taken by ports in order to operate in the green port concept.

Onshore Power Supply: Meeting the energy needs of the ships from the electricity network at the dock.

Port Operations: Handling and transportation of cargo between ship and shore and within the port, as well as pilotage and tugboat services provided to ships, etc. activities.

Port-Related Environmental Pollution: Damages to the environment as a result of operational activities in ports. For example, air pollution, water pollution, noise pollution, etc.

Sustainability: It is to ensure the continuity of production and diversity, in short, humanity by using resources effectively.

Sustainable Port: To increase the financial performance of the ports by following environmental policies and to show people-oriented approaches.

Chapter 11
Organizational Innovation Approach to Green Technological Innovation

José G. Vargas-Hernández

https://orcid.org/0000-0003-0938-4197

Posgraduate and Research Department, Tecnológico Mario Molina Unidad Zapopan, Mexico

Omar C. Vargas-González

https://orcid.org/0000-0002-6089-956X

Tecnológico Nacional de México, Ciudad Guzmán, Mexico

ABSTRACT

This study aims to analyze the implications of organizational innovation to green technological innovation departing from the assumption that organizational innovation and technological innovation are the dimensions that lead to the creation and development of green technological innovation capacities that have the potential to alleviate and ease the ecological and environmental crises. The method used is the analytical reflective based on the theoretical and empirical literature. It is concluded that the development of green technological innovation organizations tends to develop the competence to innovate and survive for a longer period in their domains.

INTRODUCTION

Organizational innovations are divided into technological innovation and management innovation (Chin & Chuang, 2015). Management innovation refers to the management strategy, structure, and systems. Technological innovation and creativity refer to the product innovation, operation processes and techniques. Organizational theory has influenced the principles of innovation management. Organizational management and technological innovation lead to higher organizational performance (Robbins & Judge, 2016).

DOI: 10.4018/978-1-6684-6815-9.ch011

Organizational innovation theory and paradigm is formulated according to its deterministic character and identified in any analysis of innovation theory (Sundbo, 1998). The identification of an innovative organization to determine the structural variables and characteristics on the innovation of processes and products are centered on the organization as the unit of analysis.

The perspectives in innovation theory are the technology-economic, entrepreneurial, and strategic which may mix elements to determine actions leading to transformational social system. (Sundbo, 1995). Elements from each perspective may be valid to mix by a specific agency. The organizational innovation processes shared in practice and theory may be supported by the system-agency relation. However, the strategic perspective is the least developed (Nyström, 1979; Sundbo, 1998; Sundbo & Fuglsang, 2002; Tidd *et al.*, 1997).

Conventional organizational design theories have investigated extensively the interrelationships between the organizational structures, environment, and organizational performance variables. The classical organizational design theory was guided by the universal organizational forms as one best way to organize. Organizations design conceptual, theorical and empirical models to support knowledge creation, learning patterns and innovative capabilities development, including lean production, high performance systems (Womack et al 1990), N-form corporation (Hedlund, 1994) and hypertext organization (Nonaka & Takeuchi, 1995), cellular forms (Miles et al 1997), modular forms (Galunic, & Eisenhardt 2001) and project-based networks (DeFillippi, 2002).

The organizational ability in knowledge-based economy to create and develop creativity, innovation and influential ideas is critical factor the viability of organizations and its impact on economic, social, and environmental change (Sørensen & Stuart, 2000). However, only a few studies deal with the relationship between organizational structure and innovation. These investigations have concluded that organizational structures facilitate the innovative creation of processes and products in relation to the environmental changes.

Institutional theories, organizational ecology, and evolutionary theories of the firm study the forces of the organizational inertia that respond incrementally to environmental changes. Industrial economics has provided theoretical and empirical foundations for the organizational structure, strategy, and innovative organization. The system theory in social sciences is the framework for explaining innovation, classify and characterize the modes.

Existing theoretical and empirical literature on organizational innovation is diverse and not integrated into a coherent framework. Empirical research on organizational innovation suggests that sources lie outside the organization (von Hippel, 1988; Lundvall, 1992). Empirical research paradigms suggest that sources of innovation lie outside an organization (von Hippel, 1988; Lundvall, 1992). There is scarce empirical research on the relationships between organizational age and propensities to produce technological innovations. The empirical analysis document the impact of organizational aging on different facets of technological innovation.

Research has the challenge to bridge the gap between the organizational action and the sources for innovative organizational change. The research streams of organizational innovation are interrelated and interacting between the different dimensions of organizational structures and innovation. Between organization and innovation there is a multi-level, dynamic and interdependent relationship between the organizational structural forms and innovativeness. Organizational design theories focus on the link between structural forms and the propensity to innovate (Burns & Stalker, 1961; Lawrence & Lorsch, 1967; Mintzberg, 1979).

ORGANIZATIONAL APPROACH

The endogenous organizational forces such as values, interest, capacity for learning and power are relevant roles in shaping organizational and technological transformation and change. Organizations can overcome inertia focusing on organizational change and adaptation to radical changes in environment leading to discontinuous organizational and technological changes.

The contingency theory proposes that the organizational environment is more related to the organizational structure and innovativeness. The organizational typologies of organic and mechanistic organizations (Burns & Stalker, 1961) differentiate the rate of complexity and change in the market and technological environment affecting organizational structures and innovation management. Mechanistic organizations have hierarchical and rigid structures more adapted to stable conditions, while the organic structures are more fluid set of arrangements to get adapted to rapid change and innovation.

The organic type of organizations has a fluid set of arrangements requiring more fluid set of arrangements for more emergent and innovative responses to the changing environmental and contextual responses. This model developed by Burns and Stalker (1961) is relevant to analyze the challenges facing organizations as innovation become relevant to manage the environmental change moving away the mechanistic towards the organic type of organization. Organizations with inertial forces respond slowly to the environmental threats and opportunities.

Organizational structure and strategy are the variables to construct the organizational forms. Certain attributes of organizational forms yield higher innovative performance leading to reduce transaction costs and cope with market failures in given environments. The organizational structure has effects on the organizational capabilities of organizations to create knowledge, learn and generate technological and organizational innovation. The interactions between organizational factors and market shapes innovative performance with little attention to social processes and internal dynamics. Some organizational attributes reduce transaction costs and cope better with capital market failures in specific environments leading to yield higher level of innovative performance.

The multi-divisional or M-form, responds to the increasing organizational scale and complexity associated to the diversification strategy in related technological and product specific areas (Chandler, 1962). The multidimensional division known also as the M form responds to the increasing organizational complexity and scale associated with a diversification strategy into related technological and product areas (Chandler, 1962). The multidimensional division is an efficient innovator in specific product markets but with limited ability to develop new competencies.

The configurational hypothesis of organizations sustains that organizations can be dominated by one of the archetypes identified by Mintzberg (1979): simple structure, machine bureaucracy, professional bureaucracy, divisional and adhocracy forms, each one with different innovative potential. Organizational simple structure is an organic type controlled by one person able to respond quickly to environmental changes, is an innovative and entrepreneurial searching for risky environments.

The professional bureaucracy structural form is a decentralized mechanistic structure with high level of autonomy, individual and functional specialization with concentration of power and status in individual experts highly innovative. Bureaucratic structures are better adapted to work in stable environments and cannot cope with the pace of environmental change and novelty and they are not innovative. In contrast, adhocracies are organic and flexible organizational forms capable of radical innovation in more volatile contextual and environmental change.

The creation and development of a social learning system amplifies the base knowledge and learning of innovative capabilities of firms operating in the innovation systems and provides the sustainability for innovative capabilities of the adhocracy. The organization is an interpretive and learning system oriented towards the internal organizational dynamics with the roles of actor's cognition and behavior aimed to shape the external environment and to achieve the outcomes of organizational change.

J-form and adhocracy are learning organizations with innovative capabilities, but with different structural forms, learning patterns and innovative competencies generated. The J-form relies more on knowledge embedded in routines. The J-forms and the adhocracy are alternative models of knowledge, learning and innovative organizations. The J-form develops an orientation towards pursuing a strategy of incremental innovation and improvements in mature technological fields. However, the firms with J-form have had limitations and difficulties in innovating in rapidly development technological fields (Lam, 2002; Whitely, 2003).

The adhocracy is a form of organization that develops the capabilities for dynamic learning and radical innovation suitable and supportive for high technology firms that increases the labor markets and other institutions of regional, sectorial and national innovation systems characterized by radical innovation and rapid commercialization in fast growing and developing new technologies (Saxenian, 1996; Bahrami & Evans, 2000; Angels, 2000; Asheim and Gerlter, 2005; Malerba, 2003) The adhocracy as an adaptive organizational form that is competitive due to its ability to reconfigure the knowledge base required to create.

The micro-economics in strategy considers that organizational structure is both cause and effect of managerial strategic choice responding to the environmental challenges and opportunities. The strategic choice perspective determines the possibility of an organizational creativity and innovative change. Organizational structure is both cause and effect of managerial strategic choice responding to the environmental opportunities. Organizational structure, strategy, and innovation are sustained in micro-economy.

The reorganization for radical organizational innovation has immediate performance effects in the case of Oticon after a partial retreat form spaghetti organization showing the difficulties of the adhocracy form of organization (Foss, 2003; Verona and Ravasi, 2003). The radical form of project-based organization known as the spaghetti organization, may stimulate entrepreneurship and innovation leading to a traditional matrix organization (Foss, 2003). The firm Oticon established a radical organizational transformation project-based organization that led to innovative benefits (Verona and Ravasi, 2003).

Organizational change and adaptation processes underlie the creation of new organizational forms focusing on the overcoming inertia and adapting to radical organizational and technological changes occurring through the selection process at the population level (Hannan & Freeman, 1977; 1984; Romanelli & Tushman, 1994).

This analysis of the implications of organizational innovation to green technological innovation departs from the assumption that organizational innovation and technological innovation are the two dimensions leading to the creation and development of green technological innovation capacities having the potential to alleviate and easy the ecological and environmental crises. The study begins with the conceptual and theoretical approaches to innovation and organizations to continue analyzing the implications of organizational innovation leading to green technological innovation. Finally, some concluding remarks are presented.

INNOVATION

Innovation is the process of bringing new ideas in problem solving (Amabile, 1988; Kanter, 1983). Innovation is a nonroutine, significant, and discontinuous organizational change that embodies a new idea that is not consistent with the current concept of the organization's business (Mezias & Glynn, 1993: 78). Innovation is a process of organizational knowledge creation and learning aimed to develop organizational capacities for change and adaptation.

Innovation is a process of learning and knowledge creation to develop new knowledge to solve new problems.

Creative destruction as conceived by Schumpeter (1950) is the factor of changes and innovation in organizations, products, processes, and new markets. Innovation is the creation process of organizational learning and knowledge and the organizational capacity for adaptation and change (Lam, 2004). Innovation is a part of the organizational system that produces it (Weick, 1979).

The innovative enterprise theory (Lazonick & West, 1998) is based on the framework of Chandler and focuses on how structure and strategy determine the competitive advantage of organizations. The innovative enterprise theory framed by the Chandler theory focuses on structure and strategy as determinants of competitive advantage of organizations (Lazonick & West, 1998). The theoretical framework enables the analysis of the leadership effects on organizational innovativeness. The innovation leadership styles presented by Bossink (2004) in a theoretical framework according to their characteristics related to process and product innovation in projects, are the charismatic, instrumental, interactive, and strategic innovation leadership.

Innovation is driven by the entrepreneurship. Innovation is driven by institutionalized routines (Nelson & Winter, 1982). The social value of innovation is represented by the entrepreneurial spirit of creativity and independence (Binks & Vale, 1990). Innovation relies on well identifiable and proven professional and technological change trajectories.

The systemic regulation of innovation is divided in modes which can be analyzed with an analytical framework (Parsons, 1951). The innovation mode is based on the system adapted to environmental changes. The mode of innovation requires an analytical scheme to compare them are related to certain values or latency, goal orientations, integrative, adaptation and creative mechanisms.

The context and the institutional frameworks affect the firm's organizational development of innovative activities in different economic and socioecological systems. Social institutions may create constrains on firms and opportunities to develop different organizational forms capable to create innovative competences and give rise to innovative projects.

The network structure is related to innovation (Powell & Grodal, 2005). Japanese firms gained a competitive advantage in some industries such as electronics and automobiles because of their organizational capacity for integrating workers and enterprise networks to coordinate specialized divisions of labor and investments innovations. Large firms and state education system driven networks train and develop members with the skills required in innovation activities. Multi-exchange firms coordinated network operations that have been ecologically dominant, which benefits the positive relationship with peripheral single-exchange firms. The multi-exchange firms ecologically dominant benefit more from single-exchange firms from this mutualism. Multi-exchange firms are ecologically dominant in controlling information and resources exchange when compared to single-exchange firms.

The development of multiple exchange systems makes the organizations possible to distinguish the indirect measures to adopt the innovation helping to explain the organizational innovation failures industry as well as the organizations to adopt the innovations to auto compete and displace. The competitive advantage is more that the result from adopting these innovations. Geographical isolation of local firms in the telephone industry encountered rivalry from a distant innovative competitor (MacMeal, 1934).

Firms sustaining their competitive advantages have benefited from a high degree of organizational integration attentive to the specific contingencies of their social structure and internal cohesiveness as innovative performance and corporate strategy. Japanese organizational integration model is adapted to work in incremental innovation and not in radical innovation of technological fields. Incremental innovation relies on upgrading of system components in sectors that are not fast-paced radical innovation such as biotechnology.

ORGANIZATIONAL INNOVATION

There is not consensus on the definition of organizational innovation since embraces a wide range of phenomena which tend to describe the relationships between the different dimensions and aspects of organizational forms and the technological innovation which may fit together. Organizational innovation as a phenomenon has different interpretations which can be classified in different streams with different focus each one. Organizational innovation refers to the creation and adoption of new ideas and behaviors in organizations (Daft, 1978; Damanpour & Evan, 1984; Damanpour, 1996). Innovation is driven by the whole organization. The innovation process tends to be more uncertain and organizations are presented as open and learning-oriented (Nonaka & Takeuchi, 1995) at open learning stage placed between the strategic choice.

Organizational innovation in management environment is identified in value-based entrepreneurial, technology-based functional and strategic reflexive modes in which the innovation system determines the action through strategy and reflexivity. The strategic reflexive perspective of organizational innovation, change is the result of interactions processes and the set of common values of the organization. Strategic reflexivity is a developed and discussed understanding innovation in marketing theory for example (Kotler, 1983; Nyström, 1990; Sundbo, 2001; Sundbo and Fuglsang, 2002). Organizational management attempts to create integration mechanisms for organizational innovation that interferes and disintegrates the organization.

The performance of the organization is dependent on the capability of the organizational innovation system to integrate innovative behaviors by structural and functional transformation. Organizational innovations are influenced by an organic structure, a complex division of labor, high-risk strategy (Hage, 2022). The strategic reflexive mode is an integrative mechanism increasingly complex and dependent on innovation management that motivates actions in attention capturing and people chasing activities of the organizational innovation nature. These variables provoke consistent results in organizational innovation, which can be also study supported by the context of knowledge societies and the theory of evolution.

Organizational and technological innovations are linked and intertwined. Organizational innovation is a precondition for technological innovation. The process of organizational innovation is based on organizational creation (Van de Ven *et al.*, 1999). Organizations may acquire the abilities to innovate as a precondition for the introduction and utilization of new technologies and inventive resources leading to challenges and complex opportunities to organizations in the emergence of new organizational forms and managerial practices.

The interconnections between the different relationships between organizational structural forms and technological innovativeness must be joined by a conceptual framework to understand the organizational innovation concept avoiding the conceptual ambiguity and confusions. New organizational forms of innovative organizations can be classified in types of organizational models, the J form that referees to an organization with cumulative learning deriving innovative capabilities from problem solving routines and collective learning competences. The second model is the adhocracy that relies on individual expertise organized in market-based projects with rapid responses to environmental changes in knowledge and skills (Mintzberg, 1979).

Conventional organizational innovativeness examines the individual, organizational and environmental determinants of propensity to innovate in organizations (Kimberly &

Evanisko 1981; Baldridge & Burnham, 1975), and focused on organizational structure (Wolfe, 1994). Coordination across functions and disciplines limits the innovative capabilities, highly innovative and adaptive, capable of learning and unlearning (Tidd et al, 1997; Lam, 2000). Adaptive and flexible forms of organization with strategic entrepreneurial may focusing on radical innovation in learning and knowledge-intensive economic activities

Organizational social interaction and group dynamics within organizations create and shape collective intelligence, organizational learning, and knowledge generation. These developments yield a relevant insight into the micro-dynamics of organizational innovative capabilities. Organizations have different structural forms that may vary in their patterns in the creation of learning and knowledge leading to different innovative capabilities. Organizational capabilities develop flexible production systems through the integration of experience and skills linking R&D, production, and marketing in a strategy of innovation based on continual upgrading and modification of components (Womack et al 1991).

Product innovation in emerging market-seeking international joint ventures (IJVs) supported by organizational ecology theory is the consequence of the organizational orientation and a response to the contingencies of local environment. Product innovation is defined as new or improved goods and services introduced in the market with innovations based on the results of new technological developments and new technological combinations or utilization of other knowledge (Laursen & Salter, 2006: 138).

Product innovation in international joint ventures is associated with conditions of ownership structure, project size, state partnership. International joint ventures operating in industry are more innovative with foreign direct investment legitimations and located in agglomeration of innovative activities (Zhou, & Li, 2008). Initial conditions are relevant as the subsequent changes affect the propensity to innovate of international joint ventures.

The structural forms of organizations underpin the nature of the organizational learning processes and the generation of innovative competences embedded in an institutional context. The structural forms of organizations develop different innovative capabilities in accordance with the vary in patterns of knowledge and learning creation. Organizational innovation from the micro-level perspective of learning and organizational knowledge creation. Organizational innovative outputs are subject to knowledge accumulation that enables to assimilate and exploit knowledge.

Firms create learning organizations capable of solving problems in continuous innovation. The social context and the organizational boundaries of learning have an influence on the organizational cognitive vision and the capacity for radical innovation and change. The role of cognition and organizational learning fosters and inhibit innovation (Cohen & Levinthal, 1990). Organizational innovation has cognitive and learning foundations. From the cognitive perspective, organizational innovation analysis sifts from organizational systems and structures toward organizational learning and knowledge creation.

The modes of organizational innovation are differentiated by the degree of determinism between the organizational system and the agency. These modes of organizational innovation are descriptions of relationships between change agencies and social systems developed overtime and simultaneously in the organization (Sundbo, 1998), but they also exist simultaneously in an organization. The organizational innovation modes are a kind of ideal type (Weber, 1958) boundary objects (Star, 1989) common understandings of innovation shared across communities and built into innovation systems.

Organizational innovation is an organizational social system that is relevant for the management environment. Organizational innovation system is in relation to the changes of social actors to determine the actions (Fuglsang & Sundbo, 2005) identify modes of innovation in the management environment: a value-based entrepreneurial, a technology-based functional and a strategic reflexive mode. In the last mode, the innovation system determines the actions of actors through strategy and reflexivity.

The other two modes of innovation, the entrepreneurial, value-based mode and the technology-based functional mode of organizational innovation are more elaborated and discussed (Sexton & Kasarda, 1992; Freeman & Soete, 1997; Tushman & Anderson, 1997; Sexton & Landström, 2000). The entrepreneurial, value-based mode of innovation has a relationship with the individual actions driving to create business (Kanter, 1983; Drucker, 1999).

Organizational learning and knowledge creation lead towards shared context and collective learning. Organizational innovation is a process of organizational and collective learning and knowledge creation leading towards shared context to develop new knowledge to solve new problems. The firm is a critical socio ecology context and environment where takes place the collective knowledge and learning creation (Nonaka & Takeuchi 1995). Organizational innovations are dependent on sharing modes to communicate the necessary number of heuristics, motivate and integrate actors during the changes.

An innovative organization is creative and intelligent (Glynn, 1996; Woodman et al 1993), capable of learning (Senge, 1990; Argyris & Schon, 1978) and creating new knowledge (Nonaka, 1994; Nonaka and Takeuchi 1995). The theory of Nonaka stresses the role of semiautonomous, decentralized project teams and group-based structure as organizing principle for creating and developing knowledge. Organizational innovative activities to create and develop the organizational capacities require the exploitation of new knowledge. The cognitive principles of organizational innovation are related to the creation processes of learning and organizational knowledge (Argyris & Schôn, 1978; Nonaka, 1994; Nonaka & Takeuchi, 1995).

The organizational structures, formal governance modes and the informal cultures and values, and the external networks of the organization have an influence on their organizational innovative activities. Organizational arrangements are suited to the different competitive environments and organizational innovation. Organizational structural perspectives treat organizational innovation as an output of some structural features.

The two types of organizational innovation are the autonomous and the systemic matching with the organizational structures (Teece, 1998). The autonomous innovation is introduced to the market without significant alternatives and modifications of processes and products. The systematic innovation favors the organizational integration requiring complex coordination among the various subsystems (Teece, 1998).

GREEN TECHNOLOGICAL INNOVATION

Drawing on organizational ecology theory, firms engage in technological innovation influenced by their resources and capabilities, the transaction-based competition, and the ownership structure (Cui, Jiao, Jiao, 2016). A well-integrated strand of literature on theories of organizational cognition and learning focusing on the micro-level organizational processes develop innovative ideas and gives support to technological innovation (Teece, 1998). The efficient innovation in specific technological and product areas its limited to the ability to develop new competencies. Technological innovation firms are well differentiated in global, international, national, and local niches, so innovation processes do not increase complementarity.

Professional, scientific, technological, and social competencies are important for organizational technological innovation. Social competencies are different that the modes of technological innovation are the change agent of competencies. Organizational technological innovation is the relationship between the social systems and the change agents. The actors are undetermined by the systems although the actions are regulated by different types of systems with different degrees of determination. The success of technological innovations may depend upon the reputation and social capital of organizations that sponsors innovations on the technical specifications (Wade, 1995; Podolny & Stuart, 1995; Tushman & Rosenkopf, 1992).

External environmental changes fit to the organizations decline over time due to the forces of organizational inertia coupled with imprinting, leading to reduce the levels of organizational and technological innovation (Aldrich & Auster, 1986). Government environmental regulations have an affirmed value on the promotion effect on green technological innovation capabilities of firms, although the internal mechanisms have not been analyzed and the advantages have not been assessed at micro-level. Different environmental regulatory methods have various effects in development of technological innovation (Jiang *et al.,* 2021).

Technological developments and advancements in work environments, offices and building systems automation innovations have the potential to stimulate innovative space designing and planning concepts (Becker, 1988). Organizational culture may enhance or constrain space designing and planning innovations in the work environment. Technology, space designing and planning, and organizational culture must be planned in an integrated approach to stimulate creativity and organizational technological innovation.

Organizational technological innovation mode is the process of actors underdetermined in social system framework. The organizational technological innovation modes which represent degrees of system determinism are the entrepreneurial, institutional and the strategic reflective. Despite that there is not a framework, the institutional environment is relevant to the organizational technological innovation and technological diffusion, including the non-market and market relationships and organizations in the commercialization of innovation (Lynn, Reddy, Aram, 1996).

Large prestigious organizations attract innovators, elaborators, and adopters of technological innovation because their resources are interdependent and distributed in reputable markets. Large organizations invest more of their slack resources in organizational and technological innovation achieving higher possession of their market power leading to higher rates of returns from innovating (Schumpeter, 1942).

Empirical findings strongly support the organizational ecology approach to technological innovation interdependence. The specific type of social competence defines the organizational technological innovation mode. Non standardized technology inhibits the advanced and standardized technological innovation.

The capacity to define and make decisions to change the innovation mode considering the consequences for action is crucial for technological innovation. The technology-based functional mode of organizational innovation is determined by the technology development to change technological trajectories (Dosi *et al.*, 1988). Firms that engage in technological innovation are shaped by their organizational attributes. High exports of firms tend to lower the probability to engage in technological innovation. High government ownership shares of firms tend to lower the probability of engage in technological innovation.

The interrelationships between the organizational structures, formal and informal, the strategy and the nature of innovation (Teece, 1998) specify the properties of technological innovation process. The nature of the relationship between organizational structural forms and technological innovativeness tend to become more complex, dynamic, multilevel, and interdependent.

New emergent entrepreneurial firms play a crucial role in economic change (Schumpeter, 1950), and by making innovations, the existing organizations develop and transform social systems. New entries into an industry in environmental change may displaces organizations already established leading to the emergence of new organizational forms to develop and evolve from the entrepreneurial activities. This perspective is consistent with the new firms involved on technological and organizational innovation to take advantage of radical technological changes (Schumpeter, 1950; Aldrich & Mueller, 1982).

Organizational radical innovation leads to the rapid emergence of technological innovations often from entrepreneurial firms (Abernathy & Utterback, 1978; Tushman & Anderson, 1986; Rosenbloom & Christensen, 1994). The new entrants into an industry sector play a critical role in organizational evolution in technological innovation in a scenario of competence destroying through the establishment of organizations better positioned for innovative organizational and technological changes in a scenario of competence-enhancement. Schumpeterian innovation model dynamics never occur in systemic industries or that the ecological perspective explains all changes in such industries.

The continuous change and technological innovations in products are supported by organizational semi-structures. Continuous organizational change for innovation (Brown & Eisenhardt, 1997) is a crucial capability for firms operating in production industries with high velocity and short cycles. Until now is not clear the organizational conditions that causes organizations to shift from one structural organizational form and archetype to another and their interactions with the dimensions of technological innovation in driving organizational changes processes.

The technology cycle model proposes that technological advancements is characterized by long periods of incremental competence enhancement organizational innovation (Anderson & Tushman 1990). A large pool of technicians, professionals and researchers in specific technological fields enable the firms to create, develop, and reconstitute their knowledge and skill base for innovative technological projects. The accumulation of organizational knowledge enhances the capability and ability to assimilate and convert this knowledge in the production of organizational technological innovations (Cohen and Levinthal, 1990). Lak of background and accumulated knowledge impedes the organizational abilities to create and develop technological innovations (Cohen & Levinthal, 1990).

Patent citations result of technological innovation building relationships (Jaffe, Trajtenberg, & Henderson,1993),

Technological innovation at the organizational level is determined by the innovation at the industry level and the passage of time through the industry lifecycles, leading to environmental changes, economic and technological contexts. The life cycle model of the industry suggests the composition of organizational technological innovation leading to changes as the consequence of maturation processes. Organizational age, size and time trend are variables of organizational technological innovation.

Organizational aging has impacts on corporate technological innovation. Organizational age is in relationship with the age and propensity of organizations to create and develop technological innovations. The relationship between organizational aging and technological innovation is relevant for the organizational determinants. The relationship between organizational aging and technological innovation is relevant as determinant of technological innovation. Older organizations are more likely to develop higher competence on organizational and technological innovations.

New start-up firms are rapidly created in an innovation system focusing on innovative projects-based firms that develop technical capabilities to assemble and reassemble teams of high-skilled technicians and scientists who engage in the dynamic organizational and technologically innovative activities. Organizational innovation is a precondition for technical innovation focusing on the internal organizational transformation processes and as the response to external environmental forces.

Organizational innovation is a social system of the firm´s management environment that is relevant for the actors during changes. Organizational innovation processes are a social system formed by organizations through the activities of actors during a period of change. The social system of innovation motivates and integrates actors who turn the innovation system into premises depending on the ability to oblige actors. The relationship between the organizational innovation system and the involved social actors determines the actions of organizational changes (Fuglsang & Sundbo 2005).

The organizational innovation system has a dialectic relationship with the actors within and outside the system on how it manifests in innovation processes. Organizational innovation as a social activity is a structured system rather than individual actors that provides a perspective on goods and services potentially in developed and changed that manages the organization.

Sylicon Valley is a good example of a regional radical innovation system with an industrial core that includes microelectronics, computer networking in both software and hardware, semiconductors, biotechnology, among others. Firms in a radical innovation system undergo continues reconfiguration and realignment to adapt to a constantly changing environment. Product certification and public listing of firms increase the probability of engaging in technological innovation. The primitive and non-standardized technology is the pattern that explains the logic of inhibited advancement that displaced the standardized innovation.

In emergent economies, firms investing in employee training, achieving product certificates and public listing have the tendency to have higher probabilities of engagements in technological innovation. High exports of firms and government ownership lead to lower probability of engagement in technological innovation. Therefore, engagements in technological innovation of firms, is an organizational phenomenon that result from resource and capabilities, market legitimation and founding conditions (Cui, Jiao, Jiao, 2016). Technological innovation of firms in BRICS shapes other organizational attributes.

The sustainability of organizational and technological innovations yield bottom-line and top-line returns (Nidumolu et al., 2009). Research on environmental regulatory methods is not focusing on the core of green technological innovation of manufacturing firms. An improvement and optimization regulatory method have not been proposed until now. Development of green technological innovation can be driven by governmental environmental regulations (Niebel, 2021).

Voluntary environmental regulation based on voluntary participation of firms has effects on technology innovation of environmental regulation arising from voluntary arrangements as governments do not impose mandatory regulations and responsibilities lie with firms who can make independent and free choices. Participation in voluntary environmental regulations helps to improve reputation and obtain government technology, funding, and policy support (Ju *et al.,* 2020). Voluntary environmental regulation enhances green product innovation capabilities, green process innovation capabilities and technology governance capabilities. Mandatory environmental regulations, protection incentives and emission reduction differ from voluntary environmental regulations.

Green technological innovation can be promoted by experienced experimentation of optimized and mature environmental regulatory methods to adapt environmental and ecological needs of protection. The incentive-based environmental regulation is a mechanism that encourages green technological innovation tax incentives, trading licenses, pollution control subsidies, support funds for cleaner production, etc. Command-based environmental regulations and technical specifications reflect the intervention of government according to local conditions in the technological innovation of production process. Command-based environmental regulations followed by incentive-based environmental regulations have a strong promotion effect (Guo & Yuan, 2020) Voluntary environmental regulations have a weak effect.

Firms investing resources to improve green innovation capabilities and the production environment and increase the use of green technologies. Incentive-based environmental regulations promote green technological innovation. Poor information reduces the effectiveness of incentive policies of regulatory authorities and the opportunistic behavior (La Nauze & Mezzetti, 2019). Pollutant discharge permits reduce the wastes emissions while advance the green technological innovation of firms.

Organizational innovation and flexibility should have a continues and proactive strategic orientation to check on technological innovation advancements to meet the stakeholder needs, take actions to respond to environmental changes and challenges, overcome or mitigate futures risks (Aspara et al., 2009; Pohle & Chapman, 2006; Carayannis et al., 2000; Carayannis, 2008).

CONCLUSION

This study aimed to analyze the implications of organizational innovation to green technological innovation departing from the assumption that organizational innovation and technological innovation are the dimensions leading to the creation and development of green technological innovation capacities, have the potential to alleviate and easy the ecological and environmental crises. The study concludes that the development of green technological innovation organizations tends to create and develop the competences that enable them to innovate and survive for a longer period in their domains.

The dimensions of organizational innovation are the management and technological innovation. The organizational innovation challenge is beyond maintaining the static balance between exploration and exploitation, change and stability, and a continuous balance to coordinate the organizational dynamics. Structure and strategy are organizational variables used to construct the organizational forms. The internal dynamics of the organization interacts with the actor learning of technological and environmental dimensions and forces leading to shape the organizational evolution. Organizational aging for dynamics and functioning has general consequences and effects in specific on technological innovation.

Technological innovation drive is level tied to innovative capabilities and abilities balanced with the experience to lower failures. Technological innovation ferment in organizations with product forms to compete in the marketplace for acceptance followed by stability with incremental innovation improvements and dominant designs, in contradiction to the radical innovation. Knowledge in novel innovations deal with high levels of technical uncertainty, complexity, and creativity in emerging new industries.

High technological innovation organizations tend to develop the competence to innovate and survive for a longer period in their domains. Organizational technological change is associated with organizational stability and tend to dominate the technological innovation frontier. The innovative activities of organizations become more insulated from external technological innovations. More experienced organizations with standing innovation routines and trajectories ten to experiment with non-local investments in technological innovation. Training employees increases the probability of firms to engage in organizational and technological innovation.

Green technological innovation capacities have the potential to alleviate and easy the ecological and environmental crises. The development of green technological innovation in manufacturing firms must be supported by the guidance to environmental protection improvement of environmental regulations. Environmental regulations may drive green technological innovations and promotes with some limitations the growth of green technological innovation capabilities. Governance approaches in the development of environmental regulations aimed to technological innovation in countries with limited resources, the universality of methods may help to improve the ecological environmental and achieve sustainable development.

Firms stimulate green technological innovation as the foundation for the implementation of voluntary environmental regulation steaming from their social responsibility. Firms invest resources to implement technological innovation, environmental protection and improve green technology innovation capabilities, production processes and governance capabilities to achieve ecological development.

Firms must meet the government requirements by investing resources to improve green innovation capabilities for environmental protection, green production processes and technological innovation. Incentive-based environmental regulation enhances firms' green product innovation capability, green process innovation capability, and technology governance capabilities.

REFERENCES

Abernathy, W. J., & Utterback, J. M. (1978). Patterns of industrial innovation. *Technology Review*, (June/July), 41–47.

Aldrich, H. E., & Auster, E. R. (1986). Even dwarfs started small: Liabilities of age and size and their strategic implications. *Research in Organizational Behavior*, 8, 165–198.

Aldrich, H. E., & Mueller, S. (1982). The Evolution of Organizational Forms: Technology, Coordination and Control. in B.M. Staw & L.L. Cummings (Eds.), Research in Organizational Behaviour. JAI Press.

Amabile, T. M. (1988). A Model of Creativity and Innovation in Organizations. In N.M. Staw & L.L. Cummings (Eds.), Research in Organizational Behavior. JAI Press.

Anderson, P., & Tushman, M. L. (1990). Technological discontinuities and dominant designs: A cyclical model of technological change. *Administrative Science Quarterly*, 35(4), 604–633. doi:10.2307/2393511

Angels, D. P. (2000). High-technology agglomeration and the labour market: The case of Silicon Valley. In K. Martin (Ed.), *Understanding Silicon Valley: The Anatomy of an Entrepreneurial Region* (pp. 125–189). Stanford University Press. doi:10.1515/9781503618381-009

Argyris, C., & Schôn, D. (1978). *Organizational Learning: A Theory of Action Perspective*. Addison-Wesley.

Argyris, C., & Schôn, D. (1987). Reasoning, action strategies, and defensive routines: The case of OD practitioners. *Research in Organizational Change and Development, 1*, 89–128.

Asheim, B., & Gertler, M. (2005). The geography of innovation. In J. Fagerberg, D. C. Mowery, & R. R. Nelson (Eds.), *The Oxford handbook of innovation.* Oxford University Press.

Aspara, J., Hietanen, J., & Tikkanen, H. (2009). Business model innovation vs. replication. *Journal of Strategic Marketing, 18*(1), 39–56. doi:10.1080/09652540903511290

Bahrami, H., & Evans, S. (2000). Flexible recylcing and high-technology entrepreneurship. In K. Martin (Ed.), *Understanding Silicon Valley: The anatomy of an entrepreneurial region* (pp. 166–189). Stanford University Press. doi:10.1515/9781503618381-011

Baldridge, J. V., & Burnham, R. A. (1975). Organizational Innovation: Individual, Organizational, and Environmental Impacts. *Administrative Science Quarterly, 20*(2), 165–176. doi:10.2307/2391692

Becker, F. D. (1988). Technological Innovation and Organizational Ecology. In *Handbook of Human-Computer Interaction.* North-Holland. https://www.sciencedirect.com/science/article/pii/B9780444705365500579

Binks, M., & Vale, P. A. (1990). *Entrepreneurship and Economic Change.* McGraw–Hill.

Bossink, B. A. G. (2004). Effectiveness of innovation leadership styles: A manager's influence on ecological innovation in construction projects. *Construction Innovation, 4*(4), 211–228. doi:10.1108/14714170410815105

Brown, S. L., & Eisenhardt, K. M. (1997). The Art of Continuous Change: Complexity Theory and Time-Paced Evolution in Relentlessly Shifting Organizations. *Administrative Science Quarterly, 42*(1), 1–34. doi:10.2307/2393807

Burgleman, E. A. (1991). Intraorganizational Ecology of Strategy Making and Organizational Adaptation: Theory and Research. *Organization Science, 2/3*(3), 239–262. doi:10.1287/orsc.2.3.239

Burns, T., & Stalker, G. M. (1961). *The Management of Innovation.* Tavistock.

Carayannis, E. G. (2008). Knowledge-driven creative destruction or leveraging knowledge for competitive advantage: Strategic Knowledge arbitrage and serendipity as real options drivers triggered by co-opetition, co-evolution, and co-specialization. *Industry and Higher Education, 22*(6), 343–353. doi:10.5367/000000008787225957

Carayannis, E. G., Alexander, J., & Ioannidis, A. (2000). Leveraging knowledge, learning, and innovation in forming strategic government–university–industry (GUI) R&D partnerships in the US, Germany, and France. *Technovation, 20*(9), 477–488. doi:10.1016/S0166-4972(99)00162-5

Chandler, A. D. (1962). *Strategy and Structure: Chapters in the History of the American Industrial Enterprise.* MIT Press.

Child, J. (1997). Strategic Choice in the Analysis of Action, Structure, Organizations and Environment: Retrospect and Prospect. *Organization Studies, 18*(1), 43–76. doi:10.1177/017084069701800104

Chin, J. M., & Chuang, C. P. (2015). The Relationships among School-Based Budgeting, Innovative Management, and School Effectiveness: A Study on Specialist Schools in Taiwan. *The Asia-Pacific Education Researcher*, *24*(4), 679–693. doi:10.100740299-014-0220-3

Cohen, W. M., & Levinthal, D. A. (1990). Absorptive Capacity: A New Perspective on Learning and Innovation. *Administrative Science Quarterly*, *35*(1), 123–138. doi:10.2307/2393553

Cui, Y., Jiao, J., Jiao, H. (2016). Technological innovation in Brazil, Russia, India, China, and South Africa (BRICS): An organizational ecology perspective. *Technological Forecasting and Social Change*, *107*, 28-36. doi:10.1016/j.techfore.2016.02.001

Daft, R. L. (1978). A Dual-Core Model of Organizational Innovation. *Academy of Management Review*, *21*, 193–210.

Damanpour, F. (1996). Organizational Complexity and Innovation: Developing and Testing Multiple Contingency Models. *Management Science*, *42*(5), 693–716. doi:10.1287/mnsc.42.5.693

Damanpour, F., & Evan, W. M. (1984). Organizational Innovation and Performance: The Problem of Organizational Lag. *Administrative Science Quarterly*, *29*(3), 392–402. doi:10.2307/2393031

DeFillipi, R. (2002). Organization Models for Collaboration in the New Economy. *Human Resource Planning*, *25*(4), 7–19.

Dosi, G., Freeman, C., Nelson, R., Silverberg, G., & Soete, L. (1988). *Technical Change and Economic Theory* (G. Dosi, C. Freeman, R. Nelson, G. Silverberg, & L. Soete, Eds.). Pinter.

Drucker, P. F. (1999). *Innovation and Entrepreneurship: Practice and Principles*. Butterworth–Heinemann.

Foss, N. J. (2003). Selective intervention and internal hybrids: Interpreting and learning from the rise and decline of the Oticon spaghetti organization. *Organization Science*, *14*(3), 331–349. doi:10.1287/orsc.14.3.331.15166

Freeman, C., & Soete, L. (1997). *The Economics of Industrial Innovation*. Pinter.

Fuglsang, L., & Sundbo. (2005). The organizational innovation system: Three modes Journal of Change Management Reframing. *Leadership and Organizational Practice*, *5*(3), 329-344.

Fuglsang, L., & Sundbo, J. (2005). The organizational innovation system: Three modes. *Journal of Change Management*, *5*(3), 329–344. doi:10.1080/14697010500258056

Galunic, D. C., & Eisenhardt, K. M. (2001). Architectural Innovation and Modular Corporate Forms. *Academy of Management Journal*, *44*(6), 1229–1249. doi:10.2307/3069398

Glynn, M. A. (1996). Innovative Genius: A Framework for Relating Individual and Organizational Intelligence to Innovation. *Academy of Management Review*, *21*(4), 1081–1111. doi:10.2307/259165

Guo, R., & Yuan, Y. (2020). Different Types of Environmental Regulations and Heterogeneous Influence on Energy Efficiency in the Industrial Sector: Evidence from Chinese Provincial Data. *Energy Policy*, *145*, 111747. doi:10. 1016/j.enpol.2020.111747

Hage, J. T. (2022). Organizational innovation and organizational change. *Annual Review of Sociology*, *25*(1), 597-622.

Hannan, M. T., & Freeman, J. (1984). Structural inertia and organizational change. *American Journal of Sociology*, *49*(2), 149–164. doi:10.2307/2095567

Hannan, M. T., & Freeman, J. (1989). *Organizational Ecology*. Harvard University Press. doi:10.4159/9780674038288

Hedlund, G. (1994). A Model of Knowledge Management and the N-Form Corporation. *Strategic Management Journal*, *15*(S2), 73–90. doi:10.1002mj.4250151006

Jaffe, A., Trajtenberg, M., & Henderson, R. (1993). Geographic localization of knowledge spillovers, as evidenced by patent citations. *The Quarterly Journal of Economics*, *108*(3), 577–598. doi:10.2307/2118401

Jiang, Z., Wang, Z., & Lan, X. (2021). How Environmental Regulations Affect Corporate Innovation? The Coupling Mechanism of Mandatory Rules and Voluntary Management. *Technol. Soc.*, *65*, 101575. Doi: .2021.101575 doi:10.1016/j.techsoc

Ju, K., Zhou, D., Wang, Q., Zhou, D., & Wei, X. (2020). What Comes after Picking Pollution Intensive Low-Hanging Fruits? Transfer Direction of Environmental Regulation in China. *J. Clean. Prod., 258*, 120405. doi:10. 1016/j.jclepro.2020.120405

Kanter, R. M. (1983). *The Change Masters: Innovations for Productivity in the American Corporation*. Unwin.

Kimberly, J. R. (1975). Environmental constraints and organizational structure: A comparative analysis of rehabilitation organizations. *Administrative Science Quarterly*, *20*(1), 1–9. doi:10.2307/2392119 PMID:10237043

Kotler, P. (1983). *Principles of Marketing*. Prentice–Hall.

La Nauze, A., & Mezzetti, C. (2019). Dynamic Incentive Regulation of Diffuse Pollution. *J. Environ. Econ. Manag., 93*, 101–124. Doi: .11.009 doi:10.1016/j.jeem.2018

Lam, A. (2000). Tacit Knowledge, Organizational Learning, Societal Institutions: An Integrated Framework. *Organization Studies*, *21*(3), 487–513. doi:10.1177/0170840600213001

Lam, A. (2002). Alternative societal models of learning and innovation in the knowledge economy. *International Social Science Journal*, *17*(1), 67–82. doi:10.1111/1468-2451.00360

Lam, A. (2004). *Organizational Innovation. Working Paper No. 1. Brunel Research in Enterprise, Innovation, Sustainability, and Ethics*. BRESE, School of Business and Management Brunel University.

Laursen, K., & Salter, A. J. (2006). Open for innovation: The role of openness in explaining innovative performance among UK manufacturing firms. *Strategic Management Journal*, *27*(2), 131–150. doi:10.1002mj.507

Lawrence, P. R., & Lorsch, J. W. (1967). Differentiation and Integration in Complex Organizations. *Administrative Science Quarterly*, *12*, 1–47.

Lazonick, W., & West, J. (1998). Organizational Integration and Competitive Advantage. In *Technology, Organization and Competitiveness*. Oxford University Press. doi:10.1093/0198290969.003.0008

Lundvall, B.-A. (Ed.). (1992). *National Systems of Innovation: Towards a Theory of Innovation and Interactive Learning*. Pinter.

Lynn, L. H., Reddy, N. M., & Aram, J. D. (1996). Linking technology and institutions: the innovation community framework, *Research Policy*, *25*(1), 91-106. https://www.sciencedirect.com/science/article/pii/0048733394008175

MacMeal, H. B. (1934). *The Story of Independent Telephony*. Independent Pioneer Telephone Association.

Malerba, F. (2003). Sectoral systems and innovation and technology policy. *Revista Brasileira de Inovação*, *2*(2), 329–375. doi:10.20396/rbi.v2i2.8648876

Mezias, S. J., & Glynn, M. A. (1993). The Three Faces of Corporate Renewal: Institution, Revolution, and Evolution. *Strategic Management Journal*, *14*(2), 77–101. doi:10.1002mj.4250140202

Miles, R. E., Snow, C. C., Mathews, J. A., Miles, G., & Coleman, H. J. Jr. (1997). Organizing in the Knowledge Age: Anticipating the Cellular Form. *The Academy of Management Executive*, *11*(4), 7–20. doi:10.5465/ame.1997.9712024836

Mintzberg, H. (1979). *The Structuring of Organization*. Prentice Hall.

Mintzberg, H. (1979). *The Structuring of Organizations: A Synthesis of the Research*. The Theory of Management Policy Series. Prentice-Hall.

Nelson, R. R., & Winter, S. G. (1982). *Evolutionary Theory of Economic Change*. Belknap Press of Harvard University Press.

Nidumolu, R., Prahalad, C. K., & Rangaswami, M. R. (2009). Why sustainability is now the key driver of innovation. *Harvard Business Review*, *87*(9), 56–64.

Niebel, C. (2021). The Impact of the General Data Protection Regulation on Innovation and the Global Political Economy. *Computer Law & Security Review*, *40*, 105523. doi:10.1016/j.clsr.2020.105523

Nonaka, I. (1994). A Dynamic Theory of Organizational Knowledge Creation. *Organization Science*, *5*(1), 14–37. doi:10.1287/orsc.5.1.14

Nonaka, I., & Takeuchi, H. (1995). *The Knowledge Creating Company*. Oxford University Press.

Nyström, H. (1979). *Creativity and Innovation*. Wiley.

Nyström, H. (1990). *Technological and Market Innovation: Strategies for Product and Company Development*. Wiley.

Parsons, T. (1951). *The Social System*. Free Press.

Podolny, J. M., & Stuart, T. E. (1995). A role-based ecology of technological change. *American Journal of Sociology*, *100*(5), 1224–1260. doi:10.1086/230637

Pohle, G., & Chapman, M. (2006). IBM's global CEO report 2006: Business model innovation matters. *Strategy and Leadership, 34*(5), 34–40. doi:10.1108/10878570610701531

Powell, W. W., & Grodal, S. (2005). Networks of Innovators. In *The Oxford Handbook of Innovation.* Oxford University Press. doi:10.1093/oxfordhb/9780199286805.003.0003

Robbins, S. P., & Judge, T. A. (2016). *Organizational behavior: Concepts, controversies, and applications* (17th ed.). Prentice Hall.

Romanelli, E., & Tushman, M. L. (1994). Organizational Transformation as Punctuated Equilibrium: An Empirical Test. *Academy of Management Journal, 37*(5), 1141–1166. doi:10.2307/256669

Rosenbloom, R. S., & Christensen, C. M. (1994). Technological discontinuities, organizational capabilities, and strategic commitments. *Industrial and Corporate Change, 3*(3), 655–685. doi:10.1093/icc/3.3.655

Saxenian, A. (1996). Beyond boundaries: Open labour markets and learning in the Silicon Valley. In M. B. Arthur & D. M. Rousseau (Eds.), *The boundaryless career: A new employment principle for a new organizational era* (pp. 23–39). Oxford University Press.

Schumpeter, J. (1950). The process of creative destruction. In J. Schumpeter (Ed.), *Capitalism, Socialism and Democracy* (3rd ed.). Allen and Unwin.

Schumpeter, J. A. (1942). *Capitalism, Socialism and Democracy.* Harper.

Senge, P. (1990). *The Fifth Discipline: The Art and Practice of the Learning Organization.* Doubleday.

Sexton, D. L., & Kasarda, J. D. (1992). The State of the Art of Entrepreneurship. PWS–Kent.

Sexton, D. L., & Landström, H. (2000). *The Blackwell Handbook of Entrepreneurship* (D. L. Sexton & H. Landström, Eds.). Blackwell.

Sørensen, J. B., & Stuart, T. E. (2000, March). Aging, Obsolescence, and Organizational Innovation. *Administrative Science Quarterly, 45*(1), 81–112. doi:10.2307/2666980

Star, S. L. (1989). The structure of ill-structured solutions: boundary objects and heterogeneous distributed problem solving. In L. Gasser & M. N. Huhns (Eds.), *Distributed Artificial Intelligence* (Vol. 2, pp. 37–54). Pitman. doi:10.1016/B978-1-55860-092-8.50006-X

Sundbo, J. (1998). *The theory of innovation: entrepreneurs, technology and strategy.* Edward Elgar.

Sundbo, J. (2001). *The Strategic Management of Innovation.* Edward Elgar.

Sundbo, J., & Fuglsang, L. (2002). *Innovation as Strategic Reflexivity* (J. Sundbo & L. Fuglsang, Eds.). Routledge. doi:10.4324/9780203219270_chapter_1

Teece, D. J. (1998). Design issues for Innovative Firms: Bureaucracy, Incentives and Industrial Structure. In A. D. Chandler Jr, P. Hagstrom, & O. Solvell (Eds.), *The Dynamic Firm.* Oxford University Press.

Tidd, J., Bessant, J., & Pavitt, K. (1997). *Managing Innovation: Integrating Technological, Market, and Organizational Change.* Wiley.

Tushman, M. L., & Anderson, P. (1997). *Managing Strategic Innovation and Change: A Collection of Readings* (M. L. Tushman & P. Anderson, Eds.). Oxford University Press.

Tushman, M. L., & Rosenkopf, L. (1992). Organizational determinants of technological change: Toward a sociology of technological evolution. *Research in Organizational Behavior, 14*, 311–347.

Van de Ven, A., Polley, D., Garud, S., & Venkataraman, S. (1999). *The Innovation Journey*. Oxford Univ. Press.

Verona, G., & Ravasi, D. (2003). Unbundling dynamic capabilities: An exploratory study of continuous product innovation. *Industrial and Corporate Change, 12*(3), 577–606. doi:10.1093/icc/12.3.577

Von Hippel, E. (1988). *The Sources of Innovation*. Oxford University Press.

Wade, J. (1995). Dynamics of organizational communities and technological bandwagons: An empirical investigation of community evolution in the microprocessor market. *Strategic Management Journal, 16*(S1), 111–133. doi:10.1002mj.4250160920

Weber, M. (1958). Religious rejections of the world and their directions. In From Max Weber: Essays in Sociology. Oxford University Press.

Weick, K. E. (1979). The Social Psychology of Organizing, Topics in Social Psychology. Addison-Wesley.

Whitley, R. (2003). The Institutional Structuring of Organizational Capabilities: The Role of Authority Sharing and Organizational Careers. *Organization Studies, 24*(5), 667–695. doi:10.1177/0170840603024005001

Wolfe, B. (1994). Organizational Innovation: Review, Critique and Suggested Research Directions. *Journal of Management Studies, 31*(3), 405–443. doi:10.1111/j.1467-6486.1994.tb00624.x

Womack, J. P., Jones, D. T., & Roos, D. (1990). *The Machine that Changed the World*. Rawson Associates.

Woodman, R. W., Sawyer, J. E., & Griffin, R. W. (1993). Toward a Theory of Organizational Creativity. *Academy of Management Review, 18*(2), 293–321. doi:10.2307/258761

Zhou, C., & Li, J. (2008). Product innovation in emerging market-based international joint ventures: An organizational ecology perspective. *Journal of International Business Studies, 39*(7), 1114–1132. doi:10.1057/jibs.2008.51

Chapter 12
Role of Corporate Social Responsibility Towards Green HRM in Selected Companies

Reshma Shrivastava
Amity University, Raipur, India

Imran Nadeem Siddiqui
Amity University, Raipur, India

Suresh Kumar Pattanayak
Amity University, Raipur, India

ABSTRACT

The majority of businesses have adopted human resource strategies that promote environmental sustainability while taking into account minimizing environmental damage and contamination. The chapter investigates how business organizations can create a sustainable environment with reference to selected companies in India. The senior management of an organization is therefore also responsible for making sure that the staff is encouraged to pursue the social, ecological, and financial benefits of living in a greener environment. The chapter highlights the value of a green environment as well as the initiatives taken by various businesses to preserve a sustainable environment. Evaluation of the green human resource management (GHRM) predicted results and anticipated challenges while attempting to create a greener environment. The chapter focuses on the corporate social responsibility effort of selected companies and how much they are spending in CSR initiatives toward a green environment.

INTRODUCTION

GHRM as an idea looks upon sustainable improvement and company responsibility. Wehrmeyer (1996) writes that if an employer is adopting a technique to defend surroundings then it will become very critical that personnel must be worried about it. There are many nations withinside the globe that' have

DOI: 10.4018/978-1-6684-6815-9.ch012

confronted detrimental impacts because of the requirement of sustainability or there is a large call for surroundings safety so it has ended up obligatory for the nations to undertake inexperienced practices. Businesses ought to now no longer simply be powerful and provide cost in the contemporary fiercely aggressive international market; additionally, they want to be responsible, which incorporates being chargeable for the surroundings. In pursuing this inexperienced agenda, scholars (Renwick et al., 2016) have contended that human useful resource control (HRM) performs a critical function. Hence, embedding inexperienced practices in HRM features may want probably beautify the chance of the organization's sustainability and cost. The HR features change into the motive force of environmental sustainability in the organization through aligning the practices and rules with sustainability desires reflecting eco-awareness. (Deepika & Karpagam, 2016). The focus of Green HRM has accelerated withinside the ultimate decade, with its popularity as one of the viable inexperienced control practices of an employer that may lessen its environmental "footprint" and makes the commercial enterprise greater sustainable. Subsequently from 2016 onwards the significance of Green HRM studies accelerated strikingly amongst scholars (Dumont et al., 2016; Guerci, Longoni, and Luzzini, 2016; Guerci, Montanari, Scapolan and Epifanio, 2016; Jabbour and Renwick, 2018; Yong et al., 2019; Yusliza et al., 2017). As a result, the look at Green HRM has accelerated exponentially. According to (Saeed et al, 2022) CSR is contributing an essential function toward Green HRM as it's the main contribution to sustainability. Green HRM and CSR together interfere with every aspect of stakeholder cost. (Malik et al 2021). Mehdi 2021 writes that inexperienced hrm and CSR develops inexperienced conduct amongst personnel. The best intention of CSR is to uphold employer principles, along with environmental safety, that's done through adopting green practices. To shift organizational structures, procedures, and climate, in addition to worker behaviors toward environmental sustainability, GHRM strategies are much like this.(Mehdi Sobokro 2021). Sustainable overall performance has been correlated with CSR and inexperienced HRM practices. This view has delivered to our knowledge of sustainability, OCBE, GHRM, and CSR. Through the lenses of motivation possibility idea and stakeholder idea, this look sought to study the mediating function of OCBE among inexperienced HRM practices, company social responsibility, and sustainable overall performance. (Malik et al 2021). The effects reveal that 3 GHRM practices—inexperienced worker engagement, inexperienced pay and rewards, and inexperienced recruitment and selection—have a good impact on employer sustainability. (Tauseef Jamal 2021).The CSR attempt can help in formulating and reaching environmental and social desires and additionally balancing those desires towards conventional economic overall performance metrics. The GHRM characteristic also can function as an accomplice in formulating company values and sustainability techniques. Although studies on Green HRM are gaining heightened attention, the point of interest regions for figuring out the relationship among the disciplines ranges widely. Hence, growing a holistic idea of this shape and a top-level view of the prevailing frame of Green HRM studies is necessary. Currently, the place suffers from a loss of complete literature critiques which have investigated and analyzed the growing frame of literature in Green HRM. Hence, a complete and improved literature evaluation on Green HRM wishes to be developed. This paper, therefore, offers in-intensity insights into and evaluation of Green HRM and the way Corporate Social Responsibility performs an essential function. The study majorly focuses on the CSR initiatives taken by Selected companies toward Green HRM. Some of the objectives are:

1. To study the CSR initiatives in selected Companies
2. To Study the Green HRM Implementation in these companies
3. To study the role of CSR towards sustainability in selected companies

BACKGROUND

Concept of Green HRM and CSR

The Green Human resource in green-oriented organizations plays a significant part in shaping the culture of the organization (Shaban S 2019). The use of green human resource management solutions is a result of the growing demand for corporate social responsibility (Cheema et al 2017). The majority of companies implement personnel strategies that promote environmental sustainability while considering minimizing environmental damage and pollution. The human resources department, through its normal operations, has made a significant contribution to environmental protection as part of the nature conservation motive. Green HRM presented his 7-dimensional multidimensional structure of Green Job Design. Environmentally friendly recruitment and selection. green training and development; green performance management; green compensation management; green health and safety; and green labor relations measurable by 28 items. As they outline new research challenges for green HRM, Jabbour, and Renwick (2018) talk about the "soft and human" aspects of creating ecologically sustainable organizations. Chandra and Mukherjee (2018) The idea of influencing environmentally conscious employees' behavior is known as "green HRM." The conceptual framework is intended to explicitly comprehend and forecast employee behavior in the workplace or throughout an organization. (Siambalapitya et al.2018) identified eight aspects of green HRM. This includes Green HRM Functions and Practices, Green Recruitment, Green Selection, Green Training and Development, Green Compensation and Rewards, Green Performance Evaluation, Green Employee Relations, and Green Complaint Management. Yusof et al. (2018), variables such as green recruitment and selection, green training and development, and green remuneration show a positive relationship with an organization's environmental performance, but the Performance ratings show no significant relationship with environmental performance. To use organizational resources sustainably for both organizations and the environment, green Practices include all management approaches, processes, and procedures. (M Jam, WN Jamal,2020). The effects of implementing Green Human Resource Management (GHRM) are a key research topic in human resource management procedures in contemporary commercial organizations. The approach for implementing GHRM is what makes the company distinctive, and its effects on green managerial innovation and green HR process innovation assist green management and sustainable green industries. (Saptaria, L., Soetjipto, B. E., & Wardoyo, C. 2022).The extensive potential of green human resource management systems can also be used to encourage organizations to adopt environmentally friendly practices(Das, S., & Dash, M. 2022). Enterprises that remove raw materials from the environment, process them and then return them to the environment as goods or services have started to run into resource issues because of the depletion of natural resources in the 21st century. Additionally, businesses don't operate in a vacuum from their environment. In other words, there is a two-way connection between businesses and their micro and macro contexts. In addition, businesses have a corporate social responsibility to the communities in which they operate. When considering all of these factors, it is evident that businesses have developed a considerably greater awareness of the environment over the previous 25 years. (Ghanem, F.2022). Sustainable development is included in corporate social responsibility (CSR) initiatives. A favorable social, economic, and environmental environment may result from it. Corporate social responsibility (CSR) is a tool for developing a distinctive brand image for the company's goods, establishing the company as a consumer-friendly brand, and upholding the ability to be trusted when it comes to the commitment to promoting social welfare. Green human resources management essentially aims to reduce the number of carbon footprints left by an organization's regular operations. The fundamental focus of GHRM is integrating Practices that really can support an approach to environmental conservation while also maintaining the organizational knowledge and understanding in the form of human resources. (Thorat, M. S., & Rose, A.2021)

FUNCTIONS OF GHRM

GHRM Concept has given various applications of HR in the new domain. GHRM policies and practices have created an impact by changing the functions of the organization in the new trend. The major functions of GHRM are.

- **Green Job Design and Analysis**

In the Real scenario, job descriptions can be used to specify environmental protection-related tasks, duties, and responsibilities. Most companies have started adopting environmental and social tasks, duties and responsibilities as far as possible in each job to protect the environment. In some companies, each job description includes at least one duty related to environmental protection and conservation. It specifically includes environmental responsibilities whenever and wherever applicable (Vijaya Lakshmi & Battu, 2018).

- **Green Human Resource Planning**

Recently few companies engage in forecasting the number of employees and types of employees, needed to implement corporate environmental management initiatives, such as ISO 14001, Environment Management Systems, etc. These are good practices that leading companies have adopted to manage their environmental issues. Corporate environmental management initiatives demand new job positions and a specific set of skills (Vijaya Lakshmi & Battu, 2018).

- **Green Recruitment**

It calls for paper-free recruitment processes with a minimum environmental impact. Applications are invited through online mediums like e-mails, online application forms, and through global talent pools. Telephonic or video-based interviews can be conducted to minimize any travel and distance-related environmental issues. Green recruitment is the process of recruiting new talent who are aware of the sustainable process, and environmental system and aware of conservation and sustainable environment (Vijaya Lakshmi & Battu, 2018) (Ashitha & Anu, 2020).

- **Green Selection**

The Company should try to select candidates who have a favorable attitude toward the green movement. Candidates who are sensitive to greener concepts and are willing to take responsibility for green initiatives should be chosen (Ashitha & Anu, 2020).

- **Green Induction**

The Induction program is conducted within the organizations to welcome new employees, make them familiar with the organization and prepare them for future jobs. In Green HRM, the induction programs are conducted in such a way as to create awareness among the recruits about the green practices followed by the organization. The induction programs should focus on the organization's green skills, working conditions, and green policies (Ashitha & Anu, 2020).

- **Green Leadership**

The green leadership mindset is required today so that leaders become equipped to create and act upon sustainable practices. This will generate larger-scale actions, and support for public policies that will ensure long-term success, well-being, and security for all segments of society (Joyce & Vijai, 2020).

- **Green Performance Appraisal & Management**

Green Performance Management is the process by which employees are encouraged to enhance their professional skills, which would help them to achieve the organizational goals and objectives in a better way(Vijaya Lakshmi & Battu, 2018)

- **Green Employee Discipline Management**

In this area, some companies have realized "discipline management" as a tool to self-regulate and control employees with environmental protection activities of the organization. These companies have developed a clear set of rules and regulations which imposes/regulate employees to be concerned with environmental protection in line with the environmental policy of the organizations. In such companies, if an employee does not abide by environmental rules and regulations, disciplinary actions (warning, fining, suspension, etc.) are taken against him/her (Vijaya Lakshmi & Battu, 2018)

- **Green Employee Relations**

Employee relations is an important aspect of HRM which is concerned with establishing cordial employer-employee relationships. The relationship facilitates motivation and morale of the employees, on the other hand, increases productivity. Employee relations involve employee participation and empowerment activities. It also helps in preventing and resolving problems arising at the workplace that may affect the quality of work. Positive employee relations are an intangible and enduring asset and a source of competitive advantage for every organization. Cordial relations will maintain economy and optimization in every aspect of work (Joyce & Vijai, 2020).

ROLE OF CHANGING ORGANISATIONS TOWARDS SUSTAINABILITY

India has an extensive collection of environmental regulations as a significant growing nation. But slowly, their number is increasing. The judiciary has played a substantial and admirable creative role. The Supreme Court of India has received numerous Public Interest Litigations against numerous industries for failing to provide adequate pollution control as well as against Pollution Control Boards to order them to take the proper actions to ensure pollution control. (Agarwal, V. K. 2005). From 2022 to 23 filing of BRSR will be mandatory for the top 1000 companies listed and their business responsibility report will change. As per the environmental law of India protection of the environment and waste management. Measures will be taken to reverse climate change. In all these efforts companies are going to play a pivotal role in sustainability. The concept of changing organization enforces " No green to Go Green". This has been the topmost agenda of the major companies in India. With due diligence of Indian Environment law of India 1986. The need of integrating sustainability measures into the human resource management system as well as the significant impact of human resource management on environmental sustainability for the achievement of long-term sustainability in corporate development (Sabokro, M., Masud, M. M., & Kayedian, A. 2021), in terms of both the economy and pollution and environmental problems, the manufacturing sector is one of the major contributors. Both internal and external stakeholders need appropriate arrangements and solutions to lessen environmental issues, which are a major concern for both parties. Because of this, it is essential to lessen environmental difficulties by introducing green initiatives and through corporate social responsibility actions in society. Companies can get a competitive edge and perform sustainably with the aid of green initiatives and CSR. Corporate social responsibility (CSR) helps companies build a positive reputation in the eyes of stakeholders, boosts brand recognition, and solves societal issues. Green initiatives aid enterprises in luring talented, dedicated, and skilled workers (Malik, S. Y., Hayat Mughal, Y., Azam, T., Cao, Y., Wan, Z., Zhu, H., & Thurasamy, R. 2021).

Ren et al. (2017) emphasize the urgent need for advanced conceptualization and scope of green HRM and develops an integrated model of precedents, consequences, and contingencies related to green HRM. Sriram and Suba (2017) Achieving green HRM is entirely based on employee commitment. It also discusses the positive and negative impact of green HRM on organizational effectiveness. Tang et al. (2017) Green HRM includes five dimensions: green recruitment and selection, green training, green performance management, green pay and compensation, and green engagement. Jabbour and de Sousa Jabbour (2016) Culture, spirit, teamwork, and empowerment underlie Green Supply Chain Management (GSCM). Internal GSCM practices and return on investment will be the first step towards a more sophisticated external GSCM and more intensive support from HRM will be required to achieve a more sustainable supply chain. Renwick et al. (2016) The articles included here provide contextual insights using theories of green recruitment, skills, employee ownership, financial/environmental performance, country culture, paradoxes, and stakeholder theories.

METHODOLOGY

In the present study, data has been collected from secondary sources. The statistics of CSR initiatives and the money spent on CSR by selected companies have been taken for study. Businesses now treat CSR as a distinct entity and give it much attention. Most businesses have a vision and purpose statement that guides their CSR initiatives, either at the corporate level or occasionally at the CSR level. The paper highlights the study on the CSR initiatives of the selected companies. Data has also been collected from secondary sources to identify the sustainable efforts of the selected companies. The paper highlights the GHRM initiatives of the selected companies and a comparative analysis has been done to derive a meaningful conclusion. Focus has also been given to the CSR spent. For analyzing the data Top 5 companies spending on CSR have been Taken. Companies selected for the study have been selected Top 5 companies Indian Companies as per sustainability 2021.

1.   Godrej Consumer Products Limited.
2.   Infosys Limited.
3.   Wipro Limited. ...
4.   Tata Chemicals Limited. ...
5.   ITC Limited. ...

DATA ANALYSIS AND DISCUSSION

For data analysis, the first company selected is:

1.   Godrej Consumer Products Limited. It is an FMCG company Godrej embraces diversity, opportunity equality, and fairness. The company recognizes that both good health and a healthy environment are necessary for sustainable economic growth and the well-being of society. Data has been collected from various secondary sources where companies' CSR initiatives and their practices of GHRM have been presented below. To aid the Green Initiative, Members who've now no longer registered their e-mail cope are asked to sign in their e-mail cope with for receiving all communique along with Annual Report, Notices, Circulars, etc. from the Company electronically with the aid of using following the process stated withinside the Note No.13. Godrej is deeply dedicated to the GOOD and GREEN techniques and success of set goals for the Godrej Group. He encourages and helps a shared imaginative and prescient price for all packages of Good and Green.

2.   The other company selected is a Major IT company in India. The company is highly technology driven and has adopted new-age HR solutions. At Infosys, HR capabilities are built across technology and process consulting. The company is very focused and adopts a stringent talent acquisition and retention policy. The brief HR policy is presented in Figure 1.

Figure 1. New age HR solutions of Infosys Private Limited.
Source: <https://www.infosys.com/> [Accessed 14 October 2022].

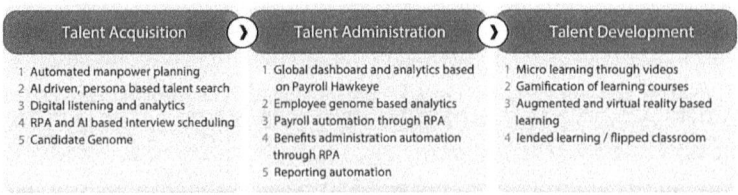

3.   Another important IT employer in India is Wipro Private Limited. Wipro HR offerings simplify lives via design-led, people-first virtual gear and techniques that assist the person that allows you to live centered at the maximum crucial tasks. Blending high-overall performance HR variations

focused on worker experience, we assist groups and HR experts in pressure enterprise transformation to construct the destiny of labour today. From fitness and wealth offerings to human capital control and patron service, our variety of skills makes us the precise accomplice for each degree of your HR transformation journey.

4. Company like Tata Chemical is one of the leading companies in CSR initiatives.. The corporation has released more than one project and initiative to preserve the surroundings and engages with nearby groups closer to remaining a sustainable and eco-friendly company. The Company spent Rs. 21 crores on its CSR applications in FY21. The corporation aided 6,878 farmers with the ability to construct, subject demonstration, and cattle control via virtual and bodily interactions withinside the ultimate economic year. Under its greening program, the corporation has planted 1.15 lakh mangroves throughout diverse websites at the side of conservation of nearby plant biodiversity at Mithapur. Overall, via its CSR projects, the corporation became capable of effect the lives of two lakh human beings withinside the ultimate economic year.

5. ITC's sustainability tasks are pushed through the notion that an enterprise wishes to serve a bigger societal motive preserving countrywide priorities in focus. The Triple Bottom Line dedication of the Company to concurrently construct economic, social, and environmental capital has orchestrated a symphony of efforts that deal with a number of the maximum tough societal problems along with sizeable poverty and environmental degradation. In the closing economic yr, the organization's Social Forestry software greened 30,439 acres of land. The organization turned instrumental in accomplishing 1/3 lakh youngsters via its schooling software. It furnished abilities to 12,470 teenagers throughout the year through vocational schooling programs. It supported the development of 640-person family bathrooms in 28 districts. ITC's waste recycling software, 'Well Being Out of Waste (WOW)', turned into accountability for the gathering of the quantum of dry waste accumulated throughout the year turned into approximately 70,900 MT from 1,067 wards. It is vital for the corporation to provoke Corporate Social Responsibility in this kind of experience so that personnel sense pleased with the corporation. CSR performs an important function in GHRM via Green schooling and development, Green Performance Appraisal, Green Selection, and Green Job description. All those 5 decided agencies have retained the Green initiative and spending extremely on CSR tasks as given in Table 1.

Table 1. CSR Spent by selected 5 companies for Sustainability

Company Name	CSR	Amount Spent Year Wise				
		2020-2021	2019-2020	2018-2019	2017-2018	2016-2017
Wipro Limited	Sustainability	246.99	181.8	185.28	186.6	186.31
Infosys Limited	Sustainability	361.82	359.94	342.04	312.6	289.44
ITC Limited	Sustainability	335.43	326.49	306.95	290.98	275.96
TATA Chemicals Limited	Sustainability	20.13	37.81	25.68	14.28	15
Godrej Consumer Products Limited	Sustainability	32.73	19.49	21.91	18.57	16.52

Source: Csr.gov.in. 2022.

From the data it is evident that comparatively from year 2016 t0 year 2021 the spent on CSR is showing an increasing trend. The company Wipro is spending on Sustainability Rs.246.99 cr. Infosys is spending 361.82 crores and ITC is spending 335.4. Tata Chemicals and Godrej is spending 20.13 and 32.73 respectively. Sustainability is an initiative towards GHRM which is basically the CSR initiative. This initiative serves the basic purpose of being green and protecting the environment.

Table 2. CSR Spent by selected 5 companies for Environment

Company Name	CSR	Amount Spent Year Wise				
		2020-2021	2019-2020	2018-2019	2017-2018	2016-2017
Wipro Limited	Environment	39.09	46.9	55.27	50.37	55.24
Infosys Limited	Environment	39.94	80.4	143.07	199.07	83.91
ITC Limited	Environment	41.81	64.61	62.5	73.04	73.99
TATA Chemicals Limited	Environment	20.01	18.14	4.22	4.63	2.65
Godrej Consumer Products Limited	Environment	2.22	1.77	5.07	4.9	5.83

Source: Csr.gov.in. 2022.

Compared to sustainability initiatives companies are also spending on the protection of the environment where all the employees play an important role. Environment protection of planet, plantation of trees, waste management and various other initiatives are there which the companies are performing under CSR activities.

CSR spent on education is one of the major initiatives of these companies which basically fosters the development of society.

Table 4 reveals the major developmental sectors of these companies, like healthcare, Education, Rural Development, Government Schemes, Eradicating poverty, Hunger and malnutrition, environmental sustainability, and Vocational eradication of poverty. Skills as well as Livelihood Enhancement Projects. These are the Top 10 developmental sectors where companies' CSR initiatives have set a remarkable trend. It's not only the initiatives of these companies but mostly many of the companies are spending on environmental sustainability it is the 4th major focus of the companies spent wisely. This is a very positive sign and shows a trend that organizations are very sensitive towards CSR and sustainability.

Table 3. CSR Spent by selected 5 companies for Education

Company Name	CSR	Amount Spent Year Wise				
		2020-2021	2019-2020	2018-2019	2017-2018	2016-2017
Wipro Limited	Education	112.65	132.1	123.51	134.99	129.1
Infosys Limited	Education	48.15	81.36	92.96	601	67.67
ITC Limited	Education	28.39	46.21	16.25	45.49	44.93
TATA Chemicals Limited	Education	104	101.7	7.43	4.82	3.54
Godrej Consumer Products Limited	Education	0.9	0.02	1.49	0.49	0.31

Source: Csr.gov.in. 2022.

Table 4. Developmental Sectors and CSR Spent

Development Sector	Total Spent FY 2016-17 (INR Cr.)	Total Spent FY 2017-18 (INR Cr.)	Total Spent FY 2018-19 (INR Cr.)	Total Spent FY 2019-20 (INR Cr.)	Total Spent FY 2020-21 (INR Cr.)
Health Care	2491.52	2776.93	3608.57	4892.28	6946.75
Education	**4505.05**	**5763.08**	**6093.63**	**7164.49**	**6391.86**
Rural Development Projects	1554.78	1724.07	2430.86	2291.38	1818.38
Poverty, Eradicating Hunger, Malnutrition	606.55	811.2	1190.66	1149.1	1236.09
Environmental Sustainability	**1076.46**	**1301.96**	**1364.21**	**1468.22**	**981.78**
Livelihood Enhancement Projects	515.47	832.4	907.49	1077.47	796.14
Vocational Skills	373.46	546.46	798.21	1165.22	630.78

Source: Csr.gov.in. 2022.

Education and Healthcare and Sustainability are significant aspects of CSR where the initiatives of companies have been enormous. This spending is a good sign for the development and growth of the GHRM practices. The vigour has started, and it will be continued.

Figure 2. Developmental Sectors and CSR Spent in Cr
Source: Csr.gov.in. 2022. Home.

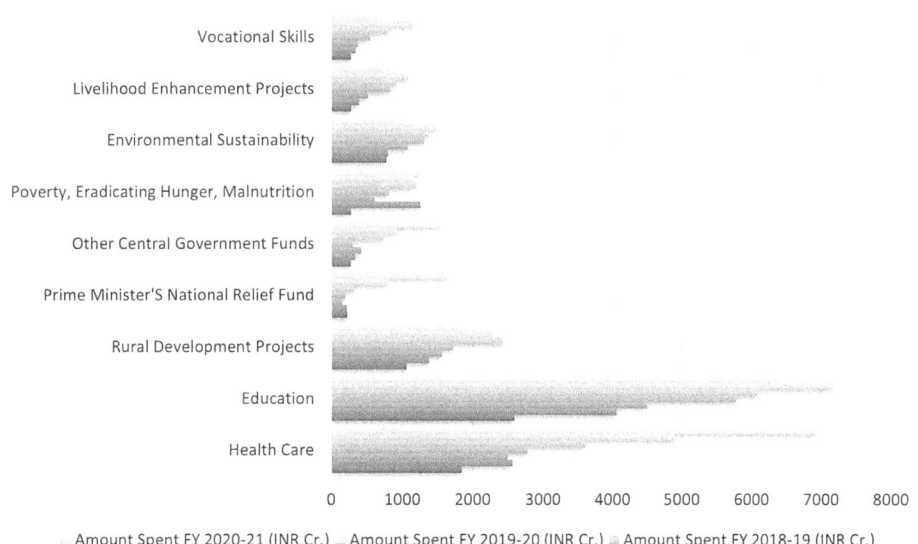

MANAGERIAL IMPLICATIONS

The 500 largest firms in the world spend about $15 billion a year on CSR. Using less energy, water, and other natural resources, and emitting fewer toxic materials is a good idea if we aspire to sustainability then we should focus on recycling, reproducing, and enhancing product quality via innovative design and minimizing packaging. Establish a management system for the environment meeting the purpose and actions for monitoring growth, reducing negativity, and exchanging best practices. Make policies for the health and safety of all workers and inform them about them. The work environment in the organization can improve by involving employees in decision-making that affects them the most. Employers should keep open discussions with their employees to discuss problem-related issues, instead of laying off the employee go for pay cuts or flexible working hours. The company should assure that all the HR policies of an organization should be known to employees and there should be no discrimination among employees. Never accept workplace humour or behavioural fun that denigrates employees due to their gender, race, age, ethnicity, disability, sexual orientation, or religion. Encourage staff members to get involved in the CSR activity by giving them financial and in-kind support. Offer some of the business's products or services to neighbourhood associations and non-profits for a donation or a charge. Look for chances to contribute extra products and unused equipment to the non-profits, community groups, and schools in your area.

FUTURE RESEARCH DIRECTION

The paper highlights the basic concept of Green HRM and Corporate Social Responsibility. How these two are interrelated as CSR focuses on sound HR practices. GHRM activities can also be studied at the individual employee level and how can it create satisfaction among employees. The green behaviour of an organization also leads to employee satisfaction as well as the sustainability of the organization. Another scope for the study is to relate CSR and GHRM practices to Employee satisfaction. These Green practices will motivate the employees to be socially responsible and will further improve the quality of work life. In the future studies can be done on how GHRM can improve the QWL of employees in companies in India.

CONCLUSION

The concept of corporate social responsibility has grown significantly. Thirty years ago, environmentalists debated CSR and sustainability; today, 93% of CEOs agree that sustainability is the key to success, and they are right. According to research, having a strong CSR program will increase staff commitment, customer satisfaction, and access to funding. Undoubtedly, a company invests a lot of money to appear ethical. According to this theory, companies must be concerned with society in order to succeed. Simply turning to the arena of profit, which is the social obligation of business, will fix all of these other judgments.

REFERENCES

Agarwal, V. K. (2005). Environmental laws in India: Challenges for enforcement. *Bulletin of the National Institute of Ecology*, *15*, 227–238.

Ashitha, A. B., & Anu, L. (2020, September). Green HRM: A Pathway to Sustainable Business. In Perspectives on Business Management & Economics (Vol. 2, pp. 106-117). Academic Press.

Cheema & Javed. (2017). *Cogent Business & Management*. doi:10.1080/23311975.2017.1310012

Das, S., & Dash, M. (2022). Role of Green HRM in Sustainable Development. *Journal of Positive School Psychology*, 4444-4451.

Deepika, R., & Karpagam, V. (2016). A study on green HRM practices in an organisation. *International Journal of Applied Research*, *2*(8), 426–429.

Dumont, J., Shen, J., & Deng, X. (2016). Effects of green HRM practices on employee workplace green behavior: The role of psychological green climate and employee green values. *Human Resource Management*, *56*(4), 613–627. doi:10.1002/hrm.21792

Ghanem, F. (n.d.). *The Potential Role Of Green Hrm Practices As An Aspect Of Environmental Concerns That Fall Under The Umbrella Of Sustainability And Corporate Social Responsibility*. Academic Press.

Godrejcp.com. (2022). *Godrej | Consumer Products - Let's make Goodness*. Available at: https://godrejcp.com/

Guerci, M., & Carollo, L. (2016). A paradox view on green human resource management: Insights from the Italian context. *International Journal of Human Resource Management*, *27*(2), 212–238. doi:10.1080/09585192.2015.1033641

Guerci, M., Longoni, A., & Luzzini, D. (2016). Translating stakeholder pressures into environmental performance – the mediating role of green HRM practices. *International Journal of Human Resource Management*, *27*(2), 262–289. doi:10.1080/09585192.2015.1065431

Guerci, M., Montanari, F., Scapolan, A., & Epifanio, A. (2016). Green and nongreen recruitment practices for attracting job applicants: Exploring independent and interactive effects. *International Journal of Human Resource Management*, *27*(2), 129–150. doi:10.1080/09585192.2015.1062040

Hacker, K. (2022). Top 100 companies in India for CSR and Sustainability in 2021. *The CSR Journal*. Available at: https://thecsrjournal.in/top-100-companies-india-csr-sustainability-2021/

Jabbour, C. J. C., & Renwick, D. W. S. (2018). The soft side of environmentally-sustainable organizations. *RAUSP Management Journal*, *53*(4), 622–627. doi:10.1108/RAUSP-07-2018-0044

Jam, M., & Jamal, W. N. (2020). Impact of Green Human Resources Management Practices on Organizational Sustainability and Employee Retention: An Empirical Study Related to Educational Institutions. iRASD. *Journal of Management*, *2*(1), 38–48.

Jamal, T., Zahid, M., Martins, J. M., Mata, M. N., Rahman, H. U., & Mata, P. N. (2021). Perceived green human resource management practices and corporate sustainability: Multigroup Analysis and major industries perspectives. *Sustainability*, *13*(6), 3045. doi:10.3390u13063045

Jyoti, K. (2019). Green HRM–People management commitment to environmental sustainability. *Proceedings of 10th International Conference on Digital Strategies for Organizational Success.*

Kim, Y.J., Kim, W.G., Choi, H., & Phetvaroon, K. (2019). The effect of green human resource management on hotel employees' eco-friendly behavior and environmental performance. *International Journal of Hospitality Management, 76*(A), 83-93. doi:10.1016/j.ijhm.2018.04.007

Lakshmi & Nagaraju. (2018). A Study on Green HRM - An Emerging Trend in HR Practices. *International Journal of Management, 9*(3), 74–82.

Leidner, S., Baden, D., & Ashleigh, M. (2019). Green (environmental) HRM: Aligning ideals with practices. *Personnel Review, 48*(5), 1169–1185. Advance online publication. doi:10.1108/PR-12-2017-0382

Longoni, A., Luzzini, D., & Guerci, M. (2016). Deploying environmental management across functions: The relationship between green human resource management and green supply chain management. *Journal of Business Ethics, 151*(4), 1–15. doi:10.100710551-016-3228-1

Malik, S. Y., Hayat Mughal, Y., Azam, T., Cao, Y., Wan, Z., Zhu, H., & Thurasamy, R. (2021). Corporate social responsibility, green human resources management, and sustainable performance: Is organizational citizenship behavior towards environment the missing link? *Sustainability, 13*(3), 1044. doi:10.3390u13031044

Matthews, B., Obereder, L., Aust, I., & Müller-Camen, M. (2018). Competing Paradigms: Status-quo and Alternative Approaches in HRM. In Contemporary Developments in Green Human Resource Management Research. Routledge.

Moraes, S. D. S., Chiappetta Jabbour, C. J., Battistelle, R. A., Rodrigues, J. M., Renwick, D. S., Foropon, C., & Roubaud, D. (2018). When knowledge management matters: Interplay between green human resources and eco-efficiency in the financial service industry. *Journal of Knowledge Management.* Advance online publication. doi:10.1108/JKM-07-2018-0414

Mukherjee, B., & Chandra, B. (2018). Conceptualizing green human resource management in predicting employees' green intention and behaviour: a conceptual framework. *Prabandhan. Indian Journal of Management, 11*(7), 36-48. doi: /2018/v11i7/129940 doi:10.17010/pijom

Ren, S., Tang, G., & Jackson, S. E. (2017). Green human resource management research in emergence: a review and future directions. *Asia Pacific Journal of Management,* 1-35. https://doi.o rg/ doi:10.1007/s10490-017-9532-1

Renwick, D. W. S., Jabbour, C. J. C., Muller-Camen, M., Redman, T., & Wilkinson, A. (2016). Contemporary developments in green (environmental) HRM scholarship. *International Journal of Human Resource Management, 27*(2), 114–128. doi:10.1080/09585192.2015.1105844

Renwick, D. W. S., Redman, T., & Maguire, S. (2013). Green human resource management: A review and research agenda. *International Journal of Management Reviews, 15*(1), 1–14. doi:10.1111/j.1468-2370.2011.00328.x

Roscoe, S., Subramanian, N., Jabbour, C. J., & Chong, T. (2019). Green human resource management and the enablers of green organisational culture: Enhancing a firm's environmental performance for sustainable development. *Business Strategy and the Environment, 28*(5), 1–13. doi:10.1002/bse.2277

Sabokro, M., Masud, M. M., & Kayedian, A. (2021). The effect of green human resources management on corporate social responsibility, green psychological climate and employees' green behavior. *Journal of Cleaner Production*, *313*, 127963. doi:10.1016/j.jclepro.2021.127963

Saeed, A., Rasheed, F., Waseem, M., & Tabash, M. I. (2021). Green human resource management and environmental performance: The role of green supply chain management practices. *Benchmarking*.

Saeed, B. B., Afsar, B., Hafeez, S., Khan, I., Tahir, M., & Afridi, M. A. (2018). Promoting employee's proenvironmental behavior through green human resource management practices. *Corporate Social Responsibility and Environmental Management*, *26*(2), 424–438. doi:10.1002/csr.1694

Saptaria, L., Soetjipto, B. E., & Wardoyo, C. (2022). Impact of the Implementation of Green Human Resources Management: A Study of Systematic Literature. *Ilomata International Journal of Management*, *3*(2), 264–283. doi:10.52728/ijjm.v3i2.471

Shaban, S. (2019). Reviewing the concept of green HRM (GHRM) and its application practices (Green Staffing) with suggested research agenda: A review from literature background and testing construction perspective. *International Business Research*, *12*(5), 86–94. doi:10.5539/ibr.v12n5p86

Siyambalapitiya, J., Zhang, X., & Liu, X. (2018). Green human resource management: A proposed model in the context of Sri Lanka's tourism industry. *Journal of Cleaner Production*, *201*(2), 542–555. doi:10.1016/j.jclepro.2018.07.305

Tang, G., Chen, Y., Jiang, Y., Paille, P., & Jia, J. (2017). Green human resource management practices: scale development and validity. *Asia Pacific Journal of Human Resources*, *56*(1), 31-55. doi:10.1111/1744-7941.12147

Thorat, M. S., & Rose, A. (n.d.). *Green HRM Move towards Corporate Social Responsibility: Review of Green HR Culture in Organzations and its Challenges*. Academic Press.

Wehrmeyer, W. (1996). Introduction. In Greening People: Human Resources and Environmental Management. Greenleaf Publishing.

Yong, J. Y., & Mohd-Yusoff, Y. (2016). Studying the influence of strategic human resource competencies on the adoption of green human resource management practices. *Industrial and Commercial Training*, *48*(8), 416–422. doi:10.1108/ICT-03-2016-0017

Yong, J. Y., Yusliza, M. Y., Ramayah, T., & Fawehinmi, O. (2019). Nexus between green intellectual capital and green human resource management. *Journal of Cleaner Production*, *215*, 364–374. doi:10.1016/j.jclepro.2018.12.306

Yusliza, M.-Y., Othman, N. Z., & Jabbour, C. J. C. (2017). Deciphering the implementation of green human resource management in an emerging economy. *Journal of Management Development*, *36*(10), 1230–1246. doi:10.1108/JMD-01-2017-0027

Yusoff, Y. M., Nejati, M., Kee, D. M. H., & Amran, A. (2018). Linking green human resource management practices to environmental performance in hotel industry. *Global Business Review*, *21*(3), 1–18. doi:10.1177/0972150918779294

Chapter 13

Sustainable Intellectual Capital:
A Comprehensive Construct for Understanding the Economic, Social, and Environmental Intangibles

Javier Martínez Falcó

https://orcid.org/0000-0001-9004-5816
University of Alicante, Spain

Bartolomé Marco Lajara

https://orcid.org/0000-0001-8811-9118
University of Alicante, Spain

Patrocinio Zaragoza-Sáez
University of Alicante, Spain

ABSTRACT

In recent years, interest in intangible assets has grown, and their identification, measurement, and management has become a topical issue. It is considered important to the recognized value of these invisible assets, called intellectual capital (IC), because they add information to traditional financial indicators that are used both to improve decision making and to demonstrate their potential to potential external users. In this context, IC that incorporates environmental and sustainable aspects (i.e., green intellectual capital [GIC] and sustainable intellectual capital [SIC]) were recently introduced in the academic literature to emphasize the importance of sustainable performance. In order to contribute new knowledge to the subject under study, the research aims to answer the following six research questions through a literature review: (1) What are the origins of IC? (2) How is IC defined? (3) What are the origins of GIC? (4) How is GIC defined? (5) What are the origins of SIC? (6) How is SIC defined?

DOI: 10.4018/978-1-6684-6815-9.ch013

INTRODUCTION

In recent years there has been a growing interest in intangible assets, at least in the private sector, and their identification, measurement and management is a topical issue. It is considered important to recognized value these invisible assets because they add information to traditional financial indicators that are used both to improve decision making and to demonstrate their potential to potential external users (Salvi et al., 2020).

Changes in the economy in recent years have made knowledge and information the most important sources of competitive advantage and success for a company or a nation. The challenge is to understand the different dynamics to which these two factors are subjected and especially the different economic laws that govern them (Xu & Liu, 2020). While on the one hand, the traditional factors of production, land, capital and labor, follow the law of diminishing marginal returns, i.e., as more of a factor is used while all other factors remain constant, the amount of output obtained per unit of additional factor tends to decrease. This means that the more a given resource is used, the lower its yield will be; on the other hand, knowledge and information enjoy increasing returns, and the more they are used, the higher their yield will be (Ali et al., 2021).

The concept of Intellectual Capital (IC) is a very new and unfamiliar topic; the term was coined in 1969 by economist John Kenneth Galbraith, who suggested that IC means intellectual action, rather than mere knowledge or pure intellect. Thus, IC can be considered both a form of value creation and an asset in its traditional sense (Galbraith, 1969). From this moment on, the definition of IC has been approached by different theorists and has been evolving over time; different elements have been included as components: Human brain potential, product and brand names, technology leadership, employee training, speed of response to customer service requests, among others. This form of capital is responsible for the fact that many companies can be sold for several times their book value.

A traditional understanding of IC is found in the approach of Benavides (2003), who argues that, generally speaking, in the literature on IC there is broad agreement in identifying three elements of IC: Human Capital (HC), Structural Capital (SC) and Relational Capital (RC).

It considers human capital as the most important factor of IC as it is the source of innovation and strategic renewal of the company. It refers not so much to people as to aspects that people possess, such as knowledge, experience, motivation, reasoning and decision-making skills, loyalty, among others. HC is aimed at improving the capabilities of the individual and the innovative capacity of work groups (Sima et al., 2018). This asset is considered to be the basis for the generation of the other elements of IC and the intangible resource par excellence, as it is inseparable from its bearer. Contacts, personal relationships, the degree of satisfaction of people in the workplace, different cognitive traits, aspects such as polyvalence and flexibility, personal skills and competencies, are factors that, when identified, allow for greater achievements in achieving an increase in the value of the organization. This makes it necessary to highlight the importance of human management in the processes of IC management (Otoo et al., 2022).

SC is the element that enables the creation of wealth through the transformation of the work of human capital. It represents the knowledge that the organization manages to make explicit, systematize and internalize and which, in principle, may be latent in the company's people and teams (Lekic et al., 2020). It includes all that structured knowledge on which the efficiency and internal effectiveness of the company depends: the structure of the organization, processes and procedures, such as those developed for the definition of products and services, strategic thinking processes, information technologies, intellectual property, available technology; in short, it represents all those mechanisms and structures of the organization that can help employees to optimize their intellectual performance and therefore their business performance (Nourani et al., 2018).

RC can be defined as the company's ability to interact positively with the business community, and thus stimulate its wealth creation potential by encouraging human and structural capital. It refers to the elements with different degrees of intangibility that are found in the relationship with customers, suppliers and other agents in the organization's environment. The essence of this dimension of IC is the knowledge that exists of the relationships external to the company, and its competitive value can be measured as a function of longevity (Wang et al., 2022).

In general terms, IC reflects intangible assets, such as: a company's ability to learn and adapt to new trends in market economics and management, with an emphasis on Knowledge Management (KM) as the most significant act of value creation. This fact has had a special impact on economic organizations, as their success is increasingly related to the investment and management of their IC; hence the need to specify the specific role of knowledge and skills in the value creation process (Martín-de Castro et al., 2019). Additionally, IC that incorporates environmental aspects, Green Intellectual Capital (GIC), was introduced by Chen (2008), becoming an emerging field of study today (Yong et al., 2019). This concept emerged in the academic literature with the aim of emphasizing the importance of the environmental intangibles possessed by the organization in order to improve the organization's competitive position.

However, as this is a relatively new field of research, there are still diverse views and no accepted or agreed position within the scientific and business community has yet been identified (Bellucci et al., 2020). In addition, recently, Zaragoza-Sáez et al. (2020) introduced the Sustainable Intellectual Capital (SIC) construct into the academic literature, defining it as the set of human, structural and relational intangibles that a company can leverage for economic, social and environmental management, allowing it to achieve competitive advantages. Thus, with the birth of this new construct, the three dimensions of sustainability (economic, social and environmental) are integrated into IC.

Correspondingly, interest in these issues is growing in the business community and definitions of IC, GIC and SIC have been developed to serve as a basis for future research related to their identification and measurement (Demartini & Beretta, 2020). Two of the most important problems in intangibles research are the lack of a common terminology and the underdevelopment of measurement scales for the constructs associated with intangibles (Garanina et al., 2021). It is quite common for each author to try to build a theory of intangibles from scratch, creating new definitions, introducing new dimensions of intangibles and IC, and trying to impose their own terminology (Bontis, 2001). This fact hinders the accumulation of knowledge, and justifies the little progress that has been made in the last twenty years in building a theory of intangibles in organizations (Gallego et al., 2020). The lack of consistency in the terminologies used has made it difficult to establish clear measurements of intangibles, especially of the dimensions of IC, which has posed an additional difficulty to progress in this area of knowledge. The objective of the present research is therefore to analyze the origin and conceptualization of IC, GIC and SIC, trying to answer the following six research questions: (1) What are the origins of IC? (2) How is IC defined? (3) What are the origins of GIC? (4) How is GIC defined? (5) What are the origins of SIC? (6) How is SIC defined?

In order to answer the following research questions, the study is structured as follows. After this brief introduction, Section 2 presents the research methodology, Section 3 the results, and finally, Section 4 the main conclusions, limitations and future lines of research.

METHODOLOGY

In this research, a narrative literature review was conducted to analyze the origins and conceptualization of IC, GIC and SIC. A literature review is considered a detailed study that aims to gather information on a given topic through the analysis of published literature (Oliver, 2012).

The aim of the narrative literature review is to synthesize fragmented knowledge from previous research on IC, GIC and SIC. The research is therefore descriptive in scope, as there are no hypotheses to test, but rather to describe and make sense of the information collected. Furthermore, the present review follows more flexible and less restrictive procedures than systematic reviews (Ferrari, 2015). Therefore, the present review does not aim to generalize the results obtained to the population (Tranfield et al., 2003), but to offer an interpretation of the literature that allows for a better understanding of the field of study of IC, GIC and SIC. To conduct the literature review, the phases proposed by Wee & Banister (2016) were followed, which are: selection of the topic, selection and reading of sources, and writing of the topic. First, the selected topic is the analysis of the origin and conceptualization of IC, GIC and SIC. Second, handbooks, readings, books, chapters and articles focusing on the evolution and conceptualization of IC, GIC and SIC were included for the research, excluding colloquium reports, seminars, doctoral theses and working papers. The time period of the publications spans from the beginnings of the IC concept in the 1990s to the present day. The Scopus and Web of Science databases were used for the selection of the publications, as they are prestigious databases containing articles published in high impact journals, which ensures that the information obtained is accurate and of high value, legitimizing reliable results. A total of 125 academic articles were reviewed and read in depth, this being the scientific production that allowed us to reflect on the concepts analyzed. Thirdly, once the article and sources had been selected and the publications had been read, the bibliographic review was carried out.

RESULTS

The results are then structured in the following three blocks: (1) IC, (2) GIC and (3) SIC.

Intellectual Capital

The Intellectual Capital View (ICV) is the academic framework under which IC has traditionally been analyzed. Said approach, which emerged at the end of the 90s of the last century, derives from the Resource-Based View (RBV) and aims to overcome the deficiencies of the latter vision, given that, although in the RBV approach, business intangible assets are considered as strategic resources to achieve a high profitability, the arguments used are excessively general and the mechanisms through which intangibles allow obtaining a superior relative position are not clarified (Priem & Butler, 2001).

The ICV is considered as complementary to the Knowledge-Based View (KBV). However, although both theories (KBV and ICV) argue the value of the company through hidden knowledge, they differ in their approach. Thus, while the KBV theory focuses on the effective use of KM through knowledge creation tools, such as organizational culture, human resource policy and Information and Communication Technologies (ICT) (Nonaka et al., 2005), the ICV theory focuses on the evaluation and measurement of intangible assets (Reed et al., 2006). Thus, while the main focus of the KBV is to "assess the effectiveness of a company's use of knowledge management tools as knowledge-generating mechanisms, such as its information technology systems and information management systems, information" (Reed et al., 2006, p. 869).

From a historical point of view, organizations have always considered as assets those tangible elements that appeared in traditional financial statements, clearly identified and valued. However, very few times other elements that did not have a dimension were conceived as assets. The term IC intends to value precisely the intangible assets, since it refers to all those assets that, even though they do not have a physical presence, contribute to generating value for the organization and achieving its objectives.

To understand the concept of IC, it is interesting to analyze the definition of the term used by Edvinsson & Malone (1999). These authors used the following simile: "A corporation is like a tree. There is a visible part (the fruits) and a part that is hidden (the roots). If we only care about the fruits, the tree may die. For the tree to grow and continue to bear fruit, the roots must be healthy and nourished." In other words, if organizations focus exclusively on the fruits (financial results) and ignore their roots (intangible assets), the company will not survive in the long term.

Two fundamental ideas can be extracted from the definition: (1) the IC is a non-financial capital and (2) it represents the gap between the market value and the book value of a company. Therefore, for the cited authors, IC refers to the set of knowledge, experiences and relationships that give the organization a competitive advantage that is sustainable over time.

According to Euroforum (1998), it is possible to define IC as the set of assets of a company that, despite not being reflected in the financial statements, produce or will produce value for the organization in the future. In this regard, derived from this accounting vision of the concept, there is a very subtle formula to calculate the value of the intangible assets of a company: the value of the IC = the market value of the organization (stock market value) - the value of the tangible assets (book value).

Bueno (2000, 2003) based on the main characteristics of the concept, proposes the following integrating proposal: "accumulation of knowledge that creates value or cognitive wealth possessed by an organization composed of a set of intangible (intellectual) assets or resources and capabilities based on knowledge, which when put into action, according to a certain strategy, in combination with physical or tangible capital, is capable of producing goods and services and of generating competitive advantages or essential competencies in the market for the organization." Likewise, the same author identifies a series of characteristics that his definition gathers:

1. It is a concept that indicates the value of accumulated wealth derived from a set of assets of an intangible nature.
2. The combination of intangible assets generates new knowledge that is transformed into business skills or the creation of a competitive advantage.
3. It is capital of an intellectual nature that represents the new source of wealth for organizations.
4. It is a capital that integrates different intangible assets, generated through a strategy based on intellectual assets.

Table 1 offers a summary of the definitions made by different authors around the concept of IC. From it two ideas emerge fundamentally. In the first place, there is a certain convergence in all the definitions when pointing out that the intangible assets derived from knowledge add value to the company and, secondly, there is an emphasis on the idea that said assets do not appear in the financial statements of the companies, generating informative asymmetries for the groups interested in them.

Table 1. IC definitions

Author	Definition
Galbraith (1969)	The difference between the market value and book value of an organization.
Bontis (1996)	The capture, coding and dissemination of information to acquire new skills.
Brooking (1997)	Set of intangible assets that allows the company to function.
Sveiby (1997)	The difference between the market value and the book value of the company.
Stewart (1998)	Intellectual components that can be harnessed to create wealth in the organization.
Euroforum (1998)	Set of assets that, despite not being reflected in the financial statements of the company, generate or will generate value for it.
Roos (1998)	The IC is the sum of the HC and the SC. The HC represents the skills and experiences of the employees, and the SC the extension and manifestation of the HC in innovations, business processes and relationships with third parties.
Sullivan (1999)	The knowledge that can become future benefits.
Edvinson & Malone (1999)	The non-financial capital that justifies the difference between the market value and the book value.
Harrison & Sullivan (2000)	Knowledge that can be turned into profit.
Viedma (2001)	The IC is made up of all those intangible assets formed by tacit or explicit knowledge that generate economic value for the company.
Heisig et al. (2001)	An intangible asset is a future collection right that has no physical or financial presence.
Ordoñez de Pablos (2003)	It is the difference between the company's market value and its book value, which contributes to the company's sustained competitive advantage.
Rastogi (2003)	IC can be thought of as a company's holistic ability to coordinate, orchestrate, and deploy its knowledge resources toward value creation in pursuit of its future vision.
Youndt et al. (2004)	IC is the sum of all the knowledge that the company uses to obtain a competitive advantage
IASB (2004)	A non-monetary, non-physical asset held for use in the production or supply of goods or services, for rental to third parties, or for administrative purposes.
García-Meca & Martinez (2005)	The knowledge, information, intellectual property and experience that can be used to create wealth.
Mavridis & Kyrmizoglou (2005)	An intangible asset with the potential to create value for the company and society itself.
Martinez-Torres (2006)	It includes the intangible assets of an organization that are not recorded in the financial statements but that may constitute 80% of the organization's market value.
Reed et al. (2006)	Core competencies of an intangible nature that enable the creation and maintenance of a competitive advantage.
Chang et al. (2008)	It represents the intangible assets related to knowledge integrated in an organization.
Hsu & Fang (2009)	The set of capabilities, knowledge, culture, strategy, processes, intellectual property and relational networks of a company that create value or competitive advantages and help the company achieve its objectives.
Mondal & Ghosh (2012)	IC can be interpreted as the set of intangible assets that do not appear explicitly in the balance sheets of a company, but that have a positive impact on the results and success of the same.
Mehralian et al. (2012)	IC is an implicit value for the company that aims to achieve a competitive advantage.
Dumay (2016)	IC is the intellectual material, knowledge, experience, intellectual property and information that can be used to create value.

Source: own elaboration from the cited authors

Based on the above definitions and the main ideas that emanate from them, we propose the following comprehensive definition:

"Intellectual capital represents a set of intangibles that justify the difference in value between the market value and the book value of the organization, and although they are increasingly recognized by the stock market, they are often omitted from the financial statements."

There are several contributions, both theoretical and practical, to classify the different elements that make up the IC. However, there is a certain consensus in dividing the IC into three dimensions: the HC, the SC and the RC (Bontis, 2001; Ordóñez de Pablos, 2003; Sánchez-Medina et al., 2007). Next, we analyze in detail how each of these three dimensions has been conceived.

In today's globalized world, organizations require workers with values, attitudes and skills that allow them to obtain critical and systematic thinking within a changing environment (Bontis, 2001). For this reason, one of the most reiterated dimensions in the different IC models is that related to HC, as it is an essential factor for the organization (Sveiby, 1997; Becker et al., 2001), whose lack negatively conditions the rest of the organization. activities that generate value for it (Edvinsson & Malone, 1999).

The HC is defined as the main source of value and innovation in the company, since the ideas of the organization emanate from it (Viedma, 2001). That is, the HC refers to the knowledge, both tacit and explicit, that the workers have, as well as their ability to put it into practice in the organization.

It is possible to classify three components within the HC: (1) competencies, made up of knowledge, skills and talent; (2) the attitude, which translates into the motivation, action and behavior of people; and (3) intellectual agility, which generates value when new knowledge is applied to transform ideas into products and services (Roos et al., 2001). Therefore, the motivation of the employees, their mental agility, their tacit and explicit knowledge, their institutional commitment or their degree of satisfaction are clear examples of HC.

Petrash (1996), Euroforum (1998) and Bontis et al. (2002) conceive HC as the stock of knowledge possessed by the members of a company. Consequently, part of the HC represents the accumulated value of the investments that organizations have made to train their employees (Skandia, 1996). Thus, although the true owner of HC is not the company, but the employees themselves (Sveiby, 1997; 2001), this is one of the main elements that make up the value of the company and, as a consequence, it must be considered as capital for the same.

From another perspective, HC has been defined as the knowledge that the organization loses when its employees decide to leave it (Sullivan, 2000; Sveiby, 2001). For this reason, organizations must try to retain the most valuable employees (Roos et al., 2001), adequately remunerating those workers who provide the greatest value to the organization (Sveiby, 2001).

Brooking (1997) conceives this dimension with the name of assets centered on the individual and incorporates assets such as: creativity, the ability to solve problems or leadership. In this same line of thought, Edvisson & Mallone (1999) and Nevado-Peña & López-Ruiz (2002) consider that the HC is made up of a set of knowledge, individual capacities, skills and experiences of the members that make up the organization.

Another of the most common dimensions within IC models is that of SC. This capital is described as that knowledge that the organization internalizes and that, therefore, remains in it despite the fact that its employees leave it (Bontis et al., 2001). Consequently, this dimension includes all the non-human intangibles of the organization, ranging from culture or internal processes to databases or information systems (Bontis et al., 2000). In addition, unlike what happens with the HC, the SC is owned by the company (Euroforum, 1998).

According to Edvinsson & Malone (1999) and Roos et al. (2001), SC can be broken down into three dimensions, these are: organizational capital, renewal and development capital, and RC. However, it is necessary to clarify that in various models these subdivisions make up their own dimensions and are not included in the SC. This happens with the renovation and development capital dimension in the Nova model (Camisón et al., 2000) and with the RC in models such as Brooking (1997), Intelect (Euroforum, 1998), the monitor of intangible assets (Sveiby, 2001).

On the one hand, organizational capital includes the value produced by the internal structure of the company and the way in which the operations and processes that take place within it are developed. Consequently, all intangibles related to culture and values, organizational structure, routines, capabilities and policies are part of said capital. On the other hand, renewal and development capital, also called technological capital, refers to those aspects that can generate future value in the organization through improvements in products and/or processes. This capital therefore includes all intangibles related to Innovation, Development and Research activities and policies (patents, copyrights, licenses, etc.).

Brooking (1997) subdivides SC into intellectual property assets and infrastructure assets. The former is related to the legal protection exercised by the organization over those assets that it considers to have a special value for it, among which can be found: manufacturing secrets, patents, copyright or design rights. As for the latter, they provide order, security and quality to the organization, such as corporate culture, databases or methodologies. Social capital is based on the consideration that organizations are not isolated systems, since they maintain relationships with their environment. In this way, the intangibles derived from the company's network of relationships are what should be considered RC.

This type of capital includes the value generated by the company's relationships with its environment, not only with its shareholders, customers and suppliers, but also with all its stakeholders (Bontis, 1996, Stewart, 1998; Ordóñez de Pablos, 2003). That is, the RC represents the knowledge that is incorporated in the links of the organization with its environment (Bontis, 1999). Customer loyalty and satisfaction, strategic alliances or the list of suppliers and distributors are clear examples of this type of intangible assets.

In the academic literature, there are numerous ways of naming this capital. Sveiby (2001), in his model *Intangible assets monitor*, designates this external component dimension, including relationships with customers and suppliers, trademarks, reputation or image. In this way, some of these elements may have legal protection, while, in others, said protection is complex. Kaplan & Norton (1997), in their model *Store card*, call the customer perspective RC and it analyzes the sources of value for the customer. Along these same lines, Edvinsson (1997) and Edvisson & Malone (1999) consider that RC is mainly made up of the value generated by the organization's relationships with its customers. However, although the Kaplan & Norton (1997) model explicitly limits this dimension to customers, it can be extrapolated to all the relationships that the company has with its environment (Olve et al., 2000).

On the other hand, Brookings (1997), in its Technology Broker model, it calls this dimension market assets, defining it as those intangible assets derived from the organization's relationship with the market. Caminsion et al. (2000), on the other hand, call it social capital, defining it as the set of knowledge-based assets from the company's relationships with customers.

Finally, it is important to note that, although each of the dimensions that make up the IC has been presented in isolation, the existence of links between them is of special importance for its proper management (Bontis, 2001).

Green Intellectual Capital

The qualifier green has gained the attention of both academics and professionals in recent decades. The academic literature shows an incipient interest in green business, characterized by: green purchasing (Zhang et al., 2018), green supply chain management (Kazancoglu et al., 2018; Zaid et al., 2018), green innovation (Li et al., 2018), green finance (Ng, 2018), green management (Mustapha et al., 2017), green information technologies (Przychodzen et al., 2018) and green human resource management (Renwick et al., 2013; Zaid et al., 2018).

In this context, Chen (2008) introduced the concept of GIC with the aim of incorporating environmental concepts into IC. The GIC allows organizations to apply strict international regulations, comply with the growing environmental awareness of consumers and create value for the organization (Huang & Kung, 2011). For this reason, their role is essential to guarantee the success of the Sustainable Development Goals (SDGs) promoted by the United Nations (Yadiati, 2019; Marco-Lajara et al., 2021a; Marco-Lajara et al., 2021b; Marco-Lajara et al., 2022a; Marco-Lajara et al., 2022b; Marco-Lajara et al., 2022c; Marco-Lajara et al., 2022d; Marco-Lajara et al., 2022e; Marco-Lajara et al., 2022f; Marco-Lajara et al., 2022g; Marco-Lajara et al., 2022h; Marco-Lajara et al., 2022i; Marco-Lajara et al., 2022j, Marco-Lajara et al., 2022k;Marco-Lajara et al., 2022l, Marco-Lajara et al., 2022m, Marco-Lajara et al., 2022n; Marco-Lajara et al. 2023c; Martínez-Falcó et al., 2023a; Martínez-Falcó et al., 2023b; Martínez-Falcó et al., 2023c, Martínez-Falcó et al., 2023d; Millan-Tudela et al., 2022a; Millan-Tudela et al., 2022b; Seva-Larrosa et al., 2022). However, GIC has only recently emerged as a major field of study (Yong et al., 2019; Yusoff et al., 2019).

Definitions of GIC are scarce in the management literature. On the one hand, Chen (2008) defined it as the total set of intangible assets, knowledge and skills related to environmental protection or ecological innovation at the individual and organizational level within an organization. Liu (2010), on the other hand, defined it as the integration of green and environmental knowledge sources in the organization to improve its competitive advantage. In the same way, López-Gamero et al. (2011) conceived it as the sum of all the knowledge that an organization is capable of taking advantage of in the environmental management process to obtain a competitive advantage. Next, each of the dimensions that make up the GIC is analyzed in detail, which, according to Chen (2008), are: Green Human Capital (GHC).

As explained in previous sections, the RBV highlights the importance of HC in the performance of the organization to obtain a competitive advantage among competitors (Barney, 2001). Chen (2008) points out the distinctive value of the GHC by defining it as the set of knowledge, skills, abilities, experiences and commitments of the employees about the protection of the environment and/or green innovation that are integrated in the employees and not in organizations.

The GHC allows an organization to recognize its intangible assets related to the environment, helping to apply green strategies in a given competitive environment. For this reason, the GHC has been considered one of the main strategic resources to obtain sustainable competitive advantages in the current dynamic organizational environment (Yusoff et al., 2019). Likewise, a higher GHC contributes more to the development of a green organization, since environmental knowledge and skills are embedded in it (Yong et al., 2019).

The scientific production related to the GHC focuses its interest on the relationship existingbetween the GHC and corporate sustainability. Yong et al. (2019) prove that the GHC has a positive effect on the management of green human resources. For their part, Chen & Chang (2013), through their research, confirm the link between the GHC and green innovation performance. Furthermore, Akhtar et al. (2018) affirm the importance of the GHC to achieve business sustainability.

The SC is conceived as the set of knowledge that houses the non-human assets of an organization, among which we can highlight: organization charts, databases, technology or process instructions (Jardon & Martos, 2012). Chen (2008), on the other hand, defined the Green Structural Capital (GSC) as the organizational assets that showed concern for the protection of the environment or green innovation within the company.

Jardon & Dasilva (2017) suggest that the organization's concern for environmental aspects is not only modified by HC, since the support of the organizational culture and systems is required to increase the level of environmental awareness in the organization. Widener (2006) states that an organization with poor systems and procedures cannot achieve its full performance. In contrast, an organization with a strong SC has a strong supportive environment that motivates its employees to generate new knowledge (Florin et al., 2003).

ICTs play a fundamental role in the development of the GSC. In fact, previous studies verify the effect of ICT on ecological practices (Yusliza et al., 2017) and green information systems for supply chain activities (Giménez et al., 2015). Likewise, Chen (2008) and Chen & Chang (2013) state that ecological innovation is essential for achieving sustainable performance. Lee & Min (2015), for their part, highlight that an organization that invests in Research and Development (R&D) activities, together with eco-innovation, tends to reduce its costs and environmental impacts.

Likewise, numerous investigations address the positive effect of GSC on business performance and environmental awareness. Chen (2008) affirmed the existence of a positive relationship between GSC and competitive advantage. Similarly, Erinos & Rahmawati (2017) demonstrated the positive impact of GSC on financial performance. On the other hand, while Huang & Kung (2011) revealed the positive effect of GSC on environmental competence and activities related to environmental commitment, Delgado-Verde et al. (2014) found a positive relationship between GSC and green product innovation.

Chen (2008) defined Green Relational Capital (GRC) as the set of intangible assets based on existing relationships between the organization and suppliers, customers, network members and partners to improve the company's environmental management and thus achieve a competitive advantage. As already described in the previous section, RC refers to an intangible asset focused on nurturing and preserving relationships with any organization, individual or group that can influence a company's position in the market. Therefore, it is essential that organizations align their interests with those of their stakeholders in order to survive and remain competitive.

Longoni & Cagliano (2018) state that the needs of different stakeholders can be addressed through the management of ecological supply chains. Likewise, other research also highlights green supply chains and the environmental perspective as powerful tools to meet the needs of stakeholders (Zhu et al., 2013; Luthra et al., 2016; Jabbour et al., 2019). Therefore, the GRC plays an important role in building strong and lasting relationships between suppliers and organizations. As far as customers are concerned, their expectations have started to focus on sustainable environmental behaviours, rather than just product, price or service (Dangelico & Pujari, 2010; Eweje, 2014). Furthermore, most of the previous studies have revealed a positive and significant effect between GRC and business results. Chen (2008) and Firmansyah (2017) demonstrated the positive link between GRC and competitive advantage. Similarly, Huang & Kung (2011) revealed the positive influence of GRC on competition and environmental commitment. Likewise, Delgado-Verde et al. (2014) found that for an organization to be successful in environmental product innovation, it must have a GRC that encourages cooperation among its employees.

Sustainable Intellectual Capital

In today's knowledge society, organizations focus their efforts on developing their intangible assets to achieve better performance (Agostini et al, 2017), as these ensure an organization's survival (Obeng et al., 2014), foster value creation (Edvinsson & Malone, 1999; Berezinets et al., 2016) and enhance its competitive advantage (Khan et al., 2019). An organization's intangibles constitute its IC (Alcaniz et al., 2011). Therefore, organizations with richer and more sophisticated IC will be able to gain greater advantages than those with poor IC (Ahmad & Ahmed, 2016).

Existing literature has repeatedly illustrated different concepts and dimensions of IC from various perspectives. However, the integration of IC with sustainability is rare and little attention has been paid to this relationship by both academics and practitioners. Against this background, the terms 'green', 'social' and 'sustainable' IC have recently entered the academic literature on corporate social and environmental responsibility management. The variety of each term is explained by their different considerations and implications (Nikolaou, 2019). Thus, under the Triple Bottom Line (TBL) approach, it is possible to state that the term GIC focuses on environmental issues (Chen, 2008; López-Gamero et al., 2009), the term Social and Environmental IC (SEIC) focuses on social and environmental issues, Social and Economic Intellectual Capital (SECIC) focuses on social and economic aspects and SIC on environmental, social and economic issues (Zaragoza-Sáez et al., 2020). Table 2 classifies, under the TCR approach, the different terms that try to integrate sustainability into IC.

Table 2. Terms integrating sustainability in the IC

	Triple Bottom Line		
	Environmental	**Social**	**Economic**
Green Intellectual Capital (GIC)	X		
Social and Environmental Intellectual Capital (SEIC)	X	X	
Social and Economic Intellectual Capital (SECIC)		X	X
Sustainable Intellectual Capital (SIC)	X	X	X

Source: own elaboration

As explained in the previous section, Chen (2008) first introduced the concept of GIC, defining it as "the total stock of all kinds of intangible assets, knowledge, capabilities and relationships, etc. on environmental protection or green innovation at the individual level and the organizational level within a company" (p. 277). GIC enables organizations to meet stringent international environmental regulations, satisfy the growing environmental awareness developed among consumers and add value to organizations (Huang & Kung, 2011). Furthermore, as with the dimensions of IC, there is some consensus in identifying three dimensions that encompass the classification of GIC: GHV, GSC and GRC.

Nikolaou (2019) introduced the concept of SEIC to address sustainable corporate intangibles not only from an environmental point of view, but also from a social point of view. He defines it as "a fine-tuning of the classical components of IC that is consistent with the requirements of corporate environmental management, corporate sustainability and corporate social responsibility". However, despite incorporating the social dimension of corporate sustainability, a holistic view of corporate sustainability is not introduced. With the aim of bringing together the economic, social and environmental perspectives, Zaragoza-Sáez et al. (2020) introduced the SIC construct into the academic literature, defining it as "the set of human, structural and relational intangibles that a company can leverage for economic, social and environmental management, enabling it to achieve competitive advantages" (p. 4). Thus, in line with the TBL approach, the authors break SIC down into two dimensions: GIC and SECIC. On the one hand, as explained above, the GIC is made up of intangible human, structural and relational capital linked to the conservation and management of natural resources. On the other hand, the SECIC is made up of human, structural and relational intangible capital linked to the impact that the company has on the social system in which it operates and to the generation of wealth through its economic activity.

CONCLUSION

Historically, organizations have always considered as assets those tangible items that appeared in traditional accounting statements, clearly identified and valued. However, other elements that did not have a spatio-temporal dimension were rarely conceived as assets. The term IC is intended to highlight intangible assets, since it refers to all those assets that, although they do not have a physical presence, contribute to generating value for the organization and to achieving its objectives.

From the definitions of IC analyzed, the idea emerges that IC represents a set of intangibles that justify the difference in value between the market value and the book value of the organization, and although they are increasingly recognized by the stock market, they are often omitted from the accounting statements. Furthermore, four fundamental characteristics are identified in the definitions studied: (1) it is a concept that indicates the value of the accumulated wealth derived from a set of assets of an intangible nature, (2) the combination of intangible assets generates new knowledge that is transformed into business competences or in the creation of a competitive advantage, (3) it is a capital of an intellectual nature that represents the new source of wealth of organizations, (4) it is a capital that integrates different intangible assets, generated through a strategy based on intellectual assets.

Concern for environmental management has gained the attention of both academics and practitioners in recent decades. In this context, Chen (2008) introduced the concept of GIC with the aim of incorporating environmental concepts into IC. GIC enables organizations to implement stringent international regulations, meet the growing environmental awareness of consumers and create value for the organization. For this reason, its role is critical to ensure the success of the SDGs promoted by the United Nations. However, GIC has only recently emerged as a major field of study. Definitions of GIC are scarce in the management literature. However, based on the conceptual review of the term, it can be considered as the sum of all the knowledge that an organization is able to leverage in the environmental management process to gain a competitive advantage. The following is a detailed analysis of each of the dimensions that make up GIC, which Chen (2008) suggests are: GHC, GSC and GRC.

However, despite incorporating the social dimension of corporate sustainability, a holistic view of corporate sustainability is not introduced. With the aim of bringing together the economic, social and environmental perspectives, Zaragoza-Sáez et al. (2020) introduced the SIC construct into the academic literature, defining it as "the set of human, structural and relational intangibles that a company can leverage for economic, social and environmental management, enabling it to achieve competitive advantages" (p. 4). Thus, in line with the TBL approach, the authors break SIC down into two dimensions: GIC and SECIC. On the one hand, as explained above, the GIC is made up of intangible human, structural and relational capital linked to the conservation and management of natural resources. On the other hand, the SECIC is made up of human, structural and relational intangible capital linked to the impact that the company has on the social system in which it operates and to the generation of wealth through its economic activity. This new construct integrates both IC and GIC, being the concept on which new knowledge can be built in the field of intangibles, given that it surpasses previous conceptualizations as it is a broader and more complete construct than the others.

This research presents several theoretical and practical contributions. On the one hand, as far as theoretical contributions are concerned, this research helps to bring clarity to an emerging field of study such as SIC. Likewise, to the best of our knowledge, there are no narrative reviews that have addressed this topic. On the other hand, the study serves as a reference guide for those professionals who are thinking of enhancing their intangible assets, since it improves the understanding of the terms, as well as the characteristics that determine each type of intangible. In such a way that the greater understanding by managers of the subject matter of the study can serve as a catalyst for improving practices that enhance the development of intangible assets.

FUTURE RESEARCH DIRECTIONS

Despite the important contributions of the study, it is important to note that the research suffers from certain limitations. The fundamental limitation of the study is methodological in nature, given that narrative reviews are dominated by the subjective criteria of the authors and do not quantitatively synthesize the data found in the different publications. To overcome these limitations of narrative reviews, a systematic review of SIC is proposed as a line of future research to increase the reproducibility of the research and increase the validity of the results obtained.

REFERENCES

Agostini, L., Nosella, A., & Filippini, R. (2017). Does intellectual capital allow improving innovation performance? A quantitative analysis in the SME context. *Journal of Intellectual Capital, 18*(2), 400–418. doi:10.1108/JIC-05-2016-0056

Ahmad, M., & Ahmed, N. (2016). Testing the relationship between intellectualcapital and a firm's performance: An empirical investigation regarding financial industries of Pakistan. *International Journal of Learning and Intellectual Capital, 13*(2-3), 250–272. doi:10.1504/IJLIC.2016.075691

Akhtar, P., Khan, Z., Frynas, J., Tse, Y., & Rao-Nicholson, R. (2018). Essential micro-foundations for contemporary business operations: Top management tangible competencies, relationship-based business networks and environmental sustainability. *British Journal of Management, 29*(1), 43–62. doi:10.1111/1467-8551.12233

Alcaniz, L., Gomez-Bezares, F., & Roslender, R. (2011). Theoretical perspectives on intellectual capital: A backward look and a proposal for going forward. *Accounting Forum, 35*(2), 104–117. doi:10.1016/j.accfor.2011.03.004

Ali, M. A., Hussin, N., Haddad, H., Al-Araj, R., & Abed, I. A. (2021). A multidimensional view of intellectual capital: The impact on innovation performance. *Journal of Open Innovation*, *7*(4), 216. doi:10.3390/joitmc7040216

Barney, J. (2001). Is the resource-based "view" a useful perspective for strategic management research? Yes. *Academy of Management Review*, *26*(1), 41–56.

Becker, B., Huselid, M., & Ulrich, D. (2001). *The HR scorecard: Linking people, strategy, and performance*. Harvard Business Press.

Bellucci, M., Marzi, G., Orlando, B., & Ciampi, F. (2020). Journal of Intellectual Capital: A review of emerging themes and future trends. *Journal of Intellectual Capital*, *22*(4), 744–767. doi:10.1108/JIC-10-2019-0239

Berezinets, I., Garanina, T., & Ilina, Y. (2016). Intellectual capital of a board of directors and its elements: Introduction to the concepts. *Journal of Intellectual Capital*, *17*(4), 632–653. doi:10.1108/JIC-01-2016-0003

Bontis, N. (1996). There is a price on your head: Managing intellectual capital strategically. *Business Quarterly*, *60*(4), 41–47.

Bontis, N. (2001). CKO wanted - Evangelical skills necessary: A review of the chief knowledge officer position. *Knowledge and Process Management*, *8*(1), 29–38. doi:10.1002/kpm.100

Bontis, N., Crossan, M., & Hulland, J. (2002). Managing an organizational learning system by aligning stocks and flows. *Journal of Management Studies*, *39*(4), 437–469. doi:10.1111/1467-6486.t01-1-00299

Brooking, A. (1997). The management of intellectual capital. *Long Range Planning*, *30*(3), 364–365. doi:10.1016/S0024-6301(97)80911-9

Bueno, E. (2000). De la sociedad de la información a la del conocimiento y el aprendizaje: La necesidad de programas de dirección del conocimiento y aprendizaje. *Jornadas Españolas de Documentación*, *7*, 647–657.

Bueno, E. (2003). Enfoques principales y tendencias en dirección del conocimiento (knowledge management). In *Dirección del conocimiento: Desarrollos teóricos y aplicaciones*. Ediciones La Coria.

Camisón, C., Palacios, D., & Devece, C. (2000). *Un modelo para la medición del capital intelectual en la empresa: el modelo Nova* [A model for the measurement of intellectual capital in the firm: the Nova model]. Available at: http://www. gestiondelconocimiento.com

Chang, S., Chen, C., & Lai, J. (2008). The Effect of Alliance Experience and Intellectual Capital on the Value Creation of International Strategic Alliances. *Omega*, *36*(2), 298–316. doi:10.1016/j.omega.2006.06.010

Chen, Y. (2008). The positive effect of green intellectual capital on competitive advantages of firms. *Journal of Business Ethics*, *77*(3), 271–286. doi:10.100710551-006-9349-1

Chen, Y., & Chang, C. (2013). Utilize structural equation modeling (SEM) to explore the influence of corporate environmental ethics: The mediation effect of green human capital. *Quality & Quantity*, *47*(1), 79–95. doi:10.100711135-011-9504-3

Dangelico, R., & Pujari, D. (2010). Mainstreaming green product innovation: Why and how companies integrate environmental sustainability. *Journal of Business Ethics*, *95*(3), 471–486. doi:10.100710551-010-0434-0

Delgado-Verde, M., Amores-Salvadó, J., Martín-de Castro, G., & Navas-López, J. (2014). Green intellectual capital and environmental product innovation: The mediating role of green social capital. *Knowledge Management Research and Practice*, *12*(3), 261–275. doi:10.1057/kmrp.2014.1

Demartini, M. C., & Beretta, V. (2020). Intellectual capital and SMEs' performance: A structured literature review. *Journal of Small Business Management*, *58*(2), 288–332. doi:10.1080/00472778.2019.1659680

Dumay, J. (2016). A critical reflection on the future of intellectual capital: From reporting to disclosure. *Journal of Intellectual Capital*, *17*(1), 168–184. doi:10.1108/JIC-08-2015-0072

Edvinsson, L., & Malone, M. (1997). *Realising your Company's True Value by Finding its Hidden Brainpower*. Harper Collins.

Edvinsson, L., & Malone, M. (1999). El capital intellectual [Intellectual capital]. *Gestion*.

Erinos, N., & Yurniwati, Y. (2018). Green intellectual capital and financial performance of manufacturing companies in Indonesia. In *First Padang International Conference On Economics Education, Economics, Business and Management, Accounting and Entrepreneurship* (pp. 613-618). Atlantis Press.

Euroforum. (1998). *Medición del Capital Intelectual. Modelo Intelect* [Intellectual Capital Measurement. Intelect Model]. Euroforum. Available at: http://gestiondelconocimiento.com/modelo_modelo_intelec.htm

Eweje, G. (2014). *Introduction: trends in corporate social responsibility and sustainability in emerging economies*. Emerald Group Publishing Limited.

Ferrari, R. (2015). Writing narrative style literature reviews. *Medical Writing*, *24*(4), 230–235. doi:10.1179/2047480615Z.000000000329

Firmansyah, A. (2017). Pengaruh green intellectual capital dan manajemen lingkungan organisasi terhadap green organizational identity dan dampaknya terhadap green competitive advantage. *Substansi: Sumber Artikel Akuntansi Auditing dan Keuangan Vokasi, 1*(1), 183-219.

Galbraith, J. (1969). The Consequences of Technology. *Journal of Accountancy*, *127*, 44–56.

Gallego, C., Mejía, G. M., & Calderón, G. (2020). Strategic design: Origins and contributions to intellectual capital in organizations. *Journal of Intellectual Capital*, *21*(6), 873–891. doi:10.1108/JIC-10-2019-0234

Garanina, T., Hussinki, H., & Dumay, J. (2021). Accounting for intangibles and intellectual capital: A literature review from 2000 to 2020. *Accounting and Finance*, *61*(4), 5111–5140. doi:10.1111/acfi.12751

García-Meca, E., & Martínez, I. (2005). Assessing the quality of disclosure on intangibles in the Spanish capital market. *European Business Review*, *17*(4), 305–313. doi:10.1108/09555340510607352

Giménez, F., Ciurana, J., Borras, F., & Pastor, D. (2013). Efficiency analysis of the designations of origin in the Spanish wine sector. *Spanish Journal of Agricultural Research*, *2*, 294–304.

Harrison, S., & Sullivan, P. Sr. (2000). Profiting from intellectual capital - learning from leading companies. *Journal of Intellectual Capital*, *1*(1), 33–46. doi:10.1108/14691930010324124

Heisig, P., Vorbeck, J., & Niebubr, J. (2001). *Intellectual capital. Knowledge Management - Best Practices in Europe*. Springer.

Hsu, Y., & Fang, W. (2009). Intellectual Capital and New Product Development Performance: The Mediating Role of Organizational Learning Capability. *Technological Forecasting and Social Change*, *76*(5), 664–677. doi:10.1016/j.techfore.2008.03.012

Huang, C., & Kung, F. (2011). Environmental consciousness and intellectual capital management: Evidence from Taiwan's manufacturing industry. *Management Decision*, *49*(9), 1405–1425. doi:10.1108/00251741111173916

IASB. (2004). Intangible Assets, International Accounting Standard. International Accounting Standards Board.

Jabbour, C., De Sousa Jabbour, A., & Sarkis, J. (2019). Unlocking effective multi-tier supply chain management for sustainability through quantitative modeling: Lessons learned and discoveries to be made. *International Journal of Production Economics*, *217*, 11–30. doi:10.1016/j.ijpe.2018.08.029

Jardon, C., & Dasilva, A. (2017). Intellectual capital and environmental concern in subsistence small businesses. *Management of Environmental Quality*, *28*(2), 214–230. doi:10.1108/MEQ-05-2015-0085

Jardon, C., & Martos, M. (2012). Intellectual capital as competitive advantage in emerging clusters in Latin America. *Journal of Intellectual Capital*, *13*(4), 462–481. doi:10.1108/14691931211276098

Kaplan, R., & Norton, D. (1997). Cuadro de mando integral [The Balance Scorecard]. *Gestion*.

Kazancoglu, Y., Kazancoglu, I., & Sagnak, M. (2018). A new holistic conceptual framework for green supply chain management performance assessment based on circular economy. *Journal of Cleaner Production*, *195*, 1282–1299. doi:10.1016/j.jclepro.2018.06.015

Khan, S., Yang, Q., & Waheed, A. (2019). Investment in intangible resources and capabilities spurs sustainable competitive advantage and firm performance. *Corporate Social Responsibility and Environmental Management*, *26*(2), 285–295. doi:10.1002/csr.1678

Lee, K., & Min, B. (2015). Green R&D for eco-innovation and its impact on carbon emissions and firm performance. *Journal of Cleaner Production*, *108*, 534–542. doi:10.1016/j.jclepro.2015.05.114

Li, T., Liang, L., & Han, D. (2018). Research on the efficiency of green technology innovation in China's provincial high-end manufacturing industry based on the RAGA-PP-SFA model. *Mathematical Problems in Engineering*, *2018*, 1–13. doi:10.1155/2018/9463707

Longoni, A., & Cagliano, R. (2018). Inclusive environmental disclosure practices and firm performance. *International Journal of Operations & Production Management*, *38*(9), 1815–1835. doi:10.1108/IJOPM-12-2016-0728

López-Gamero, M., Zaragoza-Sáez, P., Claver-Cortés, E., & Molina-Azorín, J. (2011). Sustainable development and intangibles: Building sustainable intellectual capital. *Business Strategy and the Environment*, *20*(1), 18–37. doi:10.1002/bse.666

Luthra, S., Garg, D., & Haleem, A. (2016). The impacts of critical success factors for implementing green supply chain management towards sustainability: An empirical investigation of Indian automobile industry. *Journal of Cleaner Production*, *121*, 142–158. doi:10.1016/j.jclepro.2016.01.095

Marco-Lajara, B., Falcó, J. M., Fernández, L. R., & Larrosa, P. S. (2022k). Evolución del pensamiento en la disciplina de dirección estratégica: la visión de la empresa basada en las capacidades dinámicas y en el conocimiento. [Evolution of thinking in the discipline of strategic management: the vision of the company based on dynamic capabilities and knowledge.] In *Investigación y transferencia de las ciencias sociales frente a un mundo en crisis* (pp. 1801–1826). Dykinson.

Marco-Lajara, B., García, E. S., Larrosa, P. S., & Falcó, J. M. (2022m). Knowledge creation and diffusion inspecialized environments: What are the factors involved? In *Empresa, economía y derecho. Oportunidades ante un entorno global y disruptivo* (pp. 432–459). Dykinson.

Marco-Lajara, B., Sáez, P. D. C. Z., Falcó, J. M., & García, E. S. (2022l). Las rutas del vino de España: el impacto económico derivado de las visitas a bodegas y museos. [Las rutas del vino de España: el impacto económico derivado de las visitas a bodegas y museos] In *Investigación y transferencia de las ciencias sociales frente a un mundo en crisis* (pp. 1774–1800). Dykinson.

Marco-Lajara, B., Sánchez-García, E., Martínez-Falcó, J., & Poveda-Pareja, E. (2022j). Regional Specialization, Competitive Pressure, and Cooperation: The Cocktail for Innovation. *Energies*, *15*(15), 5346.

Marco-Lajara, B., Seva-Larrosa, P., Martínez-Falcó, J., & García-Lillo, F. (2022i). Wine clusters and Protected Designations of Origin (PDOs) in Spain: An exploratory analysis. *Journal of Wine Research*, *33*(3), 1–22. doi:10.1080/09571264.2022.2110051

Marco-Lajara, B., Seva-Larrosa, P., Martinez-Falco, J., & Sanchez-Garcia, E. (2021a). How Has COVID- 19 Affected The Spanish Wine Industry? An Exploratory Analysis. *Natural Volatiles & Essential Oils Journal*, *8*(6), 2722–2731.

Marco-Lajara, B., Seva-Larrosa, P., Ruiz-Fernandez, L., & Martinez-Falco, J. (2021b). The Effect of COVID- 19 on the Spanish Wine Industry. In *Impact of Global Issues on International Trade* (pp. 211–232). IGI Global. doi:10.4018/978-1-7998-8314-2.ch012

Marco-Lajara, B., Zaragoza-Saez, P., Falcó, J. M., & Millan-Tudela, L. A. (2022a). Analysing the Relationship Between Green Intellectual Capital and the Achievement of the Sustainable Development Goals. In *Handbook of Research on Building Inclusive Global Knowledge Societies for Sustainable Development* (pp. 111–129). IGI Global. doi:10.4018/978-1-6684-5109-0.ch005

Marco-Lajara, B., Zaragoza-Sáez, P., Falcó, J. M., & Millan-Tudela, L. A. (2022f). Corporate Social Responsibility: A Narrative Literature Review. *Frameworks for Sustainable Development Goals to Manage Economic, Social, and Environmental Shocks and Disasters*, 16-34.

Marco-Lajara, B., Zaragoza-Saez, P., Falcó, J. M., & Sánchez-García, E. (2022b). COVID-19 and Wine Tourism: A Story of Heartbreak. In Handbook of Research on SDGs for Economic Development, Social Development, and Environmental Protection (pp. 90-112). IGI Global.

Marco-Lajara, B., Zaragoza-Saez, P., & Martínez-Falcó, J. (2022e). Green Innovation: Balancing Economic Efficiency With Environmental Protection. In Frameworks for Sustainable Development Goals to Manage Economic, Social, and Environmental Shocks and Disasters (pp. 239-254). IGI Global.

Marco-Lajara, B., Zaragoza-Sáez, P., Martínez-Falcó, J., & Millan-Tudela, L. A. (2023c). The Export Intensity of Spain's Autonomous Communities in Terms of the Marketing of Wine and Their Geographical Destinations. In *The Transformation of Global Trade in a New World* (pp. 1–21). IGI Global.

Marco-Lajara, B., Zaragoza-Sáez, P., Martínez-Falcó, J., & Ruiz-Fernández, L. (2022g). The Effect of Green Intellectual Capital on Green Performance in the Spanish Wine Industry: A Structural Equation Modeling Approach. *Complexity*, *2022*, 2022. doi:10.1155/2022/6024077

Marco-Lajara, B., Zaragoza-Sáez, P., Martínez-Falcó, J., & Sánchez-García, E. (2022c). Green Intellectual Capital in the Spanish Wine Industry. In Innovative Economic, Social, and Environmental Practices for Progressing Future Sustainability (pp. 102-120). IGI Global. doi:10.4018/978-1-7998-9590-9.ch006

Marco-Lajara, B., Zaragoza-Sáez, P., Martínez-Falcó, J., & Sánchez-García, E. (2022d). El capital intelectual verde como hoja de ruta para la sostenibilidad: El caso de bodegas Luzón. *GeoGraphos: Revista Digital para Estudiantes de Geografía y Ciencias Sociales*, *13*(147), 137–146.

Marco-Lajara, B., Zaragoza-Sáez, P. C., Martínez-Falcó, J., & Sánchez-García, E. (2022h). Does green intellectual capital affect green innovation performance? Evidence from the Spanish wine industry. *British Food Journal*.

Marco-Lajara, B., Zaragoza Sáez, P. D. C., & Martínez-Falcó, J. (2022n). Does Green Intellectual Capital Affect Green Performance? The Mediation of Green Innovation. *Telematiquie*, *21*(1), 4594–4602.

Martín-de Castro, G., Díez-Vial, I., & Delgado-Verde, M. (2019). Intellectual capital and the firm: Evolution and research trends. *Journal of Intellectual Capital*, *20*(4), 555–580. doi:10.1108/JIC-12-2018-0221

Martínez-Falcó, J., Marco-Lajara, B., & Zaragoza-Sáez, P. (2023b). Corporate Social Responsibility: A Comprehensive Analysis. In Positive and Constructive Contributions for Sustainable Development Goals (pp. 131-160). IGI Global.

Martínez-Falcó, J., Marco-Lajara, B., & Zaragoza-Saez, P. (2023c). Corporate Social Responsibility vs. Corporate Sustainability: Different Concepts for a Common Goal. In Positive and Constructive Contributions for Sustainable Development Goals (pp. 76-87). IGI Global.

Martínez-Falcó, J., Marco-Lajara, B., & Zaragoza-Saez, P. (2023d). Theoretical Perspectives on Corporate Social Responsibility: A Narrative Review. *Positive and Constructive Contributions for Sustainable Development Goals*, 96-113.

Martínez-Falcó, J., Marco-Lajara, B. M., Zaragoza-Sáez, P., & Ruiz-Fernández, L. (2023a). Green Intellectual Capital as a Catalyst for the Sustainable Development Goals: Evidence From the Spanish Wine Industry. In Climate Change, World Consequences, and the Sustainable Development Goals for 2030 (pp. 163-182). IGI Global.

Martínez-Torres, A. (2006). Procedure to Design a Structural and Measurement Model of Intellectual Capital: An Exploratory Study. *Information & Management*, *43*(5), 617–626. doi:10.1016/j.im.2006.03.002

Mavridis, D., & Kyrmizoglou, P. (2005). Intellectual capital performance drivers in the Greek banking sector. *Management Research News*, *28*(5), 43–62. doi:10.1108/01409170510629032

Mehralian, G., Rajabzadeh, A., Sadeh, M., & Rasekh, H. (2012). Intellectual capital and corporate performance in Iranian pharmaceutical industry. *Journal of Intellectual Capital*, *13*(1), 138–158. doi:10.1108/14691931211196259

Millan-Tudela, L. A., Marco-Lajara, B., Martínez-Falcó, J., & Sánchez-García, E. (2022b). Pursuing Business Longevity: Ways to Enhance Sustainable Development. In Frameworks for Sustainable Development Goals to Manage Economic, Social, and Environmental Shocks and Disasters (pp. 79-95). IGI Global.

Millan-Tudela, L. A. M., Marco-Lajara, B., Falcó, J. M., & Pareja, E. P. (2022a). Longevidad empresarial: revisión bibliométrica sobre la supervivencia y caída de las compañías [Corporate longevity: a bibliometric review of company survival and decline]. In Leveraging new business technology for a sustainable economic recovery (p. 170). Escuela Superior de Gestión Comercial y Marketing, ESIC.

Mondal, A., & Ghosh, S. (2012). Intellectual capital and financial performance of Indian banks. *Journal of Intellectual Capital*, *13*(4), 515–530. doi:10.1108/14691931211276115

Mustapha, M., Manan, Z., & Alwi, S. (2017). Sustainable Green Management System (SGMS)-An integrated approach towards organisational sustainability. *Journal of Cleaner Production*, *146*, 158–172. doi:10.1016/j.jclepro.2016.06.033

Nevado-Peña, D., & López-Ruiz, V. (2002). Un modelo e informe contable para la medición del capital intelectual desarrollo y aplicaciones [An accounting model and report for the measurement of intellectual capital development and applications]. *Revista de Contabilidad y Tributación*, *229*, 161–206.

Ng, A. (2018). From sustainability accounting to a green financing system: Institutional legitimacy and market heterogeneity in a global financial centre. *Journal of Cleaner Production*, *195*, 585–592. doi:10.1016/j.jclepro.2018.05.250

Nikolaou, I. (2019). A framework to explicate the relationship between CSER and financial performance: An intellectual capital-based approach and knowledge-based view of firm. *Journal of the Knowledge Economy*, *10*(4), 1427–1446. doi:10.100713132-017-0491-z

Nonaka, I., Peltokorpi, V., & Tomae, H. (2005). Strategic knowledge creation: The case of Hamamatsu Photonics. *International Journal of Technology Management*, *30*(3-4), 248–264. doi:10.1504/IJTM.2005.006709

Nourani, M., Chandran, V., Kweh, Q., & Lu, W. (2018). Measuring human, physical and structural capital efficiency performance of insurance companies. *Social Indicators Research*, *137*(1), 281–315. doi:10.100711205-017-1584-6

Obeng, B., Robson, P., & Haugh, H. (2014). Strategic entrepreneurship and small firm growth in Ghana. *International Small Business Journal*, *32*(5), 501–524. doi:10.1177/0266242612463946

Oliver, P. (2012). *Succeeding with your literature review. A handbook for students*. McGraw-Hill, Open University Press.

Olve, N., Roy, J., & Wetter, M. (2000). Implantando y gestionando el cuadro de mando integral. *Gestion*.

Ordoñez de Pablos, P. (2001). La gestión del conocimiento como base para el logro de una ventaja competitiva sostenible: La organización occidental versus japonesa [Knowledge management as a basis for achieving sustainable competitive advantage: The Western versus the Japanese organization]. *Investigaciones Europeas de Dirección y Economía de la Empresa*, *7*(3), 91–108.

Otoo, F., Kuar, M., & Otoo, E. (2022). Does human capital mediate the nexus of human resource management (HRM) practices and organizational performance? *International Journal of Research in Business and Social Science*, *11*(5), 199–209. doi:10.20525/ijrbs.v11i5.1829

Petrash, G. (1996). Dow's Journey to a knowledge value management culture. *European Management Journal*, *14*(4), 365–373. doi:10.1016/0263-2373(96)00023-0

Priem, R., & Butler, J. (2001). Is the resource-based "view" a useful perspective for strategic management research? *Academy of Management Review*, *26*(1), 22–40.

Przychodzen, W., Gómez-Bezares, F., & Przychodzen, J. (2018). Green information technologies practices and financial performance-the empirical evidence from German publicly traded companies. *Journal of Cleaner Production*, *201*, 570–579. doi:10.1016/j.jclepro.2018.08.081

Rastogi, P. (2003). The nature and role of IC - rethinking the process of value creation andsustained enterprise growth. *Journal of Intellectual Capital*, *4*(2), 227–248. doi:10.1108/14691930310472848

Reed, K., Lubatkin, M., & Srinivasa, N. (2006). Proposing and Testing an Intellectual Capital-Based View of the Firm. *Journal of Management Studies*, *43*(4), 867–893. doi:10.1111/j.1467-6486.2006.00614.x

Renwick, D., Redman, T., & Maguire, S. (2013). Green human resource management: A review and research agenda. *International Journal of Management Reviews*, *15*(1), 1–14. doi:10.1111/j.1468-2370.2011.00328.x

Roos, G. (2017). Knowledge management, intellectual capital, structural holes, economic complexity and national prosperity. *Journal of Intellectual Capital*, *18*(4), 745–770. doi:10.1108/JIC-07-2016-0072

Salvi, A., Vitolla, F., Giakoumelou, A., Raimo, N., & Rubino, M. (2020). Intellectual capital disclosure in integrated reports: The effect on firm value. *Technological Forecasting and Social Change*, *160*, 120228. doi:10.1016/j.techfore.2020.120228

Sánchez-Medina, A., Melián-González, A., & García-Falcón, J. (2007). El concepto del capital intelectual y sus dimensiones. *Investigaciones Europeas de Dirección y Economía de la Empresa*, *13*(2), 97–111.

Seva-Larrosa, P., Falcó, J. M., & Fernández, L. R. (2022). Analizando las principales variables empresariales en los clusters vinícolas españoles teniendo en cuenta la localización de las empresas y su pertenencia a una marca colectiva. [Analyzing the main business variables in Spanish wine clusters taking into account the location of the companies and their membership in a collective brand.] In *Miradas sobre el emprendimiento ante la crisis del coronavirus* (pp. 629–634). Dykinson.

Skandia. (1996). *Customer Value.* Supplement to the Annual Report. Author.

Stewart, T. (1998). *La nueva riqueza de las organizaciones: el capital intelectual* [The new wealth of organizations: Intellectual capital]. Granica.

Sullivan, P. (1999). Profiting from intellectual capital. *Journal of Knowledge Management, 3*(2), 132–142. doi:10.1108/13673279910275585

Sullivan, P. (2000). *Value driven intellectual capital: how to convert intangible corporate assets into market value.* John Wiley & Sons, Inc.

Sveiby, K. (1997). *The new organizational wealth. Managing and measuring knowledge-based assets.* Berret-Koehler Publishers, Inc.

Sveiby, K. (2001). A knowledge-based theory of the firm to guide in strategy formulation. *Journal of Intellectual Capital, 2*(4), 344–358. doi:10.1108/14691930110409651

Tranfield, D., Denyer, D., & Smart, P. (2003). Towards a methodology for developing evidence-informed management knowledge by means of systematic review. *British Journal of Management, 14*(3), 207–222. doi:10.1111/1467-8551.00375

Viedma, J. (2001). ICBS - Intellectual Capital Benchmarking System. *Journal of Intellectual Capital, 2*(2), 148–165. doi:10.1108/14691930110385937

Wee, B., & Banister, D. (2016). How to write a literature review paper? *Transport Reviews, 36*(2), 278–288. doi:10.1080/01441647.2015.1065456

Xu, J., & Liu, F. (2020). The impact of intellectual capital on firm performance: A modified and extended VAIC model. *Journal of Competitiveness, 12*(1), 161–176. doi:10.7441/joc.2010.01.10

Yadiati, W., Nissa, N., Paulus, S., Suharman, H., & Meiryani, M. (2019). The role of green intellectual capital and organizational reputation in influencing environmental performance. *International Journal of Energy Economics and Policy, 9*(3), 261–268. doi:10.32479/ijeep.7752

Yong, J., Yusliza, M., Ramayah, T., & Fawehinmi, O. (2019). Nexus between green intellectual capital and green human resource management. *Journal of Cleaner Production, 215*, 364–374. doi:10.1016/j.jclepro.2018.12.306

Youndt, M., Subramaniam, M., & Snell, S. (2004). Intellectual capital profiles: An examination of investments and returns. *Journal of Management Studies, 41*(2), 335–361. doi:10.1111/j.1467-6486.2004.00435.x

Yusliza, M., Othman, N., & Jabbour, C. (2017). Deciphering the implementation of green human resource management in an emerging economy. *Journal of Management Development, 36*(10), 1230–1246. doi:10.1108/JMD-01-2017-0027

Yusoff, Y., Omar, M., Zaman, M., & Samad, S. (2019). Do all elements of green intellectual capital contribute toward business sustainability? Evidence from the Malaysian context using the Partial Least Squares method. *Journal of Cleaner Production*, *234*, 626–637. doi:10.1016/j.jclepro.2019.06.153

Zaid, A., Jaaron, A., & Bon, A. (2018). The impact of green human resource management and green supply chain management practices on sustainable performance: An empirical study. *Journal of Cleaner Production*, *204*, 965–979. doi:10.1016/j.jclepro.2018.09.062

Zaragoza-Sáez, P., Claver-Cortés, E., Marco-Lajara, B., & Úbeda-García, M. (2020). Corporate social responsibility and strategic knowledge management as mediators between sustainable intangible capital and hotel performance. *Journal of Sustainable Tourism*, 1–23. doi:10.1080/09669582.2020.1811289

Zhang, L., Li, D., Cao, C., & Huang, S. (2018). The influence of greenwashing perception on green purchasing intentions: The mediating role of green word-of-mouth and moderating role of green concern. *Journal of Cleaner Production*, *187*, 740–750. doi:10.1016/j.jclepro.2018.03.201

Zhu, Q., Sarkis, J., & Lai, K. (2013). Institutional-based antecedents and performance outcomes of internal and external green supply chain management practices. *Journal of Purchasing and Supply Management*, *19*(2), 106–117. doi:10.1016/j.pursup.2012.12.001

ADDITIONAL READING

Benevene, P., Buonomo, I., Kong, E., Pansini, M., & Farnese, M. L. (2021). Management of Green Intellectual Capital: Evidence-Based Literature Review and Future Directions. *Sustainability*, *13*(15), 8349. doi:10.3390u13158349

Haldorai, K., Kim, W. G., & Garcia, R. F. (2022). Top management green commitment and green intellectual capital as enablers of hotel environmental performance: The mediating role of green human resource management. *Tourism Management*, *88*, 104431. doi:10.1016/j.tourman.2021.104431

Mansoor, A., Jahan, S., & Riaz, M. (2021). Does green intellectual capital spur corporate environmental performance through green workforce? *Journal of Intellectual Capital*, *22*(5), 823–839. doi:10.1108/JIC-06-2020-0181

Nisar, Q. A., Haider, S., Ali, F., Jamshed, S., Ryu, K., & Gill, S. S. (2021). Green human resource management practices and environmental performance in Malaysian green hotels: The role of green intellectual capital and pro-environmental behavior. *Journal of Cleaner Production*, *311*, 127504. doi:10.1016/j.jclepro.2021.127504

Ullah, H., Wang, Z., Mohsin, M., Jiang, W., & Abbas, H. (2022). Multidimensional perspective of green financial innovation between green intellectual capital on sustainable business: The case of Pakistan. *Environmental Science and Pollution Research International*, *29*(4), 5552–5568. doi:10.100711356-021-15919-7 PMID:34424468

KEY TERMS AND DEFINITIONS

Green Intellectual Capital: A set of human, structural, and relational intangibles that the organization possesses and whose purpose is the preservation of the environment.

Human Capital: The body of knowledge that people possess.

Intangible Asset: A business asset that cannot be physically perceived.

Intellectual Capital: A set of human, structural, and relational intangibles owned by the organization.

Relational Capital: Set of knowledge that derives from the network of relationships that the organization possesses.

Structural Capital: The body of knowledge possessed by the organization.

Compilation of References

AAPA. (2019). *Environment and Energy.* Retrieved from https://aapa.files.cms-plus.com/PDFs/Environment%20and%20 Energy%209-19.pdf

Abbott, K., Green, J., & Keohane, R. (2016). Organizational Ecology and Institutional Change in Global Governance. *International Organization*, *70*(2), 247–277. doi:10.1017/S0020818315000338

Abernathy, W. J., & Utterback, J. M. (1978). Patterns of industrial innovation. *Technology Review*, (June/July), 41–47.

Abimbola, T., Lim, M., Hillestad, T., Xie, C., & Haugland, S. A. (2010). Innovative corporate social responsibility: The founder's role in creating a trustworthy corporate brand through "green innovation." *Journal of Product and Brand Management*, *19*(6), 440–451. doi:10.1108/10610421011085758

Adda, G., Azigwe, J. B., & Awuni, A. R. (2016). Business ethics and corporate social responsibility for business success and growth. *European Journal of Business and Innovation Research*, *6*(4), 26–4.

Adler, P. S., & Kwon, S. (2002). Social capital: Prospects for a new concept. *Academy of Management Review*, *27*(1), 17–40. doi:10.2307/4134367

Afrazeh, A. (2005). *Knowledge management (concepts, models, measurement and implementation).* Amirkabir University of Technology Publication Center.

Agarwal, V. K. (2005). Environmental laws in India: Challenges for enforcement. *Bulletin of the National Institute of Ecology*, *15*, 227–238.

Agostini, L., Nosella, A., & Filippini, R. (2017). Does intellectual capital allow improving innovation performance? A quantitative analysis in the SME context. *Journal of Intellectual Capital*, *18*(2), 400–418. doi:10.1108/JIC-05-2016-0056

Aguinis, H., & Glavas, A. (2012). What We Know and Don't Know About Corporate Social Responsibility. *Journal of Management*, *38*(4), 932–968. doi:10.1177/0149206311436079

Ahmad, M., & Ahmed, N. (2016). Testing the relationship between intellectualcapital and a firm's performance: An empirical investigation regarding financial industries of Pakistan. *International Journal of Learning and Intellectual Capital*, *13*(2-3), 250–272. doi:10.1504/IJLIC.2016.075691

Aithal, P. S., & Aithal, Shubhrajyotsna (2016). Nanotechnology Innovations and Commercialization – Opportunities, Challenges & Reasons for Delay. *Proceedings of National Conference on Changing Perspectives of Management, IT, and Social Sciences in Contemporary Environment*, 14, 1-12. 10.5815/ijem.2016.06.02

Aithal, P. S. & Aithal, S. (2018). Nanotechnology based Innovations and Human Life Comfortability –Are we Marching towards Immortality? *International Journal of Applied Engineering and Management Letters*, *2*(2), 71–86.

Ajaz, T., & Ahmad, E. (2010). The effect of corruption and governance on tax revenues. *Pakistan Development Review*, *49*(4II), 405–417. doi:10.30541/v49i4IIpp.405-417

Ajina, A. S., Roy, S., Nguyen, B., Japutra, A., & Al-Hajla, A. H. (2020). Enhancing brand value using corporate social responsibility initiatives: Evidence from financial services brands in saudi arabia. *Qualitative Market Research*, *23*(4), 575–602. doi:10.1108/QMR-11-2017-0145

Ajzen, I., & Fishbein, M. (1977). Attitude-behavior relations: A theoretical analysis and review of empirical research. *Psychological Bulletin*, *84*(5), 888–918. doi:10.1037/0033-2909.84.5.888

Akhavan, P., Hosnavi, R., & Sanjaghi, M. E. (2009). Identification of knowledge management critical success factors in Iranian academic research centers. *Education, Business and Society*, *2*(4), 276–288. doi:10.1108/17537980911001107

Akhtar, C. S., Ismail, K., Ndaliman, M. A., Hussain, J., & Haider, M. (2015). Can intellectual capital of smes help in their sustainability efforts. *Journal of Management Research*, *7*(2), 82. doi:10.5296/jmr.v7i2.6930

Akhtar, P., Khan, Z., Frynas, J., Tse, Y., & Rao-Nicholson, R. (2018). Essential micro-foundations for contemporary business operations: Top management tangible competencies, relationship-based business networks and environmental sustainability. *British Journal of Management*, *29*(1), 43–62. doi:10.1111/1467-8551.12233

Al-Abdullah, M., Alsmadi, I., Aiabdullah, R., & Farkas, B. (2020). Designing Privacy-Friendly data repositories: A framework for a blockchain that follows the GDPR. *Digital Policy. Regulation & Governance*, *22*(5/6), 389–411. doi:10.1108/DPRG-04-2020-0050

Alawattage, C., & Fernando, S. (2017). Postcoloniality in corporate social and environmental accountability. *Accounting, Organizations and Society*, *60*, 1–20. doi:10.1016/j.aos.2017.07.002

Albareda, L. (2008). Corporate responsibility, governance and accountability: From self-regulation to co-regulation. *Corporate Governance: The International Journal of Business in Society*, *8*(4), 430–439. doi:10.1108/14720700810899176

Albdour, L.R.M. (2017). Principles of Corporate Governance and Ethics for Sustainable Business. *International Journal of Business and Management Invention*, *6*(4), 01-07.

Alcaniz, L., Gomez-Bezares, F., & Roslender, R. (2011, June). Theoretical perspectives on intellectual capital: A backward look and a proposal for going forward. *Accounting Forum*, *35*(2), 104–117. doi:10.1016/j.accfor.2011.03.004

Aldanondo-Ochoa, A. M., & Almansa-Sáez, C. (2009). The private provision of public environment: Consumer preferences for organic production systems. *Land Use Policy*, *26*(3), 669–682. doi:10.1016/j.landusepol.2008.09.006

Aldrich, H. E., & Mueller, S. (1982). The Evolution of Organizational Forms: Technology, Coordination and Control. in B.M. Staw & L.L. Cummings (Eds.), Research in Organizational Behaviour. JAI Press.

Aldrich, H. (2008). *Organizations and Environments*. Stanford University Press.

Aldrich, H. E. (1979). *Organizations and environments*. Prentice-Hall.

Aldrich, H. E. (1999). *Organizations evolving*. Sage.

Aldrich, H. E., & Auster, E. R. (1986). Even dwarfs started small: Liabilities of age and size and their strategic implications. *Research in Organizational Behavior*, *8*, 165–198.

Aldrich, H. E., & Pfeffer, J. (1976). Environments of organizations. *Annual Review of Sociology*, *2*(1), 79–105. doi:10.1146/annurev.so.02.080176.000455

Ali, M. A., Hussin, N., Haddad, H., Al-Araj, R., & Abed, I. A. (2021). A multidimensional view of intellectual capital: The impact on innovation performance. *Journal of Open Innovation*, *7*(4), 216. doi:10.3390/joitmc7040216

Alvesson, M. (2002). *Understanding Organisational Culture*. Sage Publications.

Alvino, F., Di Vaio, A., Hassan, R., & Palladino, R. (2020). Intellectual capital and sustainable development: A systematic literature review. *Journal of Intellectual Capital*, *22*(1), 76–94. doi:10.1108/JIC-11-2019-0259

Amabile, T. M. (1988). A Model of Creativity and Innovation in Organizations. In N.M. Staw & L.L. Cummings (Eds.), Research in Organizational Behavior. JAI Press.

Ambirar, M. C., Kemoni, N. H., & Ngulube, P. (2019). A framework for electronic records management in support of e-government in Kenya. Electronic records. *Records Management Journal*, *29*(3), 305–319. doi:10.1108/RMJ-03-2018-0006

Amburgey, T., & Hayagreeva, R. (1996). Organizational Ecology: Past, Present, and Future Directions. *Academy of Management Journal*, *39*(5), 1265–1286. doi:10.2307/256999

Ammerman, N. T. (1997). *Congregation and community*. Rutgers University Press.

Anastasopouos, A., Kolios, S., & Styios, C. (2011). How Will Greek Ports Become Green Ports? Geo-Eco-Marina, 17, 73-80.

Anaza, N. A. (2015). Relations of fit and organizational identification to employee-customer identification. *Journal of Managerial Psychology*, *30*(8), 925–939. doi:10.1108/JMP-12-2012-0389

Anderies, J. M., Janssen, M. A., & Ostrom, E. (2004). A framework to analyze the robustness of social–ecological systems from an institutional perspective. *Ecology and Society*, *9*(1), 18. doi:10.5751/ES-00610-090118

Anderson, R., Amodeo, M., & Harzfeld, J. (2010). Changing business cultures from within. The World Watch Institute. W.W. Norton.

Anderson, P., & Tushman, M. L. (1990). Technological discontinuities and dominant designs: A cyclical model of technological change. *Administrative Science Quarterly*, *35*(4), 604–633. doi:10.2307/2393511

Andersson, T., Getz, D., & Mykletun, R. (2013). Sustainable festival populations: An application of organizational ecology. *Tourism Analysis*, *18*(6), 621–634. doi:10.3727/108354213X13824558188505

Andriessen, D. (2001). Weightless Wealth: Four Modifications to Standard IC Theory. *Journal of Intellectual Capital*, *2*(3), 204–214. doi:10.1108/14691930110399941

Angels, D. P. (2000). High-technology agglomeration and the labour market: The case of Silicon Valley. In K. Martin (Ed.), *Understanding Silicon Valley: The Anatomy of an Entrepreneurial Region* (pp. 125–189). Stanford University Press. doi:10.1515/9781503618381-009

Anti-Corruption Commission Bill. (2003). Republic of South Africa.

Aramburu, N., & Sáenz, J. (2011). Structural capital, innovation capability, and size effect: An empirical study. *Journal of Management & Organization*, *17*(3), 307–325. doi:10.5172/jmo.2011.17.3.307

Argyris, C., & Schôn, D. (1978). *Organizational Learning: A Theory of Action Perspective*. Addison-Wesley.

Argyris, C., & Schôn, D. (1987). Reasoning, action strategies, and defensive routines: The case of OD practitioners. *Research in Organizational Change and Development*, *1*, 89–128.

Armstrong, M. (2006). *A handbook of human resource management practice*. Kogan Page Publishers.

Asheim, B., & Gertler, M. (2005). The geography of innovation. In J. Fagerberg, D. C. Mowery, & R. R. Nelson (Eds.), *The Oxford handbook of innovation*. Oxford University Press.

Ashitha, A. B., & Anu, L. (2020, September). Green HRM: A Pathway to Sustainable Business. In Perspectives on Business Management & Economics (Vol. 2, pp. 106-117). Academic Press.

Ashrafi, M., Walker, T., Magnan, G., Adams, M., & Acciaro, M. (2020). A review of corporate sustainability drivers in maritime ports: A multi-stakeholder perspective. Maritime Policy & Management, 1–18.

Asonitis, S., & Kostagiolas, P. A. (2010). An analytic hierarchy approach for intellectual capital: Evidence for the Greek central public libraries. *Library Management, 31*(3), 145–161. doi:10.1108/01435121011027327

Aspara, J., Hietanen, J., & Tikkanen, H. (2009). Business model innovation vs. replication. *Journal of Strategic Marketing, 18*(1), 39–56. doi:10.1080/09652540903511290

Assmann, I. (2009). Digital Audiovisual archives; Unlocking our Audio and Audiovisual heritage Potential. *ESARBICA Journal, 28*(1), 230–237. doi:10.4314/esarjo.v28i1.44406

Attila, G. (2008). Corruption, Taxation and Economic Growth: Theory and Evidence. *Centre d'Etudes et de Recherches sur le Development International working paper 2008/29*, Clermon: Ferrand.

Augier, M., & Teece, D. J. (2012). An Economics Perspective on Intellectual Capital1. In *Perspectives on intellectual capital* (pp. 3–27). Routledge.

Austin, L. L. (2012). Government's use of social media to frame health information: A review of the U.S. Centers for Disease Control and Prevention's social media practices. In S. C. Duhe (Ed.), *New Media and Public Relations* (2nd ed., pp. 209–217). Peter Lang Publishing Inc.

Avishek, B., & Javakhadze, D. (2017) Corporate Social Responsibility and Capital Allocation Efficiency. *Journal of Corporate Finance, 43*, 354-377. https://ssrn.com/abstract=3054236 or doi:10.2139/ssrn.3054236

Avishek, B., & David, J. (2017). Corporate social responsibility and capital allocation efficiency. *Journal of Corporate Finance, 43*(3), 354–377.

Aydın, S. & Tufan, F. (2018). Purchasing Behaviors of Y Generation in the Context of Sustainability and Green Concepts. *Journal of Selcuk Communication, 11*(2), 397-420. Doi:10.18094/josc.377009

Azimi, M., Hemati, A (2018). Impact of voluntary disclosure of different dimensions of intellectual capital on disclosure level of social responsibility. *Quarterly of management, accounting and economic, 2* (1), 55-69.

Baguette, M., & Stevens, V. M. (2003). Local populations and metapopulations are both natural and operational categories. *Oikos, 101*(3), 661–663. doi:10.1034/j.1600-0706.2003.12539.x

Bahrami, H., & Evans, S. (2000). Flexible recylcing and high-technology entrepreneurship. In K. Martin (Ed.), *Understanding Silicon Valley: The anatomy of an entrepreneurial region* (pp. 166–189). Stanford University Press. doi:10.1515/9781503618381-011

Baker, R. J. (2008). *Mind Over Matter: why intellectual capital is the chief source of wealth*. John Wiley & Sons Publication.

Baldridge, J. V., & Burnham, R. A. (1975). Organizational Innovation: Individual, Organizational, and Environmental Impacts. *Administrative Science Quarterly, 20*(2), 165–176. doi:10.2307/2391692

Baloyi, N., & Kotze, P. (2017). Are Organisations in South Africa Ready to Comply with Personal Data Protection or Privacy Legislation and Regulations? *IST- Africa Conference Proceedings*. IST.

Bansal, P. (2005). Evolving sustainably: A longitudinal study of corporate sustainable development. *Strategic Management Journal*, *26*(3), 197–218. doi:10.1002mj.441

Barnet, M. L. (2007). Stakeholder influence capacity and the variability of financial returns to corporate social responsibility. *Academy of Management Review*, *33*(3), 794–816. doi:10.5465/amr.2007.25275520

Barnett, W. P. (1990). The Organizational Ecology of a Technological System. *Administrative Science Quarterly*, *35*(1), 31–60. doi:10.2307/2393550

Barney, J. (1991). Firm Resources and Sustained Competitive Advantage. *Journal of Management*, *17*(1), 99–120. doi:10.1177/014920639101700108

Barney, J. (2001). Is the resource-based "view" a useful perspective for strategic management research? Yes. *Academy of Management Review*, *26*(1), 41–56.

Barrett, C. B., Brandon, K., Gibson, C., & Gjersten, H. (2001). Conserving tropical biodiversity amid weak institutions. *Bioscience*, *51*(6), 497–502. doi:10.1641/0006-3568(2001)051[0497:CTBAWI]2.0.CO;2

Bartlett, M. S. (1954). A note on the multiplying factors for various χ 2 approximations. *Journal of the Royal Statistical Society. Series B. Methodological*, *16*(2), 296–298. doi:10.1111/j.2517-6161.1954.tb00174.x

Bashar, A. (2012). *The Impact of Perceived CSR Initiatives on Consumer's Buying Behaviour: An Empirical Study*. SSRN Electronic Journal. doi:10.2139srn.3924859

Bassett, E., & Moore, S. (2013). Social capital and depressive symptoms: The association of psychosocial and network dimensions of social capital with depressive symptoms in Montreal, Canada. *Social Science & Medicine*, *86*, 96–102. doi:10.1016/j.socscimed.2013.03.005 PMID:23608098

Baum, J. A., & Shipilov, A. V. (2006). 1.2 Ecological Approaches to Organizations. The Sage handbook of organization studies, 55.

Baum, J. (1996). Organizational ecology. In S. Clegg, C. Hardy, & W. Nord (Eds.), *Handbook of organizational study* (pp. 77–115). Sage.

Baum, J. A. C. (2001). Ecologia organizacional. In S. R. Clegg (Ed.), *Hardy, C.; Nord, W. R. (orgs). Handbook de Estudos Organizacionais*. Atlas.

Baum, J., & Oliver, C. (1992). Institutional embededdness and the dynamics of organizational populations. *American Sociological Review*, *57*(4), 540–559. doi:10.2307/2096100

Bawden, R. J. (1991). Systems Thinking and Practice in Agriculture. *Journal of Dairy Science*, *74*(7), 2362–2373. doi:10.3168/jds.S0022-0302(91)78410-5

Bayliss, J., Schaafsma, M., Balmford, A., Burgess, N. D., Green, J. M. H., Madoffe, S. S., Okayasu, S., Peh, K. S. H., Platts, P. J., & Yu, D. W. (2014). The current and future value of nature-based tourism in the Eastern Arc Mountains of Tanzania. *Ecosystem Services*, *8*, 75–83. doi:10.1016/j.ecoser.2014.02.006

Béal, M., & Sabadie, W. (2018). The impact of customer inclusion in firm governance on customers' commitment and voice behaviors. *Journal of Business Research*, *92*, 1–8. doi:10.1016/j.jbusres.2018.07.019

Becker, F. D. (1988). Technological Innovation and Organizational Ecology. In *Handbook of Human-Computer Interaction*. North-Holland. https://www.sciencedirect.com/science/article/pii/B9780444705365500579

Becker, B., Huselid, M., & Ulrich, D. (2001). *The HR scorecard: Linking people, strategy, and performance*. Harvard Business Press.

Beinhocker, E. D. (2006). The adaptable corporation. *The McKinsey Quarterly*, (2), 76–87.

Bellucci, M., Marzi, G., Orlando, B., & Ciampi, F. (2020). Journal of Intellectual Capital: A review of emerging themes and future trends. *Journal of Intellectual Capital*, *22*(4), 744–767. doi:10.1108/JIC-10-2019-0239

Bender, J., Bridges, T. A., & He, C., Lester, A., & Sun, X. (2018). A Blueprint for Integrating ESG into Equity Portfolios. *Journal of Investment Management*, *16*(1).

Berardi, U., GhaffarianHoseini, A. H., & GhaffarianHoseini, A. (2014). State-of-the-art analysis of the environmental benefits of green roofs. *Applied Energy*, *115*, 411–428. doi:10.1016/j.apenergy.2013.10.047

Berezinets, I., Garanina, T., & Ilina, Y. (2016). Intellectual capital of a board of directors and its elements: Introduction to the concepts. *Journal of Intellectual Capital*, *17*(4), 632–653. doi:10.1108/JIC-01-2016-0003

Berkes, F., Colding, J., & Folke, C. (2000). Rediscovery of traditional ecological knowledge as adaptive management. *Ecological Applications*, *10*(5), 1251–1262. doi:10.1890/1051-0761(2000)010[1251:ROTEKA]2.0.CO;2

Berlin, N. (2020). *Stadt der grünen Trends-Wie Berlin den Weg der urbanen Nachhaltigkeit geht*. Available online: https://about.visitberlin.de/nachhaltiges-berlin

Bernardes, M. E. B. SÁ, F. S. (2009). Voluntarismo e determinismo em implementação de estratégias colectivas de PME: uma análise de dois processos em arranjos produtivos moveleiros [Voluntarism and determinism in implementation of collective SME strategies: An análisis of two processes in productive furniture arrangements]. In Encontro de estudos de estratégia, IV, Recife, 2009 - IV Encontro de Estudos de Estratégia. Recife: ANPAD.

Bernardini & Irvine. (2007). The 'nature' of urban sustainability: private or public greenspaces? *Transactions on Ecology and the Environment*, 661-673.

Berryman, A. A. (2002). Population: A central concept for ecology? *Oikos*, *97*(3), 439–442. doi:10.1034/j.1600-0706.2002.970314.x

Bhattacharya, C. B., & Sen, S. (2003). Consumer–Company Identification: A Framework for Understanding Consumers' Relationships with Companies. *Journal of Marketing*, *67*(2), 76–88. doi:10.1509/jmkg.67.2.76.18609

Bhatti, W. A., & Zaheer, A. (2014). The role of intellectual capital in creating and adding value to organizational performance: A conceptual analysis. *Electronic Journal of Knowledge Management*, *12*(3), 185–192.

Binks, M., & Vale, P. A. (1990). *Entrepreneurship and Economic Change*. McGraw–Hill.

Bissing-Olson, M. J., Iyer, A., Fielding, K. S., & Zacher, H. (2013). Relationships between daily affect and pro-environmental behavior at work: The moderating role of pro-environmental attitude. *Journal of Organizational Behavior*, *175*(2), 156–175. doi:10.1002/job.1788

Blakesley, I. R., & Yallop, A. C. (2019). What do you know about me? Digital privacy and online data sharing in the UK insurance sector. Journal of Information *Communication and Ethics in Society*, *18*(2), 281–303. doi:10.1108/JICES-04-2019-0046

Bock, G. W., Zmud, R. W., Kim, Y. G., & Lee, J. N. (2005). Behavioral intention formation in knowledge sharing: Examining the roles of extrinsic motivators, social-psychological forces, and organizational climate. *Management Information Systems Quarterly*, *2005*(29), 87–112. doi:10.2307/25148669

Boiral, O., & Paillé, P. (2012). Organizational citizenship behaviour for the environment: Measurement and validation. *Journal of Business Ethics*, *109*(4), 431–445. doi:10.100710551-011-1138-9

Bollen, L., Vergauwen, P., & Schnieders, S. (2005). Linking intellectual capital and intellectual property to company performance. *Management Decision*, *43*(9), 1161–1185. doi:10.1108/00251740510626254

Bontis, N. (1996). There is a price on your head: Managing intellectual capital strategically. *Business Quarterly*, *60*(4), 41–47.

Bontis, N. (1996). There's a price on your head: managing intellectual capital strategically. Business Quarterly, 60, 40-78. doi:10.1108/00251749810204142

Bontis, N. (1999). Managing organizational knowledge by diagnosing intellectual capital: Framing and advancing the state of the field. *International Journal of Technology Management*, *18*(5-8), 433–462. doi:10.1504/IJTM.1999.002780

Bontis, N. (2000). *Managing organizational knowledge by diagnosing intellectual capital. In Knowledge Management: Classic and Contemporary Works*. MIT Press.

Bontis, N. (2001). Assessing knowledge assets: A review of the models used to measure intellectual capital. *International Journal of Management Reviews*, *3*(1), 41–60. doi:10.1111/1468-2370.00053

Bontis, N. (2001). CKO wanted - Evangelical skills necessary: A review of the chief knowledge officer position. *Knowledge and Process Management*, *8*(1), 29–38. doi:10.1002/kpm.100

Bontis, N. (2002). *National intellectual capital index: Intellectual capital development in the Arab Region*. Institute for Intellectual Capital Research.

Bontis, N. (2003). Intellectual capital disclosure in Canadian corporations. *Journal of Human Resource Costing & Accounting*, *7*(1), 9–20. doi:10.1108/eb029076

Bontis, N. (2004). National intellectual capital index: A United Nations initiative for the Arab region. *Journal of Intellectual Capital*, *5*(1), 13–39. doi:10.1108/14691930410512905

Bontis, N., Crossan, M., & Hulland, J. (2002). Managing an organizational learning system by aligning stocks and flows. *Journal of Management Studies*, *39*(4), 437–469. doi:10.1111/1467-6486.t01-1-00299

Bontis, N., Dragonetti, N. C., Jacobsen, K., & Roos, G. (1999). The knowledge toolbox: A review of the tools available to measure and manage intangible resources. *European Management Journal*, *17*(4), 391–402. doi:10.1016/S0263-2373(99)00019-5

Borgman, L. C. (2018). Open Data, Grey Data, and Stewardship. *Universities at the Privacy Frontier*, *33*, 365.

Bossink, B. A. G. (2004). Effectiveness of innovation leadership styles: A manager's influence on ecological innovation in construction projects. *Construction Innovation*, *4*(4), 211–228. doi:10.1108/14714170410815105

Bozbura, F. T., Beskese, A., & Kahraman, C. (2007). Prioritization of human capital measurement indicators using fuzzy AHP. *Expert Systems with Applications*, *32*(4), 1100–1112. doi:10.1016/j.eswa.2006.02.006

Bradley, K. (1997). Intellectual capital and the new wealth of nations. *Business Strategy Review*, *8*(1), 53–62. doi:10.1111/1467-8616.00007

Brands, R. A., & Fernandez-Mateo, I. (2017). Leaning out: How negative recruitment experiences shape women's decisions to compete for executive roles. *Administrative Science Quarterly*, *62*(3), 405–442. doi:10.1177/0001839216682728

Brennan, N., & Connell, B. (2000). Intellectual capital: Current issues and policy implications. *Journal of Intellectual Capital*, *1*(3), 206–240. doi:10.1108/14691930010350792

Brimmer, S. E. (2007). The role of ethics in 21st century organizations. *Leadership advance online, 11*.

Brooking, A. (1997). Intellectual capital. In Intellectual capital. International Thomson business press.

Brooking, A. (1996). *Intellectual capital*. Cengage Learning EMEA.

Brooking, A. (1996). *Intellectual Capital: Core Assets for the Third Millennium Enterprise*. Thomson Business Press.

Brooking, A. (1997). The management of intellectual capital. *Long Range Planning*, *30*(3), 364–365. doi:10.1016/S0024-6301(97)80911-9

Brooks, C., & Oikonomou, I. (2018). The effects of environmental, social and governance disclosures and performance on firm value: A review of the literature in accounting and finance. *The British Accounting Review*, *50*(1), 1–15. doi:10.1016/j.bar.2017.11.005

Brown, J. (2009). *Intellectual Capital and Innovation: Implications for New Service Development*. Cass Business School.

Brown, J. R., Fazzari, S. M., & Petersen, B. C. (2009). Financing Innovation and Growth: Cash Flow, External Equity, and the 1990s R&D Boom. *The Journal of Finance*, *64*(1), 151–185. doi:10.1111/j.1540-6261.2008.01431.x

Brown, J., Crocamo, T. J., Bielskas, A., Ransom, E., Vanti, B. W., & Wilfong, K. (2017). Evolving skills for emerging technologies: A collaborative approach. *Library Hi Tech*, *35*(3), 346–359. doi:10.1108/LHT-12-2016-0156

Brown, S. L., & Eisenhardt, K. M. (1997). The Art of Continuous Change: Complexity Theory and Time-Paced Evolution in Relentlessly Shifting Organizations. *Administrative Science Quarterly*, *42*(1), 1–34. doi:10.2307/2393807

Bruderl, J., Preisendorfer, P., & Ziegler, R. (1992). Survival Chances of Newly Founded Business Organizations. *American Sociological Review*, *57*(2), 227–242. doi:10.2307/2096207

Brudermann, T., & Sangkakool, T. (2017). Green roofs in temperate climate cities in Europe - An analysis of key decision factors. *Urban Forestry & Urban Greening*, *21*, 224–234. doi:10.1016/j.ufug.2016.12.008

Brundtland, G. (1987). *Our Common Future: The World Commission on Environment and Development*. Oxford University Press.

Bryman, A., & Bell, E. (2011). *Business Research Methods* (3rd ed.). Oxford University Press.

Bueno, E. (2000). De la sociedad de la información a la del conocimiento y el aprendizaje: La necesidad de programas de dirección del conocimiento y aprendizaje [From the information society to the knowledge and learning society: The need for knowledge and learning management programs]. *Jornadas Españolas de Documentación*, *7*, 647–657.

Bueno, E. (2000). De la sociedad de la información a la del conocimiento y el aprendizaje: La necesidad de programas de dirección del conocimiento y aprendizaje. *Jornadas Españolas de Documentación*, *7*, 647–657.

Bueno, E. (2003). Enfoques principales y tendencias en dirección del conocimiento (knowledge management). In *Dirección del conocimiento: Desarrollos teóricos y aplicaciones*. Ediciones La Coria.

Bueno, E., Arrién, M., & Rodríguez, O. (2003). Model for the measurement and management of Intellectual Capital. *Intellectus Model. Intellectus Documents*, *5*(2), 181–192.

Bulog, I., & Grancic, I. (2017). The Benefits of Business Ethics-Ethical Behavior of Decision Makers: The Empirical Findings from Croatia. *Mediterranean Journal of Social Sciences*, *8*(4), 9–14. doi:10.2478/mjss-2018-0067

Burawat, P. (2019). The relationships among transformational leadership, sustainable leadership, lean manufacturing and sustainability performance in Thai SMEs manufacturing industry. *International Journal of Quality & Reliability Management*, *36*(6), 1014–1036. doi:10.1108/IJQRM-09-2017-0178

Burgelman, R. A. (1991). Intraorganizational Ecology of Strategy Making and Organizational Adaptation: Theory and Field Research. *Organization Science*, 239 – 262.

Burgleman, E. A. (1991). Intraorganizational Ecology of Strategy Making and Organizational Adaptation: Theory and Research. *Organization Science*, *2/3*(3), 239–262. doi:10.1287/orsc.2.3.239

Burns, T., & Stalker, G. M. (1961). *The Management of Innovation*. Tavistock.

Burszta-Adamiak, E., & Fiałkiewicza, W. (2019). Review of green roof incentives as motivators for the expansion of green infrastructure in European cities. *Scientific Review – Engineering and Environmental Sciences*, *28*(4), 641–652. DOI doi:10.22630/PNIKS.2019.28.4.5

Burszta-Adamiak, E., Stańczyk, J., & Łomotowski, J. (2019). Hydrological performance of green roofs in the context of the meteorological factors during the 5-year monitoring period. *Water and Environment Journal: the Journal / the Chartered Institution of Water and Environmental Management*, *33*(1), 144–154. doi:10.1111/wej.12385

Burt, R. (2005). *Brokerage and Closure: An Introduction to Social Capital*. Oxford University Press.

Cabello-Medina, C., López-Cabrales, A., & Valle-Cabrera, R. (2011). Leveraging theinnovative performance of human capital through HRM and social capital in Spanish firms. *International Journal of Human Resource Management*, *22*(4), 807–828. doi:10.1080/09585192.2011.555125

Cabrita, M. D. R., & Bontis, N. (2008). Intellectual capital and business performance in the Portuguese banking industry. *International Journal of Technology Management*, *43*(1-3), 212–237. doi:10.1504/IJTM.2008.019416

Çalışkan, A., & Esmer, S. (2020). An assessment of port and shipping line relationships: The value of relationship marketing. *Maritime Policy & Management*, *47*(2), 240–257. Advance online publication. doi:10.1080/03088839.2019.1690172

Camisón, C., Palacios, D., & Devece, C. (2000). *Un modelo para la medición del capital intelectual en la empresa: el modelo Nova* [A model for measuring intelectual capital in the cmopany: The Nova Model]. Disponible en: http://www.gestiondelconocimiento.com

Camisón, C., Palacios, D., & Devece, C. (2000). *Un modelo para la medición del capital intelectual en la empresa: el modelo Nova* [A model for the measurement of intellectual capital in the firm: the Nova model]. Available at: http://www.gestiondelconocimiento.com

Camus, P. A., & Lima, M. (2002). Populations, metapopulations, and the open-closed dilemma: The conflict between operational and natural population concepts. *Oikos*, *97*(3), 433–438. doi:10.1034/j.1600-0706.2002.970313.x

Capital, T. I. (1998). Exploring the concept of intellectual capital (IC). *Long Range Planning*, 31.

Caradonna, J. L. (2014). Sustainability: A History. Oxford University Press.

Carayannis, E. G. (2008). Knowledge-driven creative destruction or leveraging knowledge for competitive advantage: Strategic Knowledge arbitrage and serendipity as real options drivers triggered by co-opetition, co-evolution, and co-specialization. *Industry and Higher Education*, *22*(6), 343–353. doi:10.5367/000000008787225957

Carayannis, E. G., Alexander, J., & Ioannidis, A. (2000). Leveraging knowledge, learning, and innovation in forming strategic government–university–industry (GUI) R&D partnerships in the US, Germany, and France. *Technovation*, *20*(9), 477–488. doi:10.1016/S0166-4972(99)00162-5

Carmona-Lavado, A., Cuevas-Rodríguez, G., & Cabello-Medina, C. (2010). Social andorganizational capital: Building the context for innovation. *Industrial Marketing Management*, *39*(4), 681–690. doi:10.1016/j.indmarman.2009.09.003

Carmona-Lavado, A., Cuevas-Rodríguez, G., & Cabello-Medina, C. (2013). Service Innovativeness and Innovation Success in Technology-based Knowledge-Intensive Business Services: An Intellectual Capital Approach. *Industry and Innovation*, 20(2), 133–156. doi:10.1080/13662716.2013.771482

Carnini Pulino, S., Ciaburri, M., Magnanelli, B. S., & Nasta, L. (2022). Does ESG Disclosure Influence Firm Performance? *Sustainability*, 14(13), 7595. doi:10.3390u14137595

Carr, A. (2004). Is Business Bluffing Ethical? in Ethical Theory and Business (7th ed), Beauchamp, T. & Bowie, N. (Eds.). Prentice Hall.

Carroll (1979). A three Dimensional Conceptual Model Of Corporate Performance. *Academy of Management Review*, 4(4), 497-505.

Carroll, G. (1984). Organizational ecology. *Annual Review of Sociology*, 10(1), 71–93. doi:10.1146/annurev.so.10.080184.000443

Carroll, G. R. (1983). A stochastic model of organizational mortality: Review and reanalysis. *Social Science Research*, 12(4), 303–329. doi:10.1016/0049-089X(83)90022-4

Carroll, G. R., & Hannan, M. T. (2000). *The Demography of corporations and industries*. Princeton University Press. doi:10.1515/9780691186795

Castro, G. M., Delgado-Verde, M., Amores-Salvadó, J., & Navas-López, J. E. (2013). Linkinghuman, technological, and relational assets to technological innovation: Exploring a newapproach. *Knowledge Management Research and Practice*, 11(2), 123–132. doi:10.1057/kmrp.2013.8

Centro de Integridade Pública. (2016). The Costs of Corruption to the Mozambican Economy. *Centro de Integridade Pública Policy Brief*, 24/2016.

CFA Institute. (2018). *ESG Integration in the Americas: Markets*. Practices, and Data.

Chahal, H., & Bakshi, P. (2015). Examining intellectual capital and competitive advantagerelationship: Role of innovation and organizational learning. *International Journal of Bank Marketing*, 33(3), 376–399. doi:10.1108/IJBM-07-2013-0069

Chandler, A. D. (1962). *Strategy and Structure: Chapters in the History of the American Industrial Enterprise*. MIT Press.

Chang, N. J., & Fong, C. M. (2010). Green product quality, green corporate image, green customer satisfaction, and green customer loyalty. *African Journal of Business Management*, 4(13), 2336–2344.

Chang, S., Chen, C., & Lai, J. (2008). The Effect of Alliance Experience and Intellectual Capital on the Value Creation of International Strategic Alliances. *Omega*, 36(2), 298–316. doi:10.1016/j.omega.2006.06.010

Chang, T. W., Chen, Y. S., Yeh, Y. L., & Li, H. X. (2020). Sustainable consumption models for customers: Investigating the significant antecedents of green purchase behavior from the perspective of information asymmetry. *Journal of Environmental Planning and Management*, 2020, 1–21.

Chatterji, M. (2011). *Corporate Social Responsibility* (1st ed.). Oxford University Press.

Chauke, R. (2021). King IV municipal supplements: The impact on the municipal's approach to governance. *Technium. The Social Science Journal*, 26, 54–64.

Cheema & Javed. (2017). *Cogent Business & Management*. doi:10.1080/23311975.2017.1310012

Chen, C. -., Huang, J.-. and Hsiao, Y.-. (2010). Knowledge management and innovativeness: Therole of organizational climate and structure. International Journal of Manpower, 31(8), 848–870. doi:10.1108/01437721011088548

Chen, J., Zhao, X. and Wang, Y. (2015). A new measurement of intellectual capital and its impact on innovation performance in an open innovation paradigm. *International Journal of Technology Management, 67*(1), 1-25.

Chen, C. J., Liu, T. C., Chu, M. A., & Hsiao, Y. C. (2014). Intellectual capital and new productdevelopment. *Journal of Engineering and Technology Management, 33*, 154–173. doi:10.1016/j.jengtecman.2014.06.003

Cheng, M. Y., Lin, J. Y., Hsiao, T. Y., & Lin, T. W. (2010). Invested resource, competitive intellectual capital, and corporate performance. *Journal of Intellectual Capital, 11*(4), 433–450. doi:10.1108/14691931011085623

Chen, H., & Chen, S. (2010). Investment-cash flow sensitivity cannot be a good measure of financial constraints: Evidence from the time series. *Journal of Financial Economics, 103*(2), 393–410. doi:10.1016/j.jfineco.2011.08.009

Chen, J., Zhu, Z., & Yuan Xie, H. (2004). Measuring intellectual capital: A new model and empirical study. *Journal of Intellectual Capital, 5*(1), 195–212. doi:10.1108/14691930410513003

Chen, M. C., Cheng, S. J., & Hwang, Y. (2005). An empirical investigation of the relationship between intellectual capital and firms' market value and financial performance. *Journal of Intellectual Capital, 6*(2), 159–176. doi:10.1108/14691930510592771

Chen, Y. (2008). The positive effect of green intellectual capital on competitive advantages of firms. *Journal of Business Ethics, 77*(3), 271–286. doi:10.100710551-006-9349-1

Chen, Y. S. (2008). The driver of green innovation and green image–green core competence. *Journal of Business Ethics, 81*(3), 531–543. doi:10.100710551-007-9522-1

Chen, Y. S., & Chang, C. H. (2013). The determinants of green product development performance: Green dynamic capabilities, green transformational leadership, and green creativity. *Journal of Business Ethics, 2013*(116), 107–119. doi:10.100710551-012-1452-x

Chen, Y. S., Lai, S. B., & Wen, C. T. (2006). The influence of green innovation performance on corporate advantage in Taiwan. *Journal of Business Ethics, 2006*(67), 331–339. doi:10.100710551-006-9025-5

Chen, Y. S., Lin, S. H., Lin, C. Y., Hung, S. T., Chang, C. W., & Huang, C. W. (2020). Improving green product development performance from green vision and organizational culture perspectives. *Corporate Social Responsibility and Environmental Management, 2020*(27), 222–231. doi:10.1002/csr.1794

Chen, Y., & Chang, C. (2013). Utilize structural equation modeling (SEM) to explore the influence of corporate environmental ethics: The mediation effect of green human capital. *Quality & Quantity, 47*(1), 79–95. doi:10.100711135-011-9504-3

Chiang, H., Lin, Y.-C., & Chen, W.-W. (2022). Does family business affect the relationship between corporate social responsibility and brand value? A study in different industry taiwan. *Asia Pacific Management Review, 27*(1), 28–39. doi:10.1016/j.apmrv.2021.04.002

Chien, S. H. (2010). Market orientation and new product success: A mediator model based onintellectual capital. *Asia Pacific Management Review, 15*(3), 377–390.

Chien, S. H., & Chao, M. C. (2011). Intellectual capital and new product sale performance ofthe financial services industry in Taiwan. The Service Industries Journal, 31(16), 2641-2659.

Child, J. (1997). Strategic Choice in the Analysis of Action, Structure, Organizations and Environment: Retrospect and Prospect. *Organization Studies, 18*(1), 43–76. doi:10.1177/017084069701800104

Chin, J. M., & Chuang, C. P. (2015). The Relationships among School-Based Budgeting, Innovative Management, and School Effectiveness: A Study on Specialist Schools in Taiwan. *The Asia-Pacific Education Researcher*, *24*(4), 679–693. doi:10.100740299-014-0220-3

Chiou, T. Y., Chan, H. K., Lettice, F., & Chung, S. H. (2011). The influence of greening the suppliers and green innovation on environmental performance and competitive advantage in Taiwan. *Transp. Res. Logist. Transp. Rev*, *2011*(47), 822–836. doi:10.1016/j.tre.2011.05.016

Chisita, T. C., & Chiparausha, B. (2021). An Institutional Repository in a Developing Country: Security and Ethical Encounters at the Bindura University of Science Education, Zimbabwe. *New Review of Academic Librarianship*, *27*(1), 130–143. doi:10.1080/13614533.2020.1824925

Chiu, Lin, & Ting. (2014). Evaluation of Green Port Factors and Performance: A Fuzzy AHP Analysis. *Mathematical Problems in Engineering*. doi:10.1155/2014/802976

Cho, CH.(2007). *Organizations Legitimacy and the Strategic use of accounting information Three Studies Related to social and environmental disclosure.* [Thesis, University of Central Florida, USA].

Clarke, A. E., & Star, S. L. (2004). Symbolic Interactionist Science, Technology, Information and Biomedicine Studies. In L. T. Reynolds & N. J. Herman-Kinney (Eds.), *Handbook of Symbolic Interactionism*. Rowman & Littlefield.

Clarkson, M. B. E. (1995). A Stakeholder Framework for Analyzing and Evaluating Corporate Social Performance. *Academy of Management Review*, *20*(1), 92–117. doi:10.2307/258888

Cohen, S., & Kaimenakis, N. (2007). Intellectual capital and corporate performance in knowledge-intensive SMEs. *The Learning Organization*, *14*(3), 241–262. doi:10.1108/09696470710739417

Cohen, S., & Kaimenakis, N. (2007). Intellectual capital and corporate performance inknowledge-intensive SMEs. *The Learning Organization*, *14*(3), 241–262.

Cohen, W. M., & Levinthal, D. A. (1990). Absorptive Capacity: A New Perspective on Learning and Innovation. *Administrative Science Quarterly*, *35*(1), 123–138. doi:10.2307/2393553

Coleman, J. S. (1988), Social capital in the creation of human capital. *American Journal of Sociology*, *94*, 95.

Collins, C. J., & Clark, K. D. (2003). Strategic Human Resource Practices, Top Management Team Social Networks, and Firm Performance: The Role of Human Resource Practices in Creating Organizational Competitive Advantage. *Academy of Management Journal*, *46*(6), 740–751. doi:10.2307/30040665

Convery, N. (2014). From reactive to proactive appraisal. *Archives and Manuscripts*, *42*(2), 158–160. doi:10.1080/01576895.2014.911676

Cook, T. (2011). We are What We Keep; We keep What We are: Archival Appraisal Past, Present and Future. *Journal of the Society of Archivists*, *32*(2), 173–189. doi:10.1080/00379816.2011.619688

Coolen, H., & Meesters, J. (2012). Private and public green spaces: Meaningful but different settings. *Journal of Housing and the Built Environment*, *27*(1), 49–67. doi:10.100710901-011-9246-5

Cordeiro, J. J., & Tewari, M. (2015). Firm Characteristics, Industry Context, and Investor Reactions to Environmental CSR: A Stakeholder Theory Approach. *Journal of Business Ethics*, *130*(4), 833–849. doi:10.100710551-014-2115-x

Coss, L. D., & Dhillon, G. (2019). Cloud Privacy objectives a value-based approach. *Information & Computer Security*, *27*(2), 189–220. doi:10.1108/ICS-05-2017-0034

Costa, R. V., Fernández, C. F. J., & Dorrego, P. F. (2014). Critical elements for productinnovation at Portuguese innovative SMEs: An intellectual capital perspective. *Knowledge Management Research and Practice, 12*(3), 322–338. doi:10.1057/kmrp.2014.15

Costa, R. V., & Ramos, A. P. (2015). Designing an AHP methodology to prioritize critical elements for product innovation: An intellectual capital perspective. *Int. Journal of Business Science and Applied Management, 10*(1).

Crossan, M. M., & Apaydin, M. (2010). A multi-dimensional framework of organizationalinnovation: A systematic review of the literature. Journal of management studies, 47(6), 1154-1191.

Crouch. (2006). Modelling the Firm in its Market and Organisational Environmennt: Methodologies For studying CSR. *Organisation Studies, 27*(10), 1533-1551.

Cui, Y., Jiao, J., Jiao, H. (2016). Technological innovation in Brazil, Russia, India, China, and South Africa (BRICS): An organizational ecology perspective. *Technological Forecasting and Social Change, 107*, 28-36. doi:10.1016/j.techfore.2016.02.001

Curado, C., Henriques, L., & Bontis, N. (2011). Intellectual capital disclosure payback. *Man. Dec., 49*(7), 1080-1098.

D'Amato, V., D'Ecclesia, R., & Levantesi, S. (2022). ESG score prediction through random forest algorithm. *Computational Management Science, 19*(2), 347–373. doi:10.100710287-021-00419-3

Daft, R. L. (1978). A Dual-Core Model of Organizational Innovation. *Academy of Management Review, 21*, 193–210.

Dal Mas, F. (2019). The relationship between intellectual capital and sustainability: An analysis of practitioner's thought. In *Intellectual capital management as a driver of sustainability* (pp. 11–24). Springer. doi:10.1007/978-3-319-79051-0_2

Damanpour, F. (1996). Organizational Complexity and Innovation: Developing and Testing Multiple Contingency Models. *Management Science, 42*(5), 693–716. doi:10.1287/mnsc.42.5.693

Damanpour, F., & Evan, W. M. (1984). Organizational Innovation and Performance: The Problem of Organizational Lag. *Administrative Science Quarterly, 29*(3), 392–402. doi:10.2307/2393031

Dangelico, R., & Pujari, D. (2010). Mainstreaming green product innovation: Why and how companies integrate environmental sustainability. *Journal of Business Ethics, 95*(3), 471–486. doi:10.100710551-010-0434-0

Das, S., & Dash, M. (2022). Role of Green HRM in Sustainable Development. *Journal of Positive School Psychology*, 4444-4451.

Daum, J. H. (2003). *Intangible assets and value creation*. John Wiley & Sons.

Davenport, T. H., & Prusak, L. (1998). *Working Knowledge*. Harvard Business School Press.

Davoodi, H. R., & Tanzi, V. (1997). Corruption, public investment and growth. *In IMF Working Paper. WP/97/139*. Washington: International Monetary Fund.

De Carolis, D. M. (2010). Technological Characteristics of Industries. In V. K. Narayanan & G. Colarelli-O'Connor (Eds.), *Encyclopedia of Technology and Innovation Management* (pp. 77–79). Wiley.

de Castro, G. M., Sáez, P. L., & López, J. E. N. (2004). The role of corporate reputation in developing relational capital. *Journal of Intellectual Capital*.

de la Fuente, G., Ortiz, M., & Velasco, P. (2022). The value of a firm's engagement in ESG practices: Are we looking at the right side? *Long Range Planning, 55*(4), 102143. doi:10.1016/j.lrp.2021.102143

De Leaniz, P. M. G., & del Bosque, I. R. (2013). Intellectual capital and relational capital: The role of sustainability in developing corporate reputation. *Intangible Capital*, *9*(1), 262–280.

De Vos, A., Cumming, G. S., Moore, C. A., Maciejewski, K., & Duckworth, G. (2016). The relevance of spatial variation in ecotourism attributes for the economic sustainability of protected areas. *Ecosphere*, *7*(2), e01207. doi:10.1002/ecs2.1207

Deepika, R., & Karpagam, V. (2016). A study on green HRM practices in an organisation. *International Journal of Applied Research*, *2*(8), 426–429.

DeFillipi, R. (2002). Organization Models for Collaboration in the New Economy. *Human Resource Planning*, *25*(4), 7–19.

Degli Antoni, G., & Sacconi, L. (2011a). *Social Capital, Corporate Responsibility, Economic Behaviour and Performance*. Palgrave MacMillan.

Degli Antoni, G., & Sacconi, L. (2011b). Modeling Cognitive Social Capital and Corporate Social Responsibility as Preconditions for Sustainable Networks of Relations. In L. Sacconi & G. Degli Antoni (Eds.), *Social Capital, Corporate Responsibility, Economic Behaviour and Performance*. Palgrave MacMillan. doi:10.1057/9780230306189_8

Del Giudice, M., Di Vaio, A., Hassan, R., & Palladino, R. (2022). Digitalization and new technologies for sustainable business models at the ship–port interface: A bibliometric analysis. *Maritime Policy & Management*, *49*(3), 410–446. doi:10.1080/03088839.2021.1903600

Delgado-Verde, M., Amores-Salvadó, J., Martín-de Castro, G., & Navas-López, J. (2014). Green intellectual capital and environmental product innovation: The mediating role of green social capital. *Knowledge Management Research and Practice*, *12*(3), 261–275. doi:10.1057/kmrp.2014.1

Demartini, M. C., & Beretta, V. (2020). Intellectual capital and SMEs' performance: A structured literature review. *Journal of Small Business Management*, *58*(2), 288–332. doi:10.1080/00472778.2019.1659680

Di Giuli, A., & Kostovetsky, L. (2014). Are Red or Blue Companies More Likely to Go Green? Politics and Corporate Social Responsibility. *Journal of Financial Economics*, *111*(1), 158–180. doi:10.1016/j.jfineco.2013.10.002

Diallo, M. F., Ben Dahmane Mouelhi, N., Gadekar, M., & Schill, M. (2021). CSR actions, brand value, and willingness to pay a premium price for luxury brands: Does long-term orientation matter? *Journal of Business Ethics*, *169*(2), 241–260. doi:10.100710551-020-04486-5

Diekmann, A. (2004). The Power of Reciprocity: Fairness, Reciprocity, and Stakes in Variants of the Dictator Game. *The Journal of Conflict Resolution*, *48*(4), 487–505. doi:10.1177/0022002704265948

Dierickx, I., & Cool, K. (1989). Asset stock accumulation and sustainability of competitive advantage. *Management Science*, *35*(12), 1504–1511. doi:10.1287/mnsc.35.12.1504

DiMaggio, P., & Powell, W. W. (1983). The iron cage revisited: Collective rationality and institutional isomorphism in organizational fields. *American Sociological Review*, *48*(2), 147–160. doi:10.2307/2095101

Dingwall, R., & Strong, P. M. (1985). The Interactional Study of Organizations: A Critique and Reformulation. *Urban Life*, *14*(2), 205–231. doi:10.1177/089124168501400204

Dombin, A.N. (2012). Role of Corporate Governance in Attracting Foreign Investments in Nigeria. *Journal of Educational and Social Research*, *19*. doi:. v3n9p35. doi:10.5901/jesr.2013

Donaldson, L. (1995). *American Anti-Management Theories of Organization: A Critique of Paradigm Proliferation*. Cambridge University Press.

Dosi, G., Freeman, C., Nelson, R., Silverberg, G., & Soete, L. (1988). *Technical Change and Economic Theory* (G. Dosi, C. Freeman, R. Nelson, G. Silverberg, & L. Soete, Eds.). Pinter.

Dove, S. E. (2018). The EU General Data Protection Regulation: Implications for International Scientific Research in the Digital Era. *The Journal of Law, Medicine & Ethics*, *46*(4), 1013–1030. doi:10.1177/1073110518822003

Doyle, S. A., Moore, C. M., & Morgan, L. (2006). Supplier management in fast moving fashion retailing. *Journal of Fashion Marketing and Management*, *10*(3), 272–281. doi:10.1108/13612020610679268

Dreher, A., & Gassebner, M. (2011). *Greasing the Wheels? The Impact of Regulations and Corruption on Firm Entry*. http://corruptionresearchnetwork.org/resources/articl es/greasing-the-wheels-the-impact-of-regulations

Drucker, P. F. (1981). What is business ethic? *The Public Interest*, (63), 18.

Drucker, P. F. (1999). *Innovation and Entrepreneurship: Practice and Principles*. Butterworth–Heinemann.

Ducruet, C., & Lugo, I. (2013). Cities and transport networks in shipping and logistics research. *The Asian Journal of Shipping and Logistics*, *29*(2), 145–166. doi:10.1016/j.ajsl.2013.08.002

Dumay, J. (2016). A critical reflection on the future of intellectual capital: From reporting to disclosure. *Journal of Intellectual Capital*, *17*(1), 168–184. doi:10.1108/JIC-08-2015-0072

Dumay, J., & Garanina, T. (2013). Intellectual capital research: A critical examination of the third stage. *Journal of Intellectual Capital*, *14*(1), 10–25. doi:10.1108/14691931311288995

Dumay, J., Guthrie, J., & Puntillo, P. (2015). IC and public sector: A structured literaturereview. *Journal of Intellectual Capital*, *16*(2), 267–284. doi:10.1108/JIC-02-2015-0014

Dumay, J., Rooney, J., & Marini, L. (2013). An intellectual capital-based differentiation theory of innovation practice. *Journal of Intellectual Capital*, *14*(4), 608–633. doi:10.1108/JIC-02-2013-0024

Dumont, J., Shen, J., & Deng, X. (2016). Effects of green HRM practices on employee workplace green behavior: The role of psychological green climate and employee green values. *Human Resource Management*, *56*(4), 613–627. doi:10.1002/hrm.21792

Dzandza, E. P. (2020). Digitizing the intellectual output of Ghanaian universities. *Collection and Curation*, *39*(3), 69–75. doi:10.1108/CC-05-2019-0012

Earp, B. J., & Payton, C. F. (2001) Data Protection in the University Setting: Employee Perceptions of Student Privacy. *Proceedings of the 34th Hawaii International Conference on System Sciences*. 10.1109/HICSS.2001.927152

Eccles, R. G., Kastrapeli, M. D., & Potter, S. J. (2017). How to Integrate ESG into Investment Decision-Making: Results of a Global Survey of Institutional Investors. *Journal of Applied Corporate Finance*, *29*(4), 125–133. doi:10.1111/jacf.12267

Edmans, A., & Gabaix, X. (2016). Executive Compensation: A Modern Primer. *Journal of Economic Literature*, *54*(4), 1232–1287. doi:10.1257/jel.20161153

Edvinsson, L., & Malone, M. S. (1997). *Intellectual capital: Realizing your company's true value by finding its hidden brainpower*. harperbusiness.

Edvinsson, L. (1997). Developing intellectual capital at Skandia. *Long Range Planning*, *30*(3), 366–373. doi:10.1016/S0024-6301(97)90248-X

Edvinsson, L., & Malone, M. (1997). *Realising your Company's True Value by Finding its Hidden Brainpower*. Harper Collins.

Edvinsson, L., & Malone, M. (1999). El capital intelectual [Intellectual Capital]. *Gestion.*

Edvinsson, L., & Malone, M. (1999). El capital intellectual [Intellectual capital]. *Gestion.*

Edvinsson, L., & Malone, M. S. (1997). *Intellectual Capital.* HarperBusiness.

Edvinsson, L., & Malone, M. S. (1997). *Intellectual Capital: Realizing Your Company\'s TrueValue by Finding Its Hidden Brainpower.* Harper Collins.

Eiesland, N., & Warner, R. S. (1998). Ecology: Seeing the congregation in Contest. In N. Ammerman, J. Carroll, C. Dudley, & W. McKinney (Eds.), *Studying congregations: A new handbook* (pp. 40–77). Abingdon Press.

Eilstrup-Sangiovanni, M. (2020). Death of international organizations. The organizational ecology of intergovernmental organizations, 1815–2015. *The Review of International Organizations, 15*(2), 339–370. doi:10.100711558-018-9340-5

Eliwa, Y., Aboud, A., & Saleh, A. (2021). ESG practices and the cost of debt: Evidence from EU countries. *Critical Perspectives on Accounting, 79,* 102097. doi:10.1016/j.cpa.2019.102097

Elkington, J. (1994). Towards the sustainable corporation: Win-win-win business strategies for sustainable development. *Cal. Manag. Rev., 36*(3), 90-100.

Elkington, J. (1994). Towards the Sustainable Corporation: Win-Win-Win Business Strategies for Sustainable Development. *California Management Review, 36*(2), 90–100. doi:10.2307/41165746

Ellen, S. P., Webb, J. D., & Mohr, A. (2006). Building Corporate Associations:Consumer Attributions for CSR Programs. *Journal of the Academy of Marketing Science, 34,* 147–157. doi:10.1177/0092070305284976

Elsetouhi, A., Elbeltagi, I. and Haddoud, M.Y. (2015). Intellectual Capital And Innovations: IsOrganisational Capital A Missing Link In The Service Sector? *International Journal of Innovation Management, 19*(2), 1-29.

EPA (Environmental Protection Act). (2007). *Environmental Protection Act 1990, Chapter 43.* Retrieved January 25, 2022, from https://www.legislation.gov.uk/ukpga/1990/43/introduction

Erinos, N., & Yurniwati, Y. (2018). Green intellectual capital and financial performance of manufacturing companies in Indonesia. In *First Padang International Conference On Economics Education, Economics, Business and Management, Accounting and Entrepreneurship* (pp. 613-618). Atlantis Press.

Esmer, S., & Karataş Çetin, Ç. (2013). Liman İşletme Yönetimi. *Denizcilik İşletmeleri Yönetimi.*

Esmer, S. (2019). *Liman ve Terminal Yönetimi* [Port and Terminal Management]. Anadolu Üniversitesi Açıköğretim Fakültesi Yayını.

ESPO. (2021). Environmental Report. Retrieved September 15, 2022, from https://www.espo.be/media/ESP-2844%20(Sustainability%20Report%202021)_WEB.pdf

Esser, I.M and Delport, P.A (2018). The South African King IV Report on Corporate Governance: Is the crown shiny enough? *Company lawyer, 39*(11), 378 – 384.

Euroforum. (1998). *Medición del Capital Intelectual. Modelo Intelect* [Intellectual Capital Measurement. Intelect Model]. Euroforum. Available at: http://gestiondelconocimiento.com/modelo_modelo_intelec.htm

Eweje, G. (2014). *Introduction: trends in corporate social responsibility and sustainability in emerging economies.* Emerald Group Publishing Limited.

Ezigbo, C. A. (2013). Assessing Enforcement of Ethical Principles in the Work Place. *International Journal of Business and Social Science, 3*(22).

Fan, I. Y., & Lee, R. W. (2012). Design of a weighted and informed NK model for intellectualcapital-based innovation planning. *Expert Systems with Applications*, *39*(10), 9222–9229. doi:10.1016/j.eswa.2012.02.083

Farooq, O., Aguenaou, S., & Amor, M. A. (2015). Corporate social responsibility policy and brand value. *Journal of Applied Business Research*, *31*(6), 2013–2024. doi:10.19030/jabr.v31i6.9463

Ferenhof, H. A., Durst, S., Zaniboni Bialecki, M., & Selig, P. M. (2015). Intellectual capitaldimensions: State of the art in 2014. *Journal of Intellectual Capital*, *16*(1), 58–100. doi:10.1108/JIC-02-2014-0021

Ferguson, C. S. (2019). Assessing the King IV Corporate Governance Report in relation to business continuity and resilience. *Journal of Business Continuity & Emergency Planning*, *13*(2), 1–13. PMID:31779744

Fernandes, A. A. R., & Solimun. (2017). The mediating effect of strategic orientation and innovations on the effect of environmental uncertainties on the performance of business in the Indonesian aviation industry. *International Journal of Law and Management*, *59*(6), 1269–1278. doi:10.1108/IJLMA-10-2016-0087

Ferrari, R. (2015). Writing narrative style literature reviews. *Medical Writing*, *24*(4), 230–235. doi:10.1179/2047480615Z.000000000329

Ferrell, O. C. (2016). A framework for understanding organizational ethics. In *Business ethics: New challenges for business schools and corporate leaders* (pp. 15–29). Routledge.

Fialkiewicz, W., Burszta-Adamiak, E., Kolonko-Wiercik, A., Manzardo, A., Loss, A., Mikovits, C., & Scipioni, A. (2018). Simplified direct water footprint model to support urban water management. *Water (Basel)*, *10*(5), 630. doi:10.3390/w10050630

Fidanbas, O., & Irdan, G. (2019). The impact of intellectual capital on innovation: A literature study. *Business Management Dynamics*, *8*(12), 1.

Field, J. (2003). *Social Capital*. Routledge.

Filz, J., Blomme, R. J., & Van Rheede, A. (2016). The marketing value of CSR initiatives and potential brand equity, taste perception, and emotional value. *Advances in Hospitality and Leisure*. doi:10.1108/S1745-354220160000012006

Firer, S., & Williams, S. M. (2003). Intellectual capital and traditional measures of corporate performance. *Journal of Intellectual Capital*, *4*(3), 348–360. doi:10.1108/14691930310487806

Firmansyah, A. (2017). Pengaruh green intellectual capital dan manajemen lingkungan organisasi terhadap green organizational identity dan dampaknya terhadap green competitive advantage. *Substansi: Sumber Artikel Akuntansi Auditing dan Keuangan Vokasi, 1*(1), 183-219.

Fisher, I. (1906). *The nature of capital and income*. Macmillan and Cie. doi:10.1515/9783112351369

Fjeldstad, 0. H., & Tungodden, B. (2001). *Fiscal Corruption: A Vice or a Virtue?* (CMI Working Papers WP 2001:13).

Fong, C. M., & Chang, N. J. (2012). The impact of green learning orientation on proactive environmental innovation capability and firm performance. *African Journal of Business Management*, *6*(32), 727–735.

Forschungsanstalt Landschaftsentwicklung Landschaftsbau. (2002). *Dachbegrünungsrichtlinie. Richtlinien für die Planung, Ausführung und Pflege von Dachbegrünungen* [Green roof policy. Guidelines for the planning, execution, and maintenance of green roofs]. Bonn: Forschungsanstalt Landschaftsentwicklung Landschaftsbau.

Foss, N. J. (2003). Selective intervention and internal hybrids: Interpreting and learning from the rise and decline of the Oticon spaghetti organization. *Organization Science*, *14*(3), 331–349. doi:10.1287/orsc.14.3.331.15166

Franks, C. P. (2015). New Technologies, New Challenges: Records Retention and Disposition in a Cloud Environment. *Canadian Journal of Information and Library Science, 39*(2), 192–209. doi:10.1353/ils.2015.0011

Freeman, C., & Soete, L. (1997). *The Economics of Industrial Innovation*. Pinter.

Freeman, J., Carrol, G. R., & Hannan, M. T. (1983). The Liability ofNewness: Age Dependence in Organizational Death Rates. *American Sociological Review, 48*(5), 692–710. doi:10.2307/2094928

Fuest, C., Maffini, G., & Riedel, N. (2010). *How Does Corruption in Developing Countries Affect Investment and Tax Compliance?* https://editorialexpress.bin/conference/?

Fuglsang, L., & Sundbo. (2005). The organizational innovation system: Three modes Journal of Change Management Reframing. *Leadership and Organizational Practice, 5*(3), 329-344.

Fuglsang, L., & Sundbo, J. (2005). The organizational innovation system: Three modes. *Journal of Change Management, 5*(3), 329–344. doi:10.1080/14697010500258056

Fung, K. L. (2018). *Expanding the green network on rooftops: A study of integrating green roofs as a part of urban green innovation space planning* (Order No. 10932095). Available from ProQuest One Academic. (2124999351). Retrieved from http://wdg.biblio.udg.mx:2048/login?url=https://www.proquest.com/dissertations-theses/expanding-green-network-on-rooftops-study/docview/2124999351/se-2?accountid=28915 https://www.proquest.com/docview/2124999351?pqor igsite=gscholar&fromopenview=true

Galbraith, J. (1969). The Consequences of Technology. *Journal of Accountancy, 127*, 44–56.

Galbraith, J. K. (2007). *The new industrial state* (Vol. 9). Princeton University Press. doi:10.1515/9781400873180

Galbreath, J., & Rogers, T. (1999). Customer relationship leadership: A leadership and motivation model for the twenty-first century business. *The TQM Magazine, 11*(3), 161–171. doi:10.1108/09544789910262734

Galdeano-Gómez, E., Céspedes-Lorente, J., & Martínez-del-Río, J. (2008). Environmental performance and spillover effects on productivity: Evidence from horticultural firms. *Journal of Environmental Management, 88*(4), 1552–1561. doi:10.1016/j.jenvman.2007.07.028 PMID:17825476

Galison, P. (1996). Introduction: The Context of Disunity. In P. Galison & D. J. Stump (Eds.), *The Disunity of Science: Boundaries, Contexts, and Power* (pp. 1–33). Stanford University Press.

Gallego, C., Mejía, G. M., & Calderón, G. (2020). Strategic design: Origins and contributions to intellectual capital in organizations. *Journal of Intellectual Capital, 21*(6), 873–891. doi:10.1108/JIC-10-2019-0234

Galunic, D. C., & Eisenhardt, K. M. (2001). Architectural Innovation and Modular Corporate Forms. *Academy of Management Journal, 44*(6), 1229–1249. doi:10.2307/3069398

Gani, A. (2007). *Governance and Foreign Direct Investment Links: Evidence from Panel Data Estimations.* http://ideas.repec.org/a/taf/apeclt/v14y2007i10p753- 756.html

Gannett, L. (2003). Making populations: Bounding genes in space and time. *Philosophy of Science, 70*(5), 989–1001. doi:10.1086/377383

Garanina, T., Hussinki, H., & Dumay, J. (2021). Accounting for intangibles and intellectual capital: A literature review from 2000 to 2020. *Accounting and Finance, 61*(4), 5111–5140. doi:10.1111/acfi.12751

García-Meca, E., & Martínez, I. (2005). Assessing the quality of disclosure on intangibles in the Spanish capital market. *European Business Review, 17*(4), 305–313. doi:10.1108/09555340510607352

Garcia-Perez, A., Ghio, A., Occhipinti, Z., & Verona, R. (2020). Knowledge management and intellectual capital in knowledge-based organisations: A review and theoretical perspectives. *Journal of Knowledge Management*, *24*(7), 1719–1754. doi:10.1108/JKM-12-2019-0703

Gcaza, N., & Solms, V. R. (2017). A strategy for a Cybersecurity Culture: A South African Perspective. *The Electronic Journal of Information Systems in Developing Countries. EJISDC*, *80*(6), 1–17.

Geraie, M. S., & Rad, F. M. (2015). Mediator role of the organizational identity green in relationship between total quality management and perceived innovation with sustainable competitive advantage. *International Journal of Biology, Pharmacy and Allied Sciences*, *2015*(4), 266–276.

Gerpott, F. H., van Quaquebeke, N., Schlamp, S., & Voelpel, S. C. (2019). An Identity Perspective on Ethical Leadership to Explain Organizational Citizenship Behavior: The Interplay of Follower Moral Identity and Leader Group Prototypicality. *Journal of Business Ethics*, *156*(4), 1063–1078. doi:10.100710551-017-3625-0

Gerson, M. P. R. (1998). *The impact of fiscal policy variables on output growth*. Google Books.

Getz, G., & Andersson, T. (2016). Analyzing whole populations of festivals and events: An application of organizational ecology. *Journal of Policy Research in Tourism, Leisure & Events*, *8*(3), 249–273. doi:10.1080/19407963.2016.1158522

Ghanem, F. (n.d.). *The Potential Role Of Green Hrm Practices As An Aspect Of Environmental Concerns That Fall Under The Umbrella Of Sustainability And Corporate Social Responsibility*. Academic Press.

Gieryn, T. F. (1999). *Cultural Boundaries of Science: Credibility on the Line*. University of Chicago Press.

Giménez, F., Ciurana, J., Borras, F., & Pastor, D. (2013). Efficiency analysis of the designations of origin in the Spanish wine sector. *Spanish Journal of Agricultural Research*, *2*, 294–304.

Giuliani, M., Chiucchi, M. S., & Marasca, S. (2016). A history of intellectual capital measurements: From production to consumption. *Journal of Intellectual Capital*, *17*(3), 590–606. doi:10.1108/JIC-08-2015-0071

Glynn, M. A. (1996). Innovative Genius: A Framework for Relating Individual and Organizational Intelligence to Innovation. *Academy of Management Review*, *21*(4), 1081–1111. doi:10.2307/259165

Godrejcp.com. (2022). *Godrej | Consumer Products - Let's make Goodness*. Available at: https://godrejcp.com/

Gómez Cumpa, J. (2003). *Dossier del curso Sociología de la organización1* [Dossier of the Sociology of Organization course 1]. Escuela Profesional de Sociología Facultad de Ciencias Histórico-Sociales y Educación.

Goulden, M., Mason, M. A., & Frasch, K. (2011). Keeping women in the science pipeline. *The Annals of the American Academy of Political and Social Science*, *638*(1), 141–162. doi:10.1177/0002716211416925

Granovetter, M. (1985), Economic action and social structure: the problem of embeddedness. *American Journal of Sociology*, *91*(3), 481–510.

Grant, R. M. (1991). The resource-based theory of competitive advantage: Implications for strategy formulation. *California Management Review*, *33*(3), 114–135. doi:10.2307/41166664

Grant, R. M. (1996). Prospering in dynamically-competitive environments: Organizational capability as knowledge integration. *Organization Science*, *7*(4), 375–387. doi:10.1287/orsc.7.4.375

Graycar, A. (2015). Corruption: Classification and Analysis'. *Policy and Society*, *34*(2), 87–96. doi:10.1016/j.polsoc.2015.04.001

Green Berlin. (2020). *Capital of Green Trends: How Berlin leads the Way in Urban Sustainability*. Available online: https://about. visitberlin.de/en/greenberlin

Greene, J. C., Caracelli, V. J., & Graham, W. F. (1989). Toward a conceptual framework for mixed-method evaluation designs. *Educational Evaluation and Policy Analysis*, *11*(3), 255–274. doi:10.3102/01623737011003255

Gremler, D. D., & Gwinner, K. P. (2000). Customer-Employee Rapport in Service Relationships. *Journal of Service Research*, *3*(1), 82–104. doi:10.1177/109467050031006

Grigoropoulosi, J. E. (2019). The Role of Ethics in 21st Century Organizations. *International Journal of Progressive Education*, *15*(2), 167–175. doi:10.29329/ijpe.2019.189.12

Gross-Gołacka, E., Kusterka-Jefmańska, M., & Jefmański, B. (2020). Can elements of intellectual capital improve business sustainability?—The perspective of managers of smes in Poland. *Sustainability*, *12*(4), 1545. doi:10.3390u12041545

Guerci, M., & Carollo, L. (2016). A paradox view on green human resource management: Insights from the Italian context. *International Journal of Human Resource Management*, *27*(2), 212–238. doi:10.1080/09585192.2015.1033641

Guerci, M., Longoni, A., & Luzzini, D. (2016). Translating stakeholder pressures into environmental performance – the mediating role of green HRM practices. *International Journal of Human Resource Management*, *27*(2), 262–289. doi: 10.1080/09585192.2015.1065431

Guerci, M., Montanari, F., Scapolan, A., & Epifanio, A. (2016). Green and nongreen recruitment practices for attracting job applicants: Exploring independent and interactive effects. *International Journal of Human Resource Management*, *27*(2), 129–150. doi:10.1080/09585192.2015.1062040

Gunn, A., & Mintrom, M. (2016). Higher Education Policy Change in Europe: Academic Research Funding and the Impact Agenda. *European Education*, *48*(4), 241–257. doi:10.1080/10564934.2016.1237703

Guo, R., & Yuan, Y. (2020). Different Types of Environmental Regulations and Heterogeneous Influence on Energy Efficiency in the Industrial Sector: Evidence from Chinese Provincial Data. *Energy Policy, 145*, 111747. doi:10. 1016/j.enpol.2020.111747

Guo, Y., Wang, X., & Wang, C. (2022). Impact of privacy policy content on perceived effectiveness of privacy policy: The role of vulnerability, benevolence and privacy concern. *Journal of Enterprise Information Management*, *35*(3), 774–795. doi:10.1108/JEIM-12-2020-0481

Gupta, S. A. (2007) Determinants of Tax Revenue Efforts in Developing Countries. Washington, DC: *The International Monetary Fund*. (IMF Working Paper No.07/184).

Gupta, J., & Vegelin, C. (2016). Sustainable development goals and inclusive development. *International Environmental Agreement: Politics, Law and Economics*, *16*(3), 433–448. doi:10.100710784-016-9323-z

Gu, Q., Wang, G. G., & Wang, L. (2013). Social capital and innovation in R&D teams: The mediating roles of psychological safety and learning from mistakes. *R & D Management*, *43*(2), 89–102. doi:10.1111/radm.12002

Guthrie, J., & Dumay, J. (2015). New frontiers in the use of intellectual capital in the public sector. *Journal of Intellectual Capital*, *16*(2), 258–266. doi:10.1108/JIC-02-2015-0017

Guthrie, J., Dumay, J., Ricceri, F., & Nielsen, C. (Eds.). (2017). *The Routledge companion to intellectual capital*. Routledge. doi:10.4324/9781315393100

Guzmán, F., & Davis, D. (2017). The impact of corporate social responsibility on brand equity: Consumer responses to two types of fit. *Journal of Product and Brand Management*, *26*(5), 435–446. doi:10.1108/JPBM-06-2015-0917

Gyimah-Brempong, K. (2001). *Corruption, Economic Growth and Income Inequality in Africa.* https://link.springer.com/article/10.1007/s101010200

Hacker, K. (2022). Top 100 companies in India for CSR and Sustainability in 2021. *The CSR Journal.* Available at: https://thecsrjournal.in/top-100-companies-india-csr-sustainability-2021/

Hadavi, S. (2017). Direct and indirect effects of the physical aspects of the environment on mental well-being. *Environment and Behavior, 2017*(49), 1071–1104. doi:10.1177/0013916516679876

Hage, J. T. (2022). Organizational innovation and organizational change. *Annual Review of Sociology, 25*(1), 597-622.

Ha, H., & Janda, S. (2012). Predicting consumer intentions to purchase energy-efficient products. *Journal of Consumer Marketing, 29*(7), 461–469. doi:10.1108/07363761211274974

Hall, B. H., Jaffe, A., & Trajtenberg, M. (2005). Market Value and Patent Citations. *The RAND Journal of Economics, 36*, 16–38.

Hall, R. (1992, February). The Strategic Analysis of Intangible Resources. *Strategic Management Journal, 13*(2), 135–144. doi:10.1002mj.4250130205

Ham, S., & Han, H. (2013). Role of Perceived Fit With Hotels' Green Practices in the Formation of Customer Loyalty: Impact of Environmental Concerns. *Asia Pacific Journal of Tourism Research, 18*(7), 731–748. doi:10.1080/10941665.2012.695291

Handelman, J. M., & Arnold, S. J. (1999). The Role of Marketing Actions with a Social Dimension: Appeals to the Institutional Environment. *Journal of Marketing, 63*(3), 33–48. doi:10.1177/002224299906300303

Hannan, M. T. & Freman, J. (1991). Organizations and social structure. In *Organizational Ecology*. Harvard U. Press.

Hannan, M. T. (2005). Ecologies of organizations: Diversity and identity. *The Journal of Economic Perspectives, 19*(1), 51–70. doi:10.1257/0895330053147985

Hannan, M. T., Carroll, G. R., Dundon, E. A., & Torres, J. C. (1995). Organizational evolution in a multinational context: Entries of automobile manufacturers in Belgium, Britain, France, Germany, and Italy. *American Sociological Review, 60*(4), 509–528. doi:10.2307/2096291

Hannan, M. T., & Freeman, J. (1977). The population ecology of organizations. *American Journal of Sociology, 82*(5), 929–964. doi:10.1086/226424

Hannan, M. T., & Freeman, J. (1978). Internal politics of growth and decline. In M. Meyer (Ed.), *Environments and organizations*. Jossey-Bass.

Hannan, M. T., & Freeman, J. (1984). Structural inertia and organizational change. *American Sociological Review, 49*(2), 149–164. doi:10.2307/2095567

Hannan, M. T., & Freeman, J. (1989). Organizations and social structure. In Organizational Ecology. Harvard U. Press.

Hannan, M. T., Pólos, L., & Carroll, G. R. (2004). The evolution of inertia. *Industrial and Corporate Change, 13*(1), 213–242. doi:10.1093/icc/13.1.213

Hannan, M. T., Pólos, L., & Carroll, G. R. (2007). *Logics of organization theory: Audiences, codes, and ecologies.* Princeton University Press.

Hannan, M., & Freeman, J. (1993). *Organizational Ecology*. Harvard University Press.

Hansen, M. T., Nohria, N., & Tierney, T. (1999). What's your strategy for managing knowledge? Response. *Harvard Business Review*, *77*(3), 196–196.

Harrison, J. R. (2004, February). Models of growth in organizational ecology: A simulation assessment. *Industrial and Corporate Change*, *13*(1), 243–261. doi:10.1093/icc/13.1.243

Harrison, S., & Sullivan, P. Sr. (2000). Profiting from intellectual capital - learning from leading companies. *Journal of Intellectual Capital*, *1*(1), 33–46. doi:10.1108/14691930010324124

Hassan, L., Shaw, D., Shiu, E., Walsh, G., & Parry, S. (2013). Uncertainty in ethical consumer choice: A conceptual model. *Journal of Consumer Behaviour*, *12*(3), 182–193. doi:10.1002/cb.1409

Häubl, G., & Trifts, V. (2000). Consumer Decision Making in Online Shopping Environments: The Effects of Interactive Decision Aids. *Marketing Science*, *19*(1), 4–21. doi:10.1287/mksc.19.1.4.15178

Hawley, A. (1950). *Human ecology*. Roland.

Hedlund, G. (1994). A Model of Knowledge Management and the N-Form Corporation. *Strategic Management Journal*, *15*(S2), 73–90. doi:10.1002mj.4250151006

Heisig, P., Vorbeck, J., & Niebubr, J. (2001). *Intellectual capital. Knowledge Management - Best Practices in Europe*. Springer.

Hemphill, T. (2013). The ISO 26000 guidance on social responsibility international standard: What are the business governance implications? *Corporate Governance: The International Journal of Business in Society*, *13*(3), 305–317. doi:10.1108/CG-08-2011-0062

Henriksson, R., Livnat, J., Pfeifer, P., & Stumpp, M. (2019). Integrating ESG in Portfolio Construction. *Journal of Portfolio Management*, *45*(4), 67–81. doi:10.3905/jpm.2019.45.4.067

Hermanson, R. H. (1963). *A Method for recording all Assets and the Resulting Accounting and Economic Implications*. Michigan State University.

Hodge, T. (1997). Toward a conceptual framework for assessing progress toward sustainability. *Social Indicators Research*, *1997*(40), 5–98. doi:10.1023/A:1006847209030

Hogdson, G. M. (2001). Is Social Evolution Lamarckian or Darwinian? In J. Laurent & J. Nightingale (Eds.), *Darwinism and Evolutionary Economics* (pp. 87–118). Edward Elgar.

Hölzl, W. (2005). The Evolutionary Theory of The Firm: Routines, Complexity and Changes, Growth and Employment in Europe. Sustainability and Competitiveness, 2-18.

Houston, D. (2007). *Can Corruption Ever Improve an Economy?* http://object.cato.org/sites/cato.org/files/serials/files/cato-journal/2007/11/cj27n3-2.pdf

Howell, S. E., & Laska, S. B. (1992). The Changing Face of the Environmental Coalition. *Environment and Behavior*, *24*(1), 134–144. doi:10.1177/0013916592241006

Hsu, Y., & Fang, W. (2009). Intellectual Capital and New Product Development Performance: The Mediating Role of Organizational Learning Capability. *Technological Forecasting and Social Change*, *76*(5), 664–677. doi:10.1016/j.techfore.2008.03.012

Huang, C., & Kung, F. (2011). Environmental consciousness and intellectual capital management: Evidence from Taiwan's manufacturing industry. *Management Decision*, *49*(9), 1405–1425. doi:10.1108/00251741111173916

Huang, D. Z. X. (2021). Environmental, social and governance (ESG) activity and firm performance: A review and consolidation. *Accounting and Finance*, *61*(1), 335–360. doi:10.1111/acfi.12569

Hussinki, H., Kianto, A., Vanhala, M., & Ritala, P. (2019). Happy employees make happy customers: The role of intellectual capital in supporting sustainable value creation in organizations. In *Intellectual capital management as a driver of sustainability* (pp. 101–117). Springer. doi:10.1007/978-3-319-79051-0_6

IASB. (2004). Intangible Assets, International Accounting Standard. International Accounting Standards Board.

Ibarra, H., & Andrews, S. B. (1993). Power, social influ- ence, and sense making: Effects of network centrality and proximity on employee perceptions. *Administrative Science Quarterly*, *38*(2), 277–303. doi:10.2307/2393414

Ihnatenko, M., & Novak, N. (2018). Development of regional programs for the development of agrarian enterprises with organic production based on the European and international experience. *Baltic Journal of Economic Studies*, *4*(4), 126–133. doi:10.30525/2256-0742/2018-4-4-126-133

ILO. (2015). *News*. https://www.ilo.org/global/topics/green-jobs/news/WCMS_422575/lang--en/index.htm

Imam, P. A., & Jacobs, D. F. (2007). Effect of Corruption on Tax Revenues in the Middle East. *IMF Institute and Fiscal Affairs Department*. (IMF Working Paper No.07 /270).

In, S. Y., Rook, D., & Monk, A. (2019b). Integrating Alternative Data (Also Known as ESG Data) in Investment Decision Making. *Global Economic Review*, *48*(3), 237–260. doi:10.1080/1226508X.2019.1643059

International Integrated Reporting Council (IIRC). (2013). *Consultation draft of the international framework*. Author.

Ipinge, A., & Nengomasha, T. C. (2018). An investigation into the records management profession in the public service of Namibia. Records in Namibian Public Service. *Information and Learning Science*, *119*(7/8), 377–388. doi:10.1108/ILS-11-2017-0123

Iris, Ç., & Lam, J. S. L. (2019). A review of energy efficiency in ports: Operational strategies, technologies and energy management systems. *Renewable and Sustainable Energy Reviews, Elsevier*, *112*(C), 170–182. doi:10.1016/j.rser.2019.04.069

Isa, M. K. M. (2003). *Applying the Triple Bottom Line Approach*. Business Times.

Ishar Ali, M. S., & Siraji, M. (2021). Marketing Stimulus and its Impact on Green Product Purchase Intention of Customer: With the Mediating Role of Customer Attitude. *International Journal on Economics. Finance and Sustainable Development*, *3*(5), 36–46.

ISO. (2015). ISO 14001:2015, Third Edition: Environmental Management Systems - Requirements with Guidance for Use. American National Standards Institute.

Jääskeläinen, A., & Heikkilä, J. (2019). Purchasing and supply management practices in customer value creation. *Supply Chain Management*, *24*(3), 317–333. doi:10.1108/SCM-04-2018-0173

Jabbour, C. J. C., & Renwick, D. W. S. (2018). The soft side of environmentally-sustainable organizations. *RAUSP Management Journal*, *53*(4), 622–627. doi:10.1108/RAUSP-07-2018-0044

Jabbour, C. J. C., Santos, F. C. A., Fonseca, S. A., & Nagano, M. S. (2013). Green teams: Understanding their roles in the environmental management of companies located in Brazil. *Journal of Cleaner Production*, *2013*(46), 58–66. doi:10.1016/j.jclepro.2012.09.018

Jabbour, C., De Sousa Jabbour, A., & Sarkis, J. (2019). Unlocking effective multi-tier supply chain management for sustainability through quantitative modeling: Lessons learned and discoveries to be made. *International Journal of Production Economics*, *217*, 11–30. doi:10.1016/j.ijpe.2018.08.029

Jaeger, K., & Mykletun, R. (2009). The festivalscape of Finnmark. *Scandinavian Journal of Hospitality and Tourism*, *9*(2/3), 327–348. doi:10.1080/15022250903119520

Jaffe, A., Trajtenberg, M., & Henderson, R. (1993). Geographic localization of knowledge spillovers, as evidenced by patent citations. *The Quarterly Journal of Economics*, *108*(3), 577–598. doi:10.2307/2118401

Jain, S. K., & Kaur, G. (2004). Green marketing: An Indian perspective. *Decision*, *31*(2), 161–209.

Jamal, T., Zahid, M., Martins, J. M., Mata, M. N., Rahman, H. U., & Mata, P. N. (2021). Perceived green human resource management practices and corporate sustainability: Multigroup Analysis and major industries perspectives. *Sustainability*, *13*(6), 3045. doi:10.3390u13063045

Jam, M., & Jamal, W. N. (2020). Impact of Green Human Resources Management Practices on Organizational Sustainability and Employee Retention: An Empirical Study Related to Educational Institutions. iRASD. *Journal of Management*, *2*(1), 38–48.

Jardon, C., & Dasilva, A. (2017). Intellectual capital and environmental concern in subsistence small businesses. *Management of Environmental Quality*, *28*(2), 214–230. doi:10.1108/MEQ-05-2015-0085

Jardon, C., & Martos, M. (2012). Intellectual capital as competitive advantage in emerging clusters in Latin America. *Journal of Intellectual Capital*, *13*(4), 462–481. doi:10.1108/14691931211276098

Jiang, Z., Wang, Z., & Lan, X. (2021). How Environmental Regulations Affect Corporate Innovation? The Coupling Mechanism of Mandatory Rules and Voluntary Management. *Technol. Soc., 65*, 101575. Doi: .2021.101575 doi:10.1016/j. techsoc

Johnson, S. K. (2017). What 11 CEOs have learned about championing diversity. *Harvard Business Review.*

Johnson, S. K. (2019). *Leaking Talent How People of Color are Pushed Out of Environmental Organizations.* www. diversegreen.org https://diversegreen.org/research/leaking-talent/

Johnson, W. H. (1999). An integrative taxonomy of intellectual capital: Measuring the stock and flow of intellectual capital components in the firm. *International Journal of Technology Management*, *18*(5), 562–575. doi:10.1504/IJTM.1999.002788

Jones, R. J. III, Reilly, T. M., Cox, M. Z., & Cole, B. M. (2017). Gender Makes a Difference: Investigating Consumer Purchasing Behavior and Attitudes Toward Corporate Social Responsibility Policies. *Corporate Social Responsibility and Environmental Management*, *24*(2), 133–144. doi:10.1002/csr.1401

Joshi, M., Cahill, D., Sidhu, J., & Kansal, M. (2013). Intellectual capital and financial performance: An evaluation of the Australian financial sector. *Journal of Intellectual Capital*, *14*(2), 264–285. doi:10.1108/14691931311323887

Ju, K., Zhou, D., Wang, Q., Zhou, D., & Wei, X. (2020). What Comes after Picking Pollution Intensive Low-Hanging Fruits? Transfer Direction of Environmental Regulation in China. *J. Clean. Prod., 258*, 120405. doi:10.1016/j.jclepro.2020.120405

Jyoti, K. (2019). Green HRM–People management commitment to environmental sustainability. *Proceedings of 10th International Conference on Digital Strategies for Organizational Success.*

Kádeková, Z., Savov, R., Košičiarová, I., & Valaskova, K. (2020). CSR activities and their impact on brand value in food enterprises in slovakia based on foreign participation. *Sustainability (Switzerland)*, *12*(12). doi:10.3390/SU12124856

Kalandides, A., & Grésillon, B. (2021). The Ambiguities of "Sustainable" Berlin. *Sustainability*, *2021*(13), 1666. doi:10.3390u13041666

Kam-Sing Wong, S. (2012). The influence of green product competitiveness on the success of green product innovation: Empirical evidence from the Chinese electrical and electronics industry. *European Journal of Innovation Management*, *2012*(15), 468–490. doi:10.1108/14601061211272385

Kanter, R. M. (1983). *The Change Masters: Innovations for Productivity in the American Corporation*. Unwin.

Kaplan, R., & Norton, D. (1997). Cuadro de mando integral [The Balance Scorecard]. *Gestion.*

Kaplan, S. N., & Zingales, L. (1997). Do Investment-cash Flow Sensitivities Provide Useful Measures of Financing Constraints. *The Quarterly Journal of Economics*, *112*(1), 169–215. doi:10.1162/003355397555163

Katunian, A. (2019). Sustainability as a new approach for the human resource development in tourism sector. *Public Policy and Administration*, *18*(4), 405–417. doi:10.13165/VPA-19-18-4-03

Katuu, S. (2016). Managing digital records in a global environment. A review of the landscape of international standards and good practice guidelines. Managing digital records. *The Electronic Library*, *34*(5), 869–894. doi:10.1108/EL-04-2015-0064

Katuu, S., & Ngoepe, M. (2015). Managing digital heritage an analysis of the education and training curriculum for Africa's archives and records professionals. *Archives and Manuscripts*, *43*(2), 96–119. doi:10.1080/01576895.2015.1050677

Kazancoglu, Y., Kazancoglu, I., & Sagnak, M. (2018). A new holistic conceptual framework for green supply chain management performance assessment based on circular economy. *Journal of Cleaner Production*, *195*, 1282–1299. doi:10.1016/j.jclepro.2018.06.015

Khalique, M., Nassir Shaari, J. A., Isa, A. H. B. M., & Ageel, A. (2011). Relationship of intellectual capital with the organizational performance of pharmaceutical companies in Pakistan. *Australian Journal of Basic and Applied Sciences*, *5*(12), 1964–1969.

Khan, I., & Fatma, M. (2019). Connecting the dots between CSR and brand loyalty: The mediating role of brand experience and brand trust. *International Journal of Business Excellence*, *17*(4), 439–455. doi:10.1504/IJBEX.2019.099123

Khan, S., Yang, Q., & Waheed, A. (2019). Investment in intangible resources and capabilities spurs sustainable competitive advantage and firm performance. *Corporate Social Responsibility and Environmental Management*, *26*(2), 285–295. doi:10.1002/csr.1678

Kianto, A., Ritala, P., Spender, J. C., & Vanhala, M. (2014). The interaction of intellectual capital assets and knowledge management practices in organizational value creation. *Journal of Intellectual Capital*, *15*(3), 362–375. doi:10.1108/JIC-05-2014-0059

Kim, Y.J., Kim, W.G., Choi, H., & Phetvaroon, K. (2019). The effect of green human resource management on hotel employees' eco-friendly behavior and environmental performance. *International Journal of Hospitality Management*, *76*(A), 83-93. doi:10.1016/j.ijhm.2018.04.007

Kimberly, J. R. (1975). Environmental constraints and organizational structure: A comparative analysis of rehabilitation organizations. *Administrative Science Quarterly*, *20*(1), 1–9. doi:10.2307/2392119 PMID:10237043

Kim, H. G., Chun, W., & Wang, Z. (2021). Multiple-dimensions of corporate social responsibility and global brand value: A stakeholder theory perspective. *Journal of Marketing Theory and Practice*, *29*(4), 409–422. doi:10.1080/10696679.2020.1865109

Kim, Y., & Han, H. (2010). Intention to pay conventional-hotel prices at a green hotel – a modification of the theory of planned behavior. *Journal of Sustainable Tourism*, *18*(8), 997–1014. doi:10.1080/09669582.2010.490300

King III Report (2009). King code of governance for South Africa 2009, Institute of Directors in Southern Africa. www.ngopulse.org/sites/default/files/king_code_of_governance_for _sa_2009 _updated _june_2012.pdf

Kinnear, T. C., & Taylor, J. R. (1973). The Effect of Ecological Concern on Brand Perceptions. *JMR, Journal of Marketing Research*, *10*(2), 191–197. doi:10.1177/002224377301000210

Koh, H.-K., Burnasheva, R., & Suh, Y. G. (2022). Perceived ESG (Environmental, Social, Governance) and Consumers' Responses: The Mediating Role of Brand Credibility, Brand Image, and Perceived Quality. *Sustainability*, *14*(8), 4515. doi:10.3390u14084515

Kolomiets, T.V., & Tomashuk, I.V. (2021). Entrepreneurship and development of rural areas in Ukraine. *Colloquium-Journal, 9*(96), 29-42.

Koremenos, B., Lipson, C., & Snidal, D. (2001). The rational design of international institutions. *International Organization*, *55*(4), 761–799. doi:10.1162/002081801317193592

Kormondy, E. (1994). *Conceptos de ecología*. Alianza.

Korucuk, S., & Memiş, S. (2019). Prioritizion of Green Port Applications Performance Criteria with Dematel Method: Case of Istanbul Province. *International Journal of Euroasian Research*, *7*(16), 134–148. doi:10.33692/avrasyad.543735

Köseoğlu, M. C., & Solmaz, M. S. (2019). Green Port Approach: A Comparative Assessment Criterion of Turkey and the World Green Port. *4th National Port Congress*. Doi: 10.18872/0.2019.2

Kotler, P. (1983). *Principles of Marketing*. Prentice–Hall.

Kramer, J. P., Marinelli, E., Iammarino, S., & Diez, J. R. (2011). Intangible assets as drivers of innovation: Empirical evidence on multinational enterprises in German and UK regional systems of innovation. *Technovation*, *31*(9), 447–458. doi:10.1016/j.technovation.2011.06.005

Krebs, C. J. (2001). *Ecology: The experimental analysis of distribution and abundance* (5th ed.). Benjamin Cummings.

Kucharčíková, A. (2011). Human capital–definitions and approaches. *Human Resources Management & Ergonomics*, *5*(2), 60–70.

Kucher, A. (2019), *Sustainable soil management in the formation of competitiveness of agricultural enterprises*. Academic Publishing House «Talent». . doi:10.13140/RG.2.2.19554.07366

Kucher, L., Heldak, M., & Orlenko, A. (2018). Project management in organic agricultural production. *Agricultural and Resource Economics*, *4*(3), 104–128. doi:10.22004/ag.econ.281753

Kull, A. J., & Heath, T. B. (2016). You decide, we donate: Strengthening consumer–brand relationships through digitally co-created social responsibility. *International Journal of Research in Marketing*, *33*(1), 78–92. doi:10.1016/j.ijresmar.2015.04.005

Kumar, V., & Christodoulopoulou, A. (2014). Sustainability and branding: An integrated perspective. *Industrial Marketing Management*, *43*(1), 6–15. doi:10.1016/j.indmarman.2013.06.008

Kumar, V., Fantazy, K. A., Kumar, U., & Boyle, T. A. (2006). Implementation and management framework for supply chain flexibility. *Journal of Enterprise Information Management*, *19*(3), 303–319. doi:10.1108/17410390610658487

Kusumawardhani, T. (2012). Intellectual capital, financial profitability, and productivity: An exploratory study of the Indonesian pharmaceutical industry. *Asian Journal of Business and Accounting*, *5*(2).

La Nauze, A., & Mezzetti, C. (2019). Dynamic Incentive Regulation of Diffuse Pollution. *J. Environ. Econ. Manag.*, *93*, 101–124. Doi: .11.009 doi:10.1016/j.jeem.2018

La Torre, M., Botes, L. V., Dumay, J., & Odendaal, E. (2021). Protecting a new Achilles heel: The role of auditors within the practice of data protection. *Managerial Auditing Journal*, *36*(2), 218–239. doi:10.1108/MAJ-03-2018-1836

Lacey, H. (2000). Seeds and the Knowledge They Embody. *Peace Review*, *12*(4), 563–569. doi:10.1080/10402650020014654

Lakshmi & Nagaraju. (2018). A Study on Green HRM - An Emerging Trend in HR Practices. *International Journal of Management*, *9*(3), 74–82.

Lam, A. (2004). *Organizational Innovation. Working Paper No. 1. Brunel Research in Enterprise, Innovation, Sustainability, and Ethics*. BRESE, School of Business and Management Brunel University.

Lam, A. (2000). Tacit Knowledge, Organizational Learning, Societal Institutions: An Integrated Framework. *Organization Studies*, *21*(3), 487–513. doi:10.1177/0170840600213001

Lam, A. (2002). Alternative societal models of learning and innovation in the knowledge economy. *International Social Science Journal*, *17*(1), 67–82. doi:10.1111/1468-2451.00360

Lambsdorff, J. (2003). How Corruption Affects Economic Development. http://www.wiwi.unipassau.de/fileadmin/dokumente/lehrstuehle/lambsdorff/Papers/C_Development.pd

Lane, P. J., Salk, J. E., & Lyles, M. A. (2001). Absorptive capacity, learning, and performance in international joint ventures. *Strategic Management Journal*, *22*(12), 1139–1161. doi:10.1002mj.206

Larwood, L., Falbe, C. M., Kriger, M. P., & Miesing, P. (1995). Structure and meaning of organizational vision. *Academy of Management Journal*, *1995*(38), 740–769. doi:10.2307/256744

Laursen, K., & Salter, A. J. (2006). Open for innovation: The role of openness in explaining innovative performance among UK manufacturing firms. *Strategic Management Journal*, *27*(2), 131–150. doi:10.1002mj.507

Lawrence, P. R., & Lorsch, J. W. (1967). Differentiation and Integration in Complex Organizations. *Administrative Science Quarterly*, *12*, 1–47.

Lazonick, W., & West, J. (1998). Organizational Integration and Competitive Advantage. In *Technology, Organization and Competitiveness*. Oxford University Press. doi:10.1093/0198290969.003.0008

LEE, C., & LIM, S.-Y. (2020). Impact of Environmental Concern on Image of Internal GSCM Practices and Consumer Purchasing Behavior. *The Journal of Asian Finance. Economics and Business*, *7*(6), 241–254. doi:10.13106/jafeb.2020.vol7.no6.241

Lee, K.-H., Lee, M., & Gunarathne, N. (2019). Do green awards and certifications matter? Consumers' perceptions, green behavioral intentions, and economic implications for the hotel industry: A Sri Lankan perspective. *Tourism Economics*, *25*(4), 593–612. doi:10.1177/1354816618810563

Lee, K., & Min, B. (2015). Green R&D for eco-innovation and its impact on carbon emissions and firm performance. *Journal of Cleaner Production*, *108*, 534–542. doi:10.1016/j.jclepro.2015.05.114

Leidner, S., Baden, D., & Ashleigh, M. (2019). Green (environmental) HRM: Aligning ideals with practices. *Personnel Review*, *48*(5), 1169–1185. Advance online publication. doi:10.1108/PR-12-2017-0382

Leliaert, P. J., Candries, W., & Tilmans, R. (2003). Identifying and managing IC: a new classification. *Journal of Intellectual Capital.*

Leonidou, C. N., & Leonidou, L. C. (2011). Research into environmental marketing/management: A bibliographic analysis. *European Journal of Marketing, 45*(1/2), 68–103. doi:10.1108/03090561111095603

Lev, B. (2001). *Intangibles: management. In Measurement, and Reporting.* Brookings Institution Press.

Liao, S. H., Chang, J. C., Cheng, S. C., & Kuo, C. M. (2004). Employee relationship and knowledge sharing: A case study of a Taiwanese finance and securities firm. *Knowledge Management Research and Practice, 2004*(2), 24–34. doi:10.1057/palgrave.kmrp.8500016

Liedtka, J. (1999). Linking competitive advantage with communities of practice. *Journal of Management Inquiry, 8*(1), 5–16. doi:10.1177/105649269981002

Lim, K. S. (2001). Transforming centres of excellence- the National Heritage Board experience. *Library Review, 50*(7/8), 366–373. doi:10.1108/00242530110405364

Lin-Hi, N., & Müller, K. (2013). The CSR bottom line: Preventing corporate social irresponsibility. *Journal of Business Research, 66*(10), 1928–1936. doi:10.1016/j.jbusres.2013.02.015

Lin, Y. H., & Chen, Y. S. (2017). Determinants of green competitive advantage: The roles of green knowledge sharing, green dynamic capabilities, and green service innovation. *Quality & Quantity, 51*(4), 1663–1685. doi:10.100711135-016-0358-6

Li, T., Liang, L., & Han, D. (2018). Research on the efficiency of green technology innovation in China's provincial high-end manufacturing industry based on the RAGA-PP-SFA model. *Mathematical Problems in Engineering, 2018,* 1–13. doi:10.1155/2018/9463707

Liu, D., Jiang, K., Shalley, C. E., Keem, S., & Zhou, J. (2016). Motivational mechanisms of employee creativity: A meta-analytic examination and theoretical extension of the creativity literature. *Organizational Behavior and Human Decision Processes, 2016*(137), 236–263. doi:10.1016/j.obhdp.2016.08.001

Liu, J., Chen, J., & Tao, Y. (2015). Innovation Performance in New Product Development Teams in China's Technology Ventures: The Role of Behavioral Integration Dimensions and Collective Efficacy. *Journal of Product Innovation Management, 2015*(32), 29–44. doi:10.1111/jpim.12177

Li, Y., & Hu, X. (2022). Social network analysis of law information privacy protection of cybersecurity based on rough set theory. Law information privacy protection. *Library Hi Tech, 40*(1), 133–15. doi:10.1108/LHT-11-2018-0166

Llonch, P., Haskell, M. J., Dewhurst, R. J., & Turner, S. P. (2017). Current available strategies to mitigate greenhouse gas emissions in livestock systems: An animal welfare perspective. *Animal, 2017*(11), 274–284. doi:10.1017/S1751731116001440 PMID:27406001

Lomi, A. (1995). The Population Ecology of Organizational Founding: Location Dependence and Unobserved Heterogeneity. *Administrative Science Quarterly, 40*(1), 111–144. doi:10.2307/2393702

Longoni, A., & Cagliano, R. (2018). Inclusive environmental disclosure practices and firm performance. *International Journal of Operations & Production Management, 38*(9), 1815–1835. doi:10.1108/IJOPM-12-2016-0728

Longoni, A., Luzzini, D., & Guerci, M. (2016). Deploying environmental management across functions: The relationship between green human resource management and green supply chain management. *Journal of Business Ethics, 151*(4), 1–15. doi:10.100710551-016-3228-1

López, M., Cabrales, G., & Schmal, R. (2005) Gestion del conocimiento: una revisión teórica y sus asosiación con la universidad. *Panorama Socioeconómico*, (30).

López-Gamero, M. D., Claver-Cortés, E., & Molina-Azorín, J. F. (2008). Complementary resources and capabilities for an ethical and environmental management: A qual/quan study. *Journal of Business Ethics*, *82*(3), 701–732. doi:10.100710551-007-9587-x

López-Gamero, M., Zaragoza-Sáez, P., Claver-Cortés, E., & Molina-Azorín, J. (2011). Sustainable development and intangibles: Building sustainable intellectual capital. *Business Strategy and the Environment*, *20*(1), 18–37. doi:10.1002/bse.666

Lu, C.-S., Shang, K.-C., & Lin, C.-C. (2016). Examining sustainability performance at ports: Port managers' perspectives on developing sustainable supply chains. *Maritime Policy & Management*, *43*(8), 909–927. doi:10.1080/03088839.2016.1199918

Lundvall, B.-A. (Ed.). (1992). *National Systems of Innovation: Towards a Theory of Innovation and Interactive Learning*. Pinter.

Luthra, S., Garg, D., & Haleem, A. (2016). The impacts of critical success factors for implementing green supply chain management towards sustainability: An empirical investigation of Indian automobile industry. *Journal of Cleaner Production*, *121*, 142–158. doi:10.1016/j.jclepro.2016.01.095

Lynn, L. H., Reddy, N. M., & Aram, J. D. (1996). Linking technology and institutions: the innovation community framework, *Research Policy*, *25*(1), 91-106. https://www.sciencedirect.com/science/article/pii/0048733394008175

Maas, C. J., & Hox, J. J. (2005). Sufficient sample sizes for multilevel modeling. *Methodology*, *2005*(1), 86–92. doi:10.1027/1614-2241.1.3.86

MacMeal, H. B. (1934). *The Story of Independent Telephony*. Independent Pioneer Telephone Association.

Maditinos, D., Chatzoudes, D., Tsairidis, C., & Theriou, G. (2011). The impact of intellectual capital on firms' market value and financial performance. *Journal of Intellectual Capital*, *12*(1), 132–151. doi:10.1108/14691931111097944

Mahmood, A., & Bashir, J. (2020). How does corporate social responsibility transform brand reputation into brand equity? Economic and noneconomic perspectives of CSR. *International Journal of Engineering Business Management*, *12*, 1847979020927547. doi:10.1177/1847979020927547

Mainieri, T., Barnett, E. G., Valdero, T. R., Unipan, J. B., & Oskamp, S. (1997). Green Buying: The Influence of Environmental Concern on Consumer Behavior. *The Journal of Social Psychology*, *137*(2), 189–204. doi:10.1080/00224549709595430

Makarov, P. (2010). Intellectual capital as an indicator of a sustainable development. *Journal of Sustainable Development*, *3*(3), 85. doi:10.5539/jsd.v3n3p85

Makri, L. E., Georgiopoulou, Z., & Lambrinoudakis, C. (2020). Utilizing a privacy impact assessment method using metrics in the healthcare sector. *Information & Computer Security*, *28*(4), 503–529. doi:10.1108/ICS-01-2020-0007

Makulilo, B. A. (2012). Privacy and data protection in Africa: A state of the Art. *International Data Privacy Law*, *2*(3), 163–178. doi:10.1093/idpl/ips014

Makwae, N. E. (2021). Legal frameworks for personnel records management in support of accountability in devolved governments: A case of Garissa County Government. *Records Management Journal*, *31*(2), 109–133. doi:10.1108/RMJ-05-2019-0024

Malerba, F. (2003). Sectoral systems and innovation and technology policy. *Revista Brasileira de Inovação, 2*(2), 329–375. doi:10.20396/rbi.v2i2.8648876

Malik, M. (2015). Value-enhancing capabilities of CSR: A brief review of contemporary literature. Journal of usiness. *Ethics, 127*(2), 419–438.

Malik, S. Y., Hayat Mughal, Y., Azam, T., Cao, Y., Wan, Z., Zhu, H., & Thurasamy, R. (2021). Corporate social responsibility, green human resources management, and sustainable performance: Is organizational citizenship behavior towards environment the missing link? *Sustainability, 13*(3), 1044. doi:10.3390u13031044

Maniora, J. (2017). Is Integrated Reporting Really the Superior Mechanism for the Integration of Ethics into the Core Business Model? An Empirical Analysis. *Journal of Business Ethics, 140*(4), 755–786. doi:10.100710551-015-2874-z

Marchi, V. D. (2012). Environmental innovation and R&D cooperation: Empirical evidence from Spanish manufacturing firms. *Research Policy, 41*(3), 614–623. doi:10.1016/j.respol.2011.10.002

Marco-Lajara, B., Zaragoza-Sáez, P. C., Martínez-Falcó, J., & Sánchez-García, E. (2022h). Does green intellectual capital affect green innovation performance? Evidence from the Spanish wine industry. *British Food Journal.*

Marco-Lajara, B., Zaragoza-Saez, P., & Martínez-Falcó, J. (2022e). Green Innovation: Balancing Economic Efficiency With Environmental Protection. In Frameworks for Sustainable Development Goals to Manage Economic, Social, and Environmental Shocks and Disasters (pp. 239-254). IGI Global.

Marco-Lajara, B., Zaragoza-Sáez, P., Falcó, J. M., & Millan-Tudela, L. A. (2022f). Corporate Social Responsibility: A Narrative Literature Review. *Frameworks for Sustainable Development Goals to Manage Economic, Social, and Environmental Shocks and Disasters*, 16-34.

Marco-Lajara, B., Zaragoza-Saez, P., Falcó, J. M., & Sánchez-García, E. (2022b). COVID-19 and Wine Tourism: A Story of Heartbreak. In Handbook of Research on SDGs for Economic Development, Social Development, and Environmental Protection (pp. 90-112). IGI Global.

Marco-Lajara, B., Zaragoza-Sáez, P., Martínez-Falcó, J., & Sánchez-García, E. (2022c). Green Intellectual Capital in the Spanish Wine Industry. In Innovative Economic, Social, and Environmental Practices for Progressing Future Sustainability (pp. 102-120). IGI Global. doi:10.4018/978-1-7998-9590-9.ch006

Marco-Lajara, B., Falcó, J. M., Fernández, L. R., & Larrosa, P. S. (2022k). Evolución del pensamiento en la disciplina de dirección estratégica: la visión de la empresa basada en las capacidades dinámicas y en el conocimiento. [Evolution of thinking in the discipline of strategic management: the vision of the company based on dynamic capabilities and knowledge.] In *Investigación y transferencia de las ciencias sociales frente a un mundo en crisis* (pp. 1801–1826). Dykinson.

Marco-Lajara, B., García, E. S., Larrosa, P. S., & Falcó, J. M. (2022m). Knowledge creation and diffusion inspecialized environments: What are the factors involved? In *Empresa, economía y derecho. Oportunidades ante un entorno global y disruptivo* (pp. 432–459). Dykinson.

Marco-Lajara, B., Sáez, P. D. C. Z., Falcó, J. M., & García, E. S. (2022l). Las rutas del vino de España: el impacto económico derivado de las visitas a bodegas y museos. [Las rutas del vino de España: el impacto económico derivado de las visitas a bodegas y museos] In *Investigación y transferencia de las ciencias sociales frente a un mundo en crisis* (pp. 1774–1800). Dykinson.

Marco-Lajara, B., Sánchez-García, E., Martínez-Falcó, J., & Poveda-Pareja, E. (2022j). Regional Specialization, Competitive Pressure, and Cooperation: The Cocktail for Innovation. *Energies, 15*(15), 5346.

Marco-Lajara, B., Seva-Larrosa, P., Martínez-Falcó, J., & García-Lillo, F. (2022i). Wine clusters and Protected Designations of Origin (PDOs) in Spain: An exploratory analysis. *Journal of Wine Research*, *33*(3), 1–22. doi:10.1080/09571264.2022.2110051

Marco-Lajara, B., Seva-Larrosa, P., Martinez-Falco, J., & Sanchez-Garcia, E. (2021a). How Has COVID- 19 Affected The Spanish Wine Industry? An Exploratory Analysis. *Natural Volatiles & Essential Oils Journal*, *8*(6), 2722–2731.

Marco-Lajara, B., Seva-Larrosa, P., Ruiz-Fernandez, L., & Martinez-Falco, J. (2021b). The Effect of COVID- 19 on the Spanish Wine Industry. In *Impact of Global Issues on International Trade* (pp. 211–232). IGI Global. doi:10.4018/978-1-7998-8314-2.ch012

Marco-Lajara, B., Zaragoza Sáez, P. D. C., & Martínez-Falcó, J. (2022n). Does Green Intellectual Capital Affect Green Performance? The Mediation of Green Innovation. *Telematique*, *21*(1), 4594–4602.

Marco-Lajara, B., Zaragoza-Saez, P., Falcó, J. M., & Millan-Tudela, L. A. (2022a). Analysing the Relationship Between Green Intellectual Capital and the Achievement of the Sustainable Development Goals. In *Handbook of Research on Building Inclusive Global Knowledge Societies for Sustainable Development* (pp. 111–129). IGI Global. doi:10.4018/978-1-6684-5109-0.ch005

Marco-Lajara, B., Zaragoza-Sáez, P., Martínez-Falcó, J., & Millan-Tudela, L. A. (2023). The Export Intensity of Spain's Autonomous Communities in Terms of the Marketing of Wine and Their Geographical Destinations. In *The Transformation of Global Trade in a New World* (pp. 1–21). IGI Global.

Marco-Lajara, B., Zaragoza-Sáez, P., Martínez-Falcó, J., & Ruiz-Fernández, L. (2022g). The Effect of Green Intellectual Capital on Green Performance in the Spanish Wine Industry: A Structural Equation Modeling Approach. *Complexity*, *2022*, 2022. doi:10.1155/2022/6024077

Marco-Lajara, B., Zaragoza-Sáez, P., Martínez-Falcó, J., & Sánchez-García, E. (2022d). El capital intelectual verde como hoja de ruta para la sostenibilidad: El caso de bodegas Luzón. *GeoGraphos: Revista Digital para Estudiantes de Geografía y Ciencias Sociales*, *13*(147), 137–146.

Marco-Lajara, B., Zaragoza-Sáez, P., Martínez-Falcó, J., & Sánchez-García, E. (2023b). The Internationalization of the Spanish Wine Industry: An Analysis of Trade Flows and Their Degree of Concentration. In *The Transformation of Global Trade in a New World* (pp. 22–46). IGI Global.

Marin, L., Ruiz, S., & Rubio, A. (2009). The Role of Identity Salience in the Effects of Corporate Social Responsibility on Consumer Behavior. *Journal of Business Ethics*, *84*(1), 65–78. doi:10.100710551-008-9673-8

Marr, B. (2012). The evolution and convergence of intellectual capital as a theme. In *Perspectives on intellectual capital* (pp. 225–238). Routledge. doi:10.4324/9780080479934-24

Marr, B., & Roos, G. (2012). A strategy perspective on intellectual capital. In *Perspectives on intellectual capital* (pp. 28–41). Routledge.

Martín-de Castro, G., Díez-Vial, I., & Delgado-Verde, M. (2019). Intellectual capital and the firm: Evolution and research trends. *Journal of Intellectual Capital*, *20*(4), 555–580. doi:10.1108/JIC-12-2018-0221

Martínez-Falcó, J., Marco-Lajara, B. M., Zaragoza-Sáez, P., & Ruiz-Fernández, L. (2023a). Green Intellectual Capital as a Catalyst for the Sustainable Development Goals: Evidence From the Spanish Wine Industry. In Climate Change, World Consequences, and the Sustainable Development Goals for 2030 (pp. 163-182). IGI Global.

Martínez-Falcó, J., Marco-Lajara, B., & Zaragoza-Sáez, P. (2023b). Corporate Social Responsibility: A Comprehensive Analysis. In Positive and Constructive Contributions for Sustainable Development Goals (pp. 131-160). IGI Global.

Martínez-Falcó, J., Marco-Lajara, B., & Zaragoza-Saez, P. (2023c). Corporate Social Responsibility vs. Corporate Sustainability: Different Concepts for a Common Goal. In Positive and Constructive Contributions for Sustainable Development Goals (pp. 76-87). IGI Global.

Martínez-Falcó, J., Marco-Lajara, B., & Zaragoza-Saez, P. (2023d). Theoretical Perspectives on Corporate Social Responsibility: A Narrative Review. *Positive and Constructive Contributions for Sustainable Development Goals*, 96-113.

Martínez-Torres, A. (2006). Procedure to Design a Structural and Measurement Model of Intellectual Capital: An Exploratory Study. *Information & Management, 43*(5), 617–626. doi:10.1016/j.im.2006.03.002

Maruani, T., & Amit-Cohen, I. (2007). Open Space planning models: A review of approaches and methods. *Landscape and Urban Planning, 81*(1-2), 1–13. doi:10.1016/j.landurbplan.2007.01.003

Marutha, N. (2019). The application of legislative frameworks for the management of medical records in Limpopo Province, South Africa. *Information Development, 35*(4), 551–563. doi:10.1177/0266666918772006

Marzantowicz, Ł., & Dembinska, I. (2018). The Reasons for the Implementation of the Concept of Green Port in Sea Ports of China. *Logistics Infrastructure, 37*, 121–128.

Ma, S., & Kaplanidou, K. (2021). How corporate social responsibility and social identities lead to corporate brand equity: An evaluation in the context of sport teams as brand extensions. *Sport Marketing Quarterly, 30*(1), 16–29. doi:10.32731/SMQ.301.032021.02

Massaro, M., Dumay, J., Garlatti, A., & Dal Mas, F. (2018). Practitioners' views on intellectual capital and sustainability: From a performance-based to a worth-based perspective. *Journal of Intellectual Capital, 19*(2), 367–386. doi:10.1108/JIC-02-2017-0033

Massimo, M., & Corey, M. (2012). Everybody Needs Somebody: The Infuence of Team Network Structure on Information Technology Use. *Journal of Management Information Systems, 29*(3), 9–42. doi:10.2753/MIS0742-1222290301

Mataracı, G. D. (2016). *Green Port Approach and Sustainability in Port Authorities* [Master Thesis]. Istanbul Technical University.

Matlala, E. M., Ncube, R. T., & Parbanath, S. (2022). The State of digital records preservation in South Africa's public sector in the 21st century: A literature review. *Records Management Journal, 32*(2), 198–212. doi:10.1108/RMJ-02-2021-0004

Matthews, B., Obereder, L., Aust, I., & Müller-Camen, M. (2018). Competing Paradigms: Status-quo and Alternative Approaches in HRM. In Contemporary Developments in Green Human Resource Management Research. Routledge.

Mauro, P. (1997). *Why worry about corruption? Economic Issues*. International Monetary Fund.

Mavridis, D., & Kyrmizoglou, P. (2005). Intellectual capital performance drivers in the Greek banking sector. *Management Research News, 28*(5), 43–62. doi:10.1108/01409170510629032

Mazur, K. V., & Tomashuk, I. V. (2019). Governance, and regulation as an indispensable condition for developing the potential of rural areas. *Baltic Journal of Economic Studies, 5*(5), 67–78. doi:10.30525/2256-0742/2019-5-5-67-78

McKelvey, B. (1978, September). Organizational Systematics: Taxonomic Lessons from Biology. *Management Science, 24*(13), 1428–1440. doi:10.1287/mnsc.24.13.1428

McKelvey, B. (1982). *Organizational systematics: Taxonomy, evolution, classification*. University of California Press. doi:10.1525/9780520314696

McKelvey, B., & Aldrich, H. E. (1983). Populations, natural selection, and applied organizational science. *Administrative Science Quarterly, 28*(1), 101–128. doi:10.2307/2392389

McPherson, M. (1983). An ecology of affiliations. *American Sociological Review*, *48*(4), 519–532. doi:10.2307/2117719

Meerow, S., & Newell, J. P. (2017). Detroit, Spatial planning for multifunctional green infrastructure: Growing resilience. *Landscape and Urban Planning*, 62-75.

Mehralian, G., Rajabzadeh, A., Sadeh, M., & Rasekh, H. (2012). Intellectual capital and corporate performance in Iranian pharmaceutical industry. *Journal of Intellectual Capital*, *13*(1), 138–158. doi:10.1108/14691931211196259

Meier, M. (2011). Knowledge management in strategic alliances: A review of empirical evidence. *International Journal of Management Reviews*, *13*(1), 1–23. doi:10.1111/j.1468-2370.2010.00287.x

Mell, I. C. (2010). *Green infrastructure: Concepts, perceptions, and its use in spatial planning* [Doctoral Thesis]. School of Architecture, Planning and Landscape Newcastle University.

Melo, T., & Galan, J. I. (2011). Effects of corporate social responsibility on brand value. *Journal of Brand Management*, *18*(6), 423–437. doi:10.1057/bm.2010.54

Méndez, F., & Sepúlveda, F. (2006). *Corruption, Growth and Political Regimes: Cross Country Evidence*. http://ideas.repec.org/a/eee/poleco/v22y2006i1p82- 98.html

Mentens, J., Raes, D., & Hermy, M. (2006). Green roofs as a tool for solving the rainwater runoff problem in the urbanized 21st century? *Landscape and Urban Planning*, *77*(3), 217–226. doi:10.1016/j.landurbplan.2005.02.010

Méon, P., & Sekkat, K. (2005). Does corruption grease or sand the wheels of corruption? *Public Choice*, *122*(1-2), 69–97. doi:10.100711127-005-3988-0

Méon, P., & Weill, L. (2010). Is Corruption an Efficient Grease? *World Development*, *38*(3), 244–259. doi:10.1016/j.worlddev.2009.06.004

Mesimaki, M., Hauru, K., Kotze, D. J., & Lehvavirta, S. (2017). Neo-spaces for urban livability? Urbanities' versatile mental image of green roofs in the Helsinki metropolitan area, Finland. *Land Use Policy*, *61*, 587–600. doi:10.1016/j.landusepol.2016.11.021

Mezias, S. J., & Glynn, M. A. (1993). The Three Faces of Corporate Renewal: Institution, Revolution, and Evolution. *Strategic Management Journal*, *14*(2), 77–101. doi:10.1002mj.4250140202

Miles, R. E. & Snow, C. C. (1978). *Organizational Strategy, Structure and Process*. McGraw-Hill.

Miles, R. E., Snow, C. C., Mathews, J. A., Miles, G., & Coleman, H. J. Jr. (1997). Organizing in the Knowledge Age: Anticipating the Cellular Form. *The Academy of Management Executive*, *11*(4), 7–20. doi:10.5465/ame.1997.9712024836

Millan-Tudela, L. A. M., Marco-Lajara, B., Falcó, J. M., & Pareja, E. P. (2022a). Longevidad empresarial: revisión bibliométrica sobre la supervivencia y caída de las compañías [Corporate longevity: a bibliometric review of company survival and decline]. In Leveraging new business technology for a sustainable economic recovery (p. 170). Escuela Superior de Gestión Comercial y Marketing, ESIC.

Millan-Tudela, L. A., Marco-Lajara, B., Martínez-Falcó, J., & Sánchez-García, E. (2022b). Pursuing Business Longevity: Ways to Enhance Sustainable Development. In Frameworks for Sustainable Development Goals to Manage Economic, Social, and Environmental Shocks and Disasters (pp. 79-95). IGI Global.

Mintzberg, H. (1978). Patterns in strategy formation. *Management Science*, *24*(9), 934–948. doi:10.1287/mnsc.24.9.934

Mintzberg, H. (1979). *The Structuring of Organization*. Prentice Hall.

Mintzberg, H. (1979). *The Structuring of Organizations: A Synthesis of the Research.* The Theory of Management Policy Series. Prentice-Hall.

Mishra, D. R., & Sodok, E. (2011). Does corporate social responsibility affect the cost of capital? *Journal of Banking & Finance, 35*(9), 2388–2406. doi:10.1016/j.jbankfin.2011.02.007

Mohammed, F. (2012). *Business ethics: A case study in Gavle in Sweden.* Akademin for Utbildning Och Ekonomi.

Mohd, H. A., & Norhidayah, S. (2016), Sustainable food production: insights of Malaysian halal small and medium sized enterprises. *International Journal of Production Economics, 181*(B), 303–314. . doi:10.1016/j.ijpe.2016.06.003

Mohr, L. A., & Webb, D. J. (2005). The effects of corporate social responsibility and price on consumer responses. *The Journal of Consumer Affairs, 39*(1), 121–147. doi:10.1111/j.1745-6606.2005.00006.x

Mojapelo, M. S. (2022). Records Management in government schools in South Africa: A case study in Limpopo province. Records management in government schools. *Records Management Journal, 32*(1), 21–42. doi:10.1108/RMJ-04-2020-0012

Molina-Azorín, J. F., Claver-Cortés, E., Pereira-Moliner, J., & Tarí, J. J. (2009). Environmental practices and firm performance: An empirical analysis in the Spanish hotel industry. *Journal of Cleaner Production, 17*(5), 516–524. doi:10.1016/j.jclepro.2008.09.001

Mondal, A., & Ghosh, S. (2012). Intellectual capital and financial performance of Indian banks. *Journal of Intellectual Capital, 13*(4), 515–530. doi:10.1108/14691931211276115

Moon, J., Tang, R., & Lee, W. S. (2022). Antecedents and consequences of Starbucks' environmental, social and governance (ESG) implementation. *Journal of Quality Assurance in Hospitality & Tourism,* 1–23. doi:10.1080/1528008X.2022.2070818

Moraes, S. D. S., Chiappetta Jabbour, C. J., Battistelle, R. A., Rodrigues, J. M., Renwick, D. S., Foropon, C., & Roubaud, D. (2018). When knowledge management matters: Interplay between green human resources and eco-efficiency in the financial service industry. *Journal of Knowledge Management.* Advance online publication. doi:10.1108/JKM-07-2018-0414

Mourad, M. (2017). Quality Assurance as a driver of information management Strategy Stakeholders perspectives in Higher education. Stakeholders' perspectives in HE. Stakeholders' perspectives in HE. *Journal of Enterprise Information Management, 30*(5), 779–795. doi:10.1108/JEIM-06-2016-0104

Mouritsen, J., Bukh, P. N., & Marr, B. (2004). Reporting on intellectual capital: Why, what and how? *Measuring Business Excellence, 8*(1), 46–54. doi:10.1108/13683040410524739

Mukherjee, B., & Chandra, B. (2018). Conceptualizing green human resource management in predicting employees' green intention and behaviour: a conceptual framework. *Prabandhan. Indian Journal of Management, 11*(7), 36-48. doi: /2018/v11i7/129940 doi:10.17010/pijom

Mukherjee, T., & Sen, S. S. (2019). Intellectual capital and corporate sustainable growth: The Indian evidence. *Asian Journal of Business Environment, 9*(2), 5–15. doi:10.13106/jbees.2019.vol9.no2.5

Mullon, A., & Ngoepe, M. (2019). An integrated framework to elevate information governance to a national level in South Africa. *Records Management Journal, 29*(1/2), 103–116. doi:10.1108/RMJ-09-2018-0030

Murray, N. (2017). Urban disaster risk governance. A systemic review. PPI-Centre. UCL Institute of Education.

Musibah, A. S., Bin, W. S., & Alfattani, W. Y. (2013). Impact of Intellectual Capital on Corporate Social Responsibility Evidence from Islamic Banking Sector in GCC. *International Journal of Finance and Accounting, 2*(6), 307–311. doi:10.5923/j.ijfa.20130206.02

Mustapha, M., Manan, Z., & Alwi, S. (2017). Sustainable Green Management System (SGMS)-An integrated approach towards organisational sustainability. *Journal of Cleaner Production*, *146*, 158–172. doi:10.1016/j.jclepro.2016.06.033

Nagle, K. (2013). *Seaports: Essential to Our Economic Prosperity.* Retrieved from. http:// www.pnwa.net/wp-content/uploads/2013/03/Nagle-2013-Mission-Slides.pdf

Nahapiet, J., & Ghoshal, S. (1998). Social capital, intellectual capital, and the organizational advantage. *Academy of Management Review*, *23*(2), 242–266. doi:10.2307/259373

Nakano, C. (2007). The Significance and Limitations of Corporate Governance from the Perspective of Business Ethics: Towards the Creation of an Ethical Organizational Culture. *Asian Business & Management*, *6*(2), 163–178. doi:10.1057/palgrave.abm.9200216

Namkung, Y., & Jang, S. (2013). Effects of restaurant green practices on brand equity formation: Do green practices really matter? *International Journal of Hospitality Management*, *33*(2), 85–95. doi:10.1016/j.ijhm.2012.06.006

Nassar, S. (2018). The impact of intellectual capital on corporate performance of IT companies: Evidence from bursa Istanbul. *Journal of Accounting and Applied Business Research*, *1*(3), 1–10. doi:10.51325/ijbeg.v1i3.17

Navarro, J. G. C., Reverte, C., Melero, E. G., & Wensley, A. K. P. (2016). Linking social and economic responsibilities with financial performance: The role of innovation. *European Management Journal*, *34*(5), 530–539. doi:10.1016/j.emj.2016.02.006

Nawaz, F. (2010). *Exploring the Relationships between Corruption and Tax Revenue.* https://www.u4.no/publications/exploring-therelationships-between-corruption-and-tax-revenue/

Nekhili, M., Nagatib, H., & Tawhid, Ch. (2017). Claudia rebolledod corporate social responsibility disclosure and market value: Family versus nonfamily firms. *Journal of Business Research*, *77*(C), 41–52. doi:10.1016/j.jbusres.2017.04.001

Nelson, R. R., & Winter, S. G. (1982). *Evolutionary Theory of Economic Change.* Belknap Press of Harvard University Press.

Nelson, R., & Winter, S. (1982). *An Evolutionary Theory of Economic Change.* Harvard University Press.

Nengomasha, C. T., & Nyanga, H. E. (2012). Managing Semi current records: A case for records centers for the public services of Namibia. *Journal for Studies in Humanities and Social Sciences*, *1*(2), 231–245.

Nengomasha, T. C., & Nyanga, H. E. (2015). Access to Archives at the National Archives of Namibia. *ESARBICA Journal*, *34*, 88–103.

Nevado-Peña, D., & López-Ruiz, V. (2002). Un modelo e informe contable para la medición del capital intelectual desarrollo y aplicaciones [A model and accounting report for the measurement of intelectual capital deveopment and applications]. *Revista de Contabilidad y Tributación*, *229*, 161–206.

Ng, A. (2018). From sustainability accounting to a green financing system: Institutional legitimacy and market heterogeneity in a global financial centre. *Journal of Cleaner Production*, *195*, 585–592. doi:10.1016/j.jclepro.2018.05.250

Ngoepe, M and Mello, V (2020) Integration of records management systems at a South African Water Utility Company. *Integration of records management system.*

Ngoepe, M., & Nkwe, M. (2018). Separating the Wheat from the Chaff with the winnowing fork. The eeny meeny miny mo appraisal approach of digital records in South Africa. *Records Management Journal*, *28*(2), 130–142. doi:10.1108/RMJ-09-2017-0027

Nidumolu, R., Prahalad, C. K., & Rangaswami, M. R. (2009). Why sustainability is now the key driver of innovation. *Harvard Business Review*, *87*(9), 56–64.

Niebel, C. (2021). The Impact of the General Data Protection Regulation on Innovation and the Global Political Economy. *Computer Law & Security Review*, *40*, 105523. doi:10.1016/j.clsr.2020.105523

Nikolaou, I. (2019). A framework to explicate the relationship between CSER and financial performance: An intellectual capital-based approach and knowledge-based view of firm. *Journal of the Knowledge Economy*, *10*(4), 1427–1446. doi:10.100713132-017-0491-z

Nirino, N., Santoro, G., Miglietta, N., & Quaglia, R. (2021). Corporate controversies and company's financial performance: Exploring the moderating role of ESG practices. *Technological Forecasting and Social Change*, *162*, 120341. doi:10.1016/j.techfore.2020.120341

Nonaka, I. (1994). A Dynamic Theory of Organizational Knowledge Creation. *Organization Science*, *5*(1), 14–37. doi:10.1287/orsc.5.1.14

Nonaka, I., Peltokorpi, V., & Tomae, H. (2005). Strategic knowledge creation: The case of Hamamatsu Photonics. *International Journal of Technology Management*, *30*(3-4), 248–264. doi:10.1504/IJTM.2005.006709

Nonaka, I., & Takeuchi, H. (1995). *The Knowledge Creating Company*. Oxford University Press.

Noonan, W. D. (2016). Column: Technology Matters in Archives, Email: an appraisal approach. *Journal of Archival Organization*, *13*(3-4), 16–151. doi:10.1080/15332748.2018.1445607

Norton, T. A., Parker, S. L., Zacher, H., & Ashkanasy, N. M. (2015). Employee green behavior: A theoretical framework, multi-level review, and future research agenda. *Organization & Environment*, *2015*(28), 103–125. doi:10.1177/1086026615575773

Nourani, M., Chandran, V., Kweh, Q., & Lu, W. (2018). Measuring human, physical and structural capital efficiency performance of insurance companies. *Social Indicators Research*, *137*(1), 281–315. doi:10.100711205-017-1584-6

Nyström, H. (1979). *Creativity and Innovation*. Wiley.

Nyström, H. (1990). *Technological and Market Innovation: Strategies for Product and Company Development*. Wiley.

Obeng, B., Robson, P., & Haugh, H. (2014). Strategic entrepreneurship and small firm growth in Ghana. *International Small Business Journal*, *32*(5), 501–524. doi:10.1177/0266242612463946

Öberseder, M., Schlegelmilch, B. B., & Gruber, V. (2011). "Why Don't Consumers Care About CSR?": A Qualitative Study Exploring the Role of CSR in Consumption Decisions. *Journal of Business Ethics*, *104*(4), 449–460. doi:10.100710551-011-0925-7

OECD. (2009). *Environmental Impacts of International Shipping: A Case Study of the Port of Vancouver*. OECD Publishing.

Oldroyd, J. B., & Morris, S. S. (2012). catching falling stars: A human resource response to social capital's detrimental effect of information overload on star employees. *Academy of Management Review*, *37*(3), 396–418. doi:10.5465/amr.2010.0403

Oliver, P. (2012). *Succeeding with your literature review. A handbook for students*. McGraw-Hill, Open University Press.

Olugu, E. U. & Wong Kuan. Y. (2012). An expert fuzzy rule-based system for closedloop supply chain performance assessment in the automotive industry. *Expert Systems with Applications, 39*(1), 375-384.

Olve, N., Roy, J., & Wetter, M. (2000). Implantando y gestionando el cuadro de mando integral [Implementing and managning the balanced scorecard]. *Gestion*.

Olve, N., Roy, J., & Wetter, M. (2000). Implantando y gestionando el cuadro de mando integral. *Gestion.*

Omar, M. K., Yusoff, Y. M., & Zaman, M. D. K. (2017). The role of green intellectual capital on business sustainability. *World Applied Sciences Journal, 35*(12), 2558–2563.

Ones, D. S., & Dilchert, S. (2012). Employee green behaviors. In D. S. S. E. Jackson (Ed.), *Managing human resource for environmental sustainability* (pp. 85–116). Jossey-Bass.

Ordoñez de Pablos, P. (2001). La gestión del conocimiento como base para el logro de una ventaja competitiva sostenible: La organización occidental versus japonesa [Knowledge management as a basis for achieving a sustainable competitve advantage: The Western versus Japenese organization]. *Investigaciones Europeas de Dirección y Economía de la Empresa, 7*(3), 91–108.

Ostrom, E. (1990). *Governing the Commons: The Evolution of Institutions for Collective Action.* Cambridge University Press. doi:10.1017/CBO9780511807763

Oswald, S. L., Mossholder, K. W., & Harris, S. G. (1994). Vision salience and strategic involvement: Implications for psychological attachment to organization and job. *Strategic Management Journal, 1994*(15), 477–489. doi:10.1002mj.4250150605

Otoo, F., Kuar, M., & Otoo, E. (2022). Does human capital mediate the nexus of human resource management (HRM) practices and organizational performance? *International Journal of Research in Business and Social Science, 11*(5), 199–209. doi:10.20525/ijrbs.v11i5.1829

Özispa, N., & Arabelen, G. (2021). Prioritizing the Sustainability Strategies of Ports via AHP. *Approach Journal of Yasar University, 16*(63), 1430-1453.

Paliwal, M. (2006). *Business ethics.* New Age International. https://ebookcentral/proquest-com.acg.idm.oclc.org

Pal, T., & Hazra, M. K. (2015). *Sustainable Development.* Yadava Publication.

Parsons, T. (1951). *The Social System.* Free Press.

Paul, J., Modi, A., & Patel, J. (2016). Predicting green product consumption using theory of planned behavior and reasoned action. *Journal of Retailing and Consumer Services, 29*, 123–134. doi:10.1016/j.jretconser.2015.11.006

Pavlic, B., Cepak, F., Sucic, B., Peckaj, M., & Kandus, M. (2014). Sustainable Port Infrastructure, Practical Implementation of The Green Port Concept. *Thermal Science, 18*(3), 935–948.

Pedrini, M. (2007). Human capital convergences in intellectual capital and sustainability reports. *Journal of Intellectual Capital, 8*(2), 346–366. doi:10.1108/14691930710742880

Pell, A. N. (1996). Fixing the leaky pipeline: Women scientists in academia. *Journal of Animal Science, 74*(11), 2843–2848. doi:10.2527/1996.74112843x PMID:8923199

Peloza, J., & Shang, J. (2011). How can corporate social responsibility activities create value for stakeholders? A systematic review. *Journal of the Academy of Marketing Science, 39*(1), 117–135. doi:10.100711747-010-0213-6

Peltz, J.R (2006). Arkansas's Public Records Retention Program: Records Retention as a Cornerstone of Citizenship and Self- Government. *University of Arkansas at Little Rock Law Review, 28*(2), 175 – 249.

Penrose, E. T. (1959). *The Theory of the Growth of the Firm.* John Wiley.

Pereira, Á., & Vence, X. (2012). Key business factors for eco-innovation: An overview of recent firm-level empirical studies. *Cuadernos de Gestión, 12*, 73–103. doi:10.5295/cdg.110308ap

Petrash, G. (1996). Dow's Journey to a knowledge value management culture. *European Management Journal, 14*(4), 365–373. doi:10.1016/0263-2373(96)00023-0

Pettit, S. J., & Beresford, A. K. C. (2009). Port development: From gateways to logistics hubs. *Maritime Policy & Management, 36*(3), 253–267. doi:10.1080/03088830902861144

Petty, R., & Guthrie, J. (2000). Intellectual capital literature review: Measurement, reporting and management. *Journal of Intellectual Capital, 1*(2), 155–176. doi:10.1108/14691930010348731

Phillips, L. (1999). Green Attitudes. *American Demographics, 21*, 46–47.

Phillips, T. J. (2011). *Mergers, Acquisitions, Diverstitures and Closures Records and Information Management Checklists. AMRMA International Education Foundation.* ARMA International Educational Foundation. Pittsburgh, Rakemane, D and Mosweu, O (2021). Challenges of managing and Preserving audio-visual archives in archival institutions in Sub Saharan Africa: A Literature review. *Collection and Curation, 40*(2), 42–50.

Phiri, J. M., & Tough, G. A. (2018). Managing university records in the world of governance. Managing university records. *Records Management Journal, 28*(1), 47–61. doi:10.1108/RMJ-11-2016-0042

Pierce, J. L., Kostova, T., & Dirks, K. T. (2003). The State of Psychological Ownership: Integrating and Extending a Century of Research. *Review of General Psychology, 7*(1), 84–107. doi:10.1037/1089-2680.7.1.84

Pillay, K. (2021). *Corruption, dodgy Covid-19 procurement deals and sextortion at schools are on the rise.* Corruption Watch.

Pina e Cunha, M., Vieira da Cunha, J., & Kamoche, K. (2003). Organizational Improvisation: What, When How and Why. *International Journal of Management Reviews, 1*(3), 299–341. Advance online publication. doi:10.1111/1468-2370.00017

Plattform produktives Stadtgrün. (2020). Available online: https://www.berlin.de/gemeinschaftsgaertnern/

Podolny, J. M., & Baron, J. N. (1997). Resources and relationships: Social networks and mobility in the Putnam, R. D. (2000), Bowling Alone: The Collapse and Revival of American Community, Simon & Shuster.

Podolny, J. M., & Stuart, T. E. (1995). A role-based ecology of technological change. *American Journal of Sociology, 100*(5), 1224–1260. doi:10.1086/230637

Pohle, G., & Chapman, M. (2006). IBM's global CEO report 2006: Business model innovation matters. *Strategy and Leadership, 34*(5), 34–40. doi:10.1108/10878570610701531

Pope, S., & Kim, J. (2021). Where, When, and Who: Corporate Social Responsibility and Brand Value—A Global Panel Study. *Business & Society.* doi:10.1177/00076503211019315

Porter, M. (1980). *Competitive strategy.* The Free Press.

Porter, M. (1985). *Competitive advantage.* The Free Press.

Powell, W. W., & Grodal, S. (2005). Networks of Innovators. In *The Oxford Handbook of Innovation.* Oxford University Press. doi:10.1093/oxfordhb/9780199286805.003.0003

Pradhan, S. (2018). Role of CSR in the consumer decision making process – The case of India. *Social Responsibility Journal, 14*(1), 138–158. doi:10.1108/SRJ-06-2016-0109

PricewaterhouseCoopers. (2008). *Confronting Corruption: The Business Case for an Effective Anti-Corruption Programme.* http://www.pwc.com/gx/en/forensic-accounting dispute-consulting-services/business-case-anti-corruption-programme.jhtml

Priem, R., & Butler, J. (2001). Is the resource-based "view" a useful perspective for strategic management research? *Academy of Management Review*, 26(1), 22–40.

Przychodzen, W., Gómez-Bezares, F., & Przychodzen, J. (2018). Green information technologies practices and financial performance-the empirical evidence from German publicly traded companies. *Journal of Cleaner Production*, 201, 570–579. doi:10.1016/j.jclepro.2018.08.081

Qi, Y., Chai, Y., & Jiang, Y. (2021). Threshold effect of government subsidy, corporate social responsibility and brand value using the data of China's top 500 most valuable brands. *PLoS One*, 16(5), e0251927. doi:10.1371/journal.pone.0251927 PMID:34032810

Quinetta, M., Roberson, I., & Williamson, O. (2012). justice in self-managing teams: The role of social networks in the emergence of procedural justice climates. *Academy of Management Journal*, 55(3), 685–701. doi:10.5465/amj.2009.0491

Quintero-Quintero, W., Blanco-Ariza, A. B., & Garzón-Castrillón, M. A. (2021). Intellectual capital: A review and bibliometric analysis. *Publications*, 9(4), 46. doi:10.3390/publications9040046

Rahman, M., Rodríguez-Serrano, M., & Lambkin, M. (2019). Brand equity and firm performance: The complementary role of corporate social responsibility. *Journal of Brand Management*, 26(6), 691–704. doi:10.105741262-019-00155-9

Ramanathan, R., Ramanathan, U., & Bentley, Y. (2017). The debate on ßexibility of environmental regulations, innovation capabilities and Þnancial performance -A novel use of DEA. *Omega*, 75(5), 131–138.

Rastogi, P. N. (2003). The nature and role of IC: Rethinking the process of value creation and sustained enterprise growth. *Journal of Intellectual Capital*.

Rastogi, P. (2003). The nature and role of IC - rethinking the process of value creation and sustained enterprise growth. *Journal of Intellectual Capital*, 4(2), 227–248. doi:10.1108/14691930310472848

Raudeliuniene, J., Davidavičiene, V., & Jakubavičius, A. (2018). Knowledge management process model. *Entrep. Sustain. Issues*, 5, 542–554.

Redman, C. (2014). Should sustainability and resilience be combined or remain distinct pursuits? *Ecology and Society*, 19(2), 190–202. doi:10.5751/ES-06390-190237

Reed, K., Lubatkin, M., & Srinivasa, N. (2006). Proposing and Testing an Intellectual Capital-Based View of the Firm. *Journal of Management Studies*, 43(4), 867–893. doi:10.1111/j.1467-6486.2006.00614.x

Reeves, M., & Deimler, M. (2011). *Adaptability: The new competitive advantage*. Harvard.

Reisinger, A., & Clark, H. (2018). How much do direct livestock emissions contribute to global warming? *Global Change Biology*, 2018(24), 1749–1761. doi:10.1111/gcb.13975 PMID:29105912

Ren, S., Tang, G., & Jackson, S. E. (2017). Green human resource management research in emergence: a review and future directions. *Asia Pacific Journal of Management*, 1-35. https://doi.o rg/ doi:10.1007/s10490-017-9532-1

Renwick, D. W. S., Jabbour, C. J. C., Muller-Camen, M., Redman, T., & Wilkinson, A. (2016). Contemporary developments in green (environmental) HRM scholarship. *International Journal of Human Resource Management*, 27(2), 114–128. doi:10.1080/09585192.2015.1105844

Renwick, D., Redman, T., & Maguire, S. (2013). Green human resource management: A review and research agenda. *International Journal of Management Reviews*, 15(1), 1–14. doi:10.1111/j.1468-2370.2011.00328.x

Rexhepi, G., Ibraimi, S., & Veseli, N. (2013). Role of intellectual capital in creating enterprise strategy. *Procedia: Social and Behavioral Sciences*, 75, 44–51. doi:10.1016/j.sbspro.2013.04.006

Robbins, S. P., & Judge, T. A. (2016). *Organizational behavior: Concepts, controversies, and applications* (17th ed.). Prentice Hall.

Rodrigues, P., & Borges, A. P. (2015). Corporate social responsibility and its impact in consumer decision-making. *Social Responsibility Journal, 11*(4), 690–701. doi:10.1108/SRJ-02-2014-0026

Romanelli, E., & Tushman, M. L. (1994). Organizational Transformation as Punctuated Equilibrium: An Empirical Test. *Academy of Management Journal, 37*(5), 1141–1166. doi:10.2307/256669

Rooney, J., & Dumay, J. (2016). Intellectual capital, calculability and qualculation. *The British Accounting Review, 48*(1), 1–16. doi:10.1016/j.bar.2015.07.002

Roos, G. (2017). Knowledge management, intellectual capital, structural holes, economic complexity and national prosperity. *Journal of Intellectual Capital, 18*(4), 745–770. doi:10.1108/JIC-07-2016-0072

Roos, J., Edvinsson, L., & Dragonetti, N. C. (1997). *Intellectual capital: Navigating the new business landscape.* Springer. doi:10.1007/978-1-349-14494-5

Roscoe, S., Subramanian, N., Jabbour, C. J., & Chong, T. (2019). Green human resource management and the enablers of green organisational culture: Enhancing a firm's environmental performance for sustainable development. *Business Strategy and the Environment, 28*(5), 1–13. doi:10.1002/bse.2277

Rosenbloom, R. S., & Christensen, C. M. (1994). Technological discontinuities, organizational capabilities, and strategic commitments. *Industrial and Corporate Change, 3*(3), 655–685. doi:10.1093/icc/3.3.655

Rothstein, B., & Holberg, S. (2011). *Correlates of Corruption.* http://www.qog.pol.gu.se/digitalAssets/1357/1357840_2011_12_rothstein_holmberg.pdf

Rowe, D. B. (2011). Green Roofs as a means of pollution abatement. *Environmental Pollution, 159*(8-9), 2100–2110. doi:10.1016/j.envpol.2010.10.029 PMID:21074914

Rueda, L. I. (2022). *Teoria(s) Organizacional(es) Postmoderna(s) y la Gest(ac)ión del sujeto Postmoderno* [Tesis Doctoral]. Universidad Autónoma de Barcelona.

Ruef, M. (2000). The Emergence of Organizational Forms: A Community Ecology Approach. *American Journal of Sociology, 106*(3), 3. doi:10.1086/318963

Russo, A., & Cirella, G. (2018). Modern compact cities: How much greenery do we need? *International Journal of Environmental Research and Public Health, 15*(10), 2180. doi:10.3390/ijerph15102180 PMID:30301177

Rzempała, J., & Rzempała, A. (2015). Analysis of SME companies' awareness of the value of intellectual capital. *Scientific Journals of the University of Szczecin. Finance, Financial Markets, Insurance*, (73), 483-495.

Sabokro, M., Masud, M. M., & Kayedian, A. (2021). The effect of green human resources management on corporate social responsibility, green psychological climate and employees' green behavior. *Journal of Cleaner Production, 313*, 127963. doi:10.1016/j.jclepro.2021.127963

Saeed, A., Rasheed, F., Waseem, M., & Tabash, M. I. (2021). Green human resource management and environmental performance: The role of green supply chain management practices. *Benchmarking*.

Saeed, B. B., Afsar, B., Hafeez, S., Khan, I., Tahir, M., & Afridi, M. A. (2018). Promoting employee's proenvironmental behavior through green human resource management practices. *Corporate Social Responsibility and Environmental Management, 26*(2), 424–438. doi:10.1002/csr.1694

Sahin, A. (2018). How Principles of Business Ethics Relates to Corporate Governance and Directors? *European Journal of Economics and Business Studies, 4*(3), 22–27. doi:10.2478/ejes-2018-0056

Salimath, M. S., & Jones, R. (2011). *Population ecology theory: Implications for sustainability.* Emerald Group Publishing Limited.

Salleh, M. F. (2016). *Business Ethics and Entrepreneurship Education.* Conference: 3rd. International Conference of Business, Economics and Social Sciences (ICBESS), Bali, Indonesia.

Salvi, A., Vitolla, F., Giakoumelou, A., Raimo, N., & Rubino, M. (2020). Intellectual capital disclosure in integrated reports: The effect on firm value. *Technological Forecasting and Social Change, 160,* 120228. doi:10.1016/j.techfore.2020.120228

Sánchez Medina, A. J., Melián González, A., & Garcia Falcon, J. M. (2007). Intellectual capital and sustainable development on islands: An application to the case of Gran Canaria. *Regional Studies, 41*(4), 473–487. doi:10.1080/00343400600928327

Sánchez-Medina, A., Melián-González, A., & García-Falcón, J. (2007). El concepto del capital intelectual y sus dimensiones. *Investigaciones Europeas de Dirección y Economía de la Empresa, 13*(2), 97–111.

Sanrı, Ö. (2021). A Content Analysis of Green Port, 2009-2020. *Beykoz Akademi Dergisi, 9*(2), 50-72. Doi:10.14514/BYK.m.26515393.2021.9/2.50-72

Saptaria, L., Soetjipto, B. E., & Wardoyo, C. (2022). Impact of the Implementation of Green Human Resources Management: A Study of Systematic Literature. *Ilomata International Journal of Management, 3*(2), 264–283. doi:10.52728/ijjm.v3i2.471

Sarstedt, M., Ringle, C. M., & Hair, J. F. (2017). Partial Least Squares Structural Equation Modeling. In *Handbook of Market Research* (pp. 1–40). Springer International Publishing. doi:10.1007/978-3-319-05542-8_15-1

Satır, T., & Doğan-Sağlamtimur, N. (2018). The protection of marine aquatic life: Green Port (EcoPort) model inspired by Green Port concept in selected ports from Turkey, Europe and the USA. *Periodicals of Engineering and Natural Sciences, 6*(1), 120–129. doi:10.21533/pen.v6i1.149

Savickiene, J., & Miceikiene, A. (2018). *Sustainable economic development assessment model for family farms* (Vol. 64). Agricultural Economics. doi:10.17221/310/2017-AGRICECON

Saxenian, A. (1996). Beyond boundaries: Open labour markets and learning in the Silicon Valley. In M. B. Arthur & D. M. Rousseau (Eds.), *The boundaryless career: A new employment principle for a new organizational era* (pp. 23–39). Oxford University Press.

Saygili, E., Arslan, S., & Birkan, A. O. (2022). ESG practices and corporate financial performance: Evidence from Borsa Istanbul. *Borsa Istanbul Review, 22*(3), 525–533. doi:10.1016/j.bir.2021.07.001

Schooley, S. (2021). *What is Corporate Social Responsibility?* Business News Daily Staff.

Schumpeter, J. (1950). The process of creative destruction. In J. Schumpeter (Ed.), *Capitalism, Socialism and Democracy* (3rd ed.). Allen and Unwin.

Schumpeter, J. A. (1942). *Capitalism, Socialism and Democracy.* Harper.

Scott, D. R., & Suchard, H. T. (1992). Motivations for Australian Expenditure on Sponsorship—An Analysis. *International Journal of Advertising, 11*(4), 325–332. doi:10.1080/02650487.1992.11104508

Segaetsho, T. (2014). Preservation Risk Assessment Survey of the University of Botswana Library. *African Journal of Library Archives and Information Science, 24*(2), 176–186.

Senge, P. (1990). *The Fifth Discipline: The Art and Practice of the Learning Organization*. Doubleday.

Seva-Larrosa, P., Falcó, J. M., & Fernández, L. R. (2022). Analizando las principales variables empresariales en los clusters vinícolas españoles teniendo en cuenta la localización de las empresas y su pertenencia a una marca colectiva. [Analyzing the main business variables in Spanish wine clusters taking into account the location of the companies and their membership in a collective brand.] In *Miradas sobre el emprendimiento ante la crisis del coronavirus* (pp. 629–634). Dykinson.

Sexton, D. L., & Kasarda, J. D. (1992). The State of the Art of Entrepreneurship. PWS–Kent.

Sexton, D. L., & Landström, H. (2000). *The Blackwell Handbook of Entrepreneurship* (D. L. Sexton & H. Landström, Eds.). Blackwell.

Sexty, R. (2011). *Canadian business and society: Ethics and responsibilities* (2nd ed.). McGraw-Hill Ryerson.

Shaban, S. (2019). Reviewing the concept of green HRM (GHRM) and its application practices (Green Staffing) with suggested research agenda: A review from literature background and testing construction perspective. *International Business Research*, *12*(5), 86–94. doi:10.5539/ibr.v12n5p86

Shafique, M., Kim, R., & Rafiq, M. (2018). Green roof benefits, opportunities, and challenges– A review. *Renewable and Sustainable Energy Reviews, 90*, 757-773.

Shanks, C., Jacobson, H. K., & Kaplan, J. H. (1996). Inertia and change in the constellation of IGOs, 1981-1992. *International Organization*, *50*(4), 593–627. doi:10.1017/S002081830003352X

Sharma, K. (2016). *Child Labour in South Asia* (G. Herath, Ed.). Routledge. doi:10.4324/9781315571454

Sharma, S., & Vredenburg, H. (1998). Proactive corporate environmental strategy and the development of competitively valuable organizational capabilities. *Strategic Management Journal*, *19*(8), 729–753. doi:10.1002/(SICI)1097-0266(199808)19:8<729::AID-SMJ967>3.0.CO;2-4

Shepherd, E., Stevenson, A., & Flinn, A. (2011). Freedom of Information and Records Management in local government: Help or Hindrance? *Information Polity*, *16*(2), 111–121. doi:10.3233/IP-2011-0229

Shevchenko, A., & Petrenko, O. (2020). Current state of micro and small agribusiness in Ukraine. *Agricultural and Resource Economics*, *6*(1), 146–160. doi:10.51599/are.2020.06.01.10

Shoeb, A., & Nisar, T. (2015). Green Human Resource Management: Policies and practices. *Cogent Business & Management, 2*(1). https://www.tandfonline.com/doi/full/10.1080/23311975.2015.1030817 doi:10.1080/23311975.2015.1030817

Sila, I., & Cek, K. (2017). The Impact of Environmental, Social and Governance Dimensions of Corporate Social Responsibility on Economic Performance: Australian Evidence. *Procedia Computer Science*, *120*, 797–804. doi:10.1016/j.procs.2017.11.310

Simensky, M., & Bryer, L. G. (Eds.). (1994). *The new role of intellectual property in commercial transactions*. Wiley.

Singh, A., & Verma, P. (2018). Driving brand value through CSR initiatives: An empirical study in indian perspective. *Global Business Review*, *19*(1), 85–98. doi:10.1177/0972150917713270

Singh, D. A., & Gaur, A. S. (2009). Business Group Affiliation, Firm Governance, and Firm Performance: Evidence from China and India. *Corporate Governance*, *17*(4), 411–425. doi:10.1111/j.1467-8683.2009.00750.x

Singh, J. V., & Lumsden, Ch. J. (1990). Ecology Organizations: Theory and Investigate. *Annual Review of Sociology*, *16*, 161–195. doi:10.1146/annurev.so.16.080190.001113

Singh, J., de los Salmones Sanchez, M., & del Bosque, I. R. (2008). Understanding Corporate Social Responsibility and Product Perceptions in Consumer Markets: A Cross-cultural Evaluation. *Journal of Business Ethics*, *80*(3), 597–611. doi:10.100710551-007-9457-6

Singh, N., & Gupta, K. (2013). Environmental Attitude and Ecological Behaviour of Indian consumers. *Social Responsibility Journal*, *9*(1), 4–18. doi:10.1108/17471111311307787

Singh, S. K., Del Giudice, M., Chierici, R., & Graziano, D. (2020). Green innovation and environmental performance: The role of green transformational leadership and green human resource management. *Technological Forecasting and Social Change*, *150*, 119762. doi:10.1016/j.techfore.2019.119762

Sislian, L., Jaegler, A., & Cariou, P. (2016). A Literature Review on Port Sustainability and Ocean's Carrier Network Problem. *Research in Transportation Business & Management*, *19*, 19–26. doi:10.1016/j.rtbm.2016.03.005

Siyambalapitiya, J., Zhang, X., & Liu, X. (2018). Green human resource management: A proposed model in the context of Sri Lanka's tourism industry. *Journal of Cleaner Production*, *201*(2), 542–555. doi:10.1016/j.jclepro.2018.07.305

Skandia. (1996). *Customer Value*. Supplement to the Annual Report. Author.

Skydan, O., Nykolyuk, O., Pyvovar, P., & Martynchuk, I. (2020). Methodological approach to the evaluation of agricultural business system flexibility. *Management Theory and Studies for Rural Business and Infrastructure Development*, *41*(4), 444–462. doi:10.15544/mts.2019.36

Šlaus, I., & Jacobs, G. (2011). Human capital and sustainability. *Sustainability*, *3*(1), 97–154. doi:10.3390u3010097

Smriti, N., & Das, N. (2017). Impact of intellectual capital on business performance: evidence from Indian pharmaceutical sector. *Polish Journal of Management Studies, 15*.

Sokołowska, A. (2005). Zarzadzanie kapitałem intelektualnym w małym przedsiebiorstwie. Polskie Towarzystwo Ekonomiczne.

Sole, R. V., & Bascompte, J. (1995). Spatial Self Organization Self-Organization in complex Ecosystems. Princeton University Press.

Solove, J. D. (2008). *Understanding Privacy*. Harvard Unversity Press.

Sørensen, J. B., & Stuart, T. E. (2000, March). Aging, Obsolescence, and Organizational Innovation. *Administrative Science Quarterly*, *45*(1), 81–112. doi:10.2307/2666980

Soto Barrientos, F., & Viveros Caviedes, F. (2016). Organizaciones de la sociedad civil en Chile: Propuesta para financiamiento público y fortalecimiento institucional. *Polis*, *15*(45), 429–454. doi:10.4067/S0718-65682016000300021

Star, S. L. (1989). The structure of ill-structured solutions: boundary objects and heterogeneous distributed problem solving. In L. Gasser & M. N. Huhns (Eds.), *Distributed Artificial Intelligence* (Vol. 2, pp. 37–54). Pitman. doi:10.1016/B978-1-55860-092-8.50006-X

Stewart, T. (1998). *La nueva riqueza de las organizaciones: el capital intelectual*. Granica.

Stewart, T. A. (2010). *Intellectual Capital: The new wealth of organization*. Currency.

Stieglitz, N., Knudsen, T., & Becker, M. C. (2016). Adaptation and inertia in dynamic environments. *Strategic Management Journal*, *37*(9), 1854–1864. doi:10.1002mj.2433

Stopford, M. (2009). *Maritime Economics*. Routledge.

Stovin, V., Vesuviano, G., & Kasmin, H. (2012). The hydrological performance of a green roof test bed under UK climatic conditions. *Journal of Hydrology (Amsterdam)*, *414*, 148–161. doi:10.1016/j.jhydrol.2011.10.022

Straughan, R. D., & Roberts, J. A. (1999). Environmental segmentation alternatives: A look at green consumer behavior in the new millennium. *Journal of Consumer Marketing*, *16*(6), 558–575. doi:10.1108/07363769910297506

Strauss, A. L. (1991b). A Social World Perspective. In A. L. Strauss (Ed.), *Creating Sociological Awareness: Collective Images and Symbolic Representations* (pp. 233–244). Transaction Publishers.

Stuart, K. (2017). Methods, methodology and madness: Digital records management in the Australian government. *Records Management Journal*, *27*(2), 223–232. doi:10.1108/RMJ-05-2017-0012

Stubbs, W., & Cocklin, C. (2008). Conceptualizing a sustainability business model. *Org. Env.*, *21*(2), 103-127.

Stulz, R. M. (1961). Managerial Discretion and Optimal Financing Policies. *Journal of Financial Economics*, *26*(1), 3–27. doi:10.1016/0304-405X(90)90011-N

Suijs, J. (2005). Voluntary Disclosure of Bad News. *Journal of Business Finance <html_ent Glyph="@amp;" Ascii="&"/>. Accounting*, *32*(7–8), 1423–1435. doi:10.1111/j.0306-686X.2005.00634.x

Sullivan, P. (1999). Profiting from intellectual capital. *Journal of Knowledge Management*, *3*(2), 132–142. doi:10.1108/13673279910275585

Sullivan, P. (2000). *Value driven intellectual capital: how to convert intangible corporate assets into market value*. John Wiley & Sons, Inc.

Sultana, S., Zulkifli, N., & Zainal, D. (2018). Environmental, Social and Governance (ESG) and Investment Decision in Bangladesh. *Sustainability*, *10*(6), 1831. doi:10.3390u10061831

Sundbo, J. (1998). *The theory of innovation: entrepreneurs, technology and strategy*. Edward Elgar.

Sundbo, J. (2001). *The Strategic Management of Innovation*. Edward Elgar.

Sundbo, J., & Fuglsang, L. (2002). *Innovation as Strategic Reflexivity* (J. Sundbo & L. Fuglsang, Eds.). Routledge. doi:10.4324/9780203219270_chapter_1

Sutton, R. (2014). Aesthetics for green roofs and green walls. *The Journal of Living Architecture*, *1*(2), 1–20. doi:10.46534/jliv.2014.01.02.001

Su, X., Sun, B., & Liu, Y. (2021). Selection of cost-effective investment and output subsidies for eco-friendly products. *Journal of Cleaner Production*, *286*, 124985. doi:10.1016/j.jclepro.2020.124985

Sveiby, K. (1997). *The new organizational wealth. Managing and measuring knowledge-based assets*. Berret-Koehler Publishers, Inc.

Sveiby, K. (2001). A knowledge-based theory of the firm to guide in strategy formulation. *Journal of Intellectual Capital*, *2*(4), 344–358. doi:10.1108/14691930110409651

Swartz, P., Da Veiga, A., & Martins, N. (2021). Validating an information privacy governance questionnaire to measure the perception of employees. *Information & Computer Security*, *29*(5), 761–786. doi:10.1108/ICS-08-2020-0135

Tahazzud, H., Adams, M., & Walker, T. R. (2020). Role of sustainability in global seaports. *Ocean and Coastal Management*, *202*, 105435. doi:10.1016/j.ocecoaman.2020.105435

Talesh, S. (2015). Rule-Intermediaries in Action: How State and Business Stakeholders Influence the Meaning of Consumer Rights in Regulatory Governance Arrangements. *Law & Policy*, *37*(1–2), 1–31. doi:10.1111/lapo.12031

Tam, P. T. (2021). Impacting corporate social responsibility on brand value: A case study of commercial banks in ho chi minh city. *Academy of Strategic Management Journal, 20*(2), 1-12.

Tang, G., Chen, Y., Jiang, Y., Paille, P., & Jia, J. (2017). Green human resource management practices: scale development and validity. *Asia Pacific Journal of Human Resources, 56*(1), 31-55. doi:10.1111/1744-7941.12147

Tanzi, V. (1998). Corruption around the World: Causes Consequences, Scope and Cures. *IMF Fiscal Affairs Department*, Washington, DC: International Monetary Fund (Working Paper No. 98/63).

Tarmuji, I., Maelah, R., & Tarmuji, N. H. (2016). The Impact of Environmental, Social and Governance Practices (ESG) on Economic Performance: Evidence from ESG Score. *International Journal of Trade. Economics and Finance, 7*(3), 67–74. doi:10.18178/ijtef.2016.7.3.501

Tasaki, T., Motoshita, M., Uchida, H., & Suzuki, Y. (2013). Assessing the Replacement of Electrical Home Appliances for the Environment. *Journal of Industrial Ecology, 17*(2), 290–298. doi:10.1111/j.1530-9290.2012.00551.x

Teece, D. J. (1998). Design issues for Innovative Firms: Bureaucracy, Incentives and Industrial Structure. In A. D. Chandler Jr, P. Hagstrom, & O. Solvell (Eds.), *The Dynamic Firm*. Oxford University Press.

TEP. (2005). *Advancing the delivery of green infrastructure Targeting Issues in England's Northwest*. TEP.

Thorat, M. S., & Rose, A. (n.d.). *Green HRM Move towards Corporate Social Responsibility: Review of Green HR Culture in Organzations and its Challenges*. Academic Press.

Tidd, J., Bessant, J., & Pavitt, K. (1997). *Managing Innovation: Integrating Technological, Market, and Organizational Change*. Wiley.

Todericiu, R., & Stăniţ, A. (2015). Intellectual capital–The key for sustainable competitive advantage for the SME's sector. *Procedia Economics and Finance, 27*, 676–681. doi:10.1016/S2212-5671(15)01048-5

Todt, O., Muñoz, E., González, M., Ponce, G., & Estévez, B. (2009). Consumer attitudes and the governance of food safety. *Public Understanding of Science (Bristol, England), 18*(1), 103–114. doi:10.1177/0963662507078019 PMID:19579538

Tomashuk, I.V., & Baldynyuk, V.M. (2021). Identification of problems and prospects of rural infrastructure development of Ukraine. *Colloquium-Journal, 13*(100). doi:10.24412/2520-6990-2021-13100-58-70

Tough, G. A., & Lihoma, P. (2018). Medical record-keeping systems in Malawi. Is there a case for hybrid systems and intermediate technologies? Medical records keeping systems. *Records Management Journal, 28*(3), 265–277. doi:10.1108/RMJ-02-2018-0004

Trajtenberg, M. (1990). A Penny for Your Quotes: Patent Citations and the Value of Innovations. *The RAND Journal of Economics, 21*(1), 172–187. doi:10.2307/2555502

Tranfield, D., Denyer, D., & Smart, P. (2003). Towards a methodology for developing evidence-informed management knowledge by means of systematic review. *British Journal of Management, 14*(3), 207–222. doi:10.1111/1467-8551.00375

Transparency International. (2009). *Global Corruption Report: Corrupt. Ion and the Private Sector*.http://www.cgu.gov. br/conferenciabrocde/arquivos/English-Global-Corruption-Report 2009.pd.

Tsabetse, V., & Ngoepe, M. (2021). A Framework for quality assurance for archives and records management education in an open distance e-learning environment in Eswatini. A Framework for quality assurance for ARM. *The International Journal of Information and Learning Technology, 38*(1), 91–102. doi:10.1108/IJILT-03-2020-0033

Tsai, W., & Ghoshal, S. (1998). Social capital and value creation: The role of intrafirm networks. *Academy of Management Journal, 1998*(41), 464–476. doi:10.2307/257085

Tushman, M. L., & Anderson, P. (1997). *Managing Strategic Innovation and Change: A Collection of Readings* (M. L. Tushman & P. Anderson, Eds.). Oxford University Press.

Tushman, M. L., & Rosenkopf, L. (1992). Organizational determinants of technological change: Toward a sociology of technological evolution. *Research in Organizational Behavior*, *14*, 311–347.

Twin, A., Drury., & Perez, Y. (2021). *Business ethics.* Business Essentials.

Twinamatsiko, E., & Kumar, D. (2022). Incorporating ESG in Decision Making for Responsible and Sustainable Investments using Machine Learning. *2022 International Conference on Electronics and Renewable Systems (ICEARS)*, 1328–1334. 10.1109/ICEARS53579.2022.9752343

Ugai, T. (2016). Evaluation of sustainable roof from various aspects and benefits of agriculture roofing in urban core. *Procedia: Social and Behavioral Sciences*, *216*, 850–860. doi:10.1016/j.sbspro.2015.12.082

Ugoani, J. N. N. (2019). Business ethics and its effect on organizational sustainability. *Global Journal of Social Sciences Studies*, *5*(2), 119–131. doi:10.20448/807.5.2.119.131

Ugur, M., & Dasgupta, N. (2011). Evidence on the Economic Growth Impacts of Corruption in Low Income Countries and Beyond. Available at: http://eppi.ioe.ac.uk/cms/LinkClick.aspx

UNDP. (2020). *Environmentally Sustainable Operations.* https://www.undp.org/accountability/social-and-environmental-responsibility/sustainable-operations

Uzzi, B., Amaral, L. A. N., & Reed-Tsochas, F. (2007). Small-world networks and management science research: A review. *European Management Review*, *4*(2), 77–91. doi:10.1057/palgrave.emr.1500078

Vale, J., Miranda, R., Azevedo, G., & Tavares, M. C. (2022). The Impact of Sustainable Intellectual Capital on Sustainable Performance: A Case Study. *Sustainability*, *14*(8), 4382. doi:10.3390u14084382

Van de Ven, A., Polley, D., Garud, S., & Venkataraman, S. (1999). *The Innovation Journey.* Oxford Univ. Press.

Van Holt, T., Statler, M., Atz, U., Whelan, T., van Loggerenberg, M., & Cebulla, J. (2020). The cultural consensus of sustainability-driven innovation: Strategies for success. *Business Strategy and the Environment*, *29*(8), 3399–3409. doi:10.1002/bse.2584

Van Quaquebeke, N., Becker, J. U., Goretzki, N., & Barrot, C. (2019). Perceived Ethical Leadership Affects Customer Purchasing Intentions Beyond Ethical Marketing in Advertising Due to Moral Identity Self-Congruence Concerns. *Journal of Business Ethics*, *156*(2), 357–376. doi:10.100710551-017-3577-4

Vasiukov, D., Fernandes, P. O., & Pashkina, O. (2019). Corporate social responsibility and customer-based brand equity. Paper presented at the Proceedings of the 33rd International Business Information Management Association Conference, IBIMA 2019: Education Excellence and Innovation Management through. *Vision (Basel)*, *2020*, 4594–4604. www.scopus.com

Vázquez García, Á. W. (2022). Teorías del cambio organización: una síntesis [Theories of organization change: a synthesis]. *Revista Gestión Y Estrategia*, (39), 93-96.

Velasquez, M. G. (2014). *Business Ethics Concepts and Cases.* Pearson Education Limited.

Vereijken, P. (1992). A Methodic Way to More Sustainable Farming Systems. *Netherlands Journal of Agricultural Science*, *40*(3), 209–223. doi:10.18174/njas.v40i3.16507

Verona, G., & Ravasi, D. (2003). Unbundling dynamic capabilities: An exploratory study of continuous product innovation. *Industrial and Corporate Change*, *12*(3), 577–606. doi:10.1093/icc/12.3.577

Vetter, A. M. (2014). Archive 2.0: What Composition Students and Academic Libraries Can Gian From Digital- Collaborative Pedagogies. *Composition Studies*, *42*(1), 35–53.

Viedma, J. (2001). ICBS - Intellectual Capital Benchmarking System. *Journal of Intellectual Capital*, *2*(2), 148–165. doi:10.1108/14691930110385937

Vijayaraghavan, K. (2016). Green roofs: A critical review on the role of components, benefits, limitations, and trends. *Renewable & Sustainable Energy Reviews*, *57*, 740–752. doi:10.1016/j.rser.2015.12.119

Vincent, L. H., Bharadwaj, S. G., & Challagalla, G. N. (2004). *Does innovation mediate firm performance? A meta-analysis of determinants and consequences of organizational innovation.* Academic Press.

VisitBerlin. (Ed.). (2017). *12 mal Berliner Leben, 12 mal Berlin Erleben. Konzept für einen stadtverträglichen Berlin-Tourismus 2018+*. VisitBerlin. Available online: https://about.visitberlin.de/tourismuskonzept-2018

Visser, W. (2006). Revisiting Carroll's CSR pyramid: An African perspective. In Corporate citizenship in developing countries: New partnership perspectives. Copenhagen Business School Press.

Von Hippel, E. (1988). *The Sources of Innovation.* Oxford University Press.

Wade, J. (1995). Dynamics of organizational communities and technological bandwagons: An empirical investigation of community evolution in the microprocessor market. *Strategic Management Journal*, *16*(S1), 111–133. doi:10.1002mj.4250160920

Wakeman, R. (1996). What is a Sustainable Port? The Relationship Between Ports and Their Regions. *Journal of Urban Technology*, *3*(2), 65–79. doi:10.1080/10630739608724528

Walsh, J. P., & Ungson, G. R. (1991). Organizational Memory. *Academy of Management Review*, *16*(1), 57–91. doi:10.2307/258607

Wang, W.-Y., & Chang, C. (2005). Intellectual capital and performance in causal models: Evidence from the information technology industry in Taiwan. *Journal of Intellectual Capital*, *6*(2), 222–236. doi:10.1108/14691930510592816

Wang, Y., Hu, H., Dai, W., & Burns, K. (2021). Evaluation of industrial green development and industrial green competitiveness: Evidence from Chinese urban agglomerations. *Ecological Indicators*, *124*, 107371. doi:10.1016/j.ecolind.2021.107371

Wasiluk, K. L. (2013). Beyond eco-efficiency: Understanding CS through the IC practice lens. *Journal of Intellectual Capital*, *14*(1), 102–126. doi:10.1108/14691931311289048

Weaver-Hightower, M. (2008). An ecology metaphor for educational policy analysis: A call to complexity. *Educational Researcher*, *37*(3), 153–167. doi:10.3102/0013189X08318050

Weber, M. (1958). Religious rejections of the world and their directions. In From Max Weber: Essays in Sociology. Oxford University Press.

Wee, B. V., & Banister, D. (2016). How to write a literature review paper? *Transport Reviews*, *36*(2), 278–288. doi:10.1080/01441647.2015.1065456

Weerasinghe, I. M. S., & Dedunu, H. H. (2020). Do demographic factors matter in university-industry knowledge exchange? A study based on Sri Lankan university system. *Journal of Knowledge Management*, *25*(5), 973–988. doi:10.1108/JKM-02-2020-0092

Wehrmeyer, W. (1996). Introduction. In Greening People: Human Resources and Environmental Management. Greenleaf Publishing.

Weick, K. E. (1979). The Social Psychology of Organizing, Topics in Social Psychology. Addison-Wesley.

Wendell, H. (1991). The 1990s: A new era of formal and informal corporate disclosure. *Journal of Corporate Accounting & Finance*, *2*(3), 289–307. doi:10.1002/jcaf.3970020306

Whitley, R. (2003). The Institutional Structuring of Organizational Capabilities: The Role of Authority Sharing and Organizational Careers. *Organization Studies*, *24*(5), 667–695. doi:10.1177/0170840603024005001

Wholey, D. R., & Brittain, J. W. (1986). Organizational ecology: Findings and implications. *Academy of Management Review*, *11*(3). Advance online publication. doi:10.5465/amr.1986.57140723

Wiering, M., Liefferink, D., Boezeman, D., Kaufmann, M., Crabbé, A., & Kurstjens, N. (2020). The Wicked Problem the Water Framework Directive Cannot Solve. The Governance Approach in Dealing with Pollution of Nutrients in Surface Water in the Netherlands, Flanders, Lower Saxony, Denmark, and Ireland. *Water (Basel)*, *12*(5), 1240. doi:10.3390/w12051240

Wirtenberg, J., Harmon, K. D., Russell, W. G., & Fairfield, K. D. (2007). HR's role in building a sustainable enterprise. *Human Resource Planning*, *30*, 10–20.

Wise, V., Ali, M. M., & Wise, T. (2010). Ethical conduct in business: A case study analysis using Bangladesh experiences. *Problems and Perspectives in Management*, *8*, 4–1.

Wolfe, B. (1994). Organizational Innovation: Review, Critique and Suggested Research Directions. *Journal of Management Studies*, *31*(3), 405–443. doi:10.1111/j.1467-6486.1994.tb00624.x

Womack, J. P., Jones, D. T., & Roos, D. (1990). *The Machine that Changed the World*. Rawson Associates.

Woodman, R. W., Sawyer, J. E., & Griffin, R. W. (1993). Toward a Theory of Organizational Creativity. *Academy of Management Review*, *18*(2), 293–321. doi:10.2307/258761

World Bank. (2016). *Doing Business 2016: Measuring Regulatory Quality and Efficiency*. Washington, DC.

World Commission on Environment and Development (WCED). (1987). *"Our Common Future" report*. Retrieved January 19, 2020, from https://sustainabledevelopment.un.org/content/documents/5987our-common-future.pdf

Wright, B., & Martin, G. P. (2014). Mission, Margin, and the Role of Consumer Governance in Decision-Making at Community Health Centers. *Journal of Health Care for the Poor and Underserved*, *25*(2), 930–947. doi:10.1353/hpu.2014.0107 PMID:24858895

Wu, X. P., Xu, F. Y., & Zhou, Y. (2008). Analysis of Factors Affecting University Teachers' Job Performance. [Educational Sciences]. *Journal of East China Normal University*, *24*, 30–37.

Wysocki, J. (2021). Innovative green initiatives in the manufacturing SME sector in Poland. *Sustainability*, *13*(4), 2386. doi:10.3390u13042386

Xu, J., & Liu, F. (2020). The impact of intellectual capital on firm performance: A modified and extended VAIC model. *Journal of Competitiveness*, *12*(1), 161–176. doi:10.7441/joc.2010.01.10

Xu, J., & Wang, B. (2018). Intellectual capital, financial performance and companies' sustainable growth: Evidence from the Korean manufacturing industry. *Sustainability*, *10*(12), 4651. doi:10.3390u10124651

Xu, X. (2014). The Relation between Emerging Capital and Enterprise Performance. *Journal of Guangdong University of Finance and Economics*, *1*, 22–34.

Yadiati, W., Nissa, N., Paulus, S., Suharman, H., & Meiryani, M. (2019). The role of green intellectual capital and organizational reputation in influencing environmental performance. *International Journal of Energy Economics and Policy*, *9*(3), 261–268. doi:10.32479/ijeep.7752

Yallop, C. A., Gică, O. A., Moisescu, O. I., Coroş, M. M., & Séraphin, H. (2021). The digital traveler: Implications for data ethics and data governance in tourism and hospitality. *Journal of Consumer Marketing*. Advance online publication. doi:10.1108/JCM-12-2020-4278

Yılmaz, F. (2019). "Yeşil-Eko Liman Yaklaşımı"nın Deniz Ticareti ve Lojistik Sektörüne Katkıları: Türkiye ve AB'deki Uygulamaların Karşılaştırması [Contribution of Green-Eco Port Approach to Maritime Trade and Logistics Sector: Comparison of Practices in Turkey and EU]. *Journal of Transportation and Logistics*, *4*(2), 65–78. doi:10.26650/JTL.2019.04.02.02

Yinyoung, R., Manisha, S., & Yoon, K. (2018). CSR and financia performance: The role of CSR awareness in the restaurant industry. *International Journal of Hospitality Management*, *57*, 30–39.

Yong, J. Y., & Mohd-Yusoff, Y. (2016). Studying the influence of strategic human resource competencies on the adoption of green human resource management practices. *Industrial and Commercial Training*, *48*(8), 416–422. doi:10.1108/ICT-03-2016-0017

Yong, J., Yusliza, M., Ramayah, T., & Fawehinmi, O. (2019). Nexus between green intellectual capital and green human resource management. *Journal of Cleaner Production*, *215*, 364–374. doi:10.1016/j.jclepro.2018.12.306

Youndt, M., Subramaniam, M., & Snell, S. (2004). Intellectual capital profiles: An examination of investments and returns. *Journal of Management Studies*, *41*(2), 335–361. doi:10.1111/j.1467-6486.2004.00435.x

Young-Ferris, A., & Roberts, J. (2021). 'Looking for Something that Isn't There': A Case Study of an Early Attempt at ESG Integration in Investment Decision Making. *European Accounting Review*, 1–28. doi:10.1080/09638180.2021.2000458

Yusliza, M., Othman, N., & Jabbour, C. (2017). Deciphering the implementation of green human resource management in an emerging economy. *Journal of Management Development*, *36*(10), 1230–1246. doi:10.1108/JMD-01-2017-0027

Yusoff, Y. M., Nejati, M., Kee, D. M. H., & Amran, A. (2018). Linking green human resource management practices to environmental performance in hotel industry. *Global Business Review*, *21*(3), 1–18. doi:10.1177/0972150918779294

Yusoff, Y., Omar, M., Zaman, M., & Samad, S. (2019). Do all elements of green intellectual capital contribute toward business sustainability? Evidence from the Malaysian context using the Partial Least Squares method. *Journal of Cleaner Production*, *234*, 626–637. doi:10.1016/j.jclepro.2019.06.153

Zaid, A., Jaaron, A., & Bon, A. (2018). The impact of green human resource management and green supply chain management practices on sustainable performance: An empirical study. *Journal of Cleaner Production*, *204*, 965–979. doi:10.1016/j.jclepro.2018.09.062

Zammuto, R. F. (1988). Organizational Adaptation: Some Implications of Organizational Ecology for Strategic Choice. *Journal of Management Studies*, *25*(2), 105–112. doi:10.1111/j.1467-6486.1988.tb00026.x

Zaragoza-Sáez, P., Claver-Cortés, E., Marco-Lajara, B., & Úbeda-García, M. (2020). Corporate social responsibility and strategic knowledge management as mediators between sustainable intangible capital and hotel performance. *Journal of Sustainable Tourism*, 1–23. doi:10.1080/09669582.2020.1811289

Zdravkovic, S., Magnusson, P., & Stanley, S. M. (2010). Dimensions of fit between a brand and a social cause and their influence on attitudes. *International Journal of Research in Marketing*, *27*(2), 151–160. doi:10.1016/j.ijresmar.2010.01.005

Zhang, F., & Zhang, R. (2018). Trade-in Remanufacturing, Customer Purchasing Behavior, and Government Policy. *Manufacturing & Service Operations Management, 20*(4), 601–616. doi:10.1287/msom.2017.0696

Zhang, L., Li, D., Cao, C., & Huang, S. (2018). The influence of greenwashing perception on green purchasing intentions: The mediating role of green word-of-mouth and moderating role of green concern. *Journal of Cleaner Production, 187*, 740–750. doi:10.1016/j.jclepro.2018.03.201

Zhang, Z., & Sundaresan, S. (2010). Knowledge markets in firms: Knowledge sharing with trust and signalling. *Knowledge Management Research and Practice, 2010*(8), 322–339. doi:10.1057/kmrp.2010.22

Zhou, C., & Li, J. (2008). Product innovation in emerging market-based international joint ventures: An organizational ecology perspective. *Journal of International Business Studies, 39*(7), 1114–1132. doi:10.1057/jibs.2008.51

Zhou, Y., Thøgersen, J., Ruan, Y., & Huang, G. (2013). The moderating role of human values in planned behavior: The case of Chinese consumers' intention to buy organic food. *Journal of Consumer Marketing, 30*(4), 335–344. doi:10.1108/JCM-02-2013-0482

Zhu, B., Watts, S., & Chen, H. (2010). Visualizing social network concepts. *Decision Support Systems, 49*(2), 151–161. doi:10.1016/j.dss.2010.02.001

Zhukova, N. Y., & Melikova, A. E. (2021). Corporate social responsibility: Strengthening brand value and affecting company's financial performance. Finance. *Theory into Practice, 25*(1), 84–102. doi:10.26794/2587-5671-2021-25-1-84-102

Zhu, Q., Sarkis, J., & Lai, K. (2013). Institutional-based antecedents and performance outcomes of internal and external green supply chain management practices. *Journal of Purchasing and Supply Management, 19*(2), 106–117. doi:10.1016/j.pursup.2012.12.001

Zschockelt, F. (2009). *The importance of developing intellectual capital for innovative organizations: contributions from a HRM-perspective* [Master's thesis]. University of Twente.

Zurawicki, L., & Habib, M. (2010). Corruption and Foreign Direct Investment: What Have We Learned? *International Business & Economics Research Journal (IBER), 9*(7).

About the Contributors

Bartolomé Marco-Lajara (PhD) is Professor at the University of Alicante. His research interests are strategic management and tourism management. He is the author of several books, book chapters and international articles related to teaching methodology and the areas above mentioned. He is a member of the Tourism Research Institute at the University of Alicante since its foundation and the main researcher of a European project 'Next Tourism Generation Alliance' and of the public competitive project for the creation of the Tourist Observatory of the Valencian Community (Spain). He has taken part in others public and private projects, such as the development of the strategic plan of the Alicante province for the period 2010-2020. He is the Assistant Dean of the Economics Faculty at the University of Alicante.

Patrocinio Zaragoza-Sáez (PhD, University of Alicante, Spain) is a Professor at the Department of Business Management at the University of Alicante, Spain. She holds the position of Coordinator of the University Master's Degree in Tourism Management and Planning. Her primary research interests are knowledge management and intellectual capital, strategic management and tourism management. She has published research papers in international journals including Journal of Business Research, Regional Studies, Journal of Knowledge Management, Knowledge Management Research and Practice, Journal of Intellectual Capital, International Journal of Knowledge Management Studies, Business Strategy & Environment, Intangible Capital, International Journal of Contemporary Hospitality Management Current Issues in Tourism, Cornell Hospitality Quarterly, Tourism Economics and Tourism Management. She has been involved in several national and international scientific and academic research projects.

Javier Martínez-Falcó is Assistant Professor in the Department of Management at the University of Alicante. In the field of research, he focuses his interest on issues related to the Strategic Management of the Company, specifically in the areas of Knowledge Management and Corporate Sustainability of wine companies, on which he has written several publications in the form of articles, book chapters and contributions to conferences. He has also participated in several national research projects and teaches Strategic Management on the ADE, TADE and DADE degree courses.

* * *

Osman Arslan (PhD) is Assistant Professor in the Department of Maritime Transportation Management Engineering at the University of Kocaeli. He received his MS in Maritime Policy from the University of İstanbul in 2015. He received his Ph.D. in Maritime Transportation Management Engineering from the Piri Reis University in 2021. He worked for 5 years as 3rd and 4th captain on ships. His main fields of study are maritime labour force, maritime management, maritime transportation, and ship management.

Gazala Ashraf is Associate Professor at Amity Business School, AUC. An Academician, Researcher, Coach & Trainer since almost two decades, resource person for various workshops and MDPs including behavioural, analytical and management topics, published papers and book chapters in Scopus and UGC Care Journals, been part of review board in London Journal Press, GJBMR etc. Qualified NET, IPMA D level, AITD Coach Certification and INFS Expert.

Tlou Maggie Masenya holds a PhD in Information Science from University of South Africa and completed Masters in Information Technology at the University of Pretoria. She has seven years of work experience in academia, in the field of Information Science and Technology. She is currently a Senior Lecturer in the Department of Information Systems at Durban University of Technology. She also worked as a Senior Lecturer at University of South Africa and University of Zululand. She supervises Masters and PhD students and also serves as an external examiner for postgraduate studies. She published book chapters and articles in peer-reviewed accredited journals. She is currently reviewing articles for South African Journal of Information management, South African Journal of Library and Information Science, Mousaion, Research Metrics and Analytics Journal, Journal of South African Society of Archivists and IGI-Global book chapters. Her areas of expertise encompass ICT4D, Digital Preservation, Technopreneurship, Digital entrepreneurship, Knowledge Management, Indigenous Knowledge System, Disruptive Technologies . She is planning to be an editor for books that cover some of these arrears.

Disha Sharma is a Finance Faculty, presently working as an Assistant Professor at Amity Business School, Amity University Chhattisgarh. She has done qualified UGC-NET & SET, did master in three subjects, and completed her Ph.D. from Pt. Ravi Shankar Shukla University, Raipur. She has five years of teaching experience. She has published many papers on her credit of national and international repute. She has also written many book chapters in International and Scopus indexed books. She also has experience as Co-Principal Investigator in ICSSR Project and currently working on many other projects. She has presented various research papers at national and international conferences. She is a lifetime member of the All Indian Commerce Association and All India Accounting Association.

Imran Siddiqui is working as Assistant Professor in Amity University Chhattisgarh. His specialization is Marketing, having teaching experience of 23 years.

Omar Vargas-González is Professor and Head of Systems and Computing Department at Tecnologico Nacional de Mexico Campus Ciudad Guzman, professor at Telematic Engineering at Centro Universitario del Sur Universidad de Guadalajara with a master degree in Computer Systems. Has been trained in Innovation and Multidisciplinary Entrepreneurship at Arizona State University (2018) and a Generation of Ecosystems of Innovation, Entrepreneurship and Sustainability for Jalisco course by Harvard University T.H. Chan School of Health. At present conduct research on diverse fields such as Entrepreneurship, Economy, Statistics, Mathematics and Information and Computer Sciences. Has colaborated in the publication of over 20 scientific articles and conducted diverse Innovation and Technological Development projects.

José G. Vargas-Hernández, M.B.A., Ph.D., is a member of the National System of Researchers of Mexico and a research professor at Tecnológico Mario Molina Unidad Zapopan formerly at University Center for Economic and Managerial Sciences, University of Guadalajara. Professor Vargas-Hernández has a Ph. D. in Public Administration and a Ph.D. in Organizational Economics. He has undertaken studies in Organisational Behaviour and has a Master of Business Administration, published four books and more than 200 papers in international journals and reviews (some translated to English, French, German, Portuguese, Farsi, Chinese, etc.) and more than 300 essays in national journals and reviews. He has obtained several international Awards and recognition.

Index

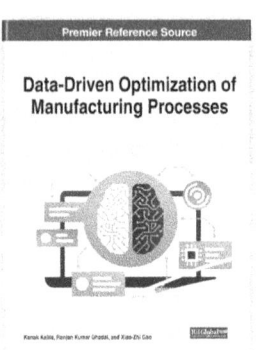

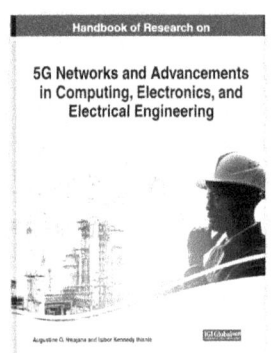
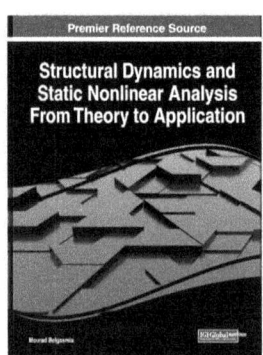

Ensure Quality Research is Introduced to the Academic Community

Become an Evaluator for IGI Global Authored Book Projects

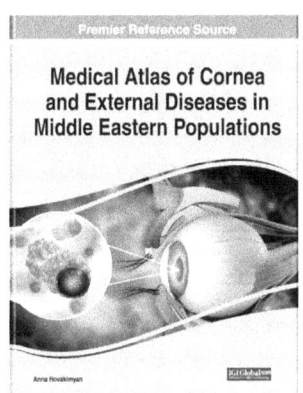

The overall success of an authored book project is dependent on quality and timely manuscript evaluations.

Applications and Inquiries may be sent to:
development@igi-global.com

Applicants must have a doctorate (or equivalent degree) as well as publishing, research, and reviewing experience. Authored Book Evaluators are appointed for one-year terms and are expected to complete at least three evaluations per term. Upon successful completion of this term, evaluators can be considered for an additional term.

If you have a colleague that may be interested in this opportunity, we encourage you to share this information with them.

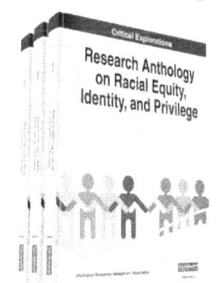